America's Top Jobs for People Re-Entering the Workforce

By Ron and Caryl Krannich

CAREER AND BUSINESS BOOKS AND SOFTWARE

101 Secrets of Highly Effective Speakers
201 Dynamite Job Search Letters
America's Top 100 Jobs for People Without a Four-Year Degree
America's Top Jobs for People Re-Entering the Workforce
America's Top Internet Job Sites
Best Jobs for the 21st Century
Change Your Job, Change Your Life
The Complete Guide to Public Employment
The Directory of Federal Jobs and Employers
Discover the Best Jobs for You!
Dynamite Cover Letters
Dynamite Resumes
Dynamite Salary Negotiations
Dynamite Tele-Search
The Educator's Guide to Alternative Jobs and Careers
The Ex-Offender's Job Hunting Guide
Find a Federal Job Fast!
From Air Force Blue to Corporate Gray
From Army Green to Corporate Gray
From Navy Blue to Corporate Gray
Get a Raise in 7 Days
High Impact Resumes and Letters
I Want to Do Something Else, But I'm Not Sure What It Is
Interview for Success
The Job Hunting Guide: Transitioning From College to Career
Job Hunting Tips for People With Hot and Not-So-Hot Backgrounds
Job Interview Tips for People With Not-So-Hot Backgrounds
Job-Power Source and *Ultimate Job Source* (software)
Jobs and Careers With Nonprofit Organizations
Military Resumes and Cover Letters
Moving Out of Education
Moving Out of Government
Nail the Cover Letter!
Nail the Job Interview!
Nail the Resume!
No One Will Hire Me!
Re-Careering in Turbulent Times
Savvy Interviewing
The Savvy Networker
The Savvy Resume Writer

TRAVEL AND INTERNATIONAL BOOKS

Best Resumes and CVs for International Jobs
The Complete Guide to International Jobs and Careers
The Directory of Websites for International Jobs
International Jobs Directory
Jobs for Travel Lovers
Mayors and Managers in Thailand
Politics of Family Planning Policy in Thailand
Shopping and Traveling in Exotic Asia
Shopping in Exotic Places
Shopping the Exotic South Pacific
Travel Planning On the Internet
Treasures and Pleasures of Australia
Treasures and Pleasures of Bermuda
Treasures and Pleasures of China
Treasures and Pleasures of Egypt
Treasures and Pleasures of Hong Kong
Treasures and Pleasures of India
Treasures and Pleasures of Indonesia
Treasures and Pleasures of Italy
Treasures and Pleasures of Mexico
Treasures and Pleasures of Paris
Treasures and Pleasures of Rio and São Paulo
Treasures and Pleasures of Santa Fe, Taos, and Albuquerque
Treasures and Pleasures of Singapore and Bali
Treasures and Pleasures of Singapore and Malaysia
Treasures and Pleasures of South America
Treasures and Pleasures of Southern Africa
Treasures and Pleasures of Thailand and Myanmar
Treasures and Pleasures of Turkey
Treasures and Pleasures of Vietnam and Cambodia

America's Top Jobs
for People
Re-Entering *the* Workforce

85 Opportunities for Jump-Starting Your Career

Ron and Caryl Krannich, Ph.Ds

IMPACT PUBLICATIONS
Manassas Park, Virginia

S

America's Top Jobs for People Re-Entering the Workforce

ISBN: 1-57023-226-1

Library of Congress: 2005920289

Publisher: For information on Impact Publications, including current and forthcoming publications, authors, press kits, online bookstore, and submission requirements, visit the left navigation bar on the front page of our main company website: www.impactpublications.com.

Publicity/Rights: For information on publicity, author interviews, and subsidiary rights, contact the Media Relations Department: Tel. 703-361-7300, Fax 703-335-9486, or email: info@impactpublications.com.

Sales/Distribution: All bookstore sales are handled through Impact's trade distributor: National Book Network, 15200 NBN Way, Blue Ridge Summit, PA 17214, Tel. 1-800-462-6420. All special sales and distribution inquiries should be directed to the publisher: Sales Department, IMPACT PUBLICATIONS, 9104 Manassas Drive, Suite N, Manassas Park, VA 20111-5211, Tel. 703-361-7300, Fax 703-335-9486, or email: info@impactpublications.com.

Contents

America's Top Jobs for People Re-Entering the Workforce

1

Jobs and Re-Entering the Workforce

FINDING A JOB UNDER THE best of circumstances is a challenging task. Assuming you have the right education and progressive experience, a good record of accomplishments, and live in an economically vibrant community with numerous employment opportunities, you still need to write a resume, network for job leads, contact employers, interview for jobs, and negotiate a compensation package. This whole roller coaster process, which involves lots of highs (invited to interviews) and lows (rejections), can take anywhere from three to six months to complete.

Facing Two Challenges

But what happens if you're re-entering the job market after a lengthy absence? Perhaps you made important personal and professional choices, such as going back to school, raising a family, joining the Peace Corps or the military, or retiring. On the other hand, perhaps you were forced by circumstances to drop out of the job market due to a major injury or illness, a lengthy period of unemployment, or incarceration. Or maybe you are now motivated by a negative situation to enter or re-enter the job market – newly divorced, face financial difficulties, closed your business, or experienced the illness, injury, or death of your spouse. Whatever your circumstances, you face two common challenges:

1. Identifying jobs and employers most receptive to people in such transition situations.

2. Convincing employers that you should be hired despite what may appear to be a red flag in your background or an objection to hiring you – the lack of continuous work experience.

This book is about the first challenge – identifying jobs appropriate for individuals re-entering the job market. Some of these jobs may relate to your previous work experience while others may appeal to your interests. All of the jobs require basic education and training, and many require more advanced education and training.

Useful Resources

A few other books identify jobs for people who need to quickly find a job or which require short-term job training – many appropriate for people re-entering the job market after a lengthy absence:

Deborah Jacobson, *150 Jobs You Can Start Today* (Broadway Books, 2003)

The Princeton Review, *Best Entry-Level Jobs* (The Princeton Review, 2005)

Paul Phifer, *Quick Prep Careers* (Facts on File, 2003)

Paul Phifer, *Great Careers in 2 Years* (Facts on File, 2003)

Laurence Shatkin, *Quick Guide to Career Training in Two Years or Less* (JIST Publishing, 2004)

Other resources deal with the second challenge, which is all about the job search itself – convincing employers that they should hire you. Six of our other books should be helpful in organizing an effective job search that deals with potential objections to your background:

Change Your Job, Change Your Life, Ron Krannich (Impact Publications, 2005)

The Ex-Offender's Job Hunting Guide, Ron and Caryl Krannich (Impact Publications, 2005)

The Job Hunting Guide: Transitioning From College to Career, Ron and Caryl Krannich (Impact Publications, 2003)

Job Hunting Tips for People With Hot and Not-So-Hot Backgrounds, Ron and Caryl Krannich (Impact Publications, 2005)

Job Interview Tips for People With Not-So-Hot Backgrounds, Caryl and Ron Krannich (Impact Publications, 2005)

Military Resumes and Cover Letters, Carl S. Savino and Ronald L. Krannich (Impact Publications, 2004)

Other resources for dealing with the job search challenge facing people re-entering the workforce include:

Expert Resumes for People Returning to Work, Wendy S. Enelow and Louise M. Kursmark (JIST Publishing, 2003)

Flex Time: A Working Mother's Guide to Balancing Career and Family, Jacqueline Foley (Avalon Publishing Group, 2003)

Jobs and the Military Spouse, Janet I. Farley (Impact Publications, 2004)

Military-to-Civilian Career Transition Guide, Janet I. Farley (JIST Publishing, 2005)

The Mom Economy, Elizabeth Wilcox (Berkley Publishing Group, 2003)

Resumes for Re-Entering the Job Market, Editors of VGM
Career Books (McGraw-Hill, 2002)

Your Unique Circumstances

Perhaps you're lucky enough to have temporarily left a job with an
employer who will rehire you. This is frequently the case with women
who decide to take a leave of absence for a year or two for child-rearing.
Many large and profitable corporations can accommodate such situations,
especially for valuable workers whom they wish to retain in the long run.

However, not many employers can afford to guarantee to rehire
employees over a long period of time. When you leave, you probably
leave for good. In addition, since you may not have kept up your work-
related skills once you were no longer working, you may be approaching
today's job market as an inexperienced entry-level worker.

Consider New Options

If you have been out of the job market for more than a year, this may be
a good time to reassess what you want to do with the rest of your work
life. Do you want to go back to what you were once doing, or do you feel
there may be other things you would like to do? Perhaps you would like
to pursue one of today's fastest growing or hottest jobs. For example, the
U.S. Department of Labor's Bureau of Labor Statistics every two years
updates its employment outlook for the coming decade and publishes the
results in the November issue of the *Monthly Labor Review* as well as in
the latest edition of the biannual *Occupational Outlook Handbook*. For
current statistics and updated projections relating to several tables presented in this chapter, please visit the website of the Bureau of Labor
Statistics: http://stats.bls.gov. You also can access online the complete text
of the popular *Occupational Outlook Handbook* through this website:
www. bls.gov/oco.

Assuming a moderate rate of economic growth in the decade ahead –
not boom-and-bust cycles – the U.S. Department of Labor projects an
average growth rate of nearly 15 percent for all occupations in the coming
decade. Technical and service occupations will grow the fastest, as
indicated in this table:

Fastest Growing Occupations, 2002-2012
(Numbers in thousands of jobs)

Occupational Title	Employment 2002	2012	Percent Change	Postsecondary Education or Training
▪ Medical assistants [3]	365	579	59	Moderate-term on-the-job training
▪ Network systems and data communications analysts [1]	186	292	57	Bachelor's degree
▪ Physician assistants [3]	63	94	49	Bachelor's degree
▪ Social and human service assistants [3]	305	454	49	Moderate-term on-the-job training
▪ Home health aides [4]	580	859	48	Short-term on-the-job training
▪ Medical records and health information technicians [3]	147	216	47	Associate degree
▪ Physical therapist aides [3]	37	54	46	Short-term on-the-job training
▪ Computer software engineers, applications [1]	394	573	46	Bachelor's degree
▪ Computer software engineers [1]	281	409	45	Bachelor's degree
▪ Physical therapist assistants [2]	50	73	45	Associate degree
▪ Fitness trainers and aerobics instructors [3]	183	264	44	Postsecondary vocational award
▪ Database administrators [1]	110	159	44	Bachelor's degree
▪ Veterinary technologists and technicians [3]	53	76	44	Associate degree
▪ Hazardous materials removal workers [2]	38	54	43	Moderate-term on-the-job training
▪ Dental hygienists [1]	148	212	43	Associate degree
▪ Occupational therapist aides [3]	8	12	43	Short-term on-the-job training
▪ Dental assistants [3]	266	379	42	Moderate-term on-the-job training
▪ Personal and home care aides [4]	608	854	40	Short-term on-the-job training
▪ Self-enrichment education teachers [2]	200	281	40	Work experience in a related occupation
▪ Computer systems analysts [1]	468	653	39	Bachelor's degree

▪ Occupational therapist assistants [2]	18	26	39	Associate degree
▪ Environmental engineers [1]	47	65	38	Bachelor's degree
▪ Postsecondary teachers [1]	1,581	1,284	38	Doctoral degree
▪ Network and computer systems administrators [1]	251	345	37	Bachelor's degree
▪ Environmental science and protection technicians, including health [2]	28	38	37	Associate degree
▪ Preschool teachers, except special education [4]	424	577	36	Postsecondary vocational award
▪ Computer and information systems managers [1]	284	387	36	Bachelor's or higher degree, plus work experience
▪ Physical therapists [1]	137	185	35	Master's degree
▪ Occupational therapists [1]	82	110	35	Bachelor's degree
▪ Respiratory therapists [2]	86	116	35	Associate degree

[1] Very high average annual earnings ($42,820 and over)
[2] High average annual earnings ($27,500 to $41,780)
[3] Low average annual earnings ($19,710 to $27,380)
[4] Very low average annual earnings (up to $19,600)

Occupations With the Largest Job Growth, 2002-2012
(Numbers in thousands of jobs)

Occupational Title	Employment 2002	2012	Percent Change	Postsecondary Education or Training
▪ Registered nurses [1]	2,284	2,908	27	Associate degree
▪ Postsecondary teachers [1]	1,581	2,184	38	Doctoral degree
▪ Retail salespersons [4]	4,076	4,672	15	Short-term on-the-job training
▪ Customer service representatives [3]	1,894	2,354	24	Moderate-term on-the-job training
▪ Combined food preparation and service workers, including fast food [3]	1,990	2,444	23	Short-term on-the-job training
▪ Cashiers, except gaming [4]	3,432	2,886	13	Short-term on-the-job training
▪ Janitors and cleaners, except maids and housekeeping cleaners [4]	2,267	2,681	18	Short-term on-the-job training

Occupation				Training
General and operations managers [1]	2,049	2,425	18	Bachelor's or higher degree + experience
Waiters and waitresses [4]	2,097	2,464	18	Short-term on-the-job training
Nursing aides, orderlies, and attendants [3]	1,375	1,718	25	Short-term on-the-job training
Truck drivers, heavy and tractor-trailer [2]	1,767	2,104	19	Moderate-term on-the-job training
Receptionists and information clerks [3]	1,100	1,425	29	Short-term on-the-job training
Security guards [4]	995	1,313	32	Short-term on-the-job training
Office clerks, general [3]	2,991	3,301	10	Short-term on-the-job training
Teacher assistants [4]	1,277	1,571	23	Short-term on-the-job training
Sales representative, wholesale and manufacturing, except technical and scientific products [1]	1,459	1,738	19	Moderate-term on-the-job training
Home health aides [4]	580	859	48	Short-term on-the-job training
Personal and home care aides [4]	608	854	40	Short-term on-the-job training
Truck drivers, light or delivery services [3]	1,022	1,259	23	Short-term on-the-job training
Landscaping and groundskeeping workers [3]	1,074	1,311	22	Short-term on-the-job training
Elementary school teachers, except special education [2]	1,467	1,690	15	Bachelor's degree
Medical assistants [3]	365	579	59	Moderate-term on-the-job training
Maintenance and repair workers, general [2]	1,266	1,472	16	Moderate-term on-the-job training
Accountants and auditors [1]	1,055	1,261	19	Bachelor's degree
Computer systems analysts [1]	468	653	39	Bachelor's degree
Secondary school teachers, except special and vocational education [1]	988	1,167	18	Bachelor's degree
Computer software engineers [1]	394	573	46	Bachelor's degree
Management analysis [1]	577	753	30	Bachelor's or higher degree, plus work experience

■ Food preparation workers [4]	850	1,022	20	Short-term on-the-job training
■ First-line supervisors/ managers of retail sales workers [2]	1,798	1,962	9	Work experience in a related occupation

[1] Very high average annual earnings ($42,820 and over)
[2] High average annual earnings ($27,500 to $41,780)
[3] Low average annual earnings ($19,710 to $27,380)
[4] Very low average annual earnings (up to $19,600)

Fastest Growing Industries, 2002-2012
(Numbers in thousands of jobs)

Industry Description	Jobs		Percent Change	Average annual rate of change
	2002	2012		
■ Software publishers	256.0	429.7	173.7	5.3
■ Management, scientific, and technical consulting services	731.8	1,137.4	405.6	4.5
■ Community care facilities for the elderly and residential care facilities	695.3	1,077.6	382.3	4.5
■ Computer systems design and related services	1,162.7	1,797.7	635.0	4.5
■ Employment services	3,248.8	5,012.3	1,763.5	4.4
■ Individual, family, community, and vocational rehabilitation services	1,238.8	1,866.6	597.3	3.9
■ Ambulatory health care services except offices of health practitioners	1,443.6	2,113.4	669.8	3.9
■ Water, sewage, and other systems	48.5	71.0	22.5	3.9
■ Internet services, data processing, and other information services	528.8	773.1	244.3	3.9
■ Child day care services	734.2	1,050.3	316.1	3.6

20 Jobs With High Median Earnings and a Significant Number of Job Openings, 2002-2012

Occupation	Average Annual Projected Job Openings, 2002-2012	Median Earnings 2002
▪ Registered nurses	110,119	$48,090
▪ Postsecondary teachers	95,980	$49,090
▪ General and operations managers	76,243	$68,210
▪ Sales representatives, wholesale and manufacturing, except technical and scientific products	66,239	$42,730
▪ Truck drivers, heavy and tractor-trailer	62,517	$33,210
▪ Elementary school teachers, except special education	54,701	$41,780
▪ First-line supervisors or managers of retail sales workers	48,645	$29,700
▪ Secondary school teachers, except special education	45,761	$43,950
▪ General maintenance and repair workers	44,978	$29,370
▪ Executive secretaries and administrative assistants	42,444	$33,410
▪ First-line supervisors or managers of office and administrative support workers	40,909	$38,820
▪ Accountants and auditors	40,465	$47,000
▪ Carpenters	31,917	$34,190
▪ Automotive service technicians and mechanics	41,887	$30,590
▪ Police and sheriff's patrol officers	31,290	$42,270
▪ Licensed practical and licensed vocational nurses	29,480	$31,440
▪ Electricians	28,485	$41,390
▪ Management analysts	25,470	$60,340
▪ Computer systems analysts	23,735	$62,890
▪ Special education teachers	23,297	$43,450

Certain patterns are clearly evident from the U.S. Department of Labor's employment projections for the coming decade:

1. The hot occupational fields are in health care and computers and involve increased technical education and training on an ongoing basis.

2. Education is closely associated with earnings – the higher the education, the higher the average annual earnings.

3. Many of the fastest growing jobs require some short- or moderate-term education.

4. Two-year associate degrees in several medical-related fields offer some of the best paying jobs.

5. Nearly 50 percent of the fastest growing jobs that generate relatively high median earnings, such as carpenters, truck drivers, repair workers, and auto mechanics, do not require a four-year degree.

Identify the "Best" Jobs for You

The fastest growing occupational fields are not necessarily the best ones for you. The best job and career for you will depend on your particular mix of skills, interests, and work and lifestyle values. Money, for example, is only one of many determiners of whether or not a job and career are particularly desirable. A job may pay a great deal of money, but it also may be very stressful, insecure, found in an undesirable location, involve long hours, and require extensive travel, including a long commute each day. The "best" job for you will be one you find rewarding in terms of your own criteria and priorities.

If you know what you do well and enjoy doing – information about yourself acquired through various self-assessment tests and exercises – you will have a better idea which jobs best fit you. Indeed, we strongly recommend conducting a self-assessment in conjunction with the information included on the various jobs profiled in this book. For details on how to identify your best fit, see our separate self-assessment volume, *I Want to Do Something Else, But I'm Not Sure What It Is* (Impact Publications, 2005).

Periodically some observers of the labor market attempt to identify what are the best, the worst, the hottest, the most lucrative, or the most promising jobs and careers of the decade. One of the most ambitious attempts to assemble a list of the "best" jobs in America is presented in the *Jobs Rated Almanac*. Similar in methodology to *Places Rated Almanac* for identifying the best places to live in America, the latest edition (2002) of this book evaluates and ranks 250 jobs in terms of six primary "job quality" criteria: income, stress, physical demands, environment, outlook, and security. According to this analysis, the 25 highest ranking ("best") jobs by accumulated score of these criteria are:

The Best Jobs in America

Job title	Overall rank
■ Biologist	1
■ Actuary	2
■ Financial planner	3
■ Computer system analyst	4
■ Accountant	5
■ Software engineer	6
■ Meteorologist	7
■ Paralegal assistant	8
■ Statistician	9
■ Astronomer	10
■ Mathematician	11
■ Parole officer	12
■ Hospital administrator	13
■ Architectural drafter	14
■ Physiologist	15
■ Dietician	16
■ Website manager	17
■ Physicist	18
■ Audiologist	19
■ Agency director (nonprofit)	20
■ Industrial designer	21
■ Chemist	22
■ Medical laboratory technician	23
■ Archeologist	24
■ Economist	25

The 20 worst jobs, or those that rank at the very bottom of the list of 250, include the following:

The Worst Jobs in America

Job title	Overall rank
■ Fisherman	250
■ Roustabout	249
■ Lumberjack	248
■ Cowboy	247
■ Ironworker	246
■ Garbage collector	245
■ Construction worker (laborer)	244
■ Taxi driver	243
■ Stevedore	242
■ Welder	241
■ Roofer	240
■ Dancer	239
■ Firefighter	238
■ Dairy farmer	237
■ Seaman	236
■ Farmer	235
■ Boilermaker	234
■ Carpenter	234
■ Sheet metal worker	232
■ Butcher	231

For the relative rankings of all 250 jobs as well as the ratings of each job on individual criterion, consult the latest edition of the *Jobs Rated Almanac*, which should be available in your local library or bookstore.

One of the most recent examinations of the best jobs in the decade ahead – those offering high pay, fast growth, and the most new jobs – is found in Ferguson's *25 Jobs That Have It All* (Chicago, IL: Ferguson Publishing Co.). This book identifies 25 jobs as the top ones:

- ■ Advertising account executives
- ■ Business managers
- ■ College professors
- ■ Computer network administrators
- ■ Computer systems programmers/analysts
- ■ Database specialists
- ■ Dental hygienists
- ■ Graphic designers
- ■ Health care managers
- ■ Management analysts and consultants

- Medical record technicians
- Occupational therapists
- Paralegals
- Pharmacy technicians
- Physician assistants
- Police officers
- Public relations specialists
- Registered nurses
- Secondary school teachers
- Software designers
- Software engineers
- Special education teachers
- Speech-language pathologists and audiologists
- Technical support specialists
- Writers and editors

Look for Exciting New Occupations

In the early 1980s the auto and related industries – steel, rubber, glass, aluminum, railroads, and auto dealers – accounted for one-fifth of all employment in the United States. Today that percentage continues to decline as service occupations further dominate America's occupational structure.

New occupations for the decade ahead will center around information, energy, high-tech, health care, and financial industries. They promise to create a new occupational structure and vocabulary relating to computers, the Internet, robotics, biotechnology, lasers, and fiber optics. By 1999, for example, the Internet reportedly was responsible for 1.3 million new jobs within a four-year period that generated more than $300 billion in business. And as these fields begin to apply new technologies to developing innovations, they in turn will generate other new occupations in the decades ahead. While most new occupations are not major growth fields – because they do not initially generate a large number of new jobs – they will present individuals with fascinating new opportunities to become leaders in pioneering new fields and industries.

Futurists agree that most new occupations in the coming decade will have two dominant characteristics:

- **They will generate fewer new jobs** in comparison to the overall growth of jobs in hundreds of more traditional service fields, such as sales workers, office clerks, truck drivers, and janitors.

- **They require a high level of education and skills** for entry into the fields as well as continuing training and retraining as each field transforms itself into an additional growth field.

If you plan to pursue an emerging occupation, expect to first acquire highly specialized skills which may require years of higher education and training.

Implications of Future Trends for You

Most growth industries and occupations require training and experience. Moving into one of these fields will require knowledge of job qualifications, the nature of the work, and sources of employment. Fortunately, the U.S. Department of Labor publishes several useful sources of information available in most libraries to help you. These include the *O*NET Dictionary of Occupational Titles*, which identifies over 1,100 job titles. The *Occupational Outlook Handbook* provides an overview of current labor market conditions and projections, as well as discusses nearly 250 occupations that account for 107 million jobs, or 87 percent of the nation's total jobs, according to several useful informational categories: nature of work; working conditions; employment; training, other qualifications, and achievement; job outlook; earnings; related occupations; and sources of additional information.

During the past eight years, the U.S. Department of Labor overhauled its traditional job classification system, which was based on an analysis of the U.S. job market of the 1960s, 1970s, and 1980s. This system had generated over 13,000 job titles as outlined in the *Dictionary of Occupational Titles* and numerous related publications. Known as the O*NET project (The Occupational Information Network), this new occupational classification system more accurately reflects the structure of today's new job market; it condenses the 13,000+ job titles into over 1,100 job titles. The new system is being gradually introduced into career education to replace the job classification system that has defined most jobs in the U.S. during the past four decades.

Anyone seeking to enter or re-enter the job market or change careers should initially consult the U.S. Department of Labor publications as well as access information on the new O*NET (www.onetcenter.org). The Department of Labor only makes this data available online (www.online.onetcenter.org). A commercial version of this system, published in book form, also is available. You should be able to find it in your local library. If not, the *O*NET Dictionary of Occupational Titles* can be ordered from Impact Publications by completing the form at the end of this book or through Impact's online bookstore: www.impactpublications.com

However, remember that labor market statistics are for industries and occupations **as a whole**. They tell you little about the shift in employment emphasis **within the industry**, and nothing about the outlook of particular jobs for you, **the individual**. For example, employment in agriculture was projected to decline by 14 percent between 1985 and 2000, but the decline consisted of an important shift in employment emphasis within the industry: there would be 500,000 fewer self-employed workers but 150,000 more wage and salary earners in the service end of agriculture. The employment statistics also assume a steady state of economic growth with consumers having more and more disposable income to stimulate a wide variety of service and trade industries.

Therefore, be careful how you interpret and use this information in making your own job and career decisions. If, for example, you want to become a college teacher, and the data tells you there will be a 10-percent decline in this occupation during the next 10 years, this does not mean you would not find employment, as well as advance, in this field. It merely means that, on the whole, competition may be keen for these jobs, and that future advancement and mobility in this occupation may not be very good – **on the whole**. At the same time, there may be numerous job opportunities available in a declining occupational field as many individuals abandon the field for more attractive occupations. In fact, you may do much better in this declining occupation than in a growing field depending on your interests, motivations, abilities, job search savvy, and level of competition. And if the decade ahead experiences more boom-and-bust cycles, expect most of these U.S. Department of Labor statistics and projections to be invalid for the economic realities of this decade.

Use this industrial and occupational data to expand your awareness of various job and career options. By no means should you make critical education, training, and occupational choices based upon this information alone. Such choices require additional types of information about you, the individual, based upon an assessment of your interests, skills, and values. If identified and used properly, this information will help clarify exactly which jobs are best for you.

The Case of Ex-Offenders

If you are re-entering the job market after being incarcerated, you face many challenges most other job seekers take for granted. You may, for example, lack money, housing, transportation, appropriate clothing, a network of helpful contacts, and other basic resources for conducting an effective job search. In addition, you need to disclose your criminal record – a big red flag that will often knock you out of the competition.

Needing immediate employment upon release, many ex-offenders look for low-skill and low-paying jobs with employers who ask few questions about their backgrounds. Not surprisingly, these also tend to be high-turnover positions as janitors, cleaners, lawn maintenance workers, home health care workers, food preparers and servers, construction laborers, packers, and retail salespeople. The construction trades, retail businesses, and lodging and food industry tend to be most receptive to hiring ex-offenders. However, many such positions are actually dead-end jobs.

If you want to find a job with a good future, you may need to acquire additional education and training. Try to quickly land your first job out in order to get work experience, but also keep an eye on some of the promising jobs outlined in this book. These jobs have a future for those who have the necessary education, training, and experience to move ahead in their careers. At the same time, we recommend reviewing our book *The Ex-Offender's Job Hunting Guide* (Impact Publications, 2005) for tips on how to find a good job despite your record.

*   *   *

The following pages outline some of the best jobs for people re-entering the workforce. Depending on your occupational interests, these jobs offer many opportunities for starting or advancing a career. Use these pages as a reference for exploring various job and career options. Our descriptions and references to additional resources should give you basic information for further exploring the best jobs for you.

2

Education Occupations

AMERICA'S ENORMOUS PUBLIC and private educational complex offers numerous opportunities for people re-entering the workforce. While most teaching positions require a bachelor's degree or higher, many other educational positions, such as teacher assistants and child day care service workers, require less than a four-year degree.

If you are leaving the military and are interested in starting a new career in teaching, be sure to contact the Troops To Teachers (TTT) program operated by the Defense Activity for Non-Traditional Education Support (DANTES – Tel. 1-800-562-6616 or visit www.dantes.doded. mil/dantes_web/). Those interested in elementary or secondary teaching positions need a bachelor's or higher degree from an accredited college. Individuals interested in teaching vocational subjects need the equivalent of one year of college and six years of related experience.

Many colleges and universities offer special certification programs for individuals interested in elementary or secondary teaching positions. Contact college and university education departments for information on special programs to fast-track individuals re-entering the job market or changing careers to become certified teachers.

Archivists, Curators, and Museum Technicians

⇨ **Annual Earnings:** $35,270
⇨ **Education/Training:** Graduate education preferred
⇨ **Outlook:** Average increase

Employment Outlook: Job opportunities for archivists, curators, and museum technicians are expected to increase about as fast as average for all occupations through 2012. Jobs are expected to grow as public and private organizations emphasize establishing archives and organizing records and information in response to increasing public interest in science, art, history, and technology. However, competition for jobs is expected to be keen because qualified applicants outnumber job openings. Graduates with highly specialized training, such as master's degrees in both library science and history, with a concentration in archives or records management, and extensive computer skills should have the best opportunities for jobs as archivists. A curator job is attractive to many people with the necessary training, but there are limited openings. So candidates may have to work part time, as an intern, or even as a volunteer assistant curator or research associate after completing their formal education. Substantial experience will be necessary for permanent status. The job outlook for conservators may be more favorable – particularly for graduates of conservation programs. The majority of jobs are available in museums, historical sites, and college and university libraries.

Nature of Work: Archivists, curators, and museum technicians acquire and preserve important documents and other valuable items for permanent storage or display. They work for museums, governments, zoos, colleges and universities, corporations, and other institutions that require experts to preserve important records. They also describe, catalogue, analyze, exhibit, and maintain valuable objects and collections for the benefit of researchers and the public. These documents and collections may include works of art, transcripts of meetings, coins and stamps, living and preserved plants and animals, and historic buildings and sites.

Archivists often specialize in an area of history or technology so they can more accurately determine what records in that area qualify for retention and should become part of the archives. Computers are being increasingly used generate and maintain archival records. **Curators** direct the acquisition, storage, and exhibition of collections, including negotiating and authorizing the purchase, sale, exchange, or loan of collections. Most curators specialize in a particular field, such as botany, art, paleontology, or history. Those working in large institutions may be highly specialized. **Conservators** manage, care for, preserve, treat, and document works of art, artifacts, and specimens – work that may require substantial historical, scientific, and archeological research. Conservators document their findings and treat items to minimize their deterioration or to restore them to their original state. Conservators usually specialize in a particular material or group of objects, such as documents and books, paintings, decorative arts, textiles, metals or architectural material.

Working Conditions: Working conditions of archivists and curators vary. Some spend most of their time working with the public, providing reference assistance and educational services. Others perform research or process records, which often means working alone or in offices with only a few people. Those who restore and install exhibits or work with bulky, heavy record containers may climb, stretch, or lift. Those in zoos, botanical gardens, and other outdoor museums or historic sites frequently walk great distances. Curators who work in large institutions may travel extensively to evaluate potential additions to the collection, organize exhibitions, and conduct research in their area of expertise.

Education, Training, Qualifications: Employment as an archivist, conservator, or curator usually requires graduate education and related work experience. While completing their formal education, many archivists and curators work in archives or museums to gain the hands-on experience that many employers seek. Although most archivists have a variety of undergraduate degrees, a graduate degree in history or library science, with courses in archival science, is preferred by most employers. Some positions may require knowledge of the discipline related to the collection, such as business or medicine.

Currently no programs offer bachelor's or master's degrees in archival science. Approximately 65 college and universities offer courses or practical training in archival science as part of their history, library science, or other curriculum. The Academy of Certified Archivists offers voluntary certification for archivists. The designation "Certified Archivist" is obtained by those with at least a master's degree and a year of appropriate archival experience.

For employment as a curator, most museums require a master's degree in an appropriate discipline of the museum's specialty – art, history, or archeology – or museum studies. Many employers prefer a doctoral degree, particularly for curators in natural history or science museums. Earning two graduate degrees – in museum studies (museology) and a specialized subject – gives a candidate a distinct advantage in this competitive job market. In small museums, curatorial positions may be available to individuals with a bachelor's degree. For some positions, an internship of full-time museum work supplemented by courses in museum practices is needed.

Earnings: Median annual earnings of archivists, curators, and museum technicians in 2002 were $35,270. Earnings vary considerably by type and size of employer and often by specialty. Salaries of curators in large, well-funded museums can be several times higher than those in small ones. The average annual salary for archivists in the federal government in nonsupervisory, supervisory, and managerial positions was $69,706 in 2003; for museum curators, $70,100; museum specialists and technicians, $48,414; and for archives technicians, $37,067.

Key Contacts: For information on archivists and on schools offering courses in archival studies, contact:

- **Society of American Archivists:** 527 South Wells Street, 5th Floor, Chicago, IL 60607-3922. Website: www.archivists.org.

For general information about careers as a curator and schools offering courses in museum studies, contact:

- **American Association of Museums:** 1575 Eye Street NW, Suite 400, Washington, DC 20005. Website: www.aam-us.org.

For information about careers and education programs in conservation and preservation, contact:

- **American Institute for Conservation of Historic and Artistic Works:** 1717 K Street NW, Suite 200, Washington, DC 20036. Website: http://aic.stanford.edu.

Childcare Workers

- ➪ **Annual Earnings:** $7.86 hourly
- ➪ **Education/Training:** Credential, experience, or two-year degree
- ➪ **Outlook:** Good

Employment Outlook: Employment of childcare workers is projected to grow about as fast as average for all occupations through the year 2012. The number of women of childbearing age (generally considered to be ages 15 to 44) in the labor force and the number of children under five years of age is expected to rise gradually over the projected 2002-12 period. Also, the proportion of youngsters enrolled full or part time in childcare and preschool programs is likely to continue to increase, spurring demand for additional childcare workers. High replacement needs should create good job opportunities for childcare workers. Qualified persons who are interested in this work should have little trouble finding and keeping a job. Opportunities for nannies should be especially good, as many workers prefer not to work in other people's homes.

Changes in perceptions of pre-primary education may lead to increased public and private spending on childcare. If more parents believe that some experience in center-based care and preschool is beneficial to children, enrollment will increase. Concern about the behavior of school-age children during non-school hours should increase demand for before- and after-school programs. Government policy often favors increased funding of early childhood education programs, and that trend will probably continue.

Nature of Work: Childcare workers play an important role in a child's development by caring for the child when parents are at work or away for other reasons. Some parents enroll their children in nursery schools or childcare centers primarily to provide them with the opportunity to interact with other children. In addition to attending to children's basic needs, childcare workers organize activities that stimulate the children's physical, emotional, intellectual, and social growth. They help children explore their interests, develop their talents and independence, build self-esteem, and learn how to get along with others.

Private household workers who are employed on an hourly basis usually are called **babysitters**. These childcare workers bathe, dress, and feed children; supervise their play; wash their clothes; and clean their rooms. They also may put them to bed and waken them, read to them, involve them in educational games, take them for doctor's visits, and discipline them. Those who are in charge of infants also prepare bottles and change diapers.

Nannies generally take care of children from birth to age 10 or 12, tending to the child's early education, nutrition, health, and other needs. They also may perform the duties of a general housekeeper, including general cleaning and laundry duties.

Childcare workers spend most of their day working with children. However, they do maintain contact with parents or guardians through informal meetings or scheduled conferences to discuss each child's progress and needs. Most childcare workers perform a combination of basic care and teaching duties. For example, a worker who shows a child how to tie a shoelace teaches the child while also providing for that child's basic care needs. Young children learn mainly through play. Recognizing the importance of play, childcare workers build their program around it.

Childcare workers in preschools greet young children as they arrive, help them to remove outer garments, and select an activity of interest. When caring for infants, they feed and change them. To ensure a well-balanced program, childcare workers prepare daily and long-term schedules of activities.

Working Conditions: Preschool or childcare facilities include private homes, schools, religious institutions, workplaces in which employers provide care for employees' children, and private buildings. Individuals who provide care in their own homes generally are called family childcare providers. Nannies and babysitters usually work in the pleasant and comfortable homes or apartments of their employers. Most are day workers who live in their own homes and travel to work. Some live in the home of their employer, generally with their own room and bath.

Watching children grow, learn, and gain new skills can be very rewarding. The work is sometimes routine; however, new activities and challenges mark each day. Childcare can be physically and emotionally taxing, as workers constantly stand, walk, bend, stoop, and lift to attend to each child's interests and problems. To ensure that children receive proper supervision, state or local regulations may require a certain ratio of workers to children. The ratio varies with the age of the children.

The work hours of childcare workers vary widely. Childcare centers usually are open year-round, with long hours so that parents can drop off and pick up their children before and after work. Some centers employ full-time and part-time staff with staggered shifts to cover the entire day. Some workers may be unable to take regular breaks during the day due to limited staffing. Family childcare providers have flexible hours and daily routines, but may work long or unusual hours to fit parents' work schedules. Live-in nannies usually work longer hours than do those who have their own homes. However, if they work evenings or weekends, they may get other time off.

Replacement needs in this occupation are high. Many childcare workers leave the occupation temporarily to fulfill family responsibilities, to study, or for other reasons. Some workers leave permanently because they are interested in pursuing other occupations or because of dissatisfaction with hours, low pay and benefits, and stressful conditions.

Education, Training, Qualifications: The training and qualifications required of childcare workers vary widely. Each state has its own licensing requirements that regulate caregiver training; these range from a high school diploma, to community college courses, to a college degree in child development or early-childhood education. Many states require continuing education for workers in this field. However, state requirements often are minimal. Childcare workers generally can obtain employment with a high school diploma and little or no experience. Local governments, private firms, and publicly funded programs may have more demanding training and education requirements.

Some employers prefer to hire childcare workers with a nationally recognized childcare development credential, secondary or postsecondary courses in child development or early-childhood education, or work experience in a childcare setting. An increasing number of employers require or prefer an associate degree in early childhood education. Schools for nannies teach early childhood education, nutrition, and childcare.

Childcare workers must anticipate and prevent problems, deal with disruptive children, provide fair but firm discipline, and be constantly alert. They must communicate effectively with the children and their parents, as well as other teachers and childcare workers. Workers should be mature, patient, understanding, and articulate, and also have energy and physical stamina. Skills in music, art, drama, and storytelling also are important. Self-employed childcare workers must have business sense and managerial skills.

Opportunities for advancement are limited. However, as childcare workers gain experience, some may advance to supervisory or administrative positions in large childcare centers or preschools. Often, these positions require additional training, such as a bachelor's or master's degree.

Earnings: Pay depends on the education attainment of the worker and the type of establishment. Although pay generally is low, more education usually means higher earnings. Median hourly earnings of wage and salary childcare workers were $7.86 in 2002. Some earned less than $5.91 whereas others earned more than $11.46. In general, workers in residential facilities earned the most at an average of $9.51 per hour, while workers in daycare services and recreation industries earned the least at just over $7.00 per hour. Earnings of self-employed childcare workers vary depending on the hours worked, the number and ages of the children, and the location. Benefits vary, but are minimal for most childcare workers. Some employers offer a full benefits package, including health insurance and paid vacations, while others offer no benefits at all. Live-in nannies get free room and board.

Key Contacts: For information on becoming a childcare provider and other resources for persons interested in childcare work, contact:

- **National Child Care Information Center**: 10530 Rosehaven Street, Suite 400, Fairfax, VA 22030. Telephone toll-free: 800-616-2242. Website: www.nccic.org.

- **The Children's Foundation**: 725 15th Street NW, Suite 505, Washington, DC 20005-2109. Website: www.childrensfounda tion.net.

For eligibility requirements and a description of the Child Development Associate credential, contact:

- **Council for Professional Recognition**: 2460 16th Street NW, Washington, DC 20009-3575. Website: www.cdacouncil.org.

For eligibility requirements and a description of the Certified Childcare Professional designation, contact:

- **National Child Care Association**: 1016 Rosser Street, Conyers, GA 30012. Website: www.nccanet.org.

For information about a career as a nanny, contact:

- **International Nanny Association**: 2020 Southwest Freeway, Suite 208, Houston, TX 77098. Telephone toll-free: 888-878-1477. Website: www.nanny.org.

State departments of human services or social services can supply state regulations and training requirements for childcare workers.

Instructional Coordinators

⇨ **Annual Earnings:** $47,350
⇨ **Education/Training:** Bachelor's degree
⇨ **Outlook:** Faster than average growth

Employment Outlook: Employment of instructional coordinators is expected to grow faster than the average for all occupations through 2012. Over the next decade, instructional coordinators will be instrumental in developing new curricula to meet the demands of a changing society and in training the teacher workforce. Opportunities are expected to be best for those who specialize in subject areas that have been targeted for improvement by the No Child Left Behind Act – namely, reading, math, and science. Additional job growth for instructional coordinators will stem from the increasing emphasis on lifelong learning and on programs for students with special needs, including those for whom English is a second language. The best opportunities are found in local government education programs. The remainder of opportunities are in individual and family services; child daycare services; scientific research and development services; and management, scientific, and technical consulting services.

Nature of Work: Instructional coordinators are also known as curriculum specialists, staff development specialists, or directors of instructional material. They develop instructional materials, train teachers, and assess educational programs in terms of quality and adherence to regulations and standards. They also assist in implementing new technology in the classroom. Instructional coordinators often specialize in specific subjects, such as reading, language arts, mathematics, or social studies. Another duty instructional coordinators have is to review textbooks, software, and other educational materials and make recommendations on purchases. They also supervise workers who catalogue, distribute, and maintain a school's educational materials and equipment.

Working Conditions: Instructional coordinators, including those employed by school districts, often work year-round, usually in offices or classrooms. Some spend much of their time traveling between schools meeting with teachers and administrators. The opportunity to shape and improve instructional curricula and work in an academic environment can be satisfying. However, some instructional coordinators find the work stressful because the occupation requires continual accountability to school administrators and it is not uncommon for people in this occupation to work long hours.

Education, Training, Qualifications: The minimum educational requirement for instructional coordinators is a bachelor's degree, usually in education. Most employers, however, prefer candidates with a master's or higher degree. Many instructional coordinators have training in curriculum development and instruction, or in a specific academic field. Instructional coordinators must have a good understanding of how to teach specific groups of students, in addition to expertise in developing educational materials. As a result, many persons transfer into instructional coordinator jobs after working for several years as teachers. Work experience in an administrator position, such as principal or assistant principal, also is beneficial.

Helpful college courses may include those in curriculum development, instructional approaches, or research design, which teach how to create and implement research studies to determine the effectiveness of a given method of curriculum or instruction, or to measure and improve student performance. Instructional coordinators usually are required to take continuing education courses to keep their skills current. Topics for continuing education courses may include teacher evaluation techniques, curriculum training, new teacher induction, consulting and teacher support, and observation and analysis of teaching.

Earnings: Median annual earnings of instructional coordinators in 2002 were $47,350. Starting salaries vary but can be expected to begin at $25,000. Depending on the job and experience level, one could earn more than $76,000.

Key Contacts: Information on requirements and job opportunities for instructional coordinators is available from local school systems and state departments of education.

Librarians

⇨ **Annual Earnings:** $43,090
⇨ **Education/Training:** Master's degree
⇨ **Outlook:** Good

Employment Outlook: Employment of librarians is expected to grow about as fast as average for all occupations through 2012. However, job opportunities are expected to be very good because a large number of librarians are expected to retire in the coming decade, creating many job openings. Also, the number of people going into this profession has fallen in recent years, resulting in more jobs than applicants in some cases. Offsetting the need for librarians are government budget cuts and the increasing use of computerized information storage and retrieval systems. Both will result in the hiring of fewer librarians and the replacement of librarians with less costly library technicians. In addition, many libraries are equipped for users to access library computers directly from their homes or offices.

Jobs for librarians outside traditional settings will grow the fastest over the decade. Nontraditional librarian jobs include working as information brokers and working for private corporations, nonprofit organizations, and consulting firms. Librarians also are hired by organizations to set up information on the Internet. Librarians working in these settings may be classified as systems analysts, database specialists and trainers, webmasters or web developers, or local area network (LAN) coordinators.

Nature of Work: Librarians increasingly are combining traditional duties with tasks involving quickly changing technology. Librarians assist people in finding information and using it effectively for personal and professional purposes. Librarians must have knowledge of a wide variety of scholarly and public information sources and must follow trends related to publishing, computers, and the media in order to oversee the selection and organization of library materials. In small libraries or information centers, librarians usually handle all aspects of the work. In large libraries, librarians often specialize in a single area, such as acquisitions, cataloguing, bibliography, reference, special collections, or administration.

Librarians are classified according to the type of library in which they work: a public library; school library media center; college, university, or other academic library; or special library. Librarians also work in information centers or libraries maintained by government agencies, corporations, law firms, advertising agencies, museums, professional associations, medical centers, hospitals, religious organizations, and research libraries. Many libraries have access to remote databases and maintain their own computerized databases. The widespread use of automation in libraries makes database-searching skills important to librarians. Librarians with computer and information systems skills can work as automated-systems librarians, planning and operating computer systems, and information architect librarians, designing information storage and retrieval systems and developing procedures for collecting, organizing, interpreting, and classifying information. More and more, librarians are applying their information management and research skills to arenas outside of libraries – for example, database development, reference tool development, information systems, publishing, Internet coordination, marketing, web content management and design, and training of database users. Entrepreneurial librarians sometimes start their own consulting practices, acting as freelance librarians or information brokers and providing services to other libraries, businesses, or government agencies.

Working Conditions: Librarians spend a significant portion of their time at their desks or in front of computer terminals; extended work at video display terminals can cause eyestrain and headaches. Assisting users in obtaining information or books for their jobs, homework, or recreational reading can be challenging and satisfying, but working with users under deadlines can be demanding and stressful. Some librarians lift and carry books, and some climb ladders to reach high stacks.

More than two out of 10 librarians work part time. Public and college librarians often work weekends and evenings, as well as some holidays. School librarians usually have the same workday and vacation schedules as classroom teachers. Special librarians usually work normal business hours, but in fast-paced industries, such as advertising or legal services, they can work longer hours when needed.

Education, Training, Qualifications: A master's degree in library science (MLS) is necessary for librarian positions in most public, academic, and special libraries and in some school libraries. The federal government requires an MLS or the equivalent in education and experience. Many colleges and universities offer MLS programs, but employers often prefer graduates of the approximately 56 schools accredited by the American Library Association. Most MLS programs require a bachelor's degree; any liberal arts major is appropriate. Most MLS programs take one year to complete; some take two. The MLS degree provides general preparation for library work, but some individuals specialize in a particular area, such as reference, technical services, or children's services. A Ph.D. degree in library and information science is advantageous for a college teaching position or for a top administrative job in a college or university library or large library system.

State certification requirements for public school librarians very widely. Most states require school librarians, often called library media specialists, to be certified as teachers and to have taken courses in library science. An MLS is needed in some cases. Some states require certification of public librarians employed in municipal, county, or regional library systems.

Earnings: Salaries of librarians vary according to the individual's qualifications and the type, size, and location of the library. Librarians with primarily administrative duties often have greater earnings. Median annual earnings of librarians in 2002 were $43,090. Some earned less than $24,510 and some earned more than $66,590. The average annual salary for all librarians in the federal government was $70,238 in 2003. Nearly one in three librarians is a member of a union or is covered under a union contract.

Key Contacts: To learn more about a career as a librarian and obtain information on accredited library education programs and scholarships, contact:

- **American Library Association**: Office for Human Resource Development and Recruitment, 50 East Huron Street, Chicago, IL 60611. Website: www.ala.org.

For information on a career as a special librarian, contact:

- **Special Libraries Association**: 331 S. Patrick Street, Alexandria, VA 22314. Website: www.sla.org.

Information on graduate schools of library and information science can be obtained from:

- **Association for Library and Information Science Education**: 1009 Commerce Park Dr., Suite 150, P.O. Box 4219, Oak Ridge, TN 37839. Website: www.alise.org.

For information on a career as a law librarian, scholarships, and a list of ALA-accredited schools offering programs in law librarianship, contact:

- **American Association of Law Libraries**: 53 West Jackson Blvd., Suite 940, Chicago, IL 60604. Website: www.aallnet.org.

Information on acquiring a job as a librarian with the federal government is available on the Internet at www.usajobs.opm.gov.

Information concerning requirements and application procedures for positions in the Library of Congress can be obtained directly from:

- **Human Resources Office, Library of Congress**: 101 Independence Avenue. SE, Washington, DC 20540-2231.

Library Technicians

⇨ **Annual Earnings:** $24,090
⇨ **Education/Training:** High school diploma
⇨ **Outlook:** Average growth

Employment Outlook: Employment of library technicians is expected to grow about as fast as the average for all occupations through 2012. In addition to jobs opening up through employment growth, some job openings will result from the need to replace library technicians who transfer to other fields or leave the labor force. The increasing use of library automation is expected to continue to spur job growth among library technicians. Computerized information systems have resulted in jobs that can now be handled by technicians rather than librarians. Although efforts to contain costs could dampen employment growth of library technicians in school, public, and college and university libraries, cost containment efforts could also result in more hiring of library technicians than librarians.

Most library technicians work in school, academic, or public libraries. Some work in hospitals and for religious organizations, mainly parochial schools. The federal government – primarily the U.S. Department of Defense and the Library of Congress – and state and local governments also employ library technicians.

Nature of Work: Library technicians both help librarians acquire, prepare, and organize material and assist users in finding information. Library technicians usually work under the supervision of a librarian, although they work independently in certain situations. Technicians in small libraries handle a range of duties; those in large libraries usually specialize. As libraries increasingly use new technologies – such as CD-ROM, the Internet, virtual libraries, and automated databases – the duties of library technicians will expand and evolve accordingly. Technicians assist with customizing databases and instruct patrons in how to use computer systems to access data. Some library technicians operate and maintain audiovisual equipment. They may also design posters, bulletin boards, or displays.

To extend library services to more patrons, many libraries operate bookmobiles, often run by library technicians. The technicians may operate the bookmobile alone or may be accompanied by another library employee. Library technicians who drive bookmobiles answer patrons' questions, receive and check out books, collect fines, maintain the book collection, shelve materials, and occasionally operate audiovisual equipment to show slides or films. In some areas, they are responsible for the maintenance of the vehicle and any photocopiers or other equipment in it. Many bookmobiles are equipped with personal computers and CD-ROM systems linked to the main library system, allowing technicians to reserve or locate books immediately. Some bookmobiles now offer Internet access to users.

Working Conditions: Technicians answer questions and provide assistance to library users. Those who prepare library materials sit at desks or computer terminals for long periods and can develop headaches or eyestrain from working at the terminals. Some duties, like calculating circulation statistics, can be repetitive and boring. Library technicians may lift and carry books, climb ladders to reach high stacks, and bend low to place books on bottom shelves. Library technicians in school libraries work regular school hours. Those in public libraries and college and university libraries also work weekends, evenings, and some holidays. Library technicians in special libraries usually work normal business hours, although they often work overtime as well.

The schedules of library technicians who drive bookmobiles depend on the size of the area being served. Some bookmobiles operate every day, while others go only on certain days. Some bookmobiles operate in the evenings and weekends, to give patrons as much access to the library as possible. Because library technicians who operate bookmobiles may be the only link some people have to the library, much of their work consists of helping the public. They may assist handicapped or elderly patrons to the bookmobile or shovel snow to ensure their safety. They may enter hospitals or nursing homes to deliver books to patrons who are bedridden.

Education, Training, Qualifications: Training requirements for library technicians vary widely, ranging from a high school diploma to specialized postsecondary training. Some employers hire individuals with work experience or other training; others train inexperienced workers on the job. Still other employers require that technicians have an associate or bachelor's degree. Given the rapid spread of automation in libraries, computer skills are needed for many jobs. Knowledge of databases, library automation systems, online library systems, online public access systems, and circulation systems is valuable. Many bookmobile drivers are required to have a commercial driver's license.

Some two-year colleges offer an associate of arts degree in library technology. Programs include both liberal arts and library-related study. Library technicians usually advance by assuming added responsibility. For example, technicians often start at the circulation desk, checking books in and out. After gaining experience, they become responsible for storing and verifying information. As they advance, they may become involved in budget and personnel matters in their departments. Some library technicians advance to supervisory positions and are in charge of the day-to-day operation of their departments.

Earnings: Median annual earnings of library technicians in 2002 were $24,090. Some earned less than $18,150, but others earned more than $31,140. Salaries of library technicians in the federal government averaged $36,788 in 2003.

Key Contacts: For information on training programs for library/media technical assistants, contact:

- **American Library Association:** Office for Human Resource Development and Recruitment, 50 East Huron Street, Chicago, IL 60611. Website: www.ala.org.

Information on acquiring a job as a library technician with the federal government may be obtained from the Office of Personnel Management at www.usajobs.opm.gov.

Teacher Assistants

- ⇨ **Annual Earnings:** $18,660
- ⇨ **Education/Training:** Varies: High school diploma to some college
- ⇨ **Outlook:** Above average growth

Employment Outlook: Employment of teacher assistants is expected to grow somewhat faster than the average for all occupations through 2012. Although school enrollments are projected to increase only slowly over the next decade, the student population for which teacher assistants are most needed – special education students and students for whom English is not their first language – is expected to increase more rapidly than the general school-age population. A greater focus on educational quality and accountability, as required by the No Child Left Behind Act, is likely to lead to an increased demand for teacher assistants. Growing numbers of teaching assistants will be needed to help teachers prepare students for standardized testing and to provide extra assistance to students who perform poorly on standardized tests. Opportunities for teacher assistant jobs are expected to be best for persons with at least two years of formal education after high school. Nearly one of three teacher assistants works for state and local government education institutions, mostly at the preschool and elementary level. Private schools, daycare centers, and religious organizations hire most of the rest.

Nature of Work: Teacher assistants provide instructional and clerical support for classroom teachers, allowing teachers more time for lesson planning and teaching. Teacher assistants tutor and assist children in learning class materials using the teacher's lesson plans, providing students with individualized attention. Teacher assistants also supervise students in the cafeteria, schoolyard, and hallways, or on field trips. Some teacher assistants perform exclusively non-instructional or clerical tasks. Most however, perform a combination of instructional and clerical duties.

Teacher assistants also work with infants and toddlers who have developmental delays or other disabilities. Under the guidance of a teacher or therapist, teacher assistants perform exercises or play games to help the child develop physically and behaviorally.

Working Conditions: Approximately four of 10 teacher assistants work part time. However, even among full-time workers, nearly 40 percent work fewer than eight hours per day. Most assistants who provide educational instruction work the traditional nine- to 10-month school year. Teacher assistants work in a variety of settings – including private homes and preschools, and local government offices, where they would deal with young adults – but most work in classrooms in elementary, middle, and secondary schools. They also work outdoors supervising recess when weather allows, and they spend much of their time standing, walking, or kneeling.

Seeing students develop and gain appreciation of the joy of learning can be very rewarding. However, working closely with students can be both physically and emotionally tiring. Teacher assistants who work with special education students often perform more strenuous tasks, including lifting, as they help students with their daily routine. Those who perform clerical work may become weary of administrative duties, such as copying materials or typing.

Education, Training, Qualifications: Educational requirements for teacher assistants vary by state or school district and range from a high school diploma to some college training, although employers increasingly prefer applicants with some college training. Teacher assistants with instructional responsibilities usually require more training than those who do not perform teaching tasks. In addition, as a result of the No Child Left Behind Act of 2001, teacher assistants in Title 1 schools – those with a high proportion of students from low-income households – will need to meet one of three requirements: have a minimum of two years of college, hold a two-year or higher degree, or pass a rigorous state and local assessment.

A number of two-year and community colleges offer associate degree programs that prepare graduates to work as teacher assistants. However, most teacher assistants receive on-the-job training. Teacher assistants must know how to operate audiovisual equipment, keep records, and prepare instructional materials, as well as have adequate computer skills.

Teacher assistants should enjoy working with children from a wide range of cultural backgrounds, and be able to handle classroom situations with fairness and patience. Teacher assistants also must demonstrate initiative and a willingness to follow a teacher's directions. They must have good writing skills and be able to communicate effectively with students and teachers. Teacher assistants who speak a second language, especially Spanish, are in great demand for communicating with growing numbers of students and parents whose primary language is not English. Advancement for teacher assistants – usually in the form of higher earnings or increased responsibility – comes primarily with experience or additional education.

Earnings: Median annual earnings of teacher assistants in 2002 were $18,660. Some earned less than $12,900 while some earned more than $29,050. Teacher assistants who work part time ordinarily do not receive benefits. Full-time workers usually receive health care coverage and other benefits. In 2002, about three out of 10 teacher assistants belonged to unions – mainly the American Federation of Teachers and the National Education Association – which bargain with school systems over wages, hours, and the terms and conditions of employment.

Key Contacts: For information on teacher assistants, including training and certifications, contact:

- **American Federation of Teachers**: Paraprofessional and School Related Personnel Division, 555 New Jersey Avenue NW, Washington, DC 20001. Website: www.aft.org.

- **National Education Association**: Educational Support Personnel Division, 1201 16th Street NW, Washington, DC 20036. Website: www.nea.org.

For information on a career as a teacher assistant, contact:

- **National Resource Center for Paraprofessionals**: 6526 Old Main Hill, Utah State University, Logan, UT 84322. Website: www.nrc para.org.

Human resource departments of school systems, school administrators, and state departments of education also can provide details about employment opportunities and required qualifications for teacher assistant jobs.

Teachers – Adult Literacy and Remedial

- ⮑ **Annual Earnings:** $17.50 per hour
- ⮑ **Education/Training:** Bachelor's degree
- ⮑ **Outlook:** Faster than average growth

Employment Outlook: Opportunities for jobs as adult literacy and remedial education teachers are expected to grow faster than average for all occupations through 2012, and a large number of job openings is expected, due to the need to replace people who leave the occupation or retire. As employers increasingly require a more literate workforce, workers' demand for adult literacy, basic education, and secondary education classes is expected to grow. Significant employment growth is anticipated, especially for ESOL (English to speakers of other languages) teachers, who will be needed by the growing number of immigrants and other residents living in this country who need to learn, or enhance their skills in, English. The demand for adult literacy and basic and secondary education often fluctuates with the economy. When the economy is good and workers are hard to find, employers relax their standards and hire workers without a degree or GED or those with limited proficiency in English. As the economy softens, more students find they need additional education to get a job. Adult education classes are often subject to changes in funding levels, which can cause the number of teaching jobs to fluctuate from year to year.

Nature of Work: Adult literacy and remedial education teachers provide adults and out-of-school youths with the education they need to read, write, and speak English and to perform elementary mathematical calculations – basic skills that equip them to solve problems well enough to become active participants in our society, to hold a job, and to further their education.

Remedial education teachers, more commonly called adult basic education teachers, teach basic courses in mathematics, languages, history, reading, writing, science, and other areas, using instructional methods geared toward adult learning. Teachers in remedial or adult basic education may have to assist students in acquiring effective study skills and the self-confidence they need to reenter an academic environment. For students who wish to get a GED credential in order to get a job or qualify for postsecondary education, adult secondary education or GED teachers provide help in acquiring the necessary knowledge and skills to pass the test. ESOL teachers help adults to speak, listen, read, and write in English, often in the context of real-life situations to promote learning. Because the teacher and students often do not share a common language, creativity is an important part of fostering communication in the classroom and achieving learning goals.

All adult literacy and remedial teachers must prepare lessons beforehand, do any related paperwork, and stay current in their fields. Many teachers must learn the latest uses for computers in the classroom, as computers are increasingly being used to supplement instruction in basic skills and in teaching ESOL.

Working Conditions: A large number of adult literacy and remedial education teachers work part time. Some have several part-time teaching assignments or work full time in addition to their part-time teaching job. Classes for adults are held on days at times that best accommodate students who may have a job or family responsibilities. Because many of these teachers work with adult students, they do not encounter some of the behavioral or social problems sometimes found with younger students. Adults attend by choice, are highly motivated, and bring years of experience to the classroom – attributes that can make teaching these students rewarding and satisfying.

Education, Training, Qualifications: Requirements for teaching adult literacy and basic and secondary education vary by state and by program. Federally funded programs run by state and local governments require high accountability and student achievement standards. Those programs run by religious, community, or volunteer organizations, rather than state-run, federally funded programs, generally develop standards based on their own needs and organizational goals. Most state and local government and educational institutions require that adult teachers have at least a bachelor's degree and, preferably, a master's degree. Some – especially school districts that hire adult education teachers – require an elementary or secondary school teaching certificate. A few have begun requiring a special certificate in ESOL or adult education. Teaching experience, especially with adults, also is preferred or required. Volunteers usually do not need a bachelor's degree, but often must attend a training program before they are allowed to work with students.

Most programs recommend that adult literacy and basic and secondary education teachers take classes or workshops on teaching adults, using technology to teach, working with learners from a variety of cultures, and teaching adults with learning disabilities. ESOL teachers also should have courses or training in second-language acquisition theory and linguistics. GED teachers should know what is required to pass the GED and be able to instruct students in the subject matter. Both part-time and full-time teachers are expected to participate in ongoing professional development activities in order to keep current on new developments in the field and to enhance skills already acquired. Opportunities for advancement vary. Some part-time teachers move into full-time teaching positions or program administrator positions, such as coordinator or director, when vacancies occur. Others may decide to use their classroom experience to move into policy work at a nonprofit organization or with the local, state, or federal government.

Earnings: Median hourly earnings of adult literacy, remedial education, and GED teachers and instructors were $17.50 in 2002. Some earned less than $10.08 per hour, while some earned more than $34.30 per hour. Part-time adult literacy and remedial education and GED instructors are usually paid by the hour or for each class they teach, and receive few benefits or none at all. Full-time teachers are generally paid a salary and receive health insurance and other benefits if they work for a school system or government.

Key Contacts: For information on adult education and family literacy programs, contact:

- **The U.S. Department of Education**: Office of Vocational and Adult Education, 4090 MES, 400 Maryland Avenue SW, Washington, DC 20202. Website: www.ed.gov/about/offices/list/ ovae.

For information on teaching English as a second language, contact:

- **Center for Adult English Language Acquisition**: 4646 40th Street NW, Washington, DC 20016. Website: www.cal.org/caela.

Teachers – Postsecondary

- ➪ **Annual Earnings:** $49,040
- ➪ **Education/Training:** Bachelor's degree/master's degree or higher preferred
- ➪ **Outlook:** Faster than average growth

Employment Outlook: Employment of postsecondary teachers is expected to grow much faster than the average for all occupations through 2012. A significant portion of these new jobs will be part-time positions. Good job opportunities are expected as retirement of current postsecondary teachers and continued increases in student enrollments create numerous openings for teachers at all types of postsecondary institutions. Projected growth in college and university enrollment over the next decade stems largely from the expected increase in the population of 18- to 24-year olds. Adults returning to college and an increase in foreign-born students also will add to the number of students. In addition, workers' growing need to regularly update their skills will continue to create new opportunities for postsecondary cater to working adults.

Postsecondary institutions are a major employer of workers holding doctoral degrees, and opportunities for Ph.D. recipients seeking jobs as postsecondary teachers are expected to be somewhat better than in previous decades. Competition will remain tight for those seeking tenure-track positions at universities, as many of the job openings are expected to be either part-time or renewable, term appointments.

Because one of the main reasons why students attend postsecondary institutions is to obtain a job, the best job prospects for postsecondary teachers are likely to be in fields where job growth is expected to be strong over the next decade. These will include fields such as business, health specialties, nursing, and computer and biological sciences. Community colleges and other institutions offering career and technical education have been among the most rapidly growing, and these institutions are expected to offer some of the best opportunities for postsecondary teachers.

Nature of Work: Postsecondary teachers instruct students in a wide variety of academic and vocational subjects beyond the high school level that may lead to a degree or simply to improvement of one's knowledge or skills. These teachers include college and university faculty, postsecondary career and technical education teachers, and graduate teaching assistants.

Faculty usually are organized into departments or divisions, based on academic subject or field. They usually teach several courses related to their subject. They may instruct undergraduate or graduate students, or both. University faculty may give lectures to several hundred students in large halls, lead small seminars, or supervise students in laboratories. They prepare lectures, exercises, and laboratory experiments; grade exams and papers; and advise and work with students individually. College and university faculty work with an increasingly varied student population made up of growing numbers of part-time, older, and culturally and racially diverse students.

Faculty members keep abreast of developments in their field by reading current literature, talking with colleagues, and participating in professional conferences. They are often expected to do their own research to expand knowledge in their field. From this process, they arrive at conclusions and publish their findings in scholarly journals, books, and electronic media. The proportion of time spent on research, teaching, administrative, and other duties varies by individual circumstance and type of institution.

Career and technical education teachers have many of the same responsibilities that other college and university faculty have. They must prepare lessons, grade papers, attend faculty meetings, and keep abreast of developments in their field.

Working Conditions: Postsecondary teachers usually have flexible schedules. They must be present for classes, generally 12 to 16 hours per week, and for faculty and committee meetings. Most establish regular office hours for student consultations, usually three to six hours per week, and most faculty now are available to students through email communication as well. Some teach night and weekend classes. This is particularly true for teachers at two-year community colleges or institutions with large enrollments of older students who have full-time jobs or family responsibilities. Most colleges and universities require teachers to work nine months of the year, which allows them the time to teach additional courses, do research, travel, or pursue nonacademic interests during the summer and school holidays. Colleges and universities usually have funds to support research or other professional development needs, including travel to conference and research sites.

About three of 10 college and university faculty worked part time in 2002. Some part-timers, known as "adjunct faculty," have primary jobs outside of academia – in government, private industry, or nonprofit research – and teach "on the side." Others prefer to work part-time hours or seek full-time jobs but are unable to obtain them due to intense competition for available openings. University faculty may experience a conflict between their responsibilities to teach students and the pressure to do research and publish their findings. Requirements to teach online classes also have added greatly to the workloads of postsecondary teachers.

Education, Training, Qualifications: Four-year colleges and universities usually consider doctoral degree holders for full-time, tenure-track positions, but may hire master's degree holders or doctoral candidates for certain disciplines. In two-year colleges, master's degree holders fill most full-time positions. However, with increasing competition for available jobs, institutions can be more selective in their hiring practices. Many two-year institutions increasingly prefer job applicants to have some teaching experience or experience with distance learning. Preference may also be given to those holding dual master's degrees, because they can teach more subjects. In addition, with competition for jobs, master's degree holders may find themselves being passed over in favor of candidates with a Ph.D. Educational requirements for teachers are generally highest at four-year research universities, but, at career and technical institutes, experience and expertise in a related occupation is the most valuable qualification.

The number of tenure-track positions is expected to decline as institutions seek flexibility in dealing with financial matters and changing student interests. Institutions will rely more heavily on limited term contracts and part-time or adjunct faculty. For most postsecondary teachers, advancement involves a move into administrative and managerial positions, such as departmental chairperson, dean, and president. At four-year institutions, such advancement requires a doctoral degree. At two-year colleges, a doctorate is helpful but not usually required, except for advancement to top administrative positions.

Earnings: Median annual earnings of all postsecondary teachers in 2002 were $49,040. Some earned less than $23,080 and others earned more than $92,430. Earnings for college faculty vary according to rank and type of institution, geographic area, and field. By rank, the average was $86,437 for professors, $61,732 for associate professors, $51,545 for assistant professors, $37,737 for instructors, and $43,914 for lecturers. In fields with high-paying nonacademic alternatives – medicine, law, engineering, and business, among others – earnings exceed those averages. In others – such as the humanities and education – they are lower.

Key Contacts: For information on the Preparing Future Faculty program, contact:

- **Association of American Colleges and Universities**: 1818 R Street NW, Washington, DC 20009. Website: www.aacu-edu.org.

General information on adult and career and technical education is available from:

- **Association for Career and Technical Education**: 1410 King Street, Alexandria, VA 22314. Website: www.acteonline.org.

Professional societies related to a field of study often provide information on academic and nonacademic employment opportunities. Special publications on higher education, such as _The Chronicle of Higher Education_ (available in libraries), list specific employment opportunities for faculty.

Teachers – Preschool, Kindergarten, Elementary, Middle, and Secondary

- ⇨ **Annual Earnings:** $42,075
- ⇨ **Education/Training:** Bachelor's degree
- ⇨ **Outlook:** Average to excellent

Employment Outlook: Job opportunities for teachers over the next decade will vary from good to excellent, depending on the locality, grade level, and subject taught. Most job openings will be attributable to the expected retirement of a large number of teachers. In addition, relatively high rates of turnover, especially among beginning teachers employed in poor, urban schools, also will lead to numerous job openings for teachers. Competition for qualified teachers among some localities will likely continue, with schools luring teachers from other states and districts with bonuses and higher pay.

Through 2012, overall student enrollments, a key factor in the demand for teachers, are expected to rise more slowly than in the past. As the children of the baby-boom generation get older, smaller numbers of young children will enter school behind them, resulting in average growth for all teachers, from preschool through secondary grades. Fast growing states in the South and West will experience the largest enrollment increases. Currently, many school districts have difficulty hiring qualified teachers in some subject areas – mathematics, science (especially chemistry and physics), bilingual education, and foreign languages. Qualified vocational teachers, both at the middle school and secondary school levels, also are currently in demand in a variety of fields. Specialties that have an adequate number of qualified teachers include general elementary education, physical education, and social studies. Teachers who are geographically mobile and who obtain licensure in more than one subject should have a distinct advantage in finding a job.

The number of teachers employed is dependent on state and local expenditures for education and on the enactment of legislation to increase the quality of education. A number of initiatives, such as reduced class size (primarily in the early elementary grades), mandatory preschool for four-year-olds, and all-day kindergarten, have been implemented in a few states, but not nationwide. Additional teachers – particularly preschool and early elementary school teachers – will be needed if states or localities implement any of these measures.

Nature of Work: Preschool, kindergarten, and elementary school teachers play a vital role in the development of children. Teachers introduce children to mathematics, language, science, and social studies. They use games, music, artwork, films, books, computers, and other tools to teach basic skills. Preschool children learn mainly through play and interactive activities. Preschool teachers capitalize on children's play to further language and vocabulary development (using storytelling, rhyming games, and acting games), improve social skills (having the children work together to build something with blocks), and introduce scientific and mathematical concepts (showing children how to balance and count blocks when building a bridge or how to mix colors when painting). Play and hands-on teaching also are used in kindergarten classrooms, but academics begin to take priority. Letter recognition, phonics, numbers, and awareness of nature and science, introduced at the preschool level, are taught primarily by kindergarten teachers.

Most elementary school teachers instruct one class of children in several subjects. Specialized teachers may teach subjects such as music or physical education to a number of classes. Middle school and secondary school teachers help students delve more deeply into subjects introduced in elementary school and expose them to more information about the world. Middle and secondary school teachers specialize in a specific subject, such as English, Spanish, mathematics, history, or biology. They can also teach subjects that are career oriented. Vocational education teachers instruct and train students to work in a wide variety of fields, such as health care, business, auto repair, communications, and, increasingly, technology. They often teach courses that are in high demand by area employers, who may provide input into the curriculum and offer internships to students.

In addition to conducting classroom activities, teachers oversee study halls and homerooms, supervise extracurricular activities, and accompany students on field trips. Secondary school teachers occasionally assist students in choosing courses, colleges, and careers.

Working Conditions: Seeing students develop new skills and learn new information can be rewarding. However, teaching may be frustrating when one is dealing with unmotivated or disrespectful students. Occasionally, teachers must cope with unruly behavior and violence in the schools. Teachers may experience stress in dealing with large classes, students from disadvantaged or multicultural backgrounds, or heavy workloads. Inner-city schools, in particular, may be run down and lack the amenities of schools in wealthier communities. Accountability standards also may increase stress levels, with teachers expected to produce students who are able to exhibit satisfactory performance on standardized tests in core subjects.

Including school duties performed outside the classroom, many teachers work more than 40 hours a week. Part-time schedules are more common among preschool and kindergarten teachers. Although some school districts have gone to all-day kindergartens, most kindergarten teachers still teach two kindergarten classes a day. Most teachers work the traditional 10-month school year with a two-month vacation during the summer. During the vacation break, those on the 10-month schedule may teach in summer sessions, take other jobs, travel, or pursue personal interests.

Education, Training, Qualifications: Requirements for regular licenses to teach kindergarten through grade 12 vary by state. However, all states require general education teachers to have a bachelor's degree and to have completed an approved teacher training program with a prescribed number of subject and education credits, as well as supervised practice teaching. Some states also require technology training and a minimum grade point average. A number of states require that teachers obtain a master's degree in education within a specified period after they begin teaching.

Almost all states require applicants for a teacher's license to be tested for competency in basic skills, such as reading and writing, and in teaching. Almost all also require the teacher to exhibit proficiency in his or her subject. Most states require continuing education for renewal of the teacher's license.

Many states have reciprocity agreements that make it easier for teachers licensed in one state to become licensed in another.

Many states offer alternative licensure programs for teachers who have bachelor's degrees in the subject they will teach, but who lack the necessary education courses required for a regular license. After working under the close supervision of experienced educators for one or two years while taking education courses outside of school hours, they receive regular licensure if they have progressed satisfactorily.

In many states, vocational teachers have many of the same requirements for teaching as their academic counterparts. However, because knowledge and experience in a particular field are an important criteria for the job, some states will license vocational education teachers without a bachelor's degree, provided they can demonstrate expertise in their field. A minimum number of hours in education courses may also be required.

Licensing requirements for preschool teachers also vary by state. Requirements for public preschool teachers are generally higher than those for private preschool teachers. Some states require a bachelor's degree in early childhood education, other require an associate degree, and still others require certification by a nationally recognized authority. The Child Development Associate (CDA) credential, the most common type of certification, requires a mix of classroom training and experience working with children, along with an independent assessment of the individual's competence.

With additional preparation, teachers may move into positions as school librarians, reading specialists, curriculum specialists, or guidance counselors. Teachers may become administrators or supervisors, although the number of these positions is limited and competition can be intense.

Earnings: Median annual earnings of kindergarten, elementary, middle, and secondary school teachers ranged from $39,810 to $44,340 in 2002. The median earnings for preschool teachers were $19,270. The estimated average salary of all public elementary and secondary school teachers in the 2001-02 school year was $44,367. Private school teachers generally earn less than public school teachers.

In 2002, more than half of all elementary, middle, and secondary school teachers belonged to unions – primarily the American Federation of Teachers and the National Education Association – that bargain with school systems over wages, hours, and other terms of employment. Fewer preschool and kindergarten teachers were union members – about 15 percent in 2002.

Teachers can boost their salary in a number of ways. In some schools, teachers receive extra pay for coaching sports and working with students in extracurricular activities. Getting a master's degree or national certification often results in a raise in pay. Some teachers earn extra income during the summer by teaching summer school or performing other jobs in the school system.

Key Contacts: Information on licensure or certification requirements and approved teacher training institutions is available from local school systems and state departments of education. Information on the teaching profession and on how to become a teacher can be obtained from:

- **Recruiting New Teachers, Inc:** 385 Concord Ave., Suite 103, Belmont, MA 02478. Website: www.rnt.org. This same organization also sponsors: www.recruitingteachers.org.

A list of institutions with accredited teacher education programs can be obtained from:

- **National Council for Accreditation of Teacher Education:** 2010 Massachusetts Avenue NW, Suite 500, Washington, DC 20036-1023. Website: www.ncate.org.

For information on vocational education and vocational education teachers, contact:

- **Association for Career and Technical Education:** 1410 King Street, Alexandria, VA 22314, Website: www.acteonline.org.

For information on careers in educating children and issues affecting preschool teachers, contact:

- **National Association for the Education of Young Children:** 1509 16th Street NW, Washington, DC 20036. Website: www.naeyc.org.

Teachers – Special Education

- ⇨ **Annual Earnings:** $42,723
- ⇨ **Education/Training:** Bachelor's degree
- ⇨ **Outlook:** Faster than average growth

Employment Outlook: Employment of special education teachers is expected to increase faster than the average for all occupations through 2012. Although slowdowns in student enrollments may constrain employment growth somewhat, additional positions for these workers will be created by continued increases in the number of special education students needing services, by legislation emphasizing training and employment for individuals with disabilities, and by educational reforms requiring higher standards for graduation. The need to replace special education teachers who switch to general education, change careers altogether, or retire will lead to additional job openings. At the same time, many school districts report shortages of qualified teachers. As a result, special education teachers should have excellent job prospects. The job outlook, however, will vary by region. Student populations are expected to increase significantly in several states in the West and South. Positions in inner cities and rural areas usually are more plentiful than job openings in suburban or wealthy urban areas.

Nature of Work: Special education teachers work with children and youths who have a variety of disabilities. A small number of special education teachers work with students with mental retardation or autism, primarily teaching them life skills and basic literacy. However, the majority of special education teachers work with children with mild to moderate disabilities, using the general education curriculum, or modifying it to meet the child's individual needs. Most special education teachers instruct students at the elementary, middle, or secondary school level, although some teachers work with infants and toddlers.

The various types of disabilities that qualify individuals for special education programs include specific learning disabilities, speech or language impairments, mental retardation, emotional disturbance, multiple disabilities, hearing impairments, orthopedic impairments, visual impairments, autism, combined deafness and blindness, traumatic brain injury, and other health impairments. Students are classified under one of the categories, and special education teachers are prepared to work with specific groups. Early identification of a child with special needs is an important part of a special education teacher's job. Early intervention is essential in educating children with disabilities.

Working Conditions: Special education teachers enjoy the challenge of working with students with disabilities and the opportunity to establish meaningful relationships with them. Although helping these students can be highly rewarding, the work can also be emotionally and physically draining. Many special education teachers are under considerable stress due to heavy workloads and administrative tasks. They must produce a substantial amount of paperwork documenting each student's progress, and they work under the threat of litigation by a student's parents if correct procedures are not followed or if the parents feel their child is not receiving an adequate education. The physical and emotional demands of the job cause some special education teachers to leave the occupation.

Some schools offer year-round education for special education students, but most special education teachers work only the traditional 10-month school year.

Education, Training, Qualifications: All states require a bachelor's degree and the completion of an approved teacher preparation program with a prescribed number of subject and education credits and supervised practice teaching. Many states require a master's degree in special education, involving at least one year of additional course work, including specialization, beyond the bachelor's degree. All 50 states and the District of Columbia require special education teachers to be licensed. The state board of education usually grants licenses, and specific requirements vary by state. In many states, special education teachers receive a general education credential to teach kindergarten through grade 12. These teachers then train in a specialty, such as learning disabilities or behavioral disorders. Some states offer general special education licenses, while others license several different specialties within special education, and still others require teachers to obtain a general education license first and an additional license in special education afterwards.

Many colleges and universities across the United States offer programs in special education at the undergraduate, master's and doctoral levels. Special education teachers usually undergo longer periods of training than do general education teachers.

Alternative and emergency licenses are available in many states, due to the need to fill special education teaching positions. Alternative licenses are designed to bring college graduates and those changing careers into teaching more quickly. Requirements for an alternative license may be less stringent than for a regular license. Requirements vary by state. In some programs, individuals begin teaching quickly under a provisional license and can obtain a regular license by teaching under the supervision of a licensed teacher for a period of one to two years while taking education courses. Emergency licenses are granted when states have difficulty finding licensed special education teachers to fill positions.

Special education teachers must be patient, able to motivate students, understanding of their students' special needs, and accepting of differences in others. Teachers must be creative and apply different types of teaching methods to reach students who are having difficulty learning. Communication and cooperation are essential traits, because special education teachers spend a great deal of time interacting with others, including students, parents, and school faculty and administrators. Special education teachers can advance to become supervisors or administrators. They may also earn advanced degrees and become instructors in colleges that prepare others to teach special education.

Earnings: Median annual earnings in 2002 of special education teachers who worked primarily in preschools, kindergartens, and elementary schools were $42,690. For those teaching in middle schools, median annual earnings were $41,350; and for special education teachers in secondary schools, median annual earnings were $44,130. In 2002, about 62 percent of special education teachers belonged to unions – mainly the American Federation of Teachers and the National Education Association – that bargain with school systems over wages, hours, and the terms and conditions of employment. In most schools, teachers receive extra pay for coaching sports and working with students in extracurricular activities. Some teachers earn extra income during the summer, working in the school system or in other jobs.

Key Contacts: For information on professions related to early intervention and education for children with disabilities, a list of accredited schools, information on teacher certification and financial aid, and general information on related personnel issues – including recruitment, retention, and supply of, and demand for, special education professionals – contact:

- **Council for Exceptional Children:** 1110 N. Glebe Road, Suite 300, Arlington, VA 22201. Website: www.cec.sped.org.

3

Health and Medical Care Jobs

HEALTH AND MEDICAL CARE jobs represent some of the fastest growing and best paying opportunities for people re-entering the workforce. Just consider the enormity of this industry: it consumes nearly $1.8 trillion a year in the United States, which represents 15 percent of the gross domestic product!

If you don't know what you want to do, seriously consider whether you would enjoy working in this field. The opportunities are numerous and the rewards are many. Indeed, you may be pleasantly surprised with the long-term career opportunities and flexible work schedules available in several career fields relating to health and medical care.

Breaking In

If you don't have the necessary educational background and credentials to qualify for entering health and medical fields, you should survey various options for acquiring basic qualifications for breaking into these high-demand fields. Most jobs require some form of post-secondary education, training, or certification. Many of the jobs require two-year associate degrees provided by community or junior colleges, while other jobs only require on-the-job training or a nine- to 24-month training program offered by hospitals, vocational schools, or community colleges.

Hot Career Fields

Five of the 10 fastest growing jobs in the decade ahead are projected to be in the health care field. Altogether, nearly 15 million people work in the health care industry. While major restructuring of health care financing and services may negatively affect some jobs in this field, especially nurses in hospitals and physicians in private practice, despite such restructuring, medicine and health care are hot career fields for the decade ahead. Entry into the medical field will most likely result in a rewarding long-term career.

Increased job opportunities are largely due to seven major changes that translate into a boom for the health care industry:

1. Increased public and private financing of health care services.

2. New medical breakthroughs for the prevention, detection, and treatment of diseases.

3. An increasingly aging population requiring and demanding more and improved health care services.

4. The increasing acceptance of alternative medical approaches.

5. Shortage of key medical professionals, such as nurses and dental hygienists.

6. Increased delegation of traditional roles of medical professionals to paramedical professionals or assistants, who are given such titles as technologists, technicians, aides, or assistants.

7. The development of numerous specialized certification and training programs, with placement services, promoted by professional associations and sponsored by hospitals, vocational schools, and community colleges.

Good Pay and Promising Growth

In general, jobs in the medical and health care industries pay better than in most other industries. They also offer good advancement opportunities for those who seek additional training and certification within or between related medical fields. The best paying jobs will go to those with high levels of education and specialized training, such as surgeons, radiologists, gynecologists, and anesthesiologists. These fields also will generate hundreds of thousands of lower paying entry-level support positions, especially for medical assistants, technicians, technologists, nursing aides, and home health aides, which require the least amounts of medical education and training.

We expect job opportunities in medicine and health care to continue to expand throughout the coming decade. New medical breakthroughs relating to genetic engineering and biochemistry will create new occupational specialties. However, don't expect this to be a constantly expanding and rosy occupational field. The organization and management of medical and health care services will continue to undergo major changes in the next decade. The field faces some difficult and challenging years ahead with hospitals and HMOs

Jobs in the medical and health care industries tend to pay better than jobs in most other industries.

being at the center of a major upheaval in managed care health services. Key service delivery centers, such as hospitals and HMOs, are experiencing numerous difficulties relating to financing and the delivery of quality services. Indeed, the health care field is undergoing a fundamental revolution in how it finances, delivers, and gets paid for its services. Many of the changes are a result of insurance companies and government legislation that largely determine how health care services will be financed and thus delivered.

Coming Changes

The revolution in medicine and health care will have a significant impact on traditional medical roles and medical providers, such as physicians, nurses, hospitals, and an army of technologists, technicians, assistants, and aides. The major factors affecting the job outlook will be the financing of health care and the restructuring of health care roles. Changes in health care financing are the key to understanding the increased demand for health care services. As health care financing undergoes major changes, expect the demand for health care services to change accordingly. The current system of health care financing, as well as proposals to increase the scope of financing, could result in an even greater demand for medical and health care services in the decade ahead. Be prepared for new approaches to health care financing as well as new roles for nurses and medical aides in delivering health care services – changes which could significantly alter future job opportunities within the health care field.

Top Jobs

Seven of the jobs appearing in this chapter are usually included on most lists of the "50 best jobs":

- Dental hygienists
- Medical assistants
- Medical records and health information technicians
- Personal and home care aides
- Physical therapy assistants and aides
- Registered nurses
- Respiratory therapists

While not necessarily the best paying jobs, they are in high demand and offer excellent entry into the expanding health care industry. Landing a job in one of these fields should result in expanding career opportunities.

Useful Resources

The jobs profiled in this chapter represent only a sampling of hundreds of different jobs that may be appropriate for individuals re-entering the workforce. The following books and websites represent a wealth of resources for further exploring opportunities in the medical and health care fields:

Books

101 Careers in Nursing, Jeanne M. Novotny, ed. (Springer Publishing Company, 2003)

Careers in Health Care, Barbara Swanson (McGraw-Hill, 2000)

Career Opportunities in Health Care, Shelly Field (Facts on File, 2002)

Guide to Careers in the Health Profession, Lynn Borders Caldwell (Princeton Review, 2001)

Health Care Explosion, Dennis Damp (Bookhaven Press, 2001)

Opportunities in Nursing Careers, Keville Fredrickson, (McGraw-Hill, 2003)

Opportunities in Physician Assistant Careers, Terence J. Sacks (McGraw-Hill, 2002)

Top 100 Health-Care Careers, Dr. Saul Wischnitzer and Edith Wischnitzer (JIST Publishing, 2005)

The Yale Guide to Careers in Medicine and the Health Professions Robert Donaldson, Kathleen Lundgren, Howard Spiro, eds. (Yale University Press, 2003)

Websites

- Monster Healthcare   http://healthcare.monster.com
- MedHunters.com   www.medhunters.com
- MedCAREERS   www.medcareers.com
- Health Care Jobs USA   www.healthcarejobusa.com
- 4 MD Jobs.com   www.4mdjobs.com
- 4 Nursing Jobs.com   www.4nursingjobs.com
- AlliedHealthCareers.com   www.alliedhealthcareers.com
- CompHealth   www.comphealth.com

- DentistJobs — www.dentistjobs.com
- DentSearch — www.dentsearch.com
- PhyJob — www.phyjob.com
- Echo-Web — www.echocareers.com
- e-Dental.com — www.e-dental.com
- Health Care Jobs Online — www.hcjobsonline.com
- Health Care Recruiters — www.hcrecruiters.com
- Health Care Job Store — www.healthcarejobstore.com
- Healthcare Jobs — http://healthcare.careerbuilder.com
- Health Care Recruitment — www.healthcarerecruitment.com
- HealthcareSource — www.healthcaresource.com
- HealthCare Works — www.healthcareworks.org
- HealthCareerWeb.com — www.healthcareerweb.com
- Health Jobsite.com — www.healthjobsite.com
- Healthlinks.net — www.healthlinks.net
- Health Network USA — www.hnusa.com
- HIPjobs.net — www.HIPjobs.net
- Hospital Jobs Online — www.hospitaljobsonline.com
- iHireNursing — www.ihirenursing.com
- iHirePhysicians.com — www.ihirephysicians.com
- JobHealthCareers — www.jobhealthcareers.net
- Jobscience — www.jobscience.com
- MDJobSite.com — www.mdjobsite.com
- Med Options — www.medoptions.com
- Medical Sales Jobs — www.medicalsalesjobs.com
- MedJobs2000 — www.medjobs2000.com
- Medjump — www.medjump.com
- MedSearch — www.medsearch.com
- MedZilla.com — www.medzilla.com
- Nursejobz.com — www.nursejobz.com
- Nurse-Recruiter.com — www.nurse-recruiter.com
- Nursing Spectrum — www.nursingspectrum.com
- Pharmaceutical Rep Jobs — www.pharmaceuticalrepjobs.com
- PhysicianBoard — www.physicianboard.com
- Physicians Employment — www.physemp.com
- PracticeChoice — www.practicechoice.com
- RTJobs.com — www.rtjobs.com
- Ultrasoundjobs.com — www.ultrasoundjobs.com
- Vital Careers — www.vitalcareers.com

Dental Assistants

- ⇨ **Annual Earnings:** $27,250
- ⇨ **Education/Training:** 9-12 month training programs
- ⇨ **Outlook:** Excellent. 16,000 annual job openings

Employment Outlook: The employment outlook for dental assistants should be excellent in the decade ahead as more individuals use dental services. More and more dentists hire dental assistants to perform routine dental tasks so they can concentrate on performing more profitable procedures. Dentists currently employ nearly 270,000 dental assistants. This number should increase by 16,000 a year.

Nature of Work: Dental assistants serve as a second pair of hands for dentists. They perform a wide range of office, patient care, and laboratory tasks. They usually work next to dentists as they examine and treat patients. Office duties include scheduling appointments, receiving patients, keeping records, sending bills, receiving payments, and ordering dental supplies. Patient care involves preparing patients for treatment, assisting dentists with instruments and materials, and keeping patients comfortable. Some dental assistants may perform the roles of dental hygienists, such as process dental x-ray film, remove sutures, and apply anesthetics. Laboratory duties include making casts of teeth and temporary crowns as well as maintaining cleanliness and quality control of appliances. They should not be confused with dental hygienists who are licensed to perform other clinical tasks and who are required to have different levels of education and training.

Working Conditions: Dental assistants work in well-lighted, clean environments where infectious diseases and dangers posed by x-ray machines are minimized by proper safety equipment and procedures – gloves, masks, eyewear, and protective clothing. Most work in private dental offices, but some also work in dental schools, hospitals, physicians' offices, and public health clinics. Nearly half of all dental assistants work part time.

Education, Training, Qualifications: While many dental assistants attend nine- to 12-month dental assisting programs sponsored by community colleges, trade schools, technical institutes, or the Armed Forces, most dental assistants pick up their skills through on-the-job experience. Many dental assistants with chairside experience go back to school to become dental hygienists. Others go on to become office managers. In 2002 the American Dental Association's Commission on Dental Accreditation approved 259 dental-assisting training programs. Most states regulate the duties of dental assistants through licensure or registration, which may require a written or practical examination.

Earnings: Median hourly earnings of dental assistants in 2002 were $13.10. The middle 50 percent earned between $10.35 and $16.20 an hour. The lowest 10 percent earned less than $8.45, and the highest 10 percent earned more than $19.41 an hour. Full-time dental assistants can expect to earn between $19,000 and $33,000 a year.

Key Contacts: Information on education and careers for dental assistants is available through:

- **American Dental Assistants Association:** 35 East Wacker Drive, Suite 1730, Chicago, IL 60601. Website: www.dentalassistant.org.

- **Commission on Dental Accreditation:** American Dental Association, 211 East Chicago Avenue, Suite 1814, Chicago, IL 60611. Website: www.ada.org/prof/ed/accred/commission/index.asp.

- **Dental Assisting National Board:** 676 North Saint Clair, Suite 1880, Chicago, IL 60611. Website: www.danb.org.

- **National Association of Dental Assistants:** 900 South Washington Street, Suite G-13, Falls Church, VA 22046.

Dental Hygienists

- ➪ **Annual Earnings:** $55,000
- ➪ **Education/Training:** Associate degree
- ➪ **Outlook:** Outstanding; 5,000 annual job openings

Employment Outlook: This continues to be one of the hottest career fields for individuals without a four-year degree. Indeed, this is a well paid growth field with excellent working conditions. Jobs in this field should be plentiful as the population continues to grow and age and requires more dental services, as incomes rise, and as dentists increasingly delegate routine procedures to dental hygienists. Over the next decade employment for dental hygienists is expected to grow much faster than other occupations – by 37.1 percent. An estimated 148,000 dental hygienists were employed in 2002. More than half of all dental hygienists work part time (less than 35 hours a week), and many hold multiple jobs.

Nature of Work: Dental hygienists provide preventive dental care and teach patients about good oral hygiene. Depending on state regulations, dental hygienists may provide any or all of these services: remove calculus, stains, and plaque; apply cavity preventive agents such as fluorides and pit and fissure sealants; and take and develop dental x-rays. In some states they also may administer anesthetics; place and carve filling materials, temporary fillings, and periodontal dressings; remove sutures; and smooth and polish metal restorations.

Working Conditions: This is a terrific career field for someone who prefers a flexible work schedule. Most dental hygienists work in dental offices where they may have a wide range of flexible work schedules – full-time, part-time, evening, and weekend. Many work two or three days a week in one office and two or three days in other offices. They normally work in clean, well-lighted rooms. Working conditions are relatively safe since they adhere to proper radiological procedures and wear safety glasses, surgical masks, and gloves to protect themselves and patients from infectious diseases.

Education, Training Qualifications: Each state licenses dental hygienists, who are required to graduate from an accredited dental hygiene school as well as pass both a written and a clinical examination. Over 265 dental hygiene programs are accredited by the Commission on Dental Accreditation. Most programs grant an associate degree, but some also offer a certificate as well as bachelor's and master's degrees. Many of these programs require applicants to have completed one year of undergraduate education with course work in biology, health, chemistry, physiology, pharmacology, and nutrition. An associate degree or certificate is required for working in private dental offices. A bachelor's or master's degree is required for research, teaching, or clinical practice in public or school health programs. High school students interested in this field are well advised to study biology, chemistry, and mathematics in preparation for such programs.

Earnings: This is a relatively well paying field for individuals with one or two years of college education. The median hourly earnings of dental hygienists in 1998 were $26.59. The middle 50 percent earned between $21.96 and $32.48 an hour. The lowest 10 percent earned less than $17.34, and the highest 10 percent earned more than $39.24 an hour.

Key Contacts: Information on careers in dental hygiene and educational requirements is available through:

- **American Dental Association:** 211 East Chicago Avenue, Suite 1814, Chicago, IL 60611. Website: www.ada.org.

- **American Dental Education Association:** 1400 K Street NW, Suite 1100, Washington, DC 20005. Website: www.adea.org.

- **American Dental Hygienists' Association:** Division of Education, 444 N. Michigan Avenue, Suite 3400, Chicago, IL 60611. Website: www.adha.org.

- **Commission on Dental Accreditation:** American Dental Association, 211 East Chicago Avenue, Suite 1814, Chicago, IL 60611. Website: www.ada.org/prof/ed/accrd/commission/index.asp.

Dental hygienists' associations operate at the local level in most states. To locate these associations, search for "dental hygienists association" in such search engines as google.com or yahoo.com.

Medical Assistants

⇨ **Annual Earnings:** $23,940
⇨ **Education/Training:** 1-2 year training program
⇨ **Outlook:** Excellent – faster than average growth

Employment Outlook: This will be one of the fastest growing occupations in the decade ahead. Growth in job opportunities reflects the overall expansion of the health care industry in response to an aging population as well as major advances in medical technology. Employment growth will be driven by the increase in the number of group practices, clinics, and other health care facilities that need a high proportion of support personnel, particularly the flexible medical assistant who can handle both administrative and clinical duties. Medical assistants work primarily in outpatient settings, which are expected to exhibit much faster than average growth.

Nature of Work: Medical assistants help physicians examine and treat patients and conduct routine office tasks. They perform numerous clerical duties, from answering telephones and greeting patients to completing insurance forms and scheduling appointments. Many arrange examining room instruments and equipment, handle supplies, and maintain waiting and examining rooms. Medical assistants held nearly 365,000 jobs in 2002. Sixty percent worked in physicians' offices; nearly 14 percent worked in public and private hospitals, including inpatient and outpatient facilities; and almost 10 percent worked in offices of other health practitioners, such as chiropractors and podiatrists. The remainder worked in outpatient care centers, public and private educational services, other ambulatory health care services, state and local government agencies, medical and diagnostic laboratories, nursing care facilities, and employment services.

Working Conditions: Medical assistants work a regular 40-hour week in medical offices. They constantly interact with patients and perform multiple responsibilities. Some work part time, evenings, or weekends.

Education, Training, Qualifications: Until recently, this was one of the few health occupations open to individuals with little formal training. Applicants normally needed a high school diploma or equivalent and were given on-the-job training. High school courses in mathematics, health, biology, typing, bookkeeping, computers, and office skills were helpful. However, most employers are now hiring graduates of formal programs in medical assisting, which are offered in vocational-technical high schools, postsecondary vocational schools, and community and junior colleges. Most of these programs last one to two years and result in a certificate, diploma, or associate degree.

Earnings: Earnings vary widely depending on experience, skill level, and location. Median annual earnings of medical assistants were $23,940 in 2002. The middle 50 percent earned between $20,260 and $28,410. The median annual earnings for medical assistants working in general medical and surgical hospitals were $24,460; offices of physicians, $24,260; outpatient care centers, $23,980; other ambulatory health care services, $23,440; and offices of other health practitioners, $21,620.

Key Contacts: For information on educational programs and careers related to medical assistants, contact:

- **American Association of Medical Assistants:** 20 N. Wacker Drive, Suite 1575, Chicago, IL 60606-2903. Website: www.aama-ntl.org.

- **American Society of Podiatric Medical Assistants:** 2124 S. Austin Blvd., Cicero, IL 60804. Website: www.aspma.org.

- **American Medical Technologists:** 710 Higgins Road, Park Ridge, IL 60068-5765. Website: www.amt1.com.

- **Accrediting Bureau of Health Education Schools:** 7777 Leesburg Pike, Suite 314 North, Falls Church, VA 22043. Website: www.abhes.org.

- **Joint Commission on Allied Health Personnel in Ophthalmology:** 2025 Woodlane Drive, St. Paul, MN 55125-2998. Website: www.jcahpo.org.

Medical Records and Health Information Technicians

⇨ **Annual Earnings:** $23,890
⇨ **Education/Training:** Associate degree
⇨ **Outlook:** Excellent

Employment Outlook: This occupational field should experience excellent job growth due to the rapid growth in the number of medical tests, treatments, and procedures that will be increasingly scrutinized by third-party payers, regulators, courts, and consumers.

Nature of Work: Medical records and health information technicians organize and evaluate medical records for completeness and accuracy. They ensure that medical charts are complete and all forms are properly identified, coded properly, signed, and on file. Much of this work is computerized and involves learning information management programs and regularly communicating with physicians and other health care professionals to clarify diagnoses or to obtain additional information. Technicians also use computer programs to tabulate and analyze data to help improve patient care, to control costs, for use in legal actions, in response to surveys, or for use in research studies.

Working Conditions: Most medical records technicians work a 40-hour week in pleasant and comfortable office settings. In hospitals, where many health information departments operate 24 hours a day, seven days a week, technicians may work day, evening, and night shifts. Their jobs require accuracy, attention to detail, and concentration. Technicians who work at computer monitors for prolonged periods must guard against eyestrain and muscle pain.

Education, Training, Qualifications: Medical records and health information technicians normally complete a two-year associate degree program at a community or junior college. Some receive training through an Independent Study Program in Medical Record Technology offered by the American Medical Record Association. Hospitals occasionally advance promising health information clerks with two to four years work experience to jobs as medical records and health information technicians. Most employers prefer hiring Accredited Record Technicians (ART), who are accredited by passing a written examination offered by the American Medical Record Association.

Earnings: The median annual earnings of medical records and health information technicians were $23,890 in 2002. The middle 50 percent earned between $19,550 and $30,600. The median annual earnings in industries employing the largest numbers of medical records and health information technicians in 2002 were $25,160 in nursing care facilities; $24,910 in general medical and surgical hospitals; $22,380 in outpatient care centers; and $21,320 in offices of physicians.

Key Contacts: For more information on careers in medical records and health information technology, including Independent Study, contact:

- American Medical Association: Commission on Allied Health Education & Accreditation, 515 N. State St., Chicago, IL 60610. Website: www.ama-assn.org.

- **American Health Information Management Association:** 233 N. Michigan Avenue, Suite 2150, Chicago, IL 60601-5800. Website: www.ahima.org.

Occupational Therapists

- ➪ **Annual Earnings:** $51,990
- ➪ **Education/Training:** Bachelor's/master's degree in occupational therapy (after 2007 the minimal requirement will be a master's)
- ➪ **Outlook:** Good to excellent

Employment Outlook: Employment of occupational therapists is expected to increase faster than the average for all occupations through 2012. Growth in demand for occupational therapists should continue due to the increasing number of individuals with disabilities or limited functions who require therapy services. The increased number of heart attacks and strokes among middle-aged people as well as a growing over-75 population will ensure the continuing demand for occupational therapy services. Hospitals will continue to employ a large number of occupational therapists to provide therapy services to acutely ill inpatients as well as to staff their outpatient rehabilitation programs.

Nature of Work: Occupational therapists help people improve their ability to perform tasks in their daily living and working environments. They work with individuals who have conditions that are mentally, physically, developmentally, or emotionally disabling. They also help them to develop, recover, or maintain daily living and working skills. Their goal is to help clients have independent, productive, and satisfying lives. They assist clients in performing activities of all types, ranging from using a computer to caring for daily needs such as dressing, cooking, and eating. Occupational therapists in mental-health settings treat individuals who are mentally ill, mentally retarded, or emotionally disturbed. Activities include time management skills, budgeting, shopping, homemaking, and the use of public transportation. Occupational therapists also may work with individuals who are dealing with alcoholism, drug abuse, depression, eating disorders, or stress-related disorders.

Working Conditions: Occupational therapists in hospital and other health care and community settings usually work a 40-hour week. Those in schools may participate in meetings and other activities during and after the school day. In 2002, more than a quarter of occupational therapists worked part time.

In large rehabilitation centers, therapists may work in spacious rooms equipped with machines, tools, and other devices generating noise. The work can be tiring, because therapists are on their feet much of the time.

Therapists increasingly are taking on supervisory roles. Due to rising health care costs, third-party payers are beginning to encourage occupational therapist assistants and aides to take more hands-on responsibilities.

Education, Training, Qualifications: Through 2006, the minimum educational requirement for entry into this field is a bachelor's degree in occupational therapy. Beginning in 2007, the minimum requirement will be a master's degree or higher. All states, Puerto Rico, and the District of Columbia regulate the practice of occupational therapy. To obtain a license, applicants must graduate from an accredited educational program and pass a national certification examination.

Earnings: Median annual earnings of occupational therapists were $51,990 in 2002. The middle 50 percent earned between $42,910 and $61,620. Median annual earnings in the industries employing the largest numbers of occupational therapists in 2002 were as follows:

- Offices of other health practitioners $53,660
- Nursing care facilities   53,930
- General medical and surgical hospitals   53,210
- Elementary and secondary schools   45,740

Key Contacts: For more information on occupational therapy as a career, contact:

- **American Occupational Therapy Association:** 4720 Montgomery Lane, Bethesda, MD 20824-1220. Website: www.aota.org.

Occupational Therapist Aides

⇨ **Annual Earnings:** $22,040
⇨ **Education/Training:** High school diploma
⇨ **Outlook:** Faster than average growth

Employment Outlook: Employment of occupational therapist aides is expected to grow much faster than the average for all occupations through 2012. The demand is likely to continue to rise due to the growth in the number of individuals with disabilities or limited function. An aging population, including the baby boom generation, will likely need more occupational therapy services. Advances in medicine that allow more people to survive will result in an increased need for rehabilitative therapy. Third-party payers, concerned with rising health care costs, are expected to encourage occupational therapists to delegate more hands-on therapy work to occupational therapist aides.

Nature of Work: Occupational therapist aides work under the direction of occupational therapists to provide rehabilitative services to persons with mental, physical, emotional, or developmental impairments. The goal is to improve clients' quality of life and ability to perform daily activities. Occupational therapist aides typically prepare materials and assemble equipment used during treatment. They are responsible for a range of clerical tasks, including scheduling appointments, answering the telephone, restocking or ordering depleted supplies, and filling out insurance forms or other paperwork. Aides are not licensed, so the law does not allow them to perform as wide a range of tasks as occupational therapist assistants.

Working Conditions: The hours and days that occupational therapist aides work vary with the facility and depend on whether they are full- or part-time employees. Many outpatient therapy offices and clinics have evening and weekend hours to be more compatible with patients' personal schedules. Occupational therapist aides need to have a moderate degree of strength, due to the physical exertion required in assisting patients with their treatment. For example, aides may need to lift patients. Constant kneeling, stooping, and standing for long periods also are part of the job.

Education, Training, Qualifications: Occupational therapist aides usually receive most of their training on the job. Qualified applicants must have a high school diploma, strong interpersonal skills, and a desire to help people in need. Applicants may increase their chances of getting a job by volunteering their services, thus displaying initiative and aptitude to prospective employers.

Aides must be responsible, patient, and willing to take directions and work as part of a team. They should be caring and genuinely want to help people who are not able to help themselves.

Earnings: Median annual earnings of occupational therapist aides were $22,040 in 2002. Some earned less than $15,400, and the highest 10 percent earned more than $38,170.

Key Contacts: For additional information on a career as an occupational therapist aide, contact:

- **American Occupational Therapy Association:** 4720 Montgomery Lane, Bethesda, MD 20824-1220. Website: www.aota.org.

Occupational Therapist Assistants

- ⇨ **Annual Earnings:** $36,660
- ⇨ **Education/Training:** Associate degree or certificate
- ⇨ **Outlook:** Much faster than average

Employment Outlook: Employment of occupational therapists is expected to grow much faster than average for all occupations through 2012. The impact of federal legislation imposing limits for reimbursement for therapy services may adversely affect the job market for occupational therapist assistants in the near term. However, over the long run, demand for occupational therapist assistants will continue to rise, due to growth in the number of individuals with disabilities or limited function. Job growth will result from an aging population, including the baby boom generation, which will need more occupational therapy services. Increasing demand also will result from advances in medicine that allow more people with critical problems to survive and then need rehabilitative therapy. Third-party payers, concerned with rising health care costs, are expected to encourage occupational therapists to delegate more hands-on therapy work to occupational therapist assistants.

Nature of Work: Occupational therapist assistants work under the direction of occupational therapists to provide rehabilitative services to persons with mental, physical, emotional, or developmental impairments. The ultimate goal is to improve clients' quality of life and ability to perform daily activities. For example, occupational therapist assistants help injured workers re-enter the labor force by teaching them how to compensate for lost motor skills, or help individuals with learning disabilities increase their independence.

Occupational therapist assistants help clients with rehabilitative activities and exercises outlined in a treatment plan developed in collaboration with an occupational therapist. Activities range from teaching the proper method of moving from a bed into a wheelchair to the best way to stretch and limber the muscles of the hand. Assistants monitor an individual's activities to make sure that they are performed correctly and to provide encouragement. They also record their client's progress for the occupational therapist, and document the billing of the client's health insurance provider.

Working Conditions: The hours and days that occupational therapist assistants work vary with the facility and with whether they are full- or part-time employees. Many outpatient therapy offices and clinics have evening and weekend hours, to help coincide with patients' personal schedules. Occupational therapist assistants need to have a moderate degree of strength, due to the physical exertion required in assisting patients with their treatment. For example, assistants may need to lift patients. Constant kneeling, stooping, and standing for long periods also are part of the job.

Education, Training, Qualifications: An associate degree or a certificate from an accredited community college or technical school is generally required to qualify for occupational therapist assistant jobs. The first year of study typically involves an introduction to health care, basic medical terminology, anatomy, and physiology. In the second year, courses are more rigorous and usually include occupational therapist courses in areas such as mental health, adult physical disabilities, gerontology, and pediatrics. Applicants to occupational therapist assistant programs can improve their chances of admission by taking high school courses in biology and health and by performing volunteer work in nursing facilities, occupational or physical therapists' offices, or other health care settings.

Occupational therapist assistants are regulated in most states and must pass a national certification examination after they graduate. Those who pass the test are awarded the title "Certified Occupational Therapist Assistant."

Earnings: Median annual earnings of occupational therapist assistants were $36,660 in 2002. Some earned less than $25,600, and the highest 10 percent earned more than $48,480.

Key Contacts: For information on a career as an occupational therapist assistant and a list of accredited programs, contact:

- **American Occupational Therapy Association:** 4720 Montgomery Lane, Bethesda, MD 20824-1220. Website: www.aota.org.

Personal and Home Care Aides

⇨ **Annual Earnings:** $7.81 hourly
⇨ **Education/Training:** On-the-job training
⇨ **Outlook:** Excellent job opportunities

Employment Outlook: Excellent job opportunities are expected for this occupation, as rapid employment growth and high replacement needs produce a large number of openings. Employment of personal and home care aides is projected to grow much faster than average through the year 2012. The number of elderly people, an age group characterized by mounting health problems and requiring some assistance, is projected to rise substantially. In addition to the elderly, patients in other age groups will increasingly rely on home care, a trend that reflects several developments, including efforts to contain costs by moving patients out of hospitals and nursing care facilities as quickly as possible, the realization that treatment can be more effective in familiar rather than clinical surroundings, and the development and improvement of medical technologies for in-home treatment.

In addition to job openings created by the increased demand for these workers, replacement needs are expected to produce numerous openings. The relatively low skill requirements, low pay, and high emotional demands of the work result in high replacement needs. For these same reasons, many people are reluctant to seek jobs in this occupation. Therefore, persons who are interested in and suited for this work – particularly those with experience or training as personal care, home health, or nursing aides – should have excellent job opportunities.

Nature of Work: Personal and home care aides help elderly, disabled, and ill persons live in their own homes or in residential care facilities instead of in a health facility. Most aides work with elderly or disabled clients who need more extensive personal and home care than family or friends can provide. Some aides work with families in which a parent is incapacitated and small children need care. Others help discharged hospital patients who have relatively short-term needs.

Personal and home care aides may provide housekeeping and routine personal care services. They clean clients' houses, do laundry, and change bed linens. Aides may plan meals, (including special diets), shop for food, and cook. Aides may also help clients move from bed, bathe, dress, and groom. Some accompany clients outside the home, serving as a guide and companion. In carrying out their work, aides may work with other health care professionals, including registered nurses, therapists, and other medical staff.

Working Conditions: The personal and home care aide's daily routine may vary. Aides may go to the same home every day for months or even years. However, most aides work with a number of different clients, each job lasting a few hours, days, or weeks. Aides often visit four or five clients on the same day. Surroundings differ from case to case. Some homes are neat and pleasant, whereas others are untidy or depressing. Some clients are pleasant and cooperative; others are angry, abusive, depressed, or otherwise difficult.

Personal and home care aides generally work on their own, with periodic visits by their supervisor. Almost a third of aides work part time, and some work weekends or evenings to suit the needs of their clients. Aides are individually responsible for getting to the client's home. They may spend a good portion of the working day traveling from one client to another. Because mechanical lifting devices that are available in institutional settings are seldom available in patients' homes, aides must be careful to avoid over-exertion or injury when they assist clients.

Education, Training, Qualifications: In some states, this occupation is open to individuals who have no formal training. On-the-job training is then generally provided. The National Association for Home Care offers national certification for personal and home care aides. Certification is a voluntary demonstration that the individual has met industry standards.

Successful personal and home care aides like to help people and do not mind hard work. They should be responsible, compassionate, emotionally stable, and cheerful. In addition, aides should be tactful, honest, and discreet, because they work in private homes. Aides also must be in good health. Advancement for personal and home care aides is limited.

Earnings: Median hourly earnings of personal and home care aides were $7.81 in 2002. Broken down by category of employment earnings were:

- Residential mental retardation, mental health
  and substance abuse facilities $8.63
- Vocational rehabilitation services $8.40
- Community care facilities for the elderly $8.14
- Individual and family services $8.12
- Home health care services $6.72

Most employers give slight pay increases with experience and added responsibility. Aides usually are paid only for the time they work in the home and normally are not paid for travel time between jobs. Employers often hire on-call hourly workers and provide no benefits.

Key Contacts: General information about training, referrals to state and local agencies about job opportunities, a list of relevant publications, and information on certification for personal and home care aides are available from:

- National Association for Home Care and Hospice: 228 7th Street SE, Washington, DC 20003. Website: www.nahc.org.

Physical Therapists

➪ **Annual Earnings:** $57,330
➪ **Education/Training:** Graduation from an accredited physical therapist education program and pass a licensure exam
➪ **Outlook:** Good to excellent

Employment Outlook: Employment of physical therapists is expected to grow faster than average for all occupations through 2012. Continuing demand is due to the growing number of individuals with disabilities, injuries, or limited functions requiring therapy services. The growing elderly population is particularly vulnerable to chronic and debilitating conditions that require therapeutic services. Also, the baby-boom generation is entering the prime age for heart attacks and strokes, increasing the demand for cardiac and physical rehabilitation. Future medical developments will permit a higher percentage of trauma victims to survive, creating additional demand for rehabilitative care. A growing number of employers also are using physical therapists to evaluate work sites, develop exercise programs, and teach safe work habits to employees in the hope of reducing injuries.

Nature of Work: Physical therapists provide services that help restore function, improve mobility, relieve pain, and prevent or limit permanent physical disabilities of patients suffering from injuries or disease. They restore, maintain, and promote overall fitness and health. Their patients include accident victims and individuals with disabling conditions such as low-back pain, arthritis, heart disease, fractures, head injuries, and cerebral palsy.

Therapists examine patients' medical histories and then test and measure the patients' strength, range of motion, balance and coordination, posture, muscle performance, respiration, and motor function. They also determine patients' ability to be independent and reintegrate into the community or workplace after injury or illness. They also develop treatment plans describing a treatment strategy, its purpose, and its anticipated outcome.

Treatment often includes exercise for patients who have been immobilized and lack flexibility, strength, or endurance. As treatment continues, physical therapists document the patient's progress, conduct periodic examinations, and modify treatments when necessary.

Some physical therapists treat a wide range of ailments; others specialize in areas such as pediatrics, geriatrics, orthopedics, sports medicine, neurology, and cardiopulmonary physical therapy.

Working Conditions: Physical therapists practice in hospitals, clinics, and private offices that have specially equipped facilities, or they treat patients in hospital rooms, homes, or schools.

Most full-time physical therapists work a 40-hour week; some work evenings and weekends to fit their patients' schedules. More than one in five physical therapists work part time.

The work of physical therapists can be physically demanding because they often stoop, kneel, crouch, lift, and stand for long periods. They also move heavy equipment and lift patients or help them turn, stand, or walk.

Education, Training, Qualifications: All states require physical therapists to pass a licensure exam before they can practice, after graduating from an accredited physical therapist educational program. Within the United States there are 203 accredited physical therapist programs, of which 113 offer master's degrees and 90 offer doctoral degrees. Physical therapists are expected to continue their professional development by participating in continuing education courses and workshops.

Earnings: Median annual earnings of physical therapists were $57,330 in 2002. The middle 50 percent earned between $48,480 and $70,050. Median annual earnings in the industries employing the largest numbers of physical therapists in 2002 were as follows:

- Home health care services $62,480
- Offices of other health practitioners $58,510
- Offices of physicians $57,640
- Nursing care facilities $57,570
- General medical and surgical hospitals $57,200

Key Contacts: Additional career information and a list of accredited education programs in physical therapy are available from:

- **American Physical Therapy Association:** 1111 North Fairfax Street, Alexandria, VA 22314-1488. Website: www.apta.org.

Physical Therapist Assistants and Aides

⇨ **Annual Earnings:** $36,080
⇨ **Education/Training:** On-the-job training to associate degree
⇨ **Outlook:** Excellent

Employment Outlook: Employment of physical therapy assistants is expected to grow much faster than average in the coming decade. This is due in part to the growing number of elderly patients experiencing chronic and debilitating conditions who require therapeutic services as well as the growing number of heart attack and stroke victims who require cardiac and physical rehabilitation. Physical therapists are expected to increasingly use assistants to reduce the cost of physical therapy services.

Nature of Work: Physical therapist assistants and aides perform components of physical therapy procedures and related tasks selected by a supervising physical therapist. They assist physical therapists in providing services that help improve mobility, relieve pain, and prevent or limit permanent physical disabilities of patients suffering from injuries or disease. Patients include accident victims and individuals with disabling conditions, such as low-back pain, arthritis, heart disease, fractures, head injuries, and cerebral palsy. Physical therapist assistants perform a variety of services that may include exercises, massages, electrical stimulation, paraffin baths, hot and cold packs, traction, and ultrasound. Physical therapist assistants record the patient's responses to treatment and report the outcome of each treatment to the physical therapist. Physical therapist aides help make therapy sessions productive, under the direct supervision of a physical therapist or physical therapist assistant. They usually are responsible for keeping the treatment area clean and organized and for preparing for each patient's therapy. Because they are not licensed, aides do not preform the clinical tasks of a physical therapist assistant.

Working Conditions: The hours and days that physical therapist assistants and aides work vary with the facility and whether they are full- or part-time employees. Many outpatient physical therapy offices and clinics have evening and weekend hours that coincide with patients' personal schedules. Since these professionals often provide physical assistance to patients, they may need to lift patients. Constant kneeling, stooping, and standing for long periods also are part of the job.

Education, Training, Qualifications: Physical therapist aides are trained on the job, but physical therapist assistants typically earn an associate degree from an accredited physical therapist assistant program. Over 40 states require licensure or registration of physical therapist assistants. Nearly 250 accredited physical therapist assistant programs operate in the United States. Most physical therapist aides receive on-the-job training.

Earnings: Median annual earnings of physical therapist assistants were $36,080 in 2002. The middle 50 percent earned between $30,260 and $42,780. Median annual earnings of physical therapist aides were $20,670 in 2002. The middle 50 percent earned between $17,430 and $24,560. Physical therapist assistants and aides working in medical and surgical hospitals tend to earn slightly more than those working elsewhere.

Key Contacts: For career information on physical therapist assistants and a list of schools offering accredited programs, contact:

- **American Physical Therapy Association:** 1111 North Fairfax Street, Alexandria, VA 22314-1488. Website: www.apta.org.

Physician Assistants

- ⇨ **Annual Earnings:** $64,670
- ⇨ **Education/Training:** Bachelor's degree/graduation from a physician assistants (PA) program
- ⇨ **Outlook:** Much faster than average growth

Employment Outlook: Employment of physician assistants (PAs) is expected to grow much faster than the average for all occupations through 2012, due to anticipated expansion of the health services industry and an emphasis on cost containment, resulting in increasing utilization of PAs by physicians and health care institutions. Physicians and institutions are expected to employ more PAs to provide primary care and to assist with medical and surgical procedures because PAs are cost-effective members of the health care team. Telemedicine – using technology to facilitate interaction between physicians and physician assistants – also will expand the use of physician assistants. Job opportunities for PAs should be good, particularly in rural and inner city clinics, because those settings have difficulty attracting physicians.

Besides the traditional office-based setting, PAs should find a growing number of jobs in institutional settings such as hospitals, academic medical centers, public clinics, and prisons. Opportunities will be best in states that allow PAs a wider scope of practice.

Nature of Work: Physician assistants provide health care services under the supervision of physicians. They should not be confused with medical assistants, who perform routine clinical and clerical tasks. PAs are formally trained to provide diagnostic, therapeutic, and preventive health care services, as delegated by a physician. Working as members of the health care team, they take medical histories, examine and treat patients, order and interpret laboratory tests and x-rays, make diagnoses, and prescribe medications. In 47 states and the District of Columbia, physician assistants may prescribe medications. PAs also may have managerial duties. Some order medical and laboratory supplies and equipment and may supervise technicians and assistants.

Physician assistants work under the supervision of a physician. However, PAs may be the principal health care providers in rural or inner city clinics, where a physician is only present for one or two days each week. In such cases, the PA confers with the supervising physician and other medical professionals as needed or as required by law. PAs may also make house calls or go to hospitals and nursing care facilities to check on patients, after which they report back to the physician. The duties of physician assistants are determined by the supervising physician and state law where they practice.

Working Conditions: Although PAs usually work in a comfortable, well-lighted environment, those in surgery often stand for long periods, and others do considerable walking. Schedules vary according to the practice setting, and often depend on the hours of the supervising physician. The workweek of hospital-based PAs may include weekends, nights, or early-morning hospital rounds to visit patients. These workers also may be on call. PAs in clinics usually work a 40-hour week.

Education, Training, Qualifications: All states require the new Pas to complete an accredited, formal education program. Most PA graduates have at least a bachelor's degree. Many have a master's degree, which is preferred. Admission requirements vary, but many programs require two years of college and some work experience in the health care field. Students should take courses in biology, English, chemistry, mathematics, psychology, and the social sciences. Most applicants to PA programs hold a bachelor's or master's degree. Many PAs have backgrounds as registered nurses, while others come from varied backgrounds, including military corpsman/medics and allied health occupations such as respiratory therapists, physical therapists, and emergency medical technicians and paramedics. PA programs usually last at least two years and are full time. Most programs are in schools of allied health, academic health centers, medical schools, or four-year colleges; a few are in community colleges, the military, or hospitals. Many accredited PA programs have clinical teaching affiliations with medical schools.

PA education includes classroom instruction in biochemistry, pathology, human anatomy, physiology, microbiology, clinical pharmacology, clinical medicine, geriatric and home health care, disease prevention, and medical ethics. Students obtain supervised clinical training in several areas, including primary care medicine, inpatient medicine, surgery, obstetrics and gynecology, geriatrics, emergency medicine, psychiatry, and pediatrics. Sometimes, PA students serve one or more "rotations" under the supervision of a physician who is seeking to hire a PA.

All states and the District of Columbia have legislation governing the qualifications or practice of physician assistants. All jurisdictions require physician assistants to pass the Physician Assistants National Certifying Exam, which is open only to graduates of accredited PA education programs. Only those successfully completing the examination may use the credential "Physician Assistant-Certified." Ongoing education and testing to be re-certified are required at a minimum of every six years.

Earnings: Median annual earnings of physician assistants were $64,670 in 2002. According to the American Academy of Physician Assistants, median income for assistants in full-time clinical practice in 2003 was about $72,457; median income for first-year graduates was about $63,437. Income varies by specialty, practice setting, geographical location, and years of experience.

Key Contacts: For information on a career as a physician assistant, as well as a list of accredited programs and a catalog of individual PA training programs, contact:

- **American Academy of Physician Assistants:** 950 North Washington St., Alexandria, VA 22314-1552. Website: www.aapa.org.

For eligibility requirements and a description of the Physician Assistant Certifying Examination, contact:

- **National Commission on Certification of Physician Assistants, Inc.,** 12000 Findley Road, Suite 200, Duluth, GA 30097. Website: www.nccpa.net.

Registered Nurses

- ⇨ **Annual Earnings:** $48,090
- ⇨ **Education/Training:** Associate to bachelor's degrees
- ⇨ **Outlook:** Excellent

Employment Outlook: Registered nurses constitute the largest health care occupation with nearly 2.3 million jobs in 2002. Jobs for registered nurses will grow much faster than for most other occupational groups. This increase responds to the overall growth in health care and the increased demand for new nurses in home health, long-term, and ambulatory care.

Nature of Work: Registered nurses provide for the physical, mental, and emotional needs of sick and injured patients. They observe, assess, and record symptoms, reactions, and progress; assist physicians during treatments and examinations; administer medications; assist in convalescence and rehabilitation; instruct patients and their families in proper care; and help individuals and groups take steps to improve or maintain their health. Hospital nurses form the largest (60 percent) group of nurses. Most are staff nurses, who provide bedside nursing care and carry out medical regimens. One of the fastest growing and most financially rewarding opportunities is for contract nurses who are hired for short-term assignments with different hospitals. Other types of nurses include office nurses, nursing care facility nurses, home health nurses, public health nurses, occupational health nurses (also known as industrial nurses), head nurses or nurse supervisors, and nurse practitioners.

Working Conditions: Most registered nurses work in well-lighted, comfortable health care facilities. They also work in a variety of settings as hospital nurses, nursing home nurses, public health nurses, private duty nurses, office nurses, occupational health or industrial nurses, and head nurses or nurse supervisors. Home health and public health nurses travel to patients' homes, schools, community centers, and other sites. Nurses may spend considerable time working and standing. Office, occupational health, and public health nurses are more likely to work regular business hours while other RNs may work in 24-hour care facilities and work nights, weekends, and holidays. Depending on the health care facility, RNs may care for individuals with infectious diseases and maybe exposed to other dangers, such as radiation, accidental needle sticks, chemicals used to sterilize instruments, and anesthetics. In addition, they are vulnerable to back injury when moving patients, shocks from electrical equipment, and hazards posed by gases.

Education, Training, Qualifications: All states require nurses to be licensed. This requirement includes graduation from an accredited nursing school and passing a national licensing examination. Individuals can acquire a nursing education through three types of programs. Nursing graduates can earn an associate degree (ADN), diploma, and bachelor of science degree (BSN) in nursing. The ADN program takes two years and is offered by community and junior colleges. BSN programs take four to five years and are offered by colleges and universities. Diploma programs are offered by hospitals and last two to three years. Licensed graduates of these three programs qualify for entry-level positions as staff nurses.

Earnings: Median annual earnings of full-time salaried registered nurses were $48,090 in 2020. The middle 50 percent earned between $40,140 and $57,490. Median annual earnings in the major industries employing the largest numbers of registered nurses in 2002 were $55,980 in employment services; $49,190 in general medical and surgical hospitals; $45,890 in home health care services; $44,870 in offices of physicians; and $43,850 in nursing care facilities. Many employers offer flexible work schedules, child care, educational benefits, and bonuses.

Key Contacts: For information on nursing careers, contact:

- **American Association of Colleges of Nursing:** 1 Dupont Circle NW, Suite 530, Washington, DC 20036. Website: www.aacn. nche.edu.

- **American Nurses Association:** 8515 Georgia Avenue, Suite 400, Silver Spring, MD 20910. Website: www.nursingworld.org.

- **National League for Nursing:** 61 Broadway, New York, NY 10006. Website: www.nln.org.

Respiratory Therapists

- ⇨ **Annual Earnings:** $40,220
- ⇨ **Education/Training:** Associate degree
- ⇨ **Outlook:** Excellent

Employment Outlook: Employment for respiratory therapists is expected to be very good in the coming decade. The number of jobs is expected to increase substantially due to an increasingly aging population. Older people are more likely to suffer from cardiopulmonary diseases such as pneumonia, chronic bronchitis, emphysema, and heart disease.

Nature of Work: Respiratory therapists held 112,000 jobs in 2002. More than four out of five jobs were in hospital departments of respiratory care, anesthesiology, or pulmonary medicine. Respiratory therapists treat all sorts of patients, from infants with lung problems to elderly people suffering from lung disease. They provide temporary relief to patients with chronic asthma or emphysema and emergency care for heart failure, stroke, drowning, or shock victims. They most commonly use oxygen or oxygen mixtures, chest physiotherapy, and aerosol medications. They apply oxygen masks, connect patients to ventilators, and regularly check on patients and equipment.

Working Conditions: Respiratory therapists usually work 35-40 hours per week in hospital departments of respiratory care, anesthesiology, or pulmonary medicine. During an emergency, therapists work under a great deal of stress. About 10 percent work with home health agencies, respiratory therapy clinics, and nursing homes. They may work evenings, nights, or weekends. Respiratory therapists employed in home health care must travel frequently to the homes of patients. Much of their work involves standing and walking.

Education, Training, Qualifications: Entry into this field requires postsecondary formal training which is provided by hospitals, medical schools, colleges and universities, trade schools, vocational-technical institutes, and the Armed Forces. Most of the Commission on Accreditation of Allied Health Education Programs (includes 59 entry-level and 319 advanced respiratory therapy programs) last two years and lead to an associate degree. Some are four-year bachelor's degree programs. Technician programs last about one year and award certificates.

Earnings: Median annual earnings for full-time respiratory therapists in 2002 were $40,220. The middle 50 percent earned between $34,430 and $46,130. In general medical and surgical hospitals, median annual earnings of respiratory therapists were $40,390 in 2002. Median annual earnings of respiratory therapy technicians were $34,130 in 2002. The middle 50 percent earned between $28,460 and $41,140.

Key Contacts: For information on respiratory therapist careers, contact:

- **American Association for Respiratory Care:** 9425 N. MacArthur Blvd., Suite 100, Irving, TX 75063. Website: www.aarc.org.

- **The National Board for Respiratory Care, Inc.:** 8310 Nieman Road, Lenexa, KS 66214-1579. Website: www.nbrc.org.

- **Committee on Accreditation of Allied Health Education Programs:** 39 East Wacker Drive, Suite 1970, Chicago, IL 60601. Website: www.caahep.org.

- **Committee on Accreditation for Respiratory Care:** 1248 Harwood Road, Bedford, TX 76021-4244. Website: www.coarc.com.

Veterinary Technologists and Technicians

- ➩ **Annual Earnings:** $22,950
- ➩ **Education/Training:** Two- to four-year programs
- ➩ **Outlook:** Excellent

Employment Outlook: Employment of veterinary technologists and technicians is expected to grow much faster than the average for all occupations during the coming decade. Keen competition is expected for veterinary technologist and technician jobs in zoos, due to expected slow growth in zoo capacity, the low turnover among workers, and high competition for a limited number of openings. As pet owners become more affluent, they are more willing to pay for advanced care of their pets. The rapidly growing number of cat owners should boost the demand for feline medicine, offsetting any reduced demand for veterinary care for dogs. Biomedical facilities, diagnostic laboratories, wildlife facilities, humane societies, animal control facilities, drug or food manufacturing companies, and food safety inspection facilities will provide more jobs for veterinary technologists and technicians.

Nature of Work: Veterinarians use the skills of veterinary technologists and technicians, who perform many of the same duties for a veterinarian that a nurse would for a physician, including routine laboratory and clinical procedures. Veterinary technologists and technicians typically conduct clinical work in a private practice under the supervision of a veterinarian – often performing various medical tests along with treating and diagnosing medical conditions and diseases in animals. They may perform laboratory tests such as urinalysis and blood counts, assist with dental prophylaxis, prepare tissue samples, take blood samples, or assist veterinarians in a variety of tests and analyses in which they often use medical equipment such as test tubes and diagnostic equipment.

Working Conditions: Veterinary technologists and technologists held about 53,000 jobs in 2002. Most worked in veterinary services. The remainder worked in boarding kennels, animal shelters, stables, grooming shops, zoos, and local, state, and federal agencies.

People who love animals get satisfaction from working with and helping them. However, some of the work may be unpleasant, physically and emotionally demanding, and sometimes dangerous. Veterinary technicians sometimes must clean cages and lift, hold, or restrain animals, risking exposure to bites or scratches. The work setting can be noisy. Veterinary technologists and technicians who witness abused animals or who euthanize unwanted, aged, or hopelessly injured animals may experience emotional stress.

Education, Training, Qualifications: Most entry-level veterinary technicians have a two-year degree, usually an associate degree, from an accredited community college program in veterinary technology, in which courses are taught in clinical and laboratory settings using live animals. In 2003, more than 80 veterinary technology programs in 41 states were accredited by the American Veterinary Medical Association. A few colleges offer four-year programs that result in a bachelor's degree in veterinary technology.

Earnings: Median annual earnings of veterinary technologists and technicians were $22,950 in 2002. The middle 50 percent earned between $19,210 and $27,890.

Key Contacts: For information on certification and careers in veterinary technology, contact:

- **American Association for Laboratory Animal Science:** 9190 Crestwyn Hills Drive, Memphis, TN 38125. Website: www.aalas. org.

- **American Veterinary Medical Association:** 1931 N. Meacham Road, Suite 100, Schaumburg, IL 60173-4360. Website: www. avma.org.

- **Association of American Veterinary Medical Colleges:** 1101 Vermont Avenue NW, Suite 301, Washington, DC 20005. Website: www.aavmc.org.

- **National Association of Veterinary Technicians in America:** P.O. Box 224, Battle Ground, IN 47920. Website: www.navta.net.

4

Government, Legal, and Security Occupations

GOVERNMENT OFFERS NUMEROUS job and career opportunities for people re-entering the workforce. Employing more than 22 million people at the federal, state, and local levels, the public sector is an enormous complex. It also generates millions of additional jobs to support its many functions, including private security forces. Despite efforts to downside government, the size of government continues to increase in response to general population growth and the demand for improved public services, from schools and highways to parks, public safety, and homeland security.

Qualifications

While education remains the largest public sector complex, most professional jobs in education require at least a four-year degree. Many other jobs, especially administrative and maintenance in nature, only require a high school diploma and on-the-job training. Many of the medical and health care jobs outlined in Chapter 3 are actually performed in local, state, and federal government hospitals and health care facilities.

Both inside and outside government, the public safety and security complexes are receptive to hiring individuals re-entering the workforce. Many of these jobs do not require a four-year degree. From police and fire protection to courts, prisons, and private security services, the public safety arena is enormous in size, and it continues to grow in response to important public safety and security issues.

The jobs outlined in this chapter represent only a few of today's many attractive opportunities in government and security. If your interests include government, public safety, security, and law, or if you're oriented toward public service, be sure to explore the many exciting opportunities available through government and the justice system. Many of these jobs offer excellent salaries, benefits, advancement, and long-term job security.

Useful Resources

Numerous resources are available for people interested in government and security jobs. For starters, you may want to the examine the following books and websites:

Books

Alternative Careers in Secret Operations, Mark Merritt (Impact Publications, 1999)

The Book of U.S. Government Jobs, Dennis V. Damp (Bookhaven Press, 2005)

The Complete Guide to Public Employment, Ron and Caryl Krannich (Impact Publications, 1995)

FBI Careers, Thomas Ackerman (JIST Publishing, 2005)

Federal Applications That Get Results, Russ Smith (Impact Publications, 1996)

Federal Jobs in Law Enforcement, Russ Smith (Impact Publications, 1996)

Federal Resume Guidebook, Kathryn Kraemer Troutman (JIST Publishing, 2004)

Find a Federal Job Fast, Ron and Caryl Krannich (Impact Publications, 1999)

Government Job Applications and Federal Resumes, Anne McKinney (PREP Publishing, 2001)

A Guide to America's Federal Jobs, Bruce Maxwell, ed. (JIST Publishing, 2005)

A Guide to Careers in Federal Law Enforcement, Thomas H. Ackerman (JIST Publishing, 2005)

Guide to Homeland Security Careers, Donald B. Hutton and Anna Mydlarz (Barron's Educational Series, 2003)

John Douglas's Guide to Landing a Career in Law Enforcement, John Douglas (McGraw-Hill, 2005)

Law Enforcement Career Starter, Mary Hesalroad (Learning Express, 2001)

Opportunities in Paralegal Careers, Alice Fins (McGraw-Hill, 1999)

Paralegal Career Guide, Chere Estrin (Prentice-Hall, 2001)

Post Office Jobs, Dennis V. Damp (Bookhaven Press, 2005)

Real KSAs – Knowledge, Skills, and Abilities – for Government Jobs, Anne McKinney (PREP Publishing, 2003)

The Successful Paralegal Job Search, Chere B. Estrin and
Stacy Hunt (Thomas Delmar Learning, 2000)

Government and Security Websites

- USA Jobs   www.usajobs.opm.gov
- Federal Jobs Central   www.fedjobs.com
- Federal Jobs Digest   www.jobsfed.com
- Lawenforcementjobs.com   www.lawenforcementjobs.com
- Careers in Government   www.careersingovernment.com
- Classified Employment   www.yourinfosource.com/
  Web Site   CLEWS
- Cop Career.com   www.copcareer.com
- Cops Online   www.copsonline.com/careers
- Corrections.com   http://database.corrections.com/
                                   career

- Federal Jobs Net   www.federaljobs.net
- Federal Times   http://federaltimes.com
- FedWorld.gov   www.fedworld.gov
- FirstGov   www.firstgov.gov
- GovernmentJobs.com   www.governmentjobs.com
- Govjobs.com   www.govjobs.com
                                   www.govtjob.net
- JobCop   www.jobcop.com
- Jobs4PublicSector (Europe)   www.jobs4publicsector.com
- Officer.com   www.officer.com
- PoliceCareer.com   www.policecareer.com
- Police Employment   www.policeemployment.com
- PSE-NET.com   www.PSE-NET.com
- StateJobs.com   www.statejobs.com
- United Nations   www.unsystem.org
- US Government Jobs.com   www.usgovernmentjobs.com
- US Intelligence Community   www.intelligence.gov

If you're interested in working for the federal government, you may
want to explore employment opportunities with these major federal
agencies:

- Agency for International
  Development (USAID)   www.usaid.gov
- Central Intelligence Agency   www.cia.gov
- Consumer Product Safety
  Commission   www.cpsc.gov
- Department of Agriculture   www.usda.gov
- Department of Commerce   www.commerce.gov
- Department of Defense   www.dod.gov
- Department of Energy   www.doe.gov
- Department of Health
  and Human Services   www.os.dhhs.gov
- Department of Homeland
  Security   www.dhs.gov
- Department of Justice   www.usdoj.gov
- Department of State   www.state.gov
- Department of
  Transportation   www.dot.gov
- Environmental Protection
  Agency   www.epa.gov
- Export-Import Bank   www.exim.gov
- Federal Communications
  Commission   www.fcc.gov
- Federal Emergency
  Management Agency   www.fema.gov
- General Services
  Administration   www.gsa.gov
- Inter-American Foundation   www.iaf.gov
- Internal Revenue Service   www.irs.ustreas.gov
- Peace Corps   www.peacecorps.com
- Smithsonian Institution   www.si.edu
- U.S. Postal Service   www.usps.gov

Legal Websites

- Legal Staff   www.legalstaff.com
- 411 Legal Info   www.411legalinfo.com/JOBS
- Attorney Job Store   www.attorneyjobstore.com
- AttorneyJobs.com   www.attorneyjobs.com

▪ CounselHounds.com	www.counselhounds.com
▪ Counsel.net	www.counsel.net
▪ Craig's List	www.craigslist.com
▪ eAttorney	www.eattorney.com
▪ Emplawyer.net	www.emplawyernet.com
▪ FindLaw Career Center	www.careers.findlaw.com
▪ Find Law Job.com	www.findlawjob.com
▪ iHire Legal	www.ihirelegal.com
▪ Jobs.LawInfo.com	www.jobs.lawinfo.com
▪ Juris Resources.com	www.jurisresources.com
▪ Law.com CareerCenter	www.lawjobs.com
▪ LawGuru.com	www.lawguru.com
▪ LawListings.com	www.lawlistings.com
▪ Law Match	www.lawmatch.com
▪ Legal Employment	www.legalemploy.com
▪ LegalHire.com	www.legalhire.com
▪ LegalStaff.com	www.legalstaff.com
▪ Legal Job Store	www.legaljobstore.com
▪ My Legal Job	www.mylegaljob.com
▪ NationJob Network	www.nationjob.com/legal
▪ Paralegal.com	www.paralegal.com
▪ Paralegal-Jobs.com	www.paralegal-jobs.com
▪ Paralegals.org	www.paralegals.org
▪ Staffwise.com	www.staffwise.com
▪ US Legal Jobs	www.uslegaljobs.com

Correctional Officers

⮕ **Annual Earnings:** $32,670
⮕ **Education/Training:** High school or two years experience
⮕ **Outlook:** Excellent

Employment Outlook: Job opportunities for correctional officers are expected to be excellent in the decade ahead. The need to replace correctional officers who transfer to other occupations, retire, or leave the labor force, coupled with rising employment demand, will generate thousands of job openings each year. In the past, some local and state corrections agencies have experienced difficulty in attracting and keeping qualified applicants, largely due to relatively low salaries and the concentration of jobs in rural locations. This situation is expected to continue.

Correctional officers held about 476,000 jobs in 2002. About three of every five jobs were in state correctional institutions such as prisons, prison camps, and youth correctional facilities. Most of the remaining jobs were in city or county jails or other institutions run by local governments. About 16,000 jobs for correctional officers were in federal correctional institutions, and about 16,000 jobs were in privately owned and managed prisons.

There are about 118 jail systems in the United States that house over 1,000 inmates each, all of which are located in urban areas. A significant number work in jails and other facilities located in law enforcement agencies throughout the country. However, most correctional officers work in institutions located in rural areas with smaller inmate populations than those in urban jails.

Nature of Work: Correctional officers are responsible for overseeing individuals who have been arrested and are awaiting trial or who have been convicted of a crime and sentenced to serve time in a jail, reformatory, or penitentiary. They maintain security and inmate accountability to prevent disturbances, assaults, or escapes. Officers have no law enforcement responsibilities outside the institution where they work. Police and sheriffs' departments in county and municipal jails or precinct station houses employ many correctional officers. Correctional officers in the U.S. jail system admit and process more than 11 million people per year, with about 500,000 offenders in jail at any given time. When individuals are first arrested, the jail staff may not know their true identity or criminal record, and violent detainees may be placed in the general population. This is the most dangerous phase of the incarceration process for correctional officers.

Most correctional officers are employed in large jails or state or federal prisons, watching over the approximately one million offenders who are incarcerated at any given time. In addition to jails and prisons, a relatively small number of correctional officers oversee individuals being held by the U.S. Immigration and Naturalization Service before they are released or deported, or they work for correctional institutions that are run by private for-profit organizations. While both jails and prisons can be dangerous places to work, prison populations are more stable than jail populations, and correctional officers in prisons know the security and custodial requirements of the prisoners with whom they are dealing.

Working Conditions: Working in a correctional institution can be stressful and hazardous. Every year, a number of correctional officers are injured in confrontations with inmates. Correctional officers may work indoors or outdoors. Some correctional institutions are well lighted, temperature controlled, and ventilated, while others are old, overcrowded, hot, and noisy.

Correctional officers usually work an eight-hour day, five days a week, on rotating shifts. Prison and jail security must be provided around the clock, which often means they work all hours of the day and night, weekends, and holidays. In addition, officers may be required to work overtime.

Education, Training, Qualifications: Most institutions require correctional officers to be at least 18 to 21 years of age and a U.S. citizen, have a high school education or its equivalent, demonstrate job stability – usually by accumulating two years of work experience, and have no felony convictions. Promotion prospects may be enhanced through obtaining a postsecondary education.

Correctional officers must be in good health. Candidates for employment are generally required to meet formal standards of physical fitness, eyesight, and hearing. Applicants are typically screened for drug abuse, subject to background checks, and required to pass a written examination. Good judgment and the ability to think and act quickly are indispensable.

Federal, state, and some local departments of corrections provide training for correctional officers. Some states have regional training academies which are available to all local agencies. All states and local correctional agencies provide on-the-job training at the conclusion of formal instruction, including legal restrictions and interpersonal relations. Many systems require firearms proficiency and self-defense skills. Officer trainees typically receive several weeks or months of training in an actual job setting under the supervision of an experienced officer. However, specific entry requirements and on-the-job training vary widely from agency to agency.

Academy trainees generally receive instruction on a number of subjects, including institutional policies, regulations, and operations, as well as custody and security procedures. As a condition of employment, new federal correctional officers must undergo 200 hours of formal training within the first year of employment. They must also complete 120 hours of specialized training at the U.S. Federal Bureau of Prisons residential training center at Glynco, Georgia within the first 60 days after appointment. Experienced officers receive annual in-service training to keep abreast of new developments and procedures.

Some correctional officers are members of prison tactical response teams, which are trained to respond to disturbances, riots, hostage situations, forced-cell moves, and other potentially dangerous confrontations. Team members receive training and practice with weapons, chemical agents, forced-entry methods, crisis management, and other tactics.

Earnings: Median annual earnings of correctional officers and jailers were $32,670 in 2002. The middle 50 percent earned between $25,950 and $42,620. The highest 10 percent earned more than $52,370. Median annual earnings in the public sector were $40,900 in the federal government;

$33,260 in state government; and $31,380 in local government. In addition to typical benefits, correctional officers employed in the public sector usually are provided with uniforms or a clothing allowance to purchase their own uniforms. Civil service systems or merit boards cover officers employed by the federal government and most state governments. Their retirement coverage entitles them to retire at age 50 after 20 years of service or at any age with 25 years of service.

Key Contacts: Information about correctional jobs in a jail setting is available from:

- **American Jail Association:** 1135 Professional Court, Hagerstown, MD 21740. Website: www.corrections.com/aja.

Information on obtaining a position as a correctional officer with the federal government is available from the Office of Personnel Management (OPM) through a telephone-based system. Consult your telephone directory under U.S. Government for a local number or call 703-724-1850 (**not** a toll-free number) or Federal Relay Service 800-877-8339.

Two Internet sites may be useful to obtain information about opportunities at the federal level:

- **Federal Bureau of Prisons** www.bop.gov
- **Office of Personnel Management** www.usajobs.opm.gov

Court Reporters

↪ **Annual Earnings:** $41,550
↪ **Education/Training:** Technical training to associate degree
↪ **Outlook:** Good to excellent

Employment Outlook: Employment of court reporters is projected to grow about as fast as the average for occupations in the coming decade. Demand for court reporter services will be spurred by the continuing need for accurate transcription of proceedings in courts and in pretrial depositions and by the growing need to create captions for live or prerecorded television and to provide other realtime transcription services for people with hearing loss. Despite the good job prospects, fewer people are going into this profession, creating a shortage of court reporters – particularly stenographic typists – and making job opportunities very good to excellent.

Court reporters held about 18,000 jobs in 2002. About 50 percent worked for state and local governments, a reflection of the large number of court reporters working in courts, legislatures, and various agencies. Most of the remaining wage and salary workers worked for court reporting agencies. Eleven percent of court reporters were self-employed.

Nature of work: Court reporters typically take verbatim reports of speeches, conversations, legal proceedings, meetings, and other events when written accounts of spoken words are necessary for correspondence, records, or legal proof. Court reporters play a critical role not only in judicial proceedings, but at every meeting where the spoken word must be preserved as a written transcript. They are responsible for ensuring a complete, accurate, and secure legal record. In addition to preparing and protecting the legal record, many court reporters assist judges and attorneys in a variety of ways, such as organizing and searching for information in the official record or making suggestions to judges and attorneys regarding courtroom administration and procedure. Increasingly, court reporters are providing closed-captioning and realtime transcription services that enable deaf and hard of hearing people to know what is being said – in classrooms, movie theaters, TV broadcasts, meetings, court proceedings, and other venues.

There are two main methods of court reporting: stenotyping and voice writing. Using a stenotype machine, stenotypists document all statements made in official proceedings. The machine allows them to press multiple keys at a time to record combinations of letters representing sounds, words, or phrases. These symbols are then recorded on computer disks or CD-ROM, which are then translated and displayed as text in a process called computer-aided transcription. The other method of court reporting is called voice writing. Using the voice-writing method, a court reporter speaks directly into a stenomask – a hand-held mask containing a microphone with a voice silencer. As the reporter repeats the testimony into the recorder, the mask and silencer prevent the reporter from being heard during testimony. Voice writers record everything that is said by judges, witnesses, attorneys, and other parties to a proceeding, including gestures and emotional reactions.

In addition to recording official proceedings in the courtroom, court reporters may take depositions for attorneys in offices and document proceedings of meetings, conventions, and other private activities. Still others capture the proceedings taking place in government agencies at all levels, from the U.S. Congress to state and local government bodies. Court reporters, both stenotypists and voice writers, who specialize in captioning live television programming for people with hearing loss are known as stenocaptioners. They work for television networks or cable stations, captioning news, emergency broadcasts, sporting events, and other programming. With Communication Access Realtime Translation (CART) and broadcast captioning, the level of understanding gained by a person with hearing loss depends entirely on the skill of the stenocaptioner. In an emergency, such as a tornado or a hurricane, hearing impaired people's safety may depend entirely on the accuracy of information provided in the form of captioning. People learning English as a second language also use captions to facilitate their English skills.

Working Conditions: The majority of court reporters work in comfortable settings, such as offices of attorneys, courtrooms, legislatures, and conventions. An increasing number of court reporters work from home-based offices as independent contractors, or freelancers. Work in this occupation presents few hazards, although sitting in the same position for long periods can be tiring, and workers can suffer wrist, back, neck, or eye problems due to strain. Workers also risk repetitive motion injuries such as carpal tunnel syndrome. In addition, the pressure to be accurate and fast can be stressful. Many official court reporters work a standard 40-hour week. Self-employed court reporters, or freelancers, usually work flexible hours, including part time, evenings, and weekends, or they can work on an on-call basis.

Education, Training, Qualifications: The amount of training required to become a court reporter varies with the type of reporting chosen. It usually takes less than a year to become a voice writer. In contrast, the average length of time it takes to become a stenotypist is 33 months. Training is offered by about 160 postsecondary vocational and technical schools and colleges. The National Court Reporters Association (NCRA) has approved about 82 programs, all of which offer courses in stenotype computer-aided transcription and realtime reporting. NCRA-approved programs require students to capture a minimum of 225 words per minute, a federal government requirement as well. Some states require court reporters to be notary publics. Others require the certified court reporter (CCR) designation, for which a reporter must pass a state certification test administered by a board of examiners. Additional certifications that demonstrate higher levels of competency may be earned. In addition to possessing speed and accuracy, court reporters must have excellent listening skills, as well as good English grammar, vocabulary, and punctuation skills. Voice writers must learn to listen and speak simultaneously and very quickly, while also identifying speakers and describing peripheral activities in the courtroom or deposition room. They must be aware of business practices and current events as well as the correct spelling of names of people, places, and events that may be mentioned in a broadcast or court proceedings. For those who work in courtrooms, an expert knowledge of legal terminology and criminal and appellate procedure is essential. Because capturing proceedings requires the use of computerized stenography or speech recognition equipment, court reporters must be knowledgeable about computer hardware and software applications.

Earnings: Court reporters had median annual earnings of $41,550 in 2002. The middle 50 percent earned between $29,770 and $55,360. The highest paid 10 percent earned more than $73,440. Median annual earnings in 2002 were $40,720 for court reporters working in local government. Both compensation and compensation methods for court reporters vary with the type of reporting job, the experience of the reporter, the level of certification achieved, and the region of the country the reporter works in. Official court reporters earn a salary and a per-page fee for transcripts. Many salaried court reporters supplement their income by doing additional freelance work. Freelance court reporters are paid per job and receive a per-page fee for transcripts. Communication Access Realtime Translation (CART) providers are paid hourly. Stenocaptioners receive a salary and benefits if they work as employees of a captioning company; stenocaptioners working as independent contractors are paid hourly.

Key Contacts: State employment service offices can provide information about job openings for court reporters. For information about careers, training, and certification in court reporting, contact any of the following sources:

- **National Court Reporters Association:** 8224 Old Courthouse Road, Vienna, VA 22182. Website: www.ncraonline.org.

- **United States Court Reporters Association:** 4731 N. Western Avenue, Chicago, IL 60625. Website: www.uscra.org.

- **National Verbatim Reporters Association:** 207 Third Avenue, Hattiesburg, MS 39401. Website: www.nvra.org.

Firefighters

⇨ **Annual Earnings:** $36,200
⇨ **Education/Training:** High school diploma plus examination
⇨ **Outlook:** Good

Employment Outlook: Prospective firefighters are expected to face keen competition for available job openings. Many people are attracted to fire-fighting because it is challenging and provides the opportunity to perform an essential public service, a high school education is usually sufficient for entry, and a pension is guaranteed upon retirement after 20 years.

Employment figures include only paid career firefighters – they do not include volunteer firefighters, who perform the same duties and may comprise the majority of firefighters in a residential area. According to the United States Fire Administration, nearly 70 percent of fire companies are staffed by volunteer firefighters. Paid career firefighters held about 282,000 jobs in 2002. First-line supervisors/managers of firefighting and prevention workers held about 63,000 jobs, and fire inspectors held about 14,000.

About nine out of 10 firefighting workers were employed by municipal or county fire departments. Some large cities have thousands of career firefighters, while many small towns have only a few. Most of the remainder worked in fire departments on federal and state installations, including airports. Private firefighting companies employ a small number of firefighters and usually operate on a subscription basis.

In response to the expanding role of firefighters, some municipalities have combined fire prevention, public fire education, safety, and emergency medical services into a single organization commonly referred to as a public safety organization. Some local and regional fire departments are being consolidated into countywide establishments in order to reduce administrative staffs and cut costs, and to establish training standards and work procedures.

Nature of Work: Firefighters are frequently the first emergency personnel at the scene of a traffic accident or medical emergency and may be called upon to put out a fire, treat injuries, or perform other vital functions. During duty hours, firefighters must be prepared to respond immediately to a fire or any other emergency that arises. Because fighting fires is dangerous and complex, it requires organization and teamwork. At every emergency scene, firefighters perform specific duties. At fires, they connect hose lines to hydrants, operate a pump to send water to high pressure hoses, and position ladders to enable them to deliver water to the fire. They also rescue victims and provide emergency medical attention as needed, ventilate smoke-filled areas, and attempt to salvage the contents of buildings. Sometimes they remain at the site of a disaster for days at a time, rescuing trapped survivors and assisting with medical treatment.

Firefighters work in a variety of settings, including urban and suburban areas, airports, chemical plants, other industrial sites, and rural areas such as grasslands and forests. In addition, some firefighters work in hazardous materials units that are trained for the control, prevention, and clean-up of oil spills and other hazardous materials incidents. Workers in urban and suburban areas, airports, and industrial sites typically use conventional firefighting equipment and tactics, while forest fires and major hazardous materials spills call for different methods.

In national forests and parks, forest fire inspectors spot fires from watchtowers and report their findings to headquarters. Forest rangers patrol to ensure campers comply with fire regulations. When fires break out, crews of firefighters are brought in to suppress the blazes using heavy equipment, hand tools, and water hoses. Forest firefighting, like urban firefighting, can be rigorous work. One of the most effective means of battling the blaze is by creating fire lines through cutting down trees and digging out grass and all other combustible vegetation, creating bare land in the path of the fire that deprives it of fuel. Elite firefighters, called smoke jumpers, parachute from airplanes to reach otherwise inaccessible areas. This can be extremely hazardous because the crews have no way to escape if the wind shifts and causes the fire to burn toward them.

Between alarms, firefighters clean and maintain equipment, conduct practice drills and fire inspections, and participate in physical activities.

Working Conditions: Firefighters spend much of their time at fire stations, which usually have features common to a residential facility like a dormitory. When an alarm sounds, firefighters respond rapidly, regardless of the weather or hour. Firefighting involves risk of death or injury from sudden cave-ins of floors, toppling walls, traffic accidents when responding to calls, and exposure to flames and smoke. Firefighters may also come in contact with poisonous, flammable, or explosive gases and chemicals, as well as radioactive or other hazardous materials that may have immediate or long-term effects on their health. For these reasons, they must wear protective gear that can be very heavy and hot.

Work hours of firefighters are longer and vary more widely than hours of most other workers. Many work more than 50 hours a week, and sometimes they may work even longer. In some agencies, they are on duty for 24 hours, then off for 48 hours, and receive an extra day off at intervals. In others, they work a day shift of 10 hours for three or four days, a night shift of 14 hours for three or four nights, have three or four days off, and then repeat the cycle. In addition, firefighters often work extra hours at fires and other emergencies and are regularly assigned to work holidays. Fire lieutenants and fire captains often work the same hours as the firefighters they supervise.

Education, Training, Qualifications: Applicants for municipal firefighting jobs generally must pass a written exam; tests of strength, physical stamina, coordination, and agility; and a medical examination that includes drug screening. Examinations are generally open to persons who are at least 18 years of age and have a high school education or its equivalent. Those who receive the highest scores in all phases of testing have the best chances of appointment. The completion of community college courses in fire science may improve an applicant's chances for appointment. In recent years, an increasing proportion of entrants to this occupation have had some post-secondary education.

As a rule, entry-level workers in large fire departments are trained for several weeks at the department's training center or academy. Through classroom instruction and practical training, the recruits study firefighting techniques, fire prevention, hazardous material control, local building codes, and emergency medical procedures, including first aid and cardiopulmonary resuscitation. They also learn how to use axes, chain saws, fire extinguishers, ladders, and other firefighting and rescue equipment. After successfully completing this training, they are assigned to a fire company, where they undergo a period of probation.

A number of fire departments have accredited apprenticeship programs lasting up to five years. These programs combine formal, technical instruction with on-the-job training under the supervision of experienced firefighters. A number of colleges offer courses leading to two- or four-year degrees in fire engineering or fire science. Many fire departments offer incentives such as tuition reimbursement or higher pay for completing advanced training.

Among the personal qualities firefighters need are mental alertness, self-discipline, courage, mechanical aptitude, endurance, strength, and a sense of public service. Initiative and good judgment are also extremely important because firefighters make quick decisions in emergencies. Because members of a crew live and work closely together under conditions of stress and danger for extended periods, they must be dependable and able to get along well with others.

Earnings: Median hourly earnings of firefighters were $17.42 in 2002 ($36,200 per year). The highest 10 percent earned more than $28.22. Median earnings were $17.92 in local government, $15.96 in the federal Government, and $13.58 in state government. Supervisors, managers, and inspectors earn higher salaries. Firefighters who average more than a certain number of hours a week are required to be paid overtime. Almost all fire departments provide protective clothing (helmets, boots, and coats) and breathing apparatus, and may also provide dress uniforms. Firefighters are generally covered by pension plans, often providing retirement at half pay after 25 years of service or if disabled in the line of duty.

Key Contacts: Information about a career as a firefighter may be obtained from local fire departments and from:

- **International Association of Fire Fighters:** 1750 New York Avenue NW, Washington, DC 20006. Website: www.iaff.org.

- **U.S. Fire Administration:** 16825 South Seton Avenue, Emmitsburg, MD 21727. Website: www.usfa.fema.gov.

Information about firefighter professional qualifications and a list of colleges offering two- or four-year degree programs in fire science or fire prevention may be obtained from:

- **National Fire Academy:** 16825 South Seton Avenue, Emmitsburg, MD 21727. Website: www.usfa.fema.gov/training/nfa.

Paralegals and Legal Assistants

⇨ **Annual Earnings:** $37,950
⇨ **Education/Training:** Associate to four-year degree
⇨ **Outlook:** Good to excellent

Employment Outlook: Paralegals and legal assistants are projected to grow faster than average for all occupations in the decade ahead. Some employment growth stems from law firms and other employers with legal staffs increasingly hiring paralegals to lower the cost and increase the availability of legal services. Additional job openings will arise as people leave the occupation. Despite projections of fast employment growth, competition for jobs should continue as many people enter the profession; however, highly skilled, formally trained paralegals with prior experience have excellent employment potential.

Private law firms will continue to be the largest employers of paralegals, but a growing array of other organizations, such as corporate legal departments, insurance companies, real estate and title insurance firms, and banks, hire paralegals. Demand for paralegals is also expected to grow as an increasing population requires legal services, especially in areas such as intellectual property, health care, international, elder, criminal, and environmental law. A growing number of experienced paralegals are expected to establish their own businesses. Job opportunities for paralegals will expand in the public sector as well. Community legal-aid programs, which provide assistance to the poor, aged, minorities, and middle-income families, will employ additional paralegals to minimize expenses and serve the most people. Federal, state, and local government agencies, consumer organizations, and the courts also should continue to hire paralegals in increasing numbers. Paralegals who provide some of the same legal services as lawyers at a lower cost, tend to fare relatively better in difficult economic conditions.

Nature of Work: While lawyers assume ultimate responsibility for legal work, they often delegate many of their tasks to paralegals. In fact, paralegals – also called legal assistants – continue to assume a growing range of tasks in the nation's legal offices and perform some of the same tasks as lawyers. Nevertheless, they are still prohibited from carrying out duties that are considered to be the practice of law, such as setting legal fees, giving legal advice, and presenting cases in court.

One of a paralegal's most important tasks is helping lawyers prepare for closings, hearings, trials, and corporate meetings. Paralegals investigate the facts of cases and ensure that all relevant information is considered. They also identify appropriate laws, judicial decisions, legal articles, and other materials that are relevant to assigned cases. After they analyze and organize the information, paralegals may prepare written reports that attorneys use in determining how cases should be handled. If attorneys decide to file lawsuits on behalf of clients, paralegals may help prepare the legal arguments, draft pleadings and motions to be filed with the court, obtain affidavits, and assist attorneys during trials. Paralegals also organize and track files of all important case documents and make them available and easily accessible to attorneys. In addition to this preparatory work, paralegals help draft contracts, mortgages, separation agreements, and trust instruments. They may also assist in preparing tax returns and planning estates. Tasks vary – depending on the employer.

Working Conditions: Paralegals employed by corporations and government usually work a standard 40-hour week. Although most paralegals work year-round, some are temporarily employed during busy times of the year, then released as the workload diminishes. Paralegals who work for law firms sometimes work very long hours when they are under pressure to meet deadlines. Some law firms reward such loyalty with bonuses and additional time off. Paralegals do most of their work at desks in offices and law libraries. Occasionally, they travel to gather information and perform other duties.

Education, Training, Qualifications: There are several ways to become a paralegal. The most common is through a community college paralegal program that leads to an associate degree. The other common method of entry, mainly for those who have a college degree, is through a certification program that leads to a certificate in paralegal studies. A small number of schools also offer bachelor's and master's degrees in paralegal studies. Some employers train paralegals on the job, hiring college graduates with no legal experience or promoting experienced legal secretaries. Other entrants have experience in a technical field that is useful to law firms, such as a background in tax preparation for tax and estate practice, criminal justice, or nursing or health administration for personal injury practice.

Formal paralegal training programs are offered by an estimated 600 colleges and universities. Approximately 250 paralegal programs are approved by the American Bar Association (ABA). Although this approval is neither required nor sought by many programs, graduation from an ABA-approved program can enhance one's employment opportunities. Paralegal programs include two-year associate degree and four-year bachelor's degree programs, and certificate programs that can take only a few months to complete. Many paralegal training programs include an internship in which students can gain practical experience by working for several months in a private law firm, office of a public defender or attorney general, bank, corporate legal department, legal-aid organization, or government agency. Experience gained in internships is an asset when seeking a job after graduation. Although most employers do not require certification, earning a voluntary certificate from a professional society may offer advantages in the labor market. Familiarity with operation and application of computers in legal research and litigation support as well as the ability to write also are increasingly important.

Earnings: Earnings of paralegals and legal assistants vary greatly. Salaries depend on education, training, experience, type and size of employer, and geographic location of the job. In general, paralegals who work for large law firms or in large metropolitan areas earn more than those who work for smaller firms or in less populated regions. In addition to a salary, many paralegals receive bonuses. In 2002, full-time, wage and salary paralegals and legal assistants had median annual earnings, including bonuses, of $37,950. The top 10 percent earned more than $61,150. Median annual earnings in the industries employing the largest numbers of paralegals in 2002 were as follow: federal government, $53,770; legal services, $36,780; local government, $36,030; and state government, $34,750.

Key Contacts: General information on a career as a paralegal can be obtained from:

- **Standing Committee on Paralegal Assistants:** American Bar Association, 321 North Clark Street, Chicago, IL 60610. Website: www.abanet.org/legalservices/paralegals/.

For information on the Certified Legal Assistant exam, schools that offer training programs in a specific state, and standards and guidelines for paralegals, contact:

- **National Association of Legal Assistants, Inc.:** 1516 South Boston St., Suite 200, Tulsa, OK 74119. Website: www.nala.org.

For information on a career as a paralegal, schools that offer training programs, job postings for paralegals, the Paralegal Advanced Competency Exam, and local paralegal associations, contact:

- **National Federation of Paralegal Associations:** 2517 Eastlake Ave. East #200, Seattle, WA 98102. Website: www.paralegals.org.

Information on paralegal training programs, including the pamphlet *How to Choose a Paralegal Education Program,* may be requested from:

- **American Association for Paralegal Education:** 407 Wekiva Springs Road, Suite 241, Longwood, FL 32779. Website: www. aafpe.org.

Police and Detectives

- ⇨ **Annual Earnings:** $42,270 - $51,410
- ⇨ **Education/Training:** High school diploma/federal and state agencies typically require college
- ⇨ **Outlook:** Faster than average growth

Employment Outlook: Employment of police and detectives is expected to grow faster than the average for all occupations through 2012. A more security conscious society and concern about drug-related crimes should contribute to the increasing demand for police services. The level of government spending determines the level of employment for police and detectives. The number of job opportunities, therefore, can vary from year to year and from place to place. Layoffs, on the other hand, are rare because retirements enable most staffing cuts to be handled through attrition. Trained law enforcement officers who lose their jobs because of budget cuts usually have little difficulty finding jobs with other agencies. The need to replace workers who retire, transfer to other occupations, or stop working for other reasons will be the source of many job openings.

Nature of Work: People depend on police officers and detectives to protect their lives and property. Law enforcement officers, some of whom are state or federal employees, perform these duties in a variety of ways, depending on the size and type of their organization. In most jurisdictions, they are expected to exercise authority when necessary, whether on or off duty.

Uniformed police officers who work in municipal police departments of various sizes, small communities, and rural areas have general law enforcement duties including maintaining regular patrols and responding to calls for service. They may direct traffic at the scene of a fire, investigate a burglary, or give first aid to an accident victim. In large police departments, officers are usually assigned to a specific type of duty. Officers may work alone, but in large agencies they often patrol with a partner. During their shift, they may identify, pursue, and arrest suspected criminals, resolve problems within the community, and enforce traffic laws. Public college and university police forces, school district police, and agencies serving transportation systems and facilities are examples of special police agencies. Some police officers specialize in such diverse fields as chemical and microscopic analysis, training and firearms instruction, or handwriting and fingerprint identification. Others work with special units such as horseback, bicycle, motorcycle or harbor patrol, canine corps, or special weapons and tactics (SWAT) or emergency response teams.

Sheriffs and deputy sheriffs enforce the law on the county level. Sheriffs are usually elected to their posts and perform duties similar to those of a local or county police chief. Police and sheriffs' deputies who provide security in city and county courts are sometimes called bailiffs.

State police officers (sometimes called **state troopers** or **highway patrol officers**) arrest criminals statewide and patrol highways to enforce motor vehicle laws and regulations. Uniformed officers are best known for issuing traffic citations to motorists who violate the law. At the scene of accidents, they may direct traffic, give first aid, and call for emergency equipment. They also write reports used to determine the cause of the accident.

Detectives are plainclothes investigators who gather facts and collect evidence for criminal cases. They conduct interviews, examine records, observe the activities of suspects, and participate in raids or arrests. Detectives and state and federal agents and inspectors usually specialize in one of a wide variety of violations such as homicide or fraud.

Working Conditions: Police work can be very dangerous and stressful. In addition to the obvious dangers of confrontations with criminals, officers need to be constantly alert and ready to deal appropriately with a number of other threatening situations. Many law enforcement officers witness death and suffering resulting from accidents and criminal behavior. A career in law enforcement may take a toll on officers' private lives. Uniformed officers, detectives, agents, and inspectors are usually scheduled to work 40-hour weeks, but paid overtime is common. Shift work is necessary because protection must be provided around the clock. Junior officers frequently work weekends, holidays, and nights. Police officers and detectives are required to work at any time their services are needed and may work long hours during investigations. In most jurisdictions, whether on or off duty, officers are expected to be armed and to exercise their arrest authority whenever necessary. The jobs of some federal agents such as U.S. Secret Service and DEA special agents require extensive travel, often on very short notice. They may relocate a number of times over the course of their careers. Some special agents in agencies such as the U.S. Border Patrol work outdoors in rugged terrain for long periods in all kinds of weather.

Education, Training, Qualifications: In larger departments, where the majority of law enforcement jobs are found, applicants usually must have at least a high school education. Federal and state agencies typically require a college degree. Civil service regulations govern the appointment of police and detectives in practically all states, large municipalities, and special police agencies, as well as in many smaller ones. Candidates must be U.S. citizens, usually at least 20 years of age, and must meet rigorous physical and personal qualifications. In the federal government, candidates must be at least 21 years of age but less than 37 years of age at the time of appointment. Physical examinations for entrance into law enforcement often include tests of vision, hearing, strength, and agility. Eligibility for appointment usually depends on performance in competitive written examinations and previous education and experience. Candidates are interviewed by senior officers, and their character traits and backgrounds are investigated. In some agencies, candidates are interviewed by a psychiatrist or a psychologist, or given a personality test. Most applicants are subjected to lie detector examinations or drug testing.

Before their first assignments, officers usually go through a period of training. In state and large local departments, recruits get training in their agency's police academy, often for 12 to 14 weeks. In small agencies, recruits often attend a regional or state academy. Training includes classroom instruction in constitutional law and civil rights, state laws and local ordinances, and accident investigation. Recruits also receive training and supervised experience in patrol, traffic control, use of firearms, self-defense, first aid, and emergency response.

Law enforcement agencies are encouraging applicants to take post-secondary school training in law enforcement-related subjects. Many entry-level applicants for police jobs have completed some formal postsecondary education and a significant number are college graduates. Many junior colleges, colleges, and universities offer programs in law enforcement or administration of justice. Other courses helpful in preparing for a career in law enforcement include accounting, finance, electrical engineering, computer science, and foreign languages. Physical education and sports are helpful in developing the competitiveness, stamina, and agility needed for many law enforcement positions. Knowledge of a foreign language is an asset in many federal agencies and urban departments. Continuing training helps police officers, detectives, and special agents improve their job performance. Many agencies pay all or part of the tuition for officers to work toward degrees in criminal justice, or public administration, and pay higher salaries to those who earn such a degree.

Earnings: Police and sheriff's patrol officers had media annual earnings of $42,270 in 2002. The highest 10 percent earned more than $65,330. Median annual earnings were $47,090 in state government, $42,020 in local government, and $41,600 in the federal government. In 2002, media annual earnings of police and detective supervisors were $61,010. The highest 10 percent earned more than $90,070. Median annual earnings were $78,230 in the federal government, $64,410 in state government, and $59,830 in local government. In 2002, median annual earnings of detectives and criminal investigators were $51,410. The highest 10 percent earned more than $80,380. Median annual earnings were $66,500 in the federal government, $47,700 in local government, and $46,600 in state government. Total earnings for local, state and special police and detectives frequently exceed the stated salary because of payments for overtime, which can be significant. In addition to the common benefits – paid vacation, sick leave, and medical and life insurance – most police and sheriffs' departments provide officers with special allowances for uniforms. Because police officers usually are covered by liberal pension plans, many retire at half-pay after 20 or 25 years of service.

Key Contacts: Information about entrance requirements may be obtained from federal, state, and local law enforcement agencies.

Information about qualifications for employment as an FBI Special Agent is available from the nearest state FBI office. The address and phone number are listed in the local telephone directory. Website: www.fbi.gov.

Information on career opportunities, qualifications, and training for U.S. Secret Service Special Agents is available from the Secret Service Personnel Division at (202) 406-5800, (888) 813-8777. Website: www.treas.gov/usss.

Information about qualifications for employment as a DEA Special Agent is available from the nearest DEA office, or call (800) DEA-4288. Website: www.usdoj.gov/dea.

Information about career opportunities, qualifications, and training to become a deputy marshal is available from: U.S. Marshals Service, Human Resources Division – Law Enforcement Recruiting, Washington, DC 20530-1000. Website: www.usmarshals.gov/careers.

For information on operations and career opportunities in the U.S. Bureau of Alcohol, Tobacco and Firearms, contact: U.S. Bureau of Alcohol, Tobacco and Firearms, Personnel Division, 650 Massachusetts Ave. NW, Room 4100, Washington, DC 20226. Website: www.atf.gov/jobs/.

Information about careers in U.S. Customs and Border Protection as available from: U.S. Customs and Border Protection, 1300 Pennsylvania Avenue NW, Washington, DC 20229. Website: www.cbp.gov.

Postal Service Workers

↪ **Annual Earnings:** $39,126
↪ **Education/Training:** High school diploma desirable, not necessarily required
↪ **Outlook:** Small decline in employment

Employment Outlook: Employment of Postal Service workers is expected to decline through 2012. Still, many jobs will become available because of the need to replace those who retire or leave the occupation. Those seeking jobs as Postal Service workers can expect to encounter keen competition. The number of applicants should continue to exceed the number of job openings due to low entry requirements and attractive wages and benefits.

Efforts by the Postal Service to provide better service may somewhat increase the demand for window clerks, but the demand for such clerks will be offset by the use of electronic communications technologies and private delivery companies. Employment of mail sorters, processors, and processing machine operators is expected to decline because of the increasing use of automated materials handling equipment and optical character readers, barcode sorters, and other automated sorting equipment.

Several factors are expected to influence demand for mail carriers. The competition from alternative delivery systems and new forms of electronic communication could decrease the total volume of mail handled. Most of the decrease is expected to consist of first-class mail. The Postal Service expects an increase in package deliveries due to the rising number of purchases made through the Internet. However, the Postal Service is moving toward more centralized mail delivery to cut down on the number of door-to-door deliveries. This trend is expected is expected to increase carrier productivity, resulting in a small decline in employment among mail carriers over the projection period.

Nature of Work: The Postal Service employs about 845,000 individuals to receive, sort and deliver billions of pieces of mail – weekly. Most Postal Service workers are clerks, mail carriers, or mail sorters, processors, and processing machine operators. Postal clerks wait on customers at post offices, whereas mail sorters, processors, and processing machine operators sort incoming and outgoing mail at post offices and mail processing centers. Mail carriers deliver mail to urban and rural residences and businesses throughout the United States. Mail carriers cover their routes on foot, by vehicle, or a combination of both. On foot, they carry a heavy load of mail in a satchel or push it on a cart. In most urban and rural areas, they use a car or small truck. Although the Postal Service provides vehicles to city carriers, most rural carriers must use their own automobiles. Deliveries are made house-to-house, to roadside mailboxes, and to large buildings such as offices or apartments, which generally have all of their tenants' mailboxes in one location. Some city carriers may have specialized duties such as delivering only parcels or picking up mail from mail collection boxes. Rural carriers provide a wider range of Postal Services. In addition to delivering and picking up mail, rural carriers may sell stamps and money orders and register, certify, and insure parcels and letters. All carriers must be able to answer customers' questions about postal regulations and services and provide change-of-address cards and other postal forms.

Working Conditions: Window clerks usually work in the public portion of clean, well-ventilated, and well-lit buildings. They have a variety of duties and frequent contact with the public, but most rarely work at night. However, in some metropolitan areas, a few large postal facilities are open until midnight. They have to be able to deal with upset customers, stand for long periods, and be held accountable for an assigned stock of stamps and funds. Depending on the size of the post office in which they work, they may also be required to sort mail.

Despite the use of automated equipment, the work of mail sorters, processors, and processing machine operators can be physically demanding. Workers may have to move heavy sacks of mail around a mail processing center. These workers are usually on their feet, reaching for sacks and trays of mail or placing packages and bundles into sacks and trays. Processing mail can be tiring and boring. Many sorters, processors, and machine operators work at night or on weekends, because most large post offices process mail around the clock, and the largest volume of mail is sorted during the evening and night shifts. Workers can experience stress as they process ever larger quantities of mail under tight production deadlines and quotas.

Most carriers begin work early in the morning – those with routes in a business district can start as early as 4am. Overtime hours are frequently required for urban carriers. Carriers who begin work early in the morning are through by early afternoon and spend most of the day on their own, relatively free from direct supervision. Carriers spend most of their time outdoors, delivering mail in all kinds of weather. Even those who drive often must walk periodically when making deliveries and must lift heavy sacks of parcel post items when loading their vehicles. In addition, carriers must be cautious of potential hazards on their routes. Wet and icy roads and sidewalks can be treacherous, and each year dogs attack numerous carriers.

Education, Training, Qualifications: Postal Service workers must be at least 18 years old. They must be U.S. citizens or have been granted permanent resident-alien status in the United States, and males must have registered with the Selective Service upon reaching age 18. Applicants should have a basic competency in English. Qualification is based on a written examination that measures speed and accuracy at checking names and numbers and the ability to memorize mail distribution procedures. Applicants must pass a physical examination and drug test, and may be asked to show that they can lift and handle mail sacks weighing 70 pounds. Applicants for mail carrier positions must have a driver's license and a good driving record, and must receive a passing grade on a road test.

Job seekers should contact the post office or mail processing center where they wish to work to determine when an exam will be given. Points are added to the test scores of honorably discharged veterans as well as veterans who were wounded in combat or are disabled. Relatively few people become postal clerks or mail carriers on their first job, because of keen competition and the customary waiting period of one to two years after passing the examination. Hence, most entrants transfer from other occupations. Postal workers often begin on a part-time, flexible basis and become regular or full time in order of seniority, as vacancies occur.

Earnings: Median annual earnings of postal mail carriers were $39,530 in 2002, while some earned over $47,500. Rural mail carriers are reimbursed for mileage put on their own vehicles while delivering mail. Median annual earnings of Postal Service clerks were $39,700, while the top 10 percent earned more than $43,750. Median annual earnings of mail sorters, processors, and processing machine operators were $38,150, with the top 10 percent earning more than $43,430. Postal Service workers receive a variety of employer-provided benefits similar to those enjoyed by federal government workers.

Key Contacts: Local post offices and state employment service offices can supply details about entrance examinations and specific employment opportunities for Postal Service workers.

Security Guards

- ➪ **Annual Earnings:** $19,140.
- ➪ **Education/Training:** High school graduate or equivalent certification
- ➪ **Outlook:** Faster than average growth

Employment Outlook: Opportunities for security guards should be favorable with employment expected to grow faster than the average for all occupations through 2012 as concern about crime, vandalism, and terrorism continue to increase the need for security. Demand for guards also will grow as private security firms increasingly perform duties – such as monitoring crowds at airports and providing security in courts – which were formerly handled by government police officers. Because enlisting the services of a security guard firm is easier and less costly than assuming direct responsibility for hiring, training, and managing a security guard force, job growth is expected to be concentrated among contract security guard agencies.

Nature of Work: Guards, who are also called security officers, patrol and inspect property to protect against fire, theft, vandalism, terrorism, and illegal activity. Security officers protect their employer's investment, enforce laws on the property, and deter criminal activity. They use radio and telephone communications to call for assistance from police, fire, or emergency services as the situation dictates. Security guards write comprehensive reports outlining their observations and activities during their assigned shift. They may interview witnesses or victims, prepare case reports, and testify in court.

Although all security guards perform many of the same duties, specific duties vary based on whether the guard works in a "static" security position or on a mobile patrol. Guards assigned to static security positions usually serve the client at one location for a specific length of time. These guards must become closely acquainted with the property and people associated with it and often monitor alarms and closed-circuit TV cameras. In contrast, guards assigned to mobile patrol duty drive or walk from location to location and conduct security checks within an assigned geographical zone. Specific job responsibilities also vary with the size, type, and location of the employer. In department stores, guards protect people, records, merchandise, money, and equipment. They often work with undercover store detectives to prevent theft by customers or store employees and help in the apprehension of shoplifting suspects prior to arrival by police. In office buildings, banks, and hospitals, guards maintain order and protect the institutions' property, staff, and customers. At air, sea, and rail terminals and other transportation facilities, guards protect people, freight, property, and equipment. They may screen passengers and visitors for weapons and explosives using metal detectors and high-tech equipment, ensure nothing is stolen while being loaded or unloaded, and watch for fires and criminals.

Working Conditions: Most security guards spend considerable time on their feet, either assigned to a specific post or patrolling buildings and grounds. Guards may be stationed at a guard desk inside a building to monitor electronic security and surveillance devices or to check the credentials of persons entering or leaving the premises. The work is usually routine, but guards must be constantly alert for threats to themselves and the property they are protecting. Guards who work during the day may have a great deal of contact with other employees and the public. Guards usually work at least eight-hour shifts for 40 hours per week and often are on call in case an emergency arises. Some employers have three shifts, and guards rotate to equally divide daytime, weekend, and holiday work. Guards usually eat on the job instead of taking a regular break away from the site. More than one in seven guards work part time, and many individuals hold a second job as a guard to supplement their primary earnings.

Education, Training, Qualifications: Many employers of unarmed guards do not have any specific educational requirements. For armed guards, employers usually prefer individuals who are high school graduates or hold an equivalent certification. Most states require that guards be licensed. To be licensed as a guard, individuals must be at least 18 years old, pass a background check, and complete classroom training in such subjects as property rights, emergency procedures, and detention of suspected criminals. Drug testing often is required, and may be random and ongoing. Many jobs require a driver's license. Guards who carry weapons must be licensed by the appropriate government authority, and some receive further certification as special police officers, which allows them to make limited types of arrests while on duty. Armed guard positions have more stringent background checks and entry requirements than those of unarmed guards because of greater insurance liability risks. Rigorous hiring and screening programs consisting of background, criminal record, and fingerprint checks are becoming the norm. Applicants are expected to have good character references, no serious police record, and good health. Applicants should be mentally alert, emotionally stable, and physically fit in order to cope with emergencies.

The amount of training guards receives varies. Training requirements are higher for armed guards because their employers are legally responsible for any use of force. Many employers give newly hired guards instruction before they start the job and also provide on-the-job training. Guards may receive training in protection, public relations, report writing, crisis deterrence, and first aid.

Earnings: Median annual earnings of security guards were $19,140 in 2002. Some earned less than $13,740 while others earned more than $31,540. Median earnings in the industries employing the largest numbers of security guards in 2002 were as follows: public schools $24,470, general medical and surgical hospitals $24,050, local government $22,120, traveler accommodation $21,390, and investigation and security services $17,910.

Key Contacts: Further information about work opportunities for guards is available from local security and guard firms and state employment service offices. Information about licensing requirements for guards may be obtained from the state licensing commission or the state police department. In states where local jurisdictions establish licensing requirements, contact a local government authority such as the sheriff, county executive, or city manager.

5

Office and Administrative Support Occupations

NUMEROUS JOB OPPORTUNITIES are available in office and administrative support occupations. Many of these jobs encompass back office operations that large corporations have been increasingly outsourcing to cheap labor markets abroad. Some of the best opportunities in these occupational fields will be found with small businesses that employ fewer than 100 individuals. These companies tend to rely on in-house personnel rather than outsource such jobs abroad.

Most of the jobs profiled in this chapter require a high school diploma and some additional training. Two jobs that appear on the U.S. Department of Labor's list of 20 jobs with high median earnings and a significant number of job openings in the decade ahead are executive secretaries and administrative assistants (see chart on page 9).

For more information on these and related office and administrative occupations, see the U.S. Department of Labor's *Occupational Outlook Handbook* and the *O*NET Dictionary of Occupational Titles* (see pages 14-15 for information on print and online editions).

Bill and Account Collectors

⇨ **Annual Earnings:** $12.88 hourly
⇨ **Education/Training:** High school diploma
⇨ **Outlook:** Faster than average growth

Employment Outlook: Employment of bill and account collectors is expected to grow faster than average for all occupations through 2012. Cash flow is becoming increasingly important to companies, which are now placing greater emphasis on collecting bad debts sooner. Thus, the workload for collectors is up as they seek to collect not only debts that are relatively old, but ones that are more recent. As more companies in a wide range of industries get involved in lending money and issuing their own credit cards, they will need to hire collectors, because debt levels will inevitably rise. The new (2005) bankruptcy law, which makes it more difficult for individuals to eliminate debts by declaring bankruptcy, should result in more collection activities on the part of banks and credit card companies. Hospitals and physicians' offices are two of the fastest growing areas requiring collectors. Government agencies also are making more use of collectors to collect on everything from parking tickets to child-support payments and past-due taxes. The Internal Revenue Service (IRS) is considering outsourcing the collection of overdue federal taxes to third-party collection agencies. If the IRS does outsource, more collectors will be required for this job. Contrary to the pattern in most occupations, employment of bill and account collectors tends to rise during recessions, reflecting the difficulty that many people have in meeting their financial obligations. However, collectors usually have more success at getting people to repay their debts when the economy is good.

Nature of Work: Bill and account collectors, called simply collectors, keep track of accounts that are overdue and attempt to collect payment on them. Some are employed by third-party collection agencies, while others – known as "in-house collectors" – work directly for the original creditors, such as department stores, hospitals, or banks.

First, collectors are called upon to locate and notify customers of delinquent accounts, usually over the telephone, but sometimes by letter. When customers move without leaving a forwarding address, collectors may check with the post office, telephone companies, credit bureaus, or former neighbors to obtain the new address. Once collectors find the debtor, they solicit payment. Collectors may also attempt to learn the cause of delay in payment. Where feasible, they offer the customer advice on how to pay off the debts, such as by taking out a bill consolidation loan. However, the collector's prime objective is always to ensure that the customer pays the debt in question. Collectors use computers and a variety of automated systems to keep track of overdue accounts. Typically, collectors work at video display terminals that are linked to computers. A computer dials the telephone number automatically, and the collector speaks only when a connection has been made.

Working Conditions: Collectors typically work in an office environment. Collectors who work for third-party collection agencies may spend most of their days on the phone in a call-center environment. However, a growing number of financial clerks – particularly medical billers – work at home, and many work part time. Collectors often have to work evenings and weekends, when it usually is easier to reach people.

Education, Training, Qualifications: Most bill and account collectors are required to have at least a high school diploma, but the completion of some college education is becoming increasingly important. The abilities to trace and locate customers who "skip out" on their debts, continually make calls to people who do not want to talk to a bill collector, and remain calm when talking to people who may get angry or even abusive on the telephone are important skills for bill collectors.

Earnings: Median hourly earnings of full-time bill and account collectors were $12.88 in 2002. In addition to their wages, some bill and account collectors receive commissions or bonuses based on the number of cases they close.

Key Contacts: Career information on bill and account collectors is available from:

- **Association of Credit and Collection Professionals:** P.O. Box 390106, Minneapolis, MN 55439. Website: www.acainternational. org.

Customer Service Representatives

- ➪ **Annual Earnings:** $26,240
- ➪ **Education/Training:** High school diploma
- ➪ **Outlook:** Excellent

Employment Outlook: Employment of customer service representatives is expected to grow faster than average for all occupations through the year 2012. Prospects for obtaining a job in this field are expected to be excellent, with more job openings than job seekers. Bilingual job seekers, in particular, may enjoy favorable job prospects. Replacement needs are expected to be significant in this large occupation because many young people work as customer service representatives before switching to other jobs. This occupation is well suited to flexible work schedules, and many opportunities for part-time work will continue to be available, particularly as organizations attempt to cut labor costs by hiring more temporary workers. There is a trend towards consolidation by centralizing call centers. As a result, employment of customer service representatives may grow at a faster rate in call centers than in other areas; however, this growth may be tempered as a variety of factors, including technological improvements, make it increasingly feasible and cost-effective for call centers to be built or relocated outside the United States. Advancements such as the Internet and automated teller machines have provided customers means of obtaining information and conducting transactions that do not entail interacting with another person. However, despite such developments, the need for customer service representatives is expected to remain strong. While jobs in some industries, such as retail trade, may be impacted by economic downturns, the occupation is generally resistant to major fluctuations in employment.

Nature of Work: Customer service representatives are employed by many different types of companies throughout the country to serve as a direct point of contact for customers. They are responsible for ensuring that their company's customers receive an adequate level of service or help with their questions and concerns. Customer service representatives interact with customers to provide information in response to inquiries about products or services and to handle and resolve complaints. Some customer service representatives handle general questions and complaints, whereas others specialize in a particular area. Many customer inquiries involve routine questions and requests such as checking on the status of an order that has been placed. Obtaining the answers to such questions usually requires simply looking up information on their computer. Some customer service representatives help people decide what types of products or services would best suit their needs. They may even aid customers in completing purchases or transactions.

In some organizations, customer service representatives spend their entire day on the telephone. In others, they may spend part of their day answering e-mails and the remainder of the day taking calls. For some, most of their contact with the public is face to face. Some customer service representatives work in call centers where there is very little time between calls; as soon as they have finished with one call they must immediately move on to another. Telephone calls may be taped and reviewed by supervisors to ensure that company policies and procedures are being followed, or a supervisor may listen in on conversations. Job responsibilities can differ, depending on the industry in which a customer service representative is employed, and at times they may assume the responsibilities of other workers, as needed.

Working Conditions: Although customer service representatives can work in a variety of settings, most work in areas that are clean and well lit. Many work in call or customer contact centers. In this type of environment, workers generally have their own workstation or cubicle space and are equipped with a telephone, headset, and computer. Because many call centers are open extended hours, beyond the traditional 9-to-5 business day, or are staffed around the clock, these positions may require workers to take on early morning, evening, or late night shifts. Weekend or holiday work may also be necessary. As a result, the occupation is well suited to flexible work schedules. About one out of seven customer service representatives works part time. The occupation also offers the opportunity for seasonal work in certain industries, often through temporary help agencies.

Call centers may be crowded and noisy, and work may be repetitious and stressful, with little time between calls. Workers usually must attempt to minimize the length of each call, while still providing excellent service. Long periods spent sitting, typing, or looking at a computer screen may cause eye and muscle strain, backaches, headaches, and repetitive motion injuries.

Customer service representatives working outside of a call center environment may interact with customers through several different means. Customers may approach them in person or contact them by telephone, computer, mail, or fax. Many of these workers will work a standard 40-hour week; however, their hours will depend on the hours of operation of the business in which they are employed. For virtually all types of customer service representatives, dealing with difficult or irate customers can be a trying task; however, the ability to directly help customers and resolve their problems has the potential to be very rewarding.

Education, Training, Qualifications: A high school diploma or the equivalent is the most common educational requirement for customer service representatives. Basic computer knowledge and good interpersonal skills also are important qualities for people who wish to be successful in this field. Because customer service representatives constantly interact with the public, strong communication and problem-solving skills are a must, particularly strong verbal communication and listening skills. For those workers who communicate through e-mail, good typing, spelling and written communication skills are necessary. High school courses in computers, English, or business are helpful in preparing for a job in customer service.

Customer service representatives play a critical role in providing an interface between the customer and the company that employs them, and for this reason employers seek out people who are able to come across in a friendly and professional manner. The ability to deal patiently with problems and complaints and to remain courteous when faced with difficult or angry people is very important. The ability to speak a foreign language is becoming increasingly necessary, and bilingual skills are considered a plus.

Training requirements vary by industry. Almost all customer service representatives are provided with some training prior to beginning work, and training continues once on the job. Although some positions may require previous industry, office, or customer service experience, many customer service jobs are entry level. Within insurance agencies and brokerages, however, a customer service job is usually not an entry-level position. Workers must have previous experience in insurance and are often required by state regulations to be licensed.

Earnings: In 2002, median annual earnings for wage and salary customer service representatives were $26,240. The highest 10 percent earned more than $42,990. Earnings for customer service representatives vary according to level of skill required, experience, training, location, and size of firm. Customer service representatives working for wired telecommunication carriers, insurance carriers, and other insurance-related activities averaged the highest wages in 2002.

Key Contacts: Some employment service offices can provide information about employment opportunities for customer service representatives.

Financial Clerks

- ⇨ **Annual Earnings:** Varies, from $20,400 to $29.600
- ⇨ **Education/Training:** High school and training
- ⇨ **Outlook:** Fair to good

Employment Outlook: Overall employment of financial clerks is expected to experience slower-than-average growth in the decade ahead despite the continued growth in business transactions. Office automation will adversely affect the demand for financial clerks. However, some financial clerks will fare better than others, especially bill collectors, who are in much demand.

Nature of Work: Financial clerks keep track of money, recording all amounts coming into or leaving an organizations. They occupy a variety of positions from which they perform various financial recordkeeping duties, from bill collectors and bookkeepers to auditing and payroll clerks. Despite the growing use of automation, interaction with the public and with co-workers remains a basic part of the job for many financial clerks.

Working Conditions: With the exception of gaming cage workers, financial clerks typically are employed in an office environment. Bill collectors who work for third-party collection agencies may spend most of their days on the phone in a call-center environment. A growing number of financial clerks – particularly medical billers – work at home, and many work part time.

Education, Training, Qualifications: Most financial clerks are required to have at least a high school diploma. Some college education, especially in accounting, is increasingly required by employers. For occupations such as bookkeepers, accounting clerks, and procurement clerks, an associate degree in business or accounting often is required.

Earnings: Salaries of financial clerks vary considerably. Median hourly earnings of full-time financial clerks in 2002 were:

- Procurement clerks $14.23
- Payroll and timekeeping clerks $13.94
- Bookkeeping, accounting, and auditing clerks $13.16
- Bill and account collectors $12.88
- Billing and posting clerks and machine operators $12.55
- Gaming cage workers $10.47
- Tellers $9.81

Key Contacts: Information on employment opportunities is available from local offices of the state employment service or through professional associations, such as:

- **Association of Credit and Collection Professionals:** P.O. Box 390106, Minneapolis, MN 55439. Website: www.acainternational.org.

- **American Institute of Professional Bookkeepers:** 6001 Montrose Road, Suite 500, Rockville, MD 20852. Website: www.aipb.org.

Information and Record Clerks

- ⇨ **Annual Earnings:** Vary by occupational setting: $17,370 to $33,010
- ⇨ **Education/Training:** High school diploma or equivalent
- ⇨ **Outlook:** Average to faster than average growth

Employment Outlook: Overall employment of information and record clerks is expected to grow about as fast as average for all occupations through 2012. In addition to the many openings occurring as businesses and organizations expand, numerous job openings for information and record clerks will result from the need to replace experienced workers who transfer to other occupations or leave the labor force. Replacement needs are expected to be significant in this large occupational group, because many young people work as clerks for a few years before switching to other, higher paying jobs. These occupations are well suited to flexible work schedules, and many opportunities for part-time work will continue to be available, particularly as organizations attempt to cut labor costs by hiring more part-time or temporary workers.

The outlook for different types of information and record clerks is expected to vary in the coming decade. Economic growth and general business expansion are expected to stimulate faster-than-average growth. Positions as hotel, motel, and resort desk clerks are expected to grow faster than average, as are positions for interviewers — especially in the health and social assistance sector. Employment of other information and record clerks is expected to experience little or no growth. Job growth for file clerks will be slowed by productivity gains stemming from office automation and the consolidation of clerical jobs.

Nature of Work: Information and record clerks are found in nearly every industry, gathering data and providing information to the public. Although their day-to-day duties differ considerably, many information and record clerks greet customers, guests, or other visitors. Many also answer telephones and either obtain information from, or provide information to, the public. **Hotel, motel, and resort desk clerks** are a guest's first contact for check-in, check-out, and other services within hotels, motels, and resorts. **Interviewers, except eligibility and loan interviewers,** found most often in medical facilities, research firms, and financial institutions, assist the public in completing forms, applications, or questionnaires. **Eligibility interviewers for government programs** determine the eligibility of individuals applying for assistance. **Receptionists and information clerks** often are a visitor's or caller's first contact within an organization, providing information and routing calls. **Reservation and transportation ticket agents and travel clerks** assist the public in making travel plans, reserving seats, and purchasing tickets for a variety of transportation services. **Other information and record clerks** focus on maintaining, updating, and processing a variety of records, ranging from payrolls to information on the shipment of goods or bank statements.

Working Conditions: Working conditions vary for different types of information and record clerks, but most clerks work in areas that are clean, well lit, and relatively quiet. This is especially true for information clerks who greet customers and visitors and usually work in highly visible areas that are furnished to make a good impression. Reservation agents and interviewing clerks who spend much of their day talking on the telephone, however, commonly work away from the public, often in large centralized reservation or phone centers. Because a number of agents or clerks may share the same workspace, it may be crowded and noisy. Interviewing clerks may conduct surveys on the street or in shopping malls, or they may go door to door.

Although most information and record clerks work a standard 40-hour week, about one out of five works part time. Some high school and college students work part time in these occupations, after school or during vacations. Some jobs – such as those in the transportation industry, hospitals, and hotels, in particular – may require working evenings, late-night shifts, weekends, and holidays. Interviewing clerks conducting surveys or other research may work mainly evenings or weekends. In general, employees with the least seniority tend to be assigned the least desirable shifts.

The work performed by information clerks may be repetitious and stressful. Many receptionists spend all day answering telephones while performing additional clerical or secretarial tasks. Reservation agents and travel clerks work under stringent time constraints or have quotas on the number of calls answered or reservations made. Additional stress is caused by technology that enables management to electronically monitor employees' use of computer systems, tape-record telephone calls, or limit the time spent on each call. Work can also be stressful when workers are trying to serve the needs of difficult or angry customers. When flights are canceled, reservations mishandled, or guests dissatisfied, these clerks must bear the brunt of the customers' anger. Hotel desk clerks and ticket agents may be on their feet most of the time, and ticket agents may have to lift heavy baggage. Prolonged exposure to a video display terminal may lead to eyestrain for the many information clerks who work with computers.

Education, Training, Qualifications: Despite the fact that hiring requirements for information and record clerk jobs vary from industry to industry, a high school diploma or its equivalent is the most common educational requirement. Increasingly, familiarity with computers and good interpersonal skills are becoming equally important as the diploma to employers. Although many employers prefer to hire information and record clerks at a higher level of education, only a few of these clerical occupations require such a level of education. Many information and record clerks deal directly with the public, so a professional appearance and a pleasant personality are important. A clear speaking voice and fluency in the English language also are essential. Good spelling and computer literacy often are needed, particularly because most work involves considerable use of the computer. In addition, speaking a foreign language fluently is becoming increasingly helpful for those wishing to enter the lodging or travel industry.

With the exception of airline reservation and transportation ticket agents, information and record clerks generally receive orientation and training on the job. New employees learn job tasks through on-the-job training under the guidance of a supervisor or an experienced clerk. Most airline reservation and ticket agents learn their skills through formal company training programs. Most banks prefer to hire college graduates for new-account clerk positions. Nevertheless, many new-account clerks without college degrees start out as bank tellers and are promoted by demonstrating excellent communication skills and the motivation to learn new skills. Some information and record clerks learn the skills they need in high schools, business schools, and community colleges. Business education programs offered by these institutions typically include courses in typing, word processing, shorthand, business communications, records management, and office systems and procedures. Order clerks in specialized technical positions obtain their training from technical institutes and two- and four-year colleges. Some entry-level clerks are college graduates with degrees in business, finance, or liberal arts. Although a degree is rarely required, many graduates accept entry-level clerical positions to get into a particular company or to enter a particular field. Workers with college degrees are likely to start at higher salaries and advance more easily than those without degrees. Advancement usually comes by transfer to a position with more responsibilities or by promotion to a supervisory position.

Earnings: Earnings vary widely by occupation and experience. Annual earnings in 2002 ranged from less than $13,020 for the lowest paid 10 percent of hotel clerks to more than $53,410 for the top 10 percent of brokerage clerks. Salaries of human resource assistants tend to be higher than for other information and record clerks, while hotel, motel, and resort desk clerks tend to earn quite a bit less. In 2003, the federal government typically paid salaries ranging from $19,898 to $23,555 a year to beginning receptionists with a high school diploma or six months of experience. The average annual salary for all receptionists employed by the federal government was about $25,704 in 2003. In addition to their hourly wage, full-time information and record clerks who work evenings, nights, weekends, or holidays may receive differential pay. Some employers offer educational assistance to their employees. Reservation and transportation ticket agents and travel clerks receive free or reduced fares for travel on their company's carriers for themselves, their immediate families, and, in some companies, friends.

Key Contacts: Information on careers in the lodging industry, as well as information about professional development and training programs, may be obtained from:

- **Educational Institute of the American Hotel and Lodging Association**: 800 N. Magnolia Avenue, Suite 1800, Orlando, FL 32803. Website: www.ei-ahma.org.

Secretaries and Administrative Assistants

⇨ **Annual Earnings:** $33,410
⇨ **Education/Training:** High school diploma
⇨ **Outlook:** Slower than average growth

Employment Outlook: Overall employment of secretaries and administrative assistants is expected to grow more slowly than the average for all occupations over the 2002-12 period. In addition to those resulting from growth, numerous job openings will result from the need to replace workers who transfer to other occupations or leave this very large occupation for other reasons each year. Opportunities should be best for applicants, particularly experienced secretaries, with extensive knowledge of software applications.

Projected employment of secretaries will vary by occupational specialty. Employment growth in the healthcare and social assistance and legal services industries should lead to average growth for medical and legal secretaries. Employment of executive secretaries and administrative assistants is projected to grow more slowly than the average for all occupations. Rapidly growing industries – such as administrative and support services, healthcare and social assistance, educational services (private), and professional, scientific, and technical services – will continue to generate most new job opportunities. A decline in employment is expected for all other secretaries, except legal, medical, or executive, who account for almost half of all secretaries and administrative assistants.

Increasingly office automation and organizational restructuring will continue to make secretaries and administrative assistants more productive in coming years. Personal computers, e-mail, scanners, and voice message systems will allow secretaries to accomplish more in the same amount of time. The use of automated equipment is also changing the distribution of work in many offices. In some cases, such traditional secretarial duties as keyboarding, filing, photocopying, and bookkeeping are being assigned to workers in other units or departments. Professionals and managers increasingly do their own word processing and data entry, and handle much of their own correspondence rather than submit the work to secretaries and other support staff. Also, in some law and medical offices, paralegals and medical assistants are assuming some tasks formerly done by secretaries. As other workers assume more of these duties, there is a trend in many offices for professionals and managers to "share" secretaries and administrative assistants. However, many secretarial and administrative duties are of a personal, interactive nature, and are not easily automated. Responsibilities such as planning conferences, working with clients, and instructing staff require tact and communication skills. Because technology cannot substitute for these personal skills, secretaries and administrative assistants will continue to play a key role in most organizations.

Nature of Work: As the reliance on technology continues to expand in offices across the country, the role of the office professional has greatly evolved. Office automation and organizational restructuring have led secretaries and administrative assistants to assume a wider range of new responsibilities once reserved for managerial and professional staff. Many secretaries and administrative assistants now provide training and orientation for new staff, conduct research on the Internet, and operate and troubleshoot new office technologies. In the midst of these changes, however, their core responsibilities have remained much the same – performing and coordinating an office's administrative activities, and storing, retrieving, and integrating information for dissemination to staff and clients.

Secretaries and administrative assistants are responsible for a variety of administrative and clerical duties necessary to run an organization efficiently. They serve as an information manager for an office, plan and schedule meetings and appointments, organize and maintain paper and electronic files, manage projects, conduct research, and provide information by using the telephone, postal mail, and e-mail. They also may handle travel arrangements. In a number of organizations, secretaries and administrative assistants work in teams in order to work flexibly and share their expertise. Specific job duties vary with experience and titles. Executive secretaries and administrative assistants, for example, perform fewer clerical tasks than do other secretaries. In addition to arranging conference calls and scheduling meetings, they may handle more complex responsibilities such as conducting research, preparing statistical reports, training employees, and supervising other clerical staff. Some secretaries and administrative assistants, such as legal and medical secretaries, perform highly specialized work requiring knowledge of technical terminology and procedures. Other technical secretaries who assist engineers or scientists may prepare correspondence, maintain the technical library, and gather and edit materials for scientific papers.

Working Conditions: Secretaries and administrative assistants usually work in schools, hospitals, corporate settings, or legal and medical offices. Their jobs often involve sitting for long periods. If they spend a lot a time typing, particularly at a video display terminal, they may encounter problems of eyestrain, stress, and repetitive motion, such as carpal tunnel syndrome.

Office work can lend itself to alternative or flexible working arrangements, such as part-time work or telecommuting – especially if the job requires extensive computer use. About one secretary in six works part time and many others work in temporary positions. A few participate in job-sharing arrangements in which two people divide responsibility for a single job. The majority of secretaries, however, are full-time employees who work a standard 40-hour week.

Education, Training, Qualifications: High school graduates who have basic office skills may qualify for entry-level secretarial positions. However, employers increasingly require extensive knowledge of software applications, such as work processing, spreadsheets, and database management. Secretaries and administrative assistants should be proficient in keyboarding and good at spelling, punctuation, grammar, and oral communication. Because secretaries and administrative assistants must be tactful in their dealings with people, employers also look for good customer service and interpersonal skills. Discretion, good judgment, organizational or management ability, initiative, and the ability to work independently are especially important for higher level administrative positions.

Secretaries and administrative assistants acquire skills in various ways. Training ranges from high school vocational education programs that teach office skills and keyboarding to one- and two-year programs in office administration offered by business schools, vocational-technical institutes, and community colleges. Many temporary placement agencies also provide formal training in computer and office skills. However, many skills tend to be acquired through on-the-job instruction by other employees or by equipment and software vendors. Specialized training programs are available for students planning to become medical or legal secretaries or administrative technology specialists. Bachelor's degrees and professional certifications are becoming increasingly important as business continues to become more global. Secretaries generally advance by being promoted to other administrative positions with more responsibilities. Qualified secretaries who broaden their knowledge of a company's operations and enhance their skills may be promoted to other positions such as senior or executive secretary, clerical supervisor, or office manager. Secretaries with word processing or data entry experience can advance to jobs as word processing or data entry trainers, supervisors, or managers within their own firms or in a secretarial, word processing, or data entry service bureau. Secretarial experience can also lead to jobs such as instructor or sales representative with manufacturers of software or computer equipment. With additional training, many legal secretaries become paralegals.

Earnings: Median annual earnings of executive secretaries and administrative assistants were $33,410 in 2002. The middle 50 percent earned between $26,980 and $41,350. The highest 10 percent earned more than $50,420. Median annual earnings of legal secretaries were $35,020 in 2002. The middle 50 percent earned between $27,540 and $44,720. The highest 10 percent earned more than $54,810. Medical secretaries earned a median annual salary of $25,430 in 2002. The middle 50 percent earned between

$21,090 and $31,070. The highest earned 10 percent more than $37,550. Median annual earnings of secretaries, except legal, medical, and executive, were about $25,290 in 2002. Salaries vary a great deal, however, reflecting differences in skills, experience, and level of responsibility. Salaries also vary in different parts of the country; earnings are usually lowest in southern cities and highest in northern and western cities. Obtaining certification in this field usually is rewarded by a higher salary.

Key Contacts: State employment offices provide information about job openings for secretaries. For information on the Certified Professional Secretary or Certified Administrative Professional designations, contact:

- **International Association of Administrative Professionals**: 10502 NW Ambassador Drive, P.O. Box 20404, Kansas City, MO 64195-0404. Website: www.iaap-hq.org.

Information on the Certified Legal Secretary Specialist (CLSS) designation can be obtained from:

- **Legal Secretaries International Inc.**: 2302 Fannin Street, Suite 500, Houston, TX 77002. Website: www.legalsecretaries.org.

Information on the Accredited Legal Secretary (ALS), Professional Legal Sceretary (PLS), and Paralegal certifications is available from:

- **NALS, Inc**: 314 East 3rd Street, Suite 210, Tulsa, OK 74120. Website: www.nals.org.

6

Sales and Related Occupations

MANY PEOPLE RE-ENTERING the workforce look toward a variety of sales positions to start new careers. Real estate and insurance sales jobs, for example, are ideal for people who prefer flexible work schedules or enjoy operating as independent contractors.

Qualifications and Education

Are you born to sell? Not many people are, but you may find you have many hidden talents that would be perfect for re-entering the job market as a salesperson. If, for example, you are self-motivated and goal-oriented, enjoy meeting strangers, can handle rejections, and are good at persuading others to buy a product or perform a service, a job or career in one of many sales fields may be right for you. While a college degree is often a plus for individuals who deal with highly technical and scientific products and services, such as pharmaceuticals, computers, weapons systems, and financial services, many sales fields, such as automotive, real estate, and insurance, are open to anyone who has demonstrated the ability to learn about a product, network for clients, and present and close deals.

Regardless of their educational backgrounds, talented salespeople working in commission-based fields selling high-ticket items can realize substantial annual earnings.

You don't need formal education credentials to be a good and productive salesperson. Effective selling skills often center on attitude, personality, communication, prospecting, perseverance, organization, and follow-through. Good salespeople can often transfer their skills from one occupational field to another because of the generic nature of their skills. An individual who starts out selling automobiles may later move into insurance and real estate.

Earnings Expectations

Earnings for salespeople can vary considerably depending on the economy, their industry, their products/services, and their talent. The least compensated tend to be part-time salespeople in retail establishments, especially in clothing and merchandising. The best compensated are generally salespeople in the financial and pharmaceutical industries.

Since most salespeople receive a base salary plus commission, their income largely depends on a combination of factors that may or may not be within their control, such as the state of the economy and their industry. Many real estate agents, for example, realized substantial increases in incomes during the hot real estate market of 2003-2005. That situation could change dramatically if and when the real estate market cools down or even declines substantially.

Nonetheless, sales is a very talent-driven type of occupation. If you are born to sell, you'll most likely do very well in any sales field. You will be sought after by many employers who readily seek such talent that immediately contributes to increasing their company's bottom line.

Advertising Sales Agents

> ⇨ **Annual Earnings:** $44,960
> ⇨ **Education/Training:** Moderate-term on-the-job training
> ⇨ **Outlook:** Good

Employment Outlook: In 2002, there were 157,000 persons working as advertising sales agents soliciting advertisements for inclusion in publications such as newspapers and magazines, television/radio advertising time, and custom-made signs. Employment for advertising sales agents in the decade ahead is expected to grow as fast as average, assuming the economy grows at a relatively steady state.

Nature of Work: Calls on prospects, advises clients of various types of programming for electronic media, layouts and design for publications, signs and displays. Sells advertising space, time, or signage; presents contract for client to sign, and may be involved in actual production of advertising.

Working Conditions: Working conditions vary. Although some work is office based, a great deal of time is spent meeting with clients and potential clients – usually at their offices.

Education, Training, Qualifications: Good sales and marketing skills for showing, promoting, and selling products and services. This includes marketing strategy, product demonstration, sales techniques, and sales control systems. Many advertising sales agents have completed some college, such as a two-year associate degree.

Earnings: Median annual earnings of advertising sales agents were $44,960 in 2002. Many sales agents work on a combination of a base salary plus commissions on sales volume or receive only a commission on their sales revenue.

Key Contacts: For information on careers in advertising, contact:

- **Advertising Educational Foundation:** 220 East 42nd Street, Suite 3300, New York, NY 10017. Website: www.aef.com/start.asp.

- **American Association of Advertising Agencies:** 405 Lexington Avenue, 18th Floor, New York, NY 10174. Website: www.aaaa.org.

- **Association of National Advertisers:** 708 Third Avenue, New York, NY 10017. Website: www.ana.net.

- **American Advertising Federation:** 1101 Vermont Avenue NW, Suite 500, Washington, DC 20005. Website: www.aaf.org.

Insurance Sales Agents

↪ **Annual Earnings:** $40,750
↪ **Education/Training:** High school diploma to college degree
↪ **Outlook:** Good

Employment Outlook: Although slower-than-average employment growth is expected among insurance agents in the decade ahead, opportunities for agents will be favorable for persons with the right qualifications and skills. Multilingual agents should be in high demand because they can serve a wider range of customers.

Nature of Work: Insurance sales agents help individuals, families, and businesses select insurance policies that provide the best protection for their lives, health, and property. Commonly referred to as "producers" in the insurance industry, these salespeople sell one or more types of insurance, such as property and casualty, life, health, disability, and long-term care. An increasing number of insurance sales agents are offering comprehensive financial planning services to their clients.

Working Conditions: Most insurance sales agents are based in small offices, from which they contact clients and provide information on the policies they sell. However, much of their time may be spent outside their offices traveling locally to meet with clients, close sales, or investigate claims. Agents usually determine their own hours of work and often schedule evening and weekend appointments for the convenience of clients. Although most agents work a 40-hour week, some work 60 hours a week or longer.

Education, Training, Qualifications: While most insurance companies and independent agencies prefer to hire college graduates – especially those who have majored in business or economics, high school graduates are occasionally hired if they have proven sales ability or have been successful in other types of work. In fact, many entrants to insurance sales agent jobs transfer from other occupations. Insurance sales agents must obtain a license in the states where they plan to do business. In most states, licenses are issued only to applicants who complete specified prelicensing courses and who pass state examinations covering insurance fundamentals and state insurance laws.

Earnings: The median annual earnings of wage-and-salary insurance sales agents were $40,750 in 2002. The middle 50 percent earned between $28,860 and $64,450. Many independent agents are paid by commission only, whereas sales workers who are employees of an agency or an insurance carrier may be paid in one of three ways: salary only, salary plus commission, or salary plus bonus.

Key Contacts: Occupational information about insurance agents is available from the home office of many life and casualty insurance companies. For information about insurance sales careers and training, contact:

- **Independent Insurance Agents and Brokers of America:** 127 S. Peyton Street, Alexandria, VA 22314. Website: www.iiaa.org.

- **National Association of Health Underwriters:** 2000 N. 14th Street, Suite 450, Arlington, VA 22201. Website: www.nahu.org.

- **Insurance Information Institute:** 110 William Street, New York, NY 10038. Website: www.iii.org.

Real Estate Brokers and Sales Agents

⇨ **Annual Earnings:** $30,930 to $50,330
⇨ **Education/Training:** Experience and training
⇨ **Outlook:** Good

Employment Outlook: Although real estate has been one of the booming sectors of the U.S. economy in the first few years of the 21st century, employment of real estate brokers and sales agents is expected to grow more slowly than the average for all occupations in the coming decade. Increasing use of information technology will continue to raise the productivity of agents and brokers, limiting the potential for job growth to a certain extent. Real estate agents and brokers will continue to experience moderate employment growth due to the increasing housing needs of a growing population, as well as the perception that real estate is a good investment.

Nature of Work: Real estate agents usually are independent sales workers who provide their services to a licensed real estate broker on a contract basis. In return, the broker pays the agent a portion of the commission earned form the agent's sale of the property. Brokers are independent businesspeople who sell real estate owned by others; they also may rent or manage properties for a fee. In addition to selling, agents and brokers spend a significant amount of time obtaining listings - agreements by owners to place properties for sale with the firm. Most real estate brokers and sales agents sell residential property. A small number, usually employed in large or specialized firms, sell commercial, industrial, agricultural, or other types of real estate.

Working Conditions: Advances in telecommunications and the ability to retrieve data about properties over the Internet allow many real estate brokers and sales agents to work out of their homes instead of real estate offices. Even with this convenience, these workers spend much of their time away from their desks – showing properties to customers, analyzing properties for sales, meeting with prospective clients, or researching the state of the market. Agents and brokers often work more than a standard 40-hour week. They usually work evenings and weekends and are always on call to suit the needs of clients. Business is usually slower during the winter season. Although the hours are long and frequently irregular, most agents and brokers have the freedom to determine their own schedule.

Education, Training, Qualifications: Real estate brokers and sales agents must be licensed. Prospective agents must be high school graduates, at least 18 years old, and pass a written test. Most states require candidates for the general sales license to complete between 30 and 90 hours of classroom instruction. Those seeking a broker's license need between 60 and 90 hours of formal training and a specific amount of experience selling real estate, usually one to three years.

Earnings: Median annual earnings of salaried real estate agents, including commissions, were $30,930 in 2002. The middle 50 percent earned between $21,010 and $52,860 a year. Median annual earnings of salaried real estate brokers, including commissions, were $50,330 in 2002. The middle 50 percent earned between $29,240 and $90,170 a year.

Key Contacts: Information about opportunities in real estate is available on the website of the following professional association:

- **National Association of Realtors:** 430 N. Michigan Avenue, Chicago, IL 60611. Website: www.realtor.org.

Retail Salespersons

⇨ **Annual Earnings:** Varies greatly, from minimum wage on up
⇨ **Education/Training:** High school diploma or equivalent
⇨ **Outlook:** Good

Employment Outlook: Employment of retail salespersons is expected to be good because of the need to replace the large number of workers who transfer to other occupations or leave the labor force each year. Employment is expected to grow about as fast as the average for all occupations in the decade ahead, reflecting rising retail sales stemming from a growing population. Opportunities for part-time work should be abundant, and demand will be strong for temporary workers during peak selling periods, such as the end-of-year holiday season. The availability of part-time and temporary work attracts many people seeking to supplement their income.

Nature of Work: These are not great paying jobs – indeed, many are minimum wage positions – but they are often significant stepping stones to other types of sales jobs and careers. Whether selling shoes, computer equipment, or automobiles, retail salespersons assist customers in finding what they are looking for and try to interest them in buying the merchandise. They describe a product's features, demonstrate its use, or show various models and colors. For some sales jobs, particularly those involving expensive and complex items, retail salespersons need special knowledge or skills.

Working Conditions: Most salespersons in retail trade work in clean, comfortable, well-lighted stores. However, they often stand for long periods and may need supervisory approval to leave the sales floor. The Monday-through-Friday, 9-to-5 workweek is the exception rather than the rule in retail sales. Most salespersons work evenings and weekends, particularly during sales and other peak retail periods. Retail salespersons held about 2.1 million wage and salary jobs in 2002.

Education, Training, Qualifications: There usually are no formal education requirements for this type of work, although a high school diploma or equivalent is preferred. Employers look for people who enjoy working with others and who have the tact and patience to deal with difficult customers. In most small stores, an experienced employee or the proprietor instructs newly hired sales personnel in making out sales checks and operating cash registers. In large stores, training programs are more formal and are usually conducted over several days.

Earnings: The starting wage for many retail sales operations is the federal minimum wage, which was $5.15 an hour in 2002. Median hourly earnings of retail salespersons, including commissions, were $8.51 in 2002. The middle 50 percent earned between $7.08 and $11.30 an hour. Median hourly earnings in the industries employing the largest numbers of retail salespersons in 2002 were as follows:

- Automobile dealers $18.25
- Building material and supplies dealers $10.41
- Department stores $8.12
- Other general merchandise stores $7.84
- Clothing stores $7.77

Compensation systems vary by type of establishment and merchandise sold. Salespersons receive hourly wages, commissions, or a combination of wages and commissions.

Key Contacts: Information on careers in retail sales may be obtained from the personnel offices of local stores or from state merchants' associations. General information about retailing is available from:

- **National Retail Federation:** 325 7th Street NW, Suite 1100, Washington, DC 20004. Website: www.nrf.com.

Information about retail sales employment opportunities is available from:

- **Retail, Wholesale, and Department Store Union:** 30 East 29th Street, 4th Floor, New York, NY 10016. Website: www.rwdsu.org.

Information about training for a career in automobile sales is available from:

- **National Automobile Dealers Association:** Public Relations Department, 8400 Westpark Drive, McLean, VA 22102-3591. Website: www.nada.org.

Sales Representatives, Wholesale, and Manufacturing

⇨ **Annual Earnings:** $55,740
⇨ **Education/Training:** Some college helpful
⇨ **Outlook:** Excellent

Employment Outlook: Employment is expected to grow about as fast as average due to continued growth in the variety and number of goods sold and from openings resulting from the need to replace workers who transfer to other occupations or leave the labor force. Job prospects for wholesale sales representatives will be better than those for manufacturing sales representatives because manufacturers are expected to continue contracting out sales duties to independent agents rather than using in-house or direct selling personnel.

Nature of Work: Regardless of the type of product they sell, sales representatives' primary duties are to capture the interest of wholesale and retail buyers and purchasing agents in their merchandise, and to address the clients' questions or concerns. Sales representatives also advise clients on methods to reduce costs, use their products, and increase sales. Sales representatives spend much of their time traveling to and visiting with prospective buyers and current clients. Obtaining new accounts is an important part of the job. Sales representatives follow leads from other clients, track advertisements in trade journals, and participate in trade shows and conferences. Sales representatives have several duties beyond selling products. They also analyze sales statistics, prepare reports, and handle administrative duties, such as filing an expense report, scheduling appointments, and making travel plans.

Manufacturers' and wholesale sales representatives held about 1.9 million jobs in 2002. About half of all salaried representatives worked in wholesale trade. Others were employed in manufacturing and mining.

Working Conditions: Some sales representatives have large territories and travel considerably. A sales region may cover several states, so they may be away from home for several days or weeks at a time. Others work near their "home base" and travel mostly by automobile. Due to the nature of their work and the amount of travel, sales representatives may work more than 40 hours per week. Sales representatives often are on their feet for long periods and may carry heavy sample products, which necessitates some physical stamina. Dealing with different types of people can be stimulating but demanding. Sales representatives often face competition from representatives of other companies. Companies usually set goals or quotas that representatives are expected to meet. Because their earnings depend on commissions, manufacturers' agents are also under pressure to maintain and expand their clientele.

Education, Training, Qualifications: The background needed for sales jobs varies by product line and market. Many employers hire individuals with previous sales experience who do not have a college degree, but often prefer those with some college education. For some consumer products, factors such as sales ability, personality, and familiarity with brands are more important than educational background. On the other hand, firms selling complex technical products may require a technical degree in addition to some sales experience. Many sales representatives attend seminars in sales techniques or take courses in marketing, economics, communication, or even a foreign language to provide the extra edge needed to make sales. Many companies have formal training programs for beginning sales representatives lasting up to two years. In some programs, trainees rotate among jobs in plants and offices to learn all phases of production, installation, and distribution of the product. New workers may get training by accompanying experienced workers on their sales calls.

Those who want to become sales representatives should be goal oriented and persuasive, and work well both independently and as part of a team. A pleasant personality and appearance, the ability to communicate well with people, and problem-solving skills are highly valued. Furthermore, completing a sale can take several months and thus requires patience and perseverance.

Earnings: Compensation methods vary significantly by the type of firm and product sold. Most employers use a combination of salary and commission or salary plus bonus. Commissions usually are based on the amount of sales, whereas bonuses may depend on individual performance, on the performance of all sales workers in the group or district, or on the company's performance.

Key Contacts: Information on careers for manufacturers' representatives and agents is available from:

- **Manufacturers' Agents National Association:** One Spectrum Pointe, Suite 150, Lake Forest, CA 92630. Website: www.mana online.org.

- **Manufacturers' Representatives Educational Research Foundation:** P.O. Box 247, Geneva, IL 60134. Website: www. mrerf.org.

Travel Agents

- ⇨ **Annual Earnings:** $26,630
- ⇨ **Education/Training:** High school diploma and training
- ⇨ **Outlook:** Fair to excellent

Employment Outlook: Employment of travel agents is expected to decline in the decade ahead. Most openings will occur as experienced agents transfer to other occupations or leave the labor force. Because of the projected decline and the fact that a number of people are attracted by the travel benefits associated with this occupation, keen competition for jobs is expected. An increasing reliance on the Internet to book travel, as well as industry consolidation, will continue to reduce the need for travel agents. Moderating the employment decline, however, are projections for increased spending on tourism and travel over the next decade. With rising household incomes, smaller families, and an increasing number of older people who are more likely to travel, more people are expected to travel on vacation – and to do so more frequently – than in the past. Business travel also should bounce back from recession and terrorism related lows as business activity expands.

While some forecasters have predicted the steady decline of travel agents due to the impact of the Internet, others see the resurgence of travel agents because of the restructuring of the traditional travel agent role. Indeed, more and more travel agencies have embraced the Internet by integrating it into their operations. But most important of all, more and more travel agents have become specialists who market cruises and specialty tours to their clients. While many travelers use the Internet to book airlines and hotel rooms and research designations, many of these same travelers are expected to use travel agents for arranging cruises and special tour packages. The future looks very bright for entrepreneurial travel agents who use the Internet to promote their services as well as offer unique travel programs to their clients.

Nature of Work: Depending on the needs of the client, travel agents give advice on destinations, make arrangements for transportation, hotel accommodations, car rentals, tours, and recreation, or plan the right vacation package or business/pleasure trip combination. They may advise on weather conditions, restaurants, tourist attractions, and recreation. For international travel, agents also provide information on customs regulations, required papers, and currency exchange rates. Travel agents may visit hotels, resorts, and restaurants to rate, firsthand, their comfort and quality.

Travel agents consult a variety of published and computer-based sources for information on departure and arrival times, fares, and hotel ratings and accommodations. Travel agents also promote their services, using telemarketing, direct mail, and the Internet. They make presentations to social and special-interest groups, arrange advertising displays, and suggest company-sponsored trips to business managers. Depending on the size of the travel agency, an agent may specialize by type of travel, such as leisure or business, or a regional or country destination, such as Europe, Africa, North America, India, Australia, or Brazil. Many are increasingly focusing on adventure travel as well as the rapidly growing lifestyle travel market that includes gay and lesbian travel, accessible travel, and luxury travel.

Working Conditions: Travel agents spend most of their time behind a desk conferring with clients, completing paperwork, contacting airlines and hotels for travel arrangements, and promoting group tours. They may work under a great deal of pressure during vacation seasons. Many agents, especially those who are self-employed, frequently work long hours. With advanced computer systems and telecommunication networks, some travel agents are able to work at home.

Travel agents held about 118,000 jobs in 2002 and are found in every part of the country. More than 8 out of 10 agents worked for travel agencies. Nearly 1 in 10 was self-employed.

Education, Training, Qualifications: Formal or specialized training is becoming increasingly important for travel agents, since few agencies are willing to train people on the job. Many vocational schools offer three- to 12-week full-time training programs, as well as evening and Saturday programs. Travel courses are also offered in public adult education programs and in community and four-year colleges. A few colleges offer a bachelor's and a master's degree in travel and tourism. Although few college courses relate directly to the travel industry, courses in computer science, geography, foreign language, and history are most useful. The American Society of Travel Agents (ASTA) and the Institute of Certified Travel Agents offer a travel correspondence course. Some people start as reservation clerks or receptionists in travel agencies. All employers require computer skills of workers whose jobs involve the operation of airline and centralized reservation systems. Experienced travel agents can take advanced self-study or group-study courses from the Travel Institute that lead to the Certified Travel Counselor (CTC) designation.

Earnings: Experience, sales ability, and the size and location of the agency determine the salary of a travel agent. Median annual earnings of travel agents were $26,630 in 2002. The middle 50 percent earned between $20,800 and $33,580. Earnings of travel agents who own their agencies depend mainly on commissions from airlines and other carriers, cruise lines, tour operators, and lodging establishments. However, commissions for booking airline tickets have dramatically declined during the past few years as airlines eliminated the traditional agency commission structure. While travel agents still book airline tickets for clients, they now charge $15 to $25 booking fees for such services. As a result, airline ticketing is no longer a major source of income for travel agents. When they travel, agents usually get substantially reduced rates for transportation and accommodations.

Key Contacts: For further information on training opportunities, contact:

- **American Society of Travel Agents:** 1101 King Street, Suite 200, Alexandria, VA 22314. Website: www.astanet.com.

For information on training and certification qualifications, contact:

- **The Travel Institute:** 148 Linden Street, Suite 305, Wellesley, MA 02482. Website: www.thetravelinstitute.com.

7

Sports, Entertainment, and Media Jobs

F EW JOB AND CAREER FIELDS have such a mass appeal as sports, entertainment, and the media. Many people would love to get paid playing their favorite sport, starring in a movie, or being before the television camera. Others would like to become a famous artist, musician, singer, or designer. And still others dream of working behind the scenes, where they put together and market productions.

Glamour Jobs

In many respects, these fields generate a disproportionate number of glamour jobs that place primary emphasis on special skills and demonstrated talents rather than education credentials. Talented and entrepreneurial individuals, who demonstrate a great deal of creativity and imagination, will find many opportunities in these fields.

Be forewarned, however, that jobs in sports, entertainment, and the media often pay much less than expected. While the top talent in these fields earn top dollar, many others working in these fields struggle for years on a part-time basis as they attempt to acquire experience and connections for making a rewarding career in a field that allows them to pursue their passions. If you have the necessary talent and drive, you'll find numerous jobs opportunities in these exciting fields.

Useful Resources

In addition to the jobs profiled in this chapter, several other books focus on related jobs and careers. McGraw-Hill, for example, publishes these career exploration titles that survey various jobs and careers in sports, entertainment, and media:

> _Careers for Film Buffs and Other Hollywood Types_
> _Careers for Music Lovers and Other Tuneful Types_
> _Careers for Sports Nuts and Other Athletic Types_
> _Careers for Writers and Others Who Have a Way With Words_
> _Careers in Journalism_
> _Opportunities in Acting Career_
> _Opportunities in Broadcasting Careers_
> _Opportunities in Cable Television Careers_
> _Opportunities in Journalism Careers_
> _Opportunities in Performing Arts Careers_
> _Opportunities in Publishing Careers_
> _Opportunities in Sports and Fitness Careers_
> _Opportunities in Television and Video Careers_

Other useful books include:

> _100 Careers in Film and Television_, Tanya Couch (Barron's Educational Series, 2002)

> _Breaking and Entering: A Career Guide About Landing Your First Job in Film Production_, April Fitzsimmons (Lone Eagle Publishing, 1997)

> _Career Opportunities in the Film Industry_, Fred and Jan Yagar (Facts on File, 2003)

Career Opportunities in the Music Industry, Shelly Field (Facts on File, 2000)

Career Opportunities in the Publishing Industry, Pat Schroeder (Facts on File, 2005)

Career Opportunities in Radio, Shelly Field (Facts on File, 2004)

Career Opportunities in the Sports Industry, Shelly Field (Facts on File, 2004)

Career Opportunities in Writing, Rosemary Ellen Guiley and Janet Frick (Facts on File, 2000)

Job Surfing: Media and Entertainment, Jeff Adams and Jim Blau (Princeton Review, 2002)

If you are interested in entertainment and/or media jobs, be sure to explore these websites:

- **Entertainment Careers**   www.entertainmentcareers.net
- **ShowBizJobs.com**   www.showbizjobs.com
- **HollywoodWeb.com**   www.hollywoodweb.com
- **440 International (Radio)**   www.440int.com
- **AM/FM Jobs**   www.amfmjobs.com
- **Entertainment Job Search**   www.dnaproductions.com/jobs. htm
- **Gigslist.org**   www.gigslist.org
- **MediaLine**   www.medialine.com
- **Media Jobz**   www.mediajobz.com
- **MediaRecruiter**   www.mediarecruiter.com
- **National Association of Broadcasters Career Center**   www.nab.org/bcc
- **Playbill Online**   www.playbill.com/jobs/find
- **TVandRadioJobs.com**   www.tvandradiojobs.com
- **TVJobs.com**   www.tvjobs.com

If you are interested in sports and recreation jobs, you'll find numerous websites related to employment opportunities in golf, tennis, mountain climbing, skiing, racing, sports medicine, coaching, sports broadcasting, summer camps, clubs, resorts, stadiums, arenas, high schools, colleges, women, and the outdoors. While most of the positions are full-time, many jobs, especially in resorts and summer camps, are seasonal and part-time:

- JobsinSports.com — www.jobsinsports.com
- CoolWorks.com — www.coolworks.com
- GolfingCareers — www.golfingcareers.com
- ActionJobs.com — www.actionjobs.com
- Camp Channel — www.campchannel.com/camp jobs
- CampJobs.com — www.campjobs.com
- Camp Staff — www.campstaff.com
- C.O.A.C.H. — www.coachhelp.com
- Coaching Jobs — www.coachingjobs.com
- Executive Sports Placement — www.prosportsjobs.com
- GolfSurfin — www.golfsurfin.com
- Summer Opportunities — www.petersons.com/summerop
- JobMonkey.com — www.jobmonkey.com
- Mountain Jobs — www.jacksonholnet.com/area_info/employment.php
- My Summers — www.mysummers.com
- NCAA Online — www.ncaa.org/employment.html
- OnlineSports.com — www.onlinesports.com
- RacingJobs.com — www.racingjobs.com
- SkiingtheNet.com — www.skiingthenet.com
- Ski Resort Jobs — www.skiresortjobs.com
- Sports Careers — www.1andall-sportsjobs.com
- Sports Medicine — www.sportsmedicinejobs.com
- Sports Workers — www.sportsworkers.com
- TeamJobs.com — www.teamjobs.com
- Tennis Jobs — www.tennisjobs.com
- Women Sports Jobs — www.womensportsjobs.com
- Work in Sports — www.workinsports.com

Actors

⇨ **Annual Earnings:** $23,470
⇨ **Education/Training:** High school diploma to college degree
⇨ **Outlook:** Good

Employment Outlook: Employment of actors is expected to grow about as fast as the average for all occupations in the decade ahead. Although a growing number of people will aspire to enter this profession, many will leave the field early because the work – when it is available – is hard, the hours are long, and the pay is low. Competition for jobs will be stiff, in part because the large number of highly trained and talented actors auditioning for roles generally exceeds the number of parts that become available. Only performers with the most stamina and talent will find regular employment.

In 2002, actors (including producers and directors) held about 139,000 jobs, primarily in motion picture and video, performing arts, and broadcast industries. Because many others were between jobs, the total number of actors available for work was higher. Employment in the theater is cyclical – higher in the fall and spring seasons – and concentrated in New York and other major cities with large commercial houses for musicals and touring productions. Actors may find work in summer festivals, on cruise lines, and in theme parks. Many smaller, nonprofit professional companies, such as repertory companies, dinner theaters, and theaters affiliated with drama schools, acting conservatories, and universities, provide employment opportunities for local amateur talent and professional entertainers.

Nature of Work: Actors express ideas and create images in theater, film, radio, television, and other performing arts media. They interpret a writer's script to entertain, inform, or instruct an audience. Although the most famous actors work in film, network television, or theater in New York or Los Angeles, far more work in local or regional television studios, theaters, or film production companies, preparing advertising, public relations, or independent, small-scale movie productions. Actors perform in stage, radio, television, video, or motion picture productions. They also work in cabarets, nightclubs, theme parks, and in "industrial" films produced for training purposes. Most actors struggle to find steady work; only a few ever achieve recognition as stars. Some actors do voice-over and narration work for advertisements, animated features, books on tape, and other electronic media. They also teach in high school or university drama departments, acting conservatories, or public programs.

Working Conditions: Actors work under constant pressure. Many face stress from the continual need to find their next job. To succeed, actors need patience and commitment to their craft. Actors strive to deliver flawless performances while working under undesirable and unpleasant conditions. Acting assignments typically are short term – ranging from one day to a few months – which means that actors frequently experience long periods of unemployment between jobs. The uncertain nature of the work results in unpredictable earnings and intense competition for even the lowest-paid jobs. Often, actors must hold other jobs in order to sustain a living.

When performing, actors typically work long, irregular hours. For example, stage actors may perform one show at night while rehearsing another during the day. They might even travel with a show when it tours the country. Movie actors may work on location, sometimes under adverse weather conditions, and may spend considerable time in their trailers or dressing rooms waiting to perform their scenes. Actors who perform in a television series often appear on camera with little or no preparation time, because scripts tend to be revised frequently or even written moments before taping. Evening and weekend work is a regular part of a stage actor's life. On weekends, more than one performance may be held per day.

Education, Training, Qualifications: Persons who become actors follow many paths. Employers generally look for people with the creative instincts, innate talent, and intellectual capacity to perform. Actors should possess a passion for performing and enjoy entertaining others. Most aspiring actors participate in high school or college plays, work in college radio stations, or perform with local community theater groups. Local and regional theater experience and work in summer stock, on cruise lines, or in theme parks help many young actors hone their skills and earn qualifying credits toward membership in one of the actors' unions.

Formal dramatic training, either through an acting conservatory or a university program, generally is necessary; however, some people successfully enter the field without it. College courses in radio and television broadcasting, communications, film, theater, drama or dramatic literature are helpful. Actors, regardless of experience level, may pursue workshop training through acting conservatories or by being mentored by a drama coach. Actors also research roles so that they can grasp concepts quickly during rehearsals and understand the story's setting and background. Sometimes actors learn a foreign language or train with a dialect coach to develop an accent to make their characters more realistic. Actors need talent, creative ability, and training that will enable them to portray different characters. A wide range of related skills, such as singing, dancing, skating, juggling, or miming, are especially useful. Physical appearance, such as the right size, weight, or features, often is one of the deciding factors in being selected for particular roles.

Earnings: Median annual earnings of salaried actors were $23,470 in 2002. The middle 50 percent earned between $15,320 and $53,320. The highest 10 percent earned more than $106,360. According to Equity, the minimum weekly salary for actors in Broadway productions as of June 2003 was $1,354. Actors in off-Broadway productions received minimums ranging from $479 to $557 a week – depending on the seating capacity of the theater. Some well-known actors – stars – earn well above the minimum; their salaries are many times the figures cited, creating the false impression that all actors are highly paid. For example, of the nearly 100,000 members of the Screen Actors' Guild, only about 50 might be considered stars.

Key Contacts: For general information about theater arts and a list of accredited college-level programs, contact:

- **National Association of Schools of Theatre:** 11250 Roger Bacon Drive, Suite 21, Reston, VA 20190. Website: http://nast.arts-accredit.org.

For general information on actors, contact any of the following:

- **Actors' Equity Association:** 165 West 46th Street, New York, NY 10036. Website: www.actorsequity.org.

- **Screen Actors Guild:** 5757 Wilshire Blvd., Los Angeles, CA 90036-3600. Website: www.sag.org.

- **American Federation of Television and Radio Artists – Screen Actors Guild:** 260 Madison Avenue, New York, NY 10016-2401. Website: www.aftra.org.

Athletes, Coaches, Umpires, and Related Workers

⇨ **Annual Earnings:** Varies greatly
⇨ **Education/Training:** Experience and training
⇨ **Outlook:** Good

Employment Outlook: Employment of athletes, coaches, umpires, and related workers is expected to increase about as fast as the average for all occupations in the decade ahead. Employment will grow as the general public continues to increasingly participate in organized sports as a form of entertainment, recreation, and physical conditioning. Job growth also will be driven by the growing numbers of baby boomers approaching retirement, during which they are expected to become more active participants of leisure-time activities, such as golf and tennis, and require instruction. The large numbers of the children of baby boomers in high schools and colleges also will be active participants in athletics and require coaches and instructors.

Expanding opportunities are expected for coaches and instructors, as a higher value is being placed upon physical fitness in our society. Opportunities should be best for persons seeking part-time umpire, referee, and other sports official jobs at the high school level, but competition is expected for higher paying jobs at the college level, and even greater competition for jobs in professional sports. Competition should be very keen for jobs as scouts, particularly for professional teams, since the number of available positions is limited.

Nature of Work: We are a nation of sports fans and sports players. Some of those who participate in amateur sports dream of becoming paid professional athletes, coaches, or sports officials, but very few beat the long and daunting odds of making a full-time living from professional athletics. Even though the chances of employment as a professional athlete are slim, there are many opportunities for at least a part-time job related to athletics as a coach, instructor, referee, or umpire in amateur athletics and in high schools, colleges, and universities.

Athletes and sports competitors compete in organized, officiated sports events to entertain spectators. The events in which they compete include both team sports – such as baseball, basketball, football, hockey, and soccer – and individual sports – such as golf, tennis, and bowling. In addition to competing in athletic events, athletes spend many hours practicing skills and teamwork under the guidance of a coach or sports instructor. Most athletes spend hours in hard practice every day. They also spend additional hours viewing videotapes, in order to critique their own performances and techniques and to scout their opponents' tendencies and weaknesses to gain a competitive advantage.

Coaches organize, instruct, and teach amateur and professional athletes in the fundamentals of individual and team sports. In individual sports, instructors may sometimes fill this role. Coaches train athletes for competition by holding practice sessions to perform drills and improve the athletes' skills and stamina. Coaches also are responsible for managing the team during both practice sessions and competitions, and for instilling good sportsmanship, a competitive spirit, and teamwork. They may also select, store, issue, and inventory equipment, materials, and supplies.

Sports instructors teach professional and nonprofessional athletes on an individual basis. They organize, instruct, train, and lead athletes in indoor and outdoor sports such as bowling, tennis, golf, and swimming. Because activities are as diverse as weight lifting, gymnastics, and scuba diving, and may include self-defense training such as karate, instructors tend to specialize in one or a few types of activities.

Umpires, referees, and other sports officials officiate at competitive athletic and sporting events. They observe the play, detect infractions of rules, and impose penalties established by the sports' rules and regulations. The job is highly stressful because officials are often required to make a decision in a matter of a split second, sometimes resulting in strong disagreement among competitors, coaches, or spectators.

Professional scouts evaluate the skills of both amateur and professional athletes to determine talent and potential. As a sports intelligence agent, the scout's primary duty is to seek out top athletic candidates for the team he or she represents, ultimately contributing to team success.

Athletes, coaches, umpires, and related workers held about 158,000 jobs in 2002. Coaches and scouts held 130,000 jobs; athletes, 15,000; and umpires, referees, and other sports officials, 14,000. Large proportions of athletes, coaches, umpires, and related workers worked part time – about 37 percent, while 17 percent maintained variable schedules. About 27 percent of workers in this occupation were self-employed, earning prize money or fees for lessons, scouting, or officiating assignments, and many other coaches and sports officials, although technically not self-employed, have such irregular or tenuous working arrangements that their working conditions resemble self-employment.

Working Conditions: Irregular work hours are the trademark of the athlete. They are common for coaches, as well as umpires, referees, and other sports officials. Athletes, coaches, umpires, and related workers often work Saturdays, Sundays, evenings, and holidays. Athletes and full-time coaches usually work more than 40 hours a week for several months during the sports season. Athletes, coaches, and sports officials who participate in competitions that are held outdoors may be exposed to all weather conditions of the season. Athletes, coaches, and some sports officials frequently travel to sporting events by bus or airplane. Many athletes are susceptible to physical injuries.

Education, Training, Qualifications: Education and training requirements for athletes, coaches, umpires, and related workers vary greatly by the level and type of sport. Regardless of the sport or occupation, jobs require immense overall knowledge of the game, usually acquired through years of experience at lower levels. Athletes usually begin competing in sports while in elementary or middle school and continue through high school and sometime college. They play in amateur tournaments and on high school and college teams, where the best attract the attention of professional scouts.

For sports instructors, certification is highly desirable for those interested in becoming a tennis, golf, karate, or any other kind of instructor. Often, one must be at least 18 years old and CPR certified.

Each sport has specific requirements for umpires, referees, and other sports officials. Referees, umpires, and other officials often begin their careers by volunteering for intramural, community, and recreational league competitions.

Standards are stringent for officials in professional sports. For umpire jobs in professional baseball, for example, a high school diploma or equivalent is usually sufficient, plus 20/20 vision and quick reflexes. To qualify for the professional ranks, however, prospective candidates must attend professional umpire training school.

Earnings: Median annual earnings of athletes were $45,320 in 2002. The lowest 10 percent earned less than $14,090, and the highest 10 percent earned more than $145,600. Similar to actors, the very top paid professionals made millions. Median annual earnings of umpires and related workers were $20,540 in 2002. The middle 50 percent earned between $16,210 and $29,490. Median annual earnings of coaches and scouts were $27,880 in 2002. The middle 50 percent earned between $17,890 and $42,250.

Key Contacts: For information about sports officiating for team and individual sports, contact:

- **National Association of Sports Officials:** 2017 Lathrop Avenue, Racine, WI 53405. Website: www.naso.org.

Artists and Related Workers

⇨ **Annual Earnings:** Varies greatly
⇨ **Education/Training:** Training and experience
⇨ **Outlook:** Good

Employment Outlook: Employment of artists and related workers is expected to grow about as fast as the average in the decade ahead. Because the arts attract many talented people with creative ability, the number of aspiring artists continues to grow. Consequently, competition for both salaried jobs and freelance work in some areas is expected to be keen. The need for artists to illustrate and animate materials for magazines, journals, and other printed or electronic productions will spur demand for illustrators and animators of all types. Growth in the motion picture and video industries will provide new job opportunities for illustrators, cartoonists, and animators. Competition for most jobs, however, will be strong, because job opportunities are relatively few and the number of people interested in these positions usually exceeds the number of available openings.

Nature of Work: Artists create art to communicate ideas, thoughts, or feelings. They use a variety of methods – painting, sculpting, or illustration – and an assortment of materials, including oils, watercolors, acrylics, pastels, pencils, pen and ink, plaster, clay, and computers. Artists generally fall into one of three categories: **Art directors** formulate design concepts and presentation approaches for visual communications media. **Fine artists, including painters, sculptors, and illustrators**, create original artwork, using a variety of media and techniques, and display their work in museums, commercial art galleries, corporate collections, and private homes; some of their artwork may be commissioned. **Multimedia artists and animators** create special effects, animation, or other visual images on film, or video, or with computers or other electronic media. They primarily work in motion picture and video industries, advertising, and computer systems design services.

Working Conditions: Many artists work in fine- or commercial-art studios located in office buildings, warehouses, or lofts. Others work in private studios in their homes. Some fine artists share studio space. Studio surroundings usually are well lighted and ventilated; however, fine artists may be exposed to fumes from glue, paint, ink, and other materials and to dust or other residue from filings, splattered paint, or spilled fluids. Artists employed by publishing companies, advertising agencies, and design firms generally work a standard workweek. Self-employed artists can set their own hours, but may spend much time and effort selling their artwork to potential customers or clients and building a reputation. Artists held about 149,000 jobs in 2002. More than half were self-employed.

Of the artists who were not self-employed, many worked in advertising and related services; newspaper, periodical, book, and software publishers; motion picture and video industries; specialized design services; and computer systems design and related services. Some self-employed artists offered their services to advertising agencies, design firms, publishing houses, and other businesses on a contract or freelance basis.

Education, Training, Qualifications: Training requirements for artists vary by specialty. Although formal training is not strictly necessary for fine artists, it is very difficult to become skilled enough to make a living without some training. Independent schools of art and design offer postsecondary studio training in the fine arts leading to an Associate in Art or a Bachelor in Fine Arts degree. Typically, these programs focus more intensively on studio work than do the academic programs in a university setting. Illustrators learn drawing and sketching skills through training in art programs and through extensive practice. Evidence of appropriate talent and skill, displayed in an artist's portfolio, is an important factor used by art directors, clients, and others in deciding whether to hire an individual or to contract out work.

Earnings: Median annual earnings of salaried art directors were $61,850 in 2002. Median annual earnings of salaried fine artists, including painters, sculptors, and illustrators, were $35,260 in 2002. Median annual earnings of salaried multimedia artists and animators were $43,980 in 2002. Earnings for self-employed artists vary widely. Some charge only a nominal fee while they gain experience and build a reputation for their work. Others, such as well-established freelance fine artists and illustrators, can earn more than salaried artists. Many, however, find it difficult to rely solely on income earned from selling paintings or other works of art.

Key Contacts: For general information about art and design and a list of accredited college-level programs, contact:

- **National Association of Schools of Art and Design:** 11250 Roger Bacon Drive, Suite 21, Reston, VA 20190. Website: http://nasad.arts-accredit.org.

For information on careers in medical illustration, contact:

- **Association of Medical Illustrators:** 245 1st Street, Suite 1800, Cambridge, MA 02142. Website: www.ami.org.

Broadcast and Sound Engineering Technicians and Radio Operators

- ➪ **Annual:** $27,760 to $36,970
- ➪ **Education/Training:** Technical school to college training
- ➪ **Outlook:** Good

Employment Outlook: People seeking entry-level jobs as technicians in broadcasting are expected to face strong competition in major metropolitan areas, where pay generally is higher and the number of qualified job seekers typically exceeds the number of openings. Overall employment of broadcast and sound engineering technicians and radio operators is expected to grow about as fast as the average for all occupations in the decade ahead. Job growth in radio and television broadcasting will be limited by consolidation of ownership of radio and television stations, and by labor-saving technical advances such as computer-controlled programming and remotely controlled transmitters. Projected job growth varies among detailed occupations in this field. For example, employment of broadcast technicians is expected to grow about as fast as the average for all occupations in the decade ahead, as improved technology enhances the capabilities of technicians to produce higher quality radio and television programming. Employment of radio operators is expected to decline as more stations operate transmitters that control programming remotely. Employment of audio and video equipment technicians and sound engineering technicians is expected to grow faster than the average for all occupations.

Nature of Work: Broadcast and sound engineering technicians and radio operators set up, operate, and maintain a wide variety of electrical and electronic equipment involved in almost any radio or television broadcast, concert, play, musical recording, television show, or movie. There are many specialized occupations within the field. **Audio and video equipment technicians** set up and operate audio and video equipment, including microphones, sound speakers, video screens, projectors, video monitors, recording equipment, connecting wires and cables, sound and mixing boards, and related electronic equipment for concerts, sports events, meetings and conventions, presentations, and news conferences. **Broadcast technicians** set up, operate, and maintain equipment that regulates the signal strength, clarity, and range of sounds and colors of radio or television broadcasts. **Sound engineering technicians** operate machines and equipment to record, synchronize, mix, or reproduce music, voices, or sound effects in recording studios, sporting arenas, theater productions, or movie and video productions. **Radio operators** mainly receive and transmit communications using a variety of tools. They also are responsible for repairing equipment.

Broadcast and sound engineering technicians and radio operators held about 93,000 jobs in 2002 in the following occupations:

- Audio and video equipment technicians   42,000
- Broadcast technicians   35,000
- Sound engineering technicians   13,000
- Radio operators   3,000

Working Conditions: Broadcast and sound engineering technicians and radio operators generally work indoors in pleasant surroundings. However, those who broadcast news and other programs from locations outside the studio may work outdoors in all types of weather.

Technicians at large stations and the networks usually work a 40-hour week under great pressure to meet broadcast deadlines, and may occasionally work overtime. Those who work on motion pictures may be on a tight schedule and may work long hours to meet contractual deadlines.

Education, Training, Qualifications: The best way to prepare for a broadcast and sound engineering technician job is to obtain technical school, community college, or college training in electronics, computer networking, or broadcast technology. In the motion picture industry, people are hired as apprentice editorial assistants and work their way up to more skilled jobs. Employers in the motion picture industry usually hire experienced freelance technicians on a picture-by-picture basis. Reputation and determination are important in getting jobs.

Beginners learn skills on the job from experienced technicians and supervisors. They often begin their careers in small stations and, once experienced, move on to larger ones. Large stations usually hire only technicians with experience.

Audio and video equipment technicians generally need a high school diploma. Many recent entrants have a community college degree or other forms of postsecondary degrees, although that is not always a requirement.

Earnings: Television stations usually pay higher salaries than do radio stations; commercial broadcasting usually pays more than public broadcasting; and stations in large markets pay more than those in small markets.

Median annual earnings of broadcast technicians in 2002 were $27,760. The middle 50 percent earned between $18,860 and $45,200. Median annual earnings of sound engineering technicians in 2002 were $36,350. The middle 50 percent earned between $24,330 and $57,350. Median annual earnings of audio and video equipment technicians in 2002 were $31,110. The middle 50 percent earned between $22,670 and $43,950. Median annual earnings of radio operators in 2002 were $31,530. The middle 50 percent earned between $24,000 and $41,430.

Key Contacts: For career information and links to employment resources, contact:

- **National Association of Broadcasters:** 1771 N Street NW, Washington, DC 20036. Website: www.nab.org.

- **Society of Broadcast Engineers:** 9247 North Meridian Street, Suite 305, Indianapolis, IN 46260. Website: www.sbe.org.

Designers

⇨ **Annual Earnings:** Varies from $19,480 to $52,260
⇨ **Education/Training:** Experience to bachelor's degree
⇨ **Outlook:** Good to excellent

Employment Outlook: Overall employment of designers is expected to grow about as fast as the average for all occupations in the decade ahead as the economy expands and consumers, businesses, and manufacturers continue to rely on the services provided by designers. However, designers in most fields – with the exception of floral design – are expected to face keen competition for available positions. Many talented individuals are attracted to careers as designers. Individuals with little or no formal education in design, as well as those who lack creativity and perseverance, will find it very difficult to establish and maintain a career in this occupation. Among the design specialties, graphic designers are projected to provide the most new jobs. Demand for graphic designers should increase because of the rapidly expanding market for Web-based information and expansion of the video entertainment market, including television, movies, video, and made-for-Internet outlets. Rising demand for interior design of private homes, offices, restaurants and other retail establishments, and institutions that care for the rapidly growing elderly population should spur employment growth of interior designers. New jobs for floral designers are expected to stem mostly from the relatively high replacement needs in retail florists that result from comparatively low starting pay and limited opportunities for advancement. Increased demand for industrial designers will come from continued emphasis on the quality and safety of products, demand for new products that are easy and comfortable to use, and the development of high-technology products in medicine, transportation, and other fields.

Nature of Work: Designers are people with a desire to create. They combine practical knowledge with artistic ability to turn abstract ideas into formal designs for the merchandise we buy, the clothes we wear, the website we use, the publications we read, and the living and office space we inhabit. Designers usually specialize in a particular area of design, such as automobiles, industrial or medical equipment, home appliances, clothing and textiles, floral arrangements, publications, websites, logos, signage, movie or TV credits, interiors of homes or office buildings, merchandise displays, or movie, television, and theater sets. **Commercial and industrial designers** develop countless manufactured products, including airplanes, cars, children's toys, computer equipment, furniture, home appliances, and medical, office, and recreational equipment. **Fashion designers** design clothing and accessories. **Floral designers** cut and arrange live, dried, or artificial flowers and foliage into designs, according to the customer's order. **Graphic designers** plan, analyze, and create visual solutions to communications problems. **Interior designers** enhance the function, safety, and quality of interior spaces of private homes, public buildings, and business or international facilities, such as offices, restaurants, retail establishments, hospitals, hotels, and theaters. **Merchandise displayers and window dressers, or visual merchandisers**, plan and erect commercial displays, such as those in windows and interiors of retail stores or at trade exhibitions. **Set and exhibit designers** create sets for movie, television, and theater productions and design special exhibition displays.

Designers held about 532,000 jobs in 2002. Approximately one-third were self-employed. Employment was distributed as follows:

- Graphic designers   212,000
- Floral designers   104,000
- Merchandise displayers and window trimmers   77,000
- Interior designers   60,000
- Commercial and industrial designers   52,000
- Fashion designers   15,000
- Set and exhibit designers   12,000

Working Conditions: Working conditions and places of employment vary. Designers employed by manufacturing establishments, large corporations, or design firms generally work regular hours in well-lighted and comfortable settings. Designers in small design consulting firms, or those who freelance, generally work on a contract, or job, basis. They frequently adjust their workday to suit their clients' schedules and deadlines, meeting with the clients during evening or weekend hours when necessary. Consultants and self-employed designers tend to work longer hours and in smaller, more congested environments. Designers may transact business in their own offices or studios, or in clients' homes or offices. They also may travel to other locations, such as showrooms, design centers, clients' exhibit sites, and manufacturing facilities.

Education, Training, Qualifications: Creativity is crucial in all design occupations. People in this field must have a strong sense of the esthetic – an eye for color and detail, a sense of balance and proportion, and an appreciation for beauty. A good portfolio – a collection of examples of a person's best work – often is the deciding factor in getting a job.

While a bachelor's degree is required for most entry-level design positions, many other positions, such as floral design and visual merchandising, primarily require experience and talent. Interior design is the only design field subject to government regulation. Passing the National Council for Interior Design qualification examination is required for registration or licensure. In fashion design, employers seek individuals with a two- or four-year degree who are knowledgeable in the areas of textiles, fabrics, and ornamentation, and about trends in the fashion world. Most floral designers learn their skills on the job. Formal training for some design professions is available in two- and three-year professional schools that award certificates or associate degrees in design. Employers increasingly expect new designers to be familiar with computer-aided design software as a design tool. Beginning designers usually receive on-the-job training and normally need one to three years of training before they can advance to higher level positions.

Earnings: Median annual earnings for commercial and industrial designers were $52,260 in 2002. The middle 50 percent earned between $39,240 and $67,430. Median annual earnings for fashion designers were $51,290 in 2002. The middle 50 percent earned between $35,550 and $75,970. Median annual earnings for floral designers were $19,480 in 2002. The middle 50 percent earned between $15,880 and $23,560. Median annual earnings for graphic designers were $36,680 in 2002. The middle 50 percent earned between $28,140 and $48,820. Median annual earnings for interior designers were $39,180 in 2002. The middle 50 percent earned between $29,070 and $53,060. Median annual earnings of merchandise displayers and window dressers were $22,550 in 2002. The middle 50 percent earned between $18,320 and $29,070. Median annual earnings for set and exhibit designers were $33,870 in 2000. The middle 50 percent earned between $24,780 and $46,350. The American Institute of Graphic Arts reported 2002 median annual earnings for staff-level graphic designers was $40,000. Senior designers with supervisory and decision-making responsibilities made $55,000. Solo designers, who freelanced or worked under contract to another company, reported median earnings of $55,000.

Key Contacts: For information about graphic, communication, or interaction design careers, contact:

- **American Institute of Graphic Arts:** 164 Fifth Avenue, New York, NY 10010. Website: www.aiga.org.

For information on degree, continuing education, and licensure programs in interior design and interior design research, contact:

- **American Society of Interior Designers:** 608 Massachusetts Avenue NE, Washington, DC 20002-6006. Website: www.asid.org.

For a list of schools with accredited programs in interior design, contact:

- **Foundation for Interior Design Education Research:** 146 Monroe Center, NW, Suite 1318, Grand Rapids, MI 49503. Website: www.fider.org.

For information on careers, continuing education, and certification programs in the interior design specialty of residential kitchen and bath design, contact:

- **National Kitchen and Bath Association:** 687 Willow Grove Street, Hackettstown, NJ 07840. Website: www.nkba.org/student.

For information about careers in floral design, contact:

- **Society of American Florists:** 1601 Duke Street, Alexandria, VA 22314. Website: www.safnow.org.

Desktop Publishers

- ➪ **Annual Earnings:** $31,620
- ➪ **Education/Training:** High school diploma/related certificate or coursework helpful
- ➪ **Outlook:** Faster than average growth

Employment Outlook: Employment of desktop publishers is expected to grow faster than average for all occupations through 2012, as more page layout and design work is performed in-house using computers and sophisticated publishing software. Many new jobs for desktop publishers are expected to emerge in commercial printing and publishing establishments. In addition to employment growth, many job openings for desktop publishers will result from the need to replace workers who move into managerial positions, transfer to other occupations, or who leave the labor force.

Nature of Work: Using computer software, desktop publishers format and combine text, numerical data, photographs, charts, and other visual graphic elements to produce publication-ready material. Depending on the nature of a particular project, desktop publishers may write and edit text, create graphics to accompany text, convert photographs and drawings into digital images and then manipulate those images, design page layouts, create proposals, develop presentations and advertising campaigns, typeset and do color separation, and translate electronic information onto film or other traditional forms. Desktop publishers produce books, business cards, calendars, magazines, newsletters, newspapers, packaging, slides, and tickets.

Desktop publishers use a keyboard to enter and select formatting properties, such as the size and style of type, column width, and spacing, and store them in the computer, which then displays and arranges columns of type on a video display terminal or computer monitor. An entire newspaper, catalog, or book page, complete with artwork and graphics, can be created on the screen exactly as it will appear in print. Operators transmit the pages for production either into film and then into printing plates, or directly into plates. Instead of receiving typed text from customers, desktop publishers get the material over the Internet or on a computer disk. In addition, because most materials today often are published on the Internet, desktop publishers may need to know electronic-publishing technologies, such as Hypertext

Markup Language (HTML), and may be responsible for converting text and graphics to an Internet-ready format.

Working Conditions: Desktop publishers usually work in clean, air-conditioned office areas with little noise. They generally work an eight-hour day, five days a week. Some employees work night shifts, weekends, and holidays. Desktop publishers often are subject to stress and the pressures of short deadlines and tight work schedules. Like other workers who spend long hours working in front of a computer monitor, they may be susceptible to eyestrain, back discomfort, and hand and wrist problems.

Education, Training, Qualifications: Although formal training is not always required, those with certificates or degrees will have the best job opportunities. Most employers prefer to hire people who have at least a high school diploma and who possess good communication skills, basic computer skills, and a strong work ethic. Most workers qualify for jobs as desktop publishers by taking classes or completing certificate programs at vocational schools, universities, and colleges or through the Internet. Programs range in length, but the average certificate program takes approximately one year. However, some desktop publishers train on the job to develop the necessary skills. The length of on-the-job training varies by company. An internship or part-time desktop publishing assignment is another way to gain experience as a desktop publisher.

Students interested in pursuing a career in desktop publishing may obtain an associate degree in applied science or a bachelor's degree in graphic arts, graphic communications, or graphic design. The skills learned earning a bachelor's degree are intended for students who may eventually move into management positions, while two-year associate degree programs are designed to train skilled workers.

Desktop publishers should be able to deal courteously with people, because in small shops they may have to take customers' orders. They also may have to add, subtract, multiply, divide, and compute ratios to estimate job costs. Desktop publishers need good manual dexterity, and they must be able to pay attention to detail and work independently. Good eyesight, including visual acuity, depth perception, a wide field of view, color vision, and the ability to focus quickly also are assets. Artistic ability often is a plus. Workers with limited training and experience may start as helpers. As workers gain experience, they advance to positions with greater responsibilities. Some move into supervisory or management positions. Other desktop publishers may start their own company or work as independent consultants, while those with more artistic talent and further education may find opportunities in graphic design or commercial art.

Earnings: Earnings for desktop publishers vary according to level of experience, training, location, and size of firm. Median annual earnings of desktop publishers were $31,620 in 2002. The highest 10 percent earned more than $52,540 a year. Printing and related support activities paid the most, averaging $35,140, whereas those working for newspaper, periodical, book, and directory publishers averaged earnings of $26,050.

Key Contacts: Details about apprenticeship and other training programs may be obtained from local employers such as newspapers and printing shops or from the local offices of the state employment service.

For information on careers and training in printing, desktop publishing, and graphic arts, write to either of the following sources:

- **Graphic Communications Council:** 1899 Preston White Drive, Reston, VA 20191. Website: www.npes.org/education/index.html.

- **Graphic Arts Technical Foundation:** 200 Deer Run Road, Sewickley, PA 15143. Website: www.gatf.org.

Gaming Services

- ⇨ **Annual Earnings:** Varies from $14,090 to $39,290
- ⇨ **Education/Training:** High school or GED plus training
- ⇨ **Outlook:** Excellent

Employment Outlook: With demand for gaming showing no sign of waning, employment in gaming services occupations is projected to grow faster than the average for all occupations in the decade ahead. Even during the recent downturn in the economy, profits at casinos have risen. With many states benefiting from casino gambling in the form of tax revenue or compacts with Indian tribes, additional states are rethinking their opposition to legalized gambling and will likely approve the building of more casinos and other gaming formats in the coming decade. The increase in gaming reflects growth in the population and in its disposable income, both of which are expected to continue.

Nature of Work: Legalized gambling in the United States today includes casino gaming, state lotteries, parimutuel wagering on contests such as horse or dog racing, and charitable gaming. Gaming, the playing of games of chance, is a multibillion-dollar industry that is responsible for the creation of a number of unique service occupations. Gaming services occupations held 192,000 jobs in 2002:

- Gaming dealers   78,000
- Gaming supervisors   39,000
- Slot key persons   21,000
- Gaming and sports book writers & runners   14,000
- All other gaming service workers   40,000

Gaming services workers are found mainly in the traveler accommodation and gaming industries. Most are employed in commercial casinos, including land-based or riverboats in 11 states. The largest number works in land-based casinos in Nevada, and the second largest group works in similar establishments in New Jersey. Mississippi, which boasts the greatest number of riverboat casinos in operation, employs the most workers in that venue. In addition, 23 states have Indian casinos. Legal lotteries are held in 40 states and the District of Columbia, and parimutuel wagering is legal in 41 states.

Like nearly every business establishment, casinos have workers who direct and oversee day-to-day operations. **Gaming supervisors** oversee the gaming operations and personnel in an assigned area. They circulate among the tables and observe the operations to ensure that all of the stations and games are covered for each shift. Some gaming occupations demand specially acquired skills – dealing blackjack, for example – that are unique to casino work. Others require skills common to most businesses, such as the ability to conduct financial transactions. **Slot key persons**, also called slot attendants or slot technicians, coordinate and supervise the slot department and its workers. **Gaming and sportsbook writers and runners** assist in the operations of games such as bingo and keno, in addition to taking bets on sporting events. **Gaming dealers** operate table games such as craps, blackjack, and roulette. Standing or sitting behind the table, dealers provide dice, dispense cards to players, or run the equipment.

Working Conditions: The atmosphere in casinos is generally filled with fun and often considered glamorous. However, casino work can also be physically demanding. Most occupations require that workers stand for long periods; some require the lifting of heavy items. The "glamorous" atmosphere exposes casino workers to certain hazards, such as cigarette, cigar, and pipe smoke. Noise from slot machines, gaming tables, and chattering workers and patrons may be distracting to some, although workers wear protective headgear in areas where loud machinery is used to count money.

Education, Training, Qualifications: There usually are no minimum educational requirements for entry-level gaming jobs, although most employers prefer a high school diploma or GED. However, entry-level gaming services workers are required to have a license issued by a regulatory agency, such as a state casino control board or commission. Each casino establishes its own requirements for education, training, and experience. Almost all provide some in-house training in addition to requiring certification. Many institutions of higher learning give training toward certification in gaming, as well as offering an associate's, bachelor's, or master's degree in a hospitality-related field.

Earnings: Wage earnings for gaming services workers vary according to occupation, level of experience, training, location, and size of the gaming establishment. The following were median earnings for various gaming services occupations in 2002:

- Gaming supervisors $39,290
- Slot key persons $22,870
- Gaming and sports book writers & runners $18,660
- Gaming dealers $14,090

Key Contacts: For additional information on careers in gaming, visit your public library and your state gaming regulatory agency or casino control commission. Information on careers in gaming also is available from:

- **American Gaming Association:** 555 13th Street NW, Suite 1010 East, Washington, DC 20004. Website: www.americangaming.org.

Musicians, Singers, and Related Workers

- ⇨ **Annual Earnings:** $36,290
- ⇨ **Education/Training:** Experience, training, and college
- ⇨ **Outlook:** Good

Employment Outlook: Competition for jobs for musicians, singers, and related workers is expected to be keen. The vast number of persons with the desire to perform will exceed the number of openings. Overall employment of musicians, singers, and related workers is expected to grow about as fast as the average for all occupations in the decade ahead. Most new wage and salary jobs for musicians will arise in religious organizations. Slower-than-average growth is expected for self-employed musicians, who generally perform in nightclubs, concert tours, and other venues.

Musicians, singers, and related workers held about 215,000 jobs in 2002. Almost 40 percent worked part-time, and more than one-third were self-employed. Many found jobs in cities in which entertainment and recording activities are concentrated, such as New York, Los Angeles, Chicago, and Nashville. Musicians, singers, and related workers are employed in a variety of settings. Of those who earn a wage or salary, more than one-half are employed by religious organizations and one-fourth by performing arts companies, such as professional orchestras, small chamber music groups, musical theater companies, and ballet troupes. Musicians and singers also perform in nightclubs and restaurants and for weddings and other events. Well-known musicians and groups may perform in concerts, appear on radio and television broadcasts, and make recordings and music videos. The Armed Forces also offers careers in their bands and smaller musical groups.

Nature of Work: Musicians, singers, and related workers play musical instruments, sing, compose or arrange music, or conduct groups in instrumental or vocal performances. They may perform solo or as part of a group. Although most of these entertainers play for live audiences, many perform exclusively for recording or production studios. Regardless of the setting, musicians, singers, and related workers spend considerable time practicing, alone and with their band, orchestra, or other musical ensemble.

Musicians often gain their reputation or professional standing in a particular kind of music or performance. However, **instrumental musicians** who learn several related instruments, such as flute and clarinet, and who can perform equally well in several musical styles, have better employment opportunities. **Singers** are often classified according to their voice range – soprano, contralto, tenor, baritone, or bass – or the type of music they sing, such as opera, rock, popular, folk, rap, or country and western. **Music directors** and **conductors** lead groups of musicians. These leaders usually audition and select the musicians, choose the music most appropriate for their talents and abilities – as well as the situation or audience, and direct rehearsals and performances. **Composers** create original music such as symphonies, operas, sonatas, radio and television jingles, film scores, or popular songs. Although most composers and songwriters practice their craft on instruments and transcribe the notes with pen and paper, some use computer software to compose and edit their music. **Arrangers** transcribe and adapt musical compositions to a particular style for orchestras, bands, choral groups, or individuals. Components of music – including tempo, volume, and the mix of instruments needed – are arranged to express the composer's message. While some arrangers write directly into a musical composition, others use computer software to make changes.

Working Conditions: Musicians typically perform at night and on weekends. They spend much of their remaining time practicing or in rehearsal. Full-time musicians with long-term employment contracts, such as those with symphony orchestras or television and film production companies, enjoy steady work and less travel. Nightclub, solo, or recital musicians frequently travel to perform in a variety of local settings and may tour nationally or internationally. Because many musicians find only part-time or intermittent work, experiencing unemployment between engagements, they often supplement their income with other types of jobs. The stress of constantly looking for work leads many musicians to accept permanent, full-time jobs in other occupations, while working only part time as musicians.

Although they usually work indoors, some perform outdoors for parades, concerts, and dances. In some nightclubs and restaurants, smoke and odors may be present, and lighting and ventilation may be inadequate.

Education, Training, Qualifications: Aspiring musicians begin studying an instrument at an early age. They may gain valuable experience playing in a school or community band or orchestra or with a group of friends. Participation in school musicals or choirs provides good early training and experience. Although there are no mandated credentials such as certificates or degrees, and a few musicians gain success through natural talent and hard work, formal training is helpful and necessary for most people. Formal training may be obtained through private study with an accomplished musician, in a college or university music program, or in a music conservatory.

Young people considering careers in music should have musical talent, versatility, creativity, poise, and a good stage presence. Because quality performance requires constant study and practice, self-discipline is vital. Musicians who play in concerts or in nightclubs and those who tour must have physical stamina to endure frequent travel and an irregular performance schedule. Musicians and singers must always make their performances look effortless; therefore, preparation and practice are important. They also must be prepared to face the anxiety of intermittent employment and of rejection when auditioning for work.

Earnings: Median annual earnings of salaried musicians and singers were $36,290 in 2002. The middle 50 percent earned between $18,660 and $59,970. Median earnings were $43,060 in performing arts companies and $18,160 in religious organizations. Earnings often depend upon the number of hours and weeks worked, a performer's professional reputation, and the setting. The most successful musicians earn performance or recording fees that far exceed the median earnings.

Key Contacts: For general information about music and music teacher education and a list of accredited college-level programs, contact:

- **National Association of Schools of Music:** 11250 Roger Bacon Drive, Suite 21, Reston, VA 20190. Website: http://nasm.arts-accredit.org.

Photographers

⇨ **Annual Earnings:** $24,040
⇨ **Education/Training:** Experience to associate degree
⇨ **Outlook:** Good

Employment Outlook: Photographers can expect keen competition for job openings because the work is attractive to many people. Employment of photographers is expected to increase about as fast as the average for all occupations in the decade ahead. Demand for portrait photographers should increase as the population grows. Job growth, however, will be constrained somewhat by the widespread use of digital photography and the falling price of digital equipment.

Photographers held about 130,000 jobs in 2002. More than half were self-employed, a much higher proportion than the average for all occupations. Some self-employed photographers have contracts with advertising agencies, magazines, or other places to do individual projects for a predetermined fee, while others operate portrait studios or provide photographs to stock photo agencies. Most salaried photographers work in portrait or commercial photography studios. Newspapers, magazines, television broadcasters, and advertising agencies employ most of the rest. Most photographers work in metropolitan areas.

Nature of Work: Photographers produce and preserve images that paint a picture, tell a story, or record an event. To create commercial quality photographs, photographers need both technical expertise and creativity. Producing a successful picture requires choosing and presenting a subject to achieve a particular effect, and selecting the appropriate equipment. Photographers use either a traditional camera that records images on film that is developed into prints or a digital camera that electronically records images. Some photographers send their film to laboratories for processing and printing. Other photographers, especially those who use black and white film or who require special effects, prefer to develop their own film. Using computers and specialized software, photographers also can manipulate and enhance the scanned or digital image to create the desired effect. Some photographers specialize in areas such as portrait, commercial and industrial, scientific, news, or fine art photography. Self-employed, or freelance, photographers may license the use of their photographs through stock photo agencies or contract with clients or agencies to provide photographs as necessary.

Working Conditions: Working conditions for photographers vary considerably. Photographers employed in government and advertising agencies usually work a five-day, 40-hour week. On the other hand, news photographers often work long, irregular hours and must be available to work on short notice. Many photographers work part-time or variable schedules. Portrait photographers usually work in their own studios but also may travel to take photographs at the client's location, such as a school, a company office, or a private home. News and commercial photographers frequently travel locally, stay overnight on assignments, or travel to distant places for long periods. Some photographers work in uncomfortable or even dangerous surroundings, especially news photographers covering accidents, natural disasters, civil unrest, or military conflicts. Many photographers must wait long hours in all kinds of weather for an event to take place and stand or walk for long periods while carrying heavy equipment. News photographers often work under strict deadlines. Self-employment allows greater autonomy; however, income can be uncertain and the continuous, time-consuming search for new clients can be stressful.

Education, Training, Qualifications: Employers usually seek applicants with a "good eye," imagination, and creativity, as well as a good technical understanding of photography. Many community and junior colleges, vocational-technical institutes, private trade and technical schools, and universities offer photography courses. Qualifications required vary widely depending on the type of photography position sought. Experience gained through an internship or as an assistant to an experienced photographer is useful and can substitute for formal training for many positions. A degree from a community or junior college will strengthen an applicant's job chances. Entry-level positions in photojournalism or in industrial or scientific photography generally require a college degree in journalism or photography.

Photographers who operate their own businesses, or freelance, need business skills as well as talent. These individuals must know how to prepare a business plan; submit bids; write contracts; market their work; hire models, if needed; get permission to shoot on locations that normally are not open to the public; obtain releases to use photographs of people; license and price photographs; secure copyright protection for their work; and keep financial records. Some photographers teach at technical schools, film schools, or universities.

Earnings: Median annual earnings of salaried photographers were $24,040 in 2002. The middle 50 percent earned between $17,740 and $34,910. The highest 10 percent earned more than $49,920. Median hourly earnings in the industries employing the largest numbers of salaried photographers were $15.12 for newspapers and periodicals and $10.51 for other professional or scientific services. Salaried photographers – more of whom work full time –

tend to earn more than those who are self-employed. Because most freelance photographers purchase their own equipment, they incur considerable expense acquiring and maintaining cameras and accessories.

Key Contacts: Career information on photography is available from:

- **Professional Photographers of America, Inc.:** 229 Peachtree Street NE, Suite 2200, Atlanta, GA 30303. Website: www.ppa. com.

- **National Press Photographers Association, Inc.:** 3200 Croasdaile Drive, Suite 306, Durham, NC 27705. Website: www. nppa.org.

Public Relations Specialists

⇨ **Annual Earnings:** $41,710
⇨ **Education/Training:** Internships or associate degree
⇨ **Outlook:** Excellent

Employment Outlook: Employment of public relations specialists is expected to increase faster than the average for all occupations in the coming decade. Keen competition will likely continue for entry-level public relations jobs, as the number of qualified applicants is expected to exceed the number of job openings. Many people are attracted to this profession due to the high-profile nature of the work. While college graduates who combine a degree in journalism, public relations, advertising, or another communications-related field with a public relations internship or other work experience will have the best opportunities, individuals without a four-year degree can also succeed in this field.

Public relations specialists held about 158,000 jobs in 2002. Public relations specialists are concentrated in service-providing industries such as advertising and related services: health care, and social assistance, educational services, and government. Others worked for communications firms, financial institutions, and government agencies. About 11,000 public relations specialists were self-employed. Public relations specialists are concentrated in large cities, where press services and other communications facilities are readily available and many businesses and trade associations have their headquarters. Cities such as New York, Los Angeles, San Francisco, Chicago, and Washington, DC have a disproportionate number of such firms. There is a trend, however, for public relations jobs to be dispersed throughout the country – closer to clients.

Nature of Work: Public relations specialists – also referred to as **communications specialists** and **media specialists** – serve as advocates for businesses, nonprofit associations, universities, hospitals and other organizations, and build positive relationships with the public. Public relations specialists handle organizational functions such as media, community, consumer, industry, and governmental relations; political campaigns; interest-group representation; conflict mediation; or employee and investor relations. They help an organization and its public adapt mutually to each other. Informing the general public, interest groups, and stockholders of an organization's policies, activities, and accomplishments is an important part of a public relations specialist's job.

Working Conditions: Some public relations specialists work a standard 35- to 40-hour week, but unpaid overtime is common. Occasionally, they must be at the job or on call around the clock, especially if there is an emergency or crisis. Public relations offices are busy places; work schedules can be irregular and frequently interrupted. Schedules often have to be rearranged so that workers can meet deadlines, deliver speeches, attend meetings and community activities, or travel.

Education, Training, Qualifications: There are no defined standards for entry into a public relations career. A degree from a two-year (four-year preferred) college combined with some experience gained through an internship or summer job is considered good preparation for public relations work. In fact, internships are becoming vital to obtaining employment. The ability to communicate effectively is essential. Many entry-level public relations specialists have a college major in public relations, journalism, advertising, or communication. Some firms seek graduates who have worked in electronic or print journalism. Other employers seek applicants with demonstrated communication skills and training or experience in a field related to the firm's business – information technology, health science, engineering, sales, or finance, for example. Many colleges help students gain part-time internships in public relations that provide valuable training and experience. The U.S. Armed Forces also can be an excellent place to gain training and experience. Membership in local chapters of the Public Relations Student Society of America or the International Association of Business Communicators provides an opportunity for students to exchange views with public relations specialists and to make professional contacts that may help them find a job in the field. A portfolio of published articles, television or radio programs, slide presentations, and other work is an asset in finding a job. Writing for a school publication or television or radio station provides valuable experience and material for one's portfolio.

People who choose public relations as a career need an outgoing personality, self-confidence, an understanding of human psychology, and an enthusiasm for motivating people. They should be competitive, yet able to function as part of a team and open to new ideas.

Earnings: Median annual earnings for salaried public relations specialists were $41,710 in 2002. Median annual earnings in the industries employing the largest numbers of public relations specialists in 2002 were: advertising and related services, $48,070; local government, $42,000; business, professional, labor, political, and similar organizations, $39,330; and colleges, universities, and professional schools, $36,820.

Key Contacts: For additional information on public relations careers, contact:

- **Public Relations Society of America, Inc.:** 33 Maiden Lane, 11th Floor, New York, NY 10038-5150. Website: www.prsa.org.

- **International Association of Business Communicators:** One Hallidie Plaza, Suite 600, San Francisco, CA 94102. Website: www.iabc.com.

Recreation and Fitness Workers

- ⇨ **Annual Earnings:** Recreation workers $8.69 per hour; fitness trainers, $11.51 per hour
- ⇨ **Education/Training:** High school to graduate degree, depending on the position
- ⇨ **Outlook:** Faster than average growth

Employment Outlook: Overall employment of recreation and fitness workers is expected to grow faster than the average for all occupations through 2012, as an increasing number of people spend more time and money on recreation, fitness, and leisure services and as more businesses recognize the benefits of recreation and fitness, and wellness programs. Employment growth may be inhibited somewhat by budget constraints that some local governments may face during this period. Employment of fitness workers who are concentrated in the rapidly growing arts, entertainment, and recreation industries, is expected to increase much faster than average due to rising interest in personal training, aerobics instruction, and other fitness activities. However, competition will be keen for career positions as recreation workers because the field attracts many applicants and because the number of career positions is limited compared with the number of lower level seasonal jobs. Opportunities for staff positions should be best for persons with formal training and experience gained in part-time or seasonal recreational jobs.

Those with graduate degrees should have the best opportunities for supervisory or administrative positions. Opportunities are expected to be good for fitness trainers and aerobics instructors because of relatively rapid growth in employment. Job openings for both recreation and fitness workers also will result from the need to replace the large numbers of workers who leave these occupations each year.

Nature of Work: Recreation and fitness workers plan, organize, and direct activities such as aerobics, arts and crafts, the performing arts, and sports at local playgrounds and recreation areas, parks, community centers, health clubs, fitness centers, camps, theme parks, and tourist attractions. Increasingly, recreational and fitness workers also are found in workplaces, where they organize and direct leisure activities and athletic programs for employees of all ages.

Recreation workers hold a variety of positions at different levels of responsibility. **Recreation leaders**, who are responsible for a recreation program's daily operation, primarily organize and direct participants. Workers who provide instruction and coach groups in specialties such as art, music, drama, swimming, or tennis may be called **activity specialists**. **Recreation supervisors** oversee recreation leaders and plan, organize, and manage recreational activities to meet the needs of a variety of populations. **Directors of recreation and parks** develop and manage comprehensive recreation programs in parks, playgrounds, and other settings.

Camp counselors lead and instruct children and teenagers in outdoor-oriented forms of recreation, such as swimming, hiking, horseback riding, and camping. Fitness workers instruct or coach groups or individuals in various exercise activities. Because gyms and health clubs offer a variety of exercise activities such as weightlifting, yoga, aerobics, and karate, fitness workers typically specialize in only a few areas. **Fitness trainers** help clients assess their level of physical fitness and help them set and reach fitness goals. **Personal trainers** work with clients on a one-to-one basis in either a gym or the client's home. **Aerobics instructors** conduct group exercise sessions that involve aerobic exercise, stretching, and muscle conditioning. **Fitness directors** oversee the operation of a health club or fitness center. Their work involves creating and maintaining programs that meet the needs of the club's members.

Working Conditions: Recreation and fitness workers may work in a variety of settings – a health club, cruise ship, woodland recreational park, or playground in the center of a large urban community. Regardless of the setting, most recreation workers spend much of their time outdoors and may work in a variety of weather conditions, whereas most fitness workers spend their time indoors at fitness centers and health clubs. Recreation and fitness directors and supervisors, however, typically spend most of their time in an office, planning programs and special events. Directors and supervisors generally engage in less physical activity than do lower level recreation and fitness workers. Nevertheless, recreation and fitness workers at all levels risk suffering injuries during physical activities. Many recreation and fitness workers work about 40 hours a week. People entering this field, especially camp counselors, should expect some night and weekend work and irregular hours. About 36 percent work part time and many recreational jobs are seasonal.

Education, Training, Qualifications: Educational requirements for recreation workers range from a high school diploma – or sometimes less for many summer jobs – to graduate degrees for some administrative positions in large public recreation systems. Full-time career professional positions usually require a college degree with a major in parks and recreation or leisure studies, but a bachelor's degree in any liberal arts field may be sufficient for some jobs in the private sector. In industrial recreation, or "employee services" as it is more commonly called, companies prefer to hire those with a bachelor's degree in recreation or leisure studies and a background in business administration. Specialized training or experience in a particular field, such as art, music, drama, or athletics, is an asset for many jobs. Some jobs require certification. For example, a lifesaving certificate is a prerequisite for teaching or coaching water-related activities. Graduates of associate degree programs in parks and recreation, social work, and other human services disciplines also enter some career recreation positions. High school graduates occasionally enter some career recreation positions, but this is not common. Some college students work part time as recreation workers while earning degrees. This is a good way to gain experience.

Generally fitness trainers and aerobics instructors must obtain a certification in the fitness field to obtain employment. An increasing number of employers require fitness workers to have a bachelor's degree in a field related to health or fitness, such as exercise science or physical education. Some employers allow workers to substitute a college degree for certification, while others require both a degree and certification. A bachelor's degree, and in some cases a master's degree, usually is required to advance to management positions in a health club or fitness center. College courses in management, business administration, accounting, and personnel management are helpful for advancement to supervisory or managerial jobs.

Earnings: While this is not a well paid occupational field, it does offer attractive job-related activities, especially if you have a passion for recreation, fitness, and the outdoors. Indeed, many people in this field get paid, however meager, for what they really love to do. Many self-employed individuals in this field, especially those who own their own recreation and fitness businesses or serve as personal trainers and consultants, do very well financially.

Median annual earnings vary considerably in this field. Median hourly earnings of recreation workers who worked full time in 2002 were $8.59 ($18,100 per year). The middle 50 percent earned between $7.09 and $11.36, while the top 10 percent earned $15.72 or more. However, earnings of recreation directors and others in supervisory or managerial positions can be substantially higher. Median hourly earnings in the industries employing the largest numbers of recreation workers in 2002 were:

- Nursing care facilities $9.30
- Local government $8.98
- Individual and family services $8.71
- Civic and social organizations $7.73
- Other amusement and recreation industries $7.53

Median hourly earnings of fitness trainers and aerobics instructors in 2002 were $11.51. The middle percent earned between $8.06 and $18.18, while the top 10 percent earned $26.22 or more. Earnings of successful self-employed personal trainers can be much higher. Median hourly earnings in the industries employing the largest numbers of fitness trainers and aerobics instructors in 2002 were:

- Other amusement and recreation industries $13.81
- Civic and social organizations $9.24
- Other schools and instruction $8.93

Key Contacts: For information on jobs in recreation, contact employers such as local government departments of parks and recreation, nursing and personal care facilities, the Boy or Girl Scouts, or local social or religious organizations.

For information on careers, certification, and academic programs in parks and recreation, contact:

- **National Recreation and Park Association:** Division of Professional Services, 22377 Belmont Ridge Road, Ashburn, VA 20148-4150. Website: www.nrpa.org.

For career information about camp counselors, contact:

- **American Camp Association:** 5000 State Road 67 North, Martinsville, IN 46151. Website: www.acacamps.org.

For information on careers and certification in the fitness field, contact:

- **American Council on Exercise:** 4851 Paramount Drive, San Diego, CA 92123. Website: www.acefitness.org.

- **National Strength and Conditioning Association:** 1885 Bob Johnson Drive, Colorado Springs, CO 80906. Website: www.nsca-lift.org.

- **American College of Sports Medicine:** P.O. Box 1440, Indianapolis, IN 46206-1440. Website: www.acsm.org.

Television, Video, and Motion Picture Camera Operators and Editors

⇨ **Annual Earnings:** $32,720
⇨ **Education/Training:** Experience and training
⇨ **Outlook:** Good

Employment Outlook: Television, video, and motion picture camera operators and editors can expect keen competition for job openings because the work is attractive to many people. Employment of camera operators and editors is expected to grow about as fast as the average for all occupations in the decade ahead. Rapid expansion of the entertainment market, especially motion picture production and distribution, will spur growth of camera operators. In addition, computer and Internet services will provide new outlets for interactive productions. Growth will be tempered, however, by the increased off-shore production of motion pictures. Camera operators will be needed to film made-for-the-Internet broadcasts, such as live music videos, digital movies, sports features, and general information on entertainment programming.

Nature of Work: Television, video, and motion picture camera operations produce images that tell a story, inform or entertain an audience, or record an event. Film and video editors edit sound tracks, film, and video for the motion picture, cable, and broadcast television industries. Some camera operators do their own editing. Camera operators use television, video, or motion picture cameras to shoot a wide range of material, including television series, studio programs, news and sporting events, music videos, motion pictures, documentaries, and training sessions. Some camera operators film or videotape private ceremonies and special events. Studio camera operators work in a broadcast studio and usually videotape their subjects from a fixed position. News camera operations, also called **electronic news gathering (ENG) operators**, work as part of a reporting team, following newsworthy events as they unfold. Camera operators employed in the entertainment field use motion picture cameras to film movies, television programs, and commercials. Those who film motion pictures are also known as **cinematographers**.

Working Conditions: Working conditions for camera operators and editors vary considerably. Those employed in government, television and cable networks, and advertising agencies usually work a five-day, 40-hour week. By contrast, ENG operators often work long, irregular hours and must be available to work on short notice. Camera operators and editors working in motion picture production also may work long, irregular hours. Some camera operators – especially ENG operators covering accidents, natural disasters, civil unrest, or military conflicts – work in uncomfortable or even dangerous surroundings. Many camera operators must wait long hours in all kinds of weather for an event to take place, and must stand or walk for long periods while carrying heavy equipment.

Education, Training, Qualifications: Employers usually seek applicants with a "good eye," imagination, and creativity, as well as a good technical understanding of how the camera operates. Television, video, and motion picture camera operators and editors usually acquire their skills through on-the-job training or formal postsecondary training at vocational schools, colleges, universities, or photographic institutes. Formal education may be required for some positions. Many universities, community and junior colleges, vocational-technical institutes, and private trade and technical schools offer courses in camera operation and videography.

Earnings: Median annual earnings for television, video, and motion picture camera operators were $32,720 in 2002. The middle 50 percent earned between $20,610 and $51,000. Median annual earnings were $46,540 in the motion picture and video industries and $25,830 in radio and television broadcasting. Median annual earnings for film and video editors were $38,270 in 2002. The middle 50 percent earned between $26,780 and $55,300. Median annual earnings were $41,440 in the motion picture and video industries, which employ the largest numbers of film and video editors.

Key Contacts: Information about career and employment opportunities for camera operators and film and video editors is available from local offices of state employment service agencies, local offices of the relevant trade unions, and local television and film production companies that employ these workers. Some camera operators belong to unions, including the International Alliance of Theatrical Stage Employees and the National Association of Broadcast Employees and Technicians.

8

Construction Trades and Related Jobs

T HE CONSTRUCTION TRADES offer numerous job opportunities for people re-entering the workforce. They offer many jobs
for people without a four-year degree. Ex-offenders re-entering
communities often quickly find jobs in these trades. These jobs
are especially plentiful in communities experiencing population and
housing growth. Indeed, in many parts of the country experiencing a
housing boom, it's difficult to find people in these trades.

Turnover Occupations

The construction trades have always been cyclical occupational fields.
When economic times are good, individuals in these fields have plenty of
work, and their skills command top dollar. However, during recessions
many of these workers have difficulty finding full-time employment, and
some leave their trade for other types of employment.

Working in these trades often involves hard work, uncomfortable working conditions, stressful projects, and unpredictable employment. Many people drop out of these trades because of unhappy experiences. Given the constant turnover of employees in the construction trades, opportunities regularly open for skilled and enterprising workers. But if you are very skilled and enjoy this type of work, you'll find excellent opportunities in the construction and related trades.

Many people without a four-year degree enter these trades because entry into the trades is based more on interests, skills, and on-the-job training than on education requirements. Many individuals with or without a high school diploma initially break into the building and construction trades through apprenticeship programs, where they acquire the necessary skills and experience to advance into their respective trades.

Useful Online Resources

Individuals interested in job and career opportunities in the construction and related trades should explore the following websites:

- Construction Jobs   www.constructionjobs.com
- ConstructionJobStore   www.constructionjobstore.com
- Architect Jobs   www.architectjobs.com
- Carpenter Jobs   www.carpenterjobs.com
- ConstructionGigs.com   www.constructiongigs.com
- Construction Manager Jobs   www.constructionmanager job.com

- Electrician Jobs   www.electricianjobs.com
- Engineer Employment   www.engineeremployment.com
- Estimator Jobs   www.estimatorjobs.com
- iHireConstruction   www.ihireconstruction.com
- Jobsite   www.jobsite.com
- New Home Sales Jobs   www.newhomesalesjobs.com
- PlumberJobs   www.plumberjobs.com
- Project Manager Jobs   www.projectmanagerjobs.com
- TradeJobsOnline   www.tradejobsonline.com

Brickmasons, Blockmasons, and Stonemasons

⇨ **Annual Earnings:** $41,800
⇨ **Education/Training:** Experience and vocational education
⇨ **Outlook:** Excellent

Employment Outlook: Employment opportunities for brickmasons, blockmasons, and stonemasons are expected to be excellent in the decade ahead. Many openings will result from the need to replace workers who retire, transfer to other occupations, or leave these trades for other reasons. There may be fewer applicants than needed because many potential workers prefer to work under less strenuous, more comfortable conditions. Employment in these trades is expected to increase about as fast as the average for all occupations as population and business growth create a need for new houses, industrial facilities, schools, hospitals, offices, and other structures. Employment of brickmasons, blockmasons, and stonemasons, like that of many other construction workers, is sensitive to changes in the economy. When the level of construction activity falls, workers in these trades can experience periods of unemployment.

Nature of Work: Brickmasons, blockmasons, and stonemasons work in closely related trades creating attractive, durable surfaces, and structures. The work varies in complexity, from laying a simple masonry walkway to installing an ornate exterior on a high-rise building. Breakmasons and blockmasons – who often are called simply **bricklayers** – build and repair walls, floors, partitions, fireplaces, chimneys, and other structures with bricks, precast masonry panels, concrete block, and other masonry materials. Some brickmasons specialize in installing firebrick linings in industrial furnaces. Stonemasons build stone walls, as well as set stone exteriors and floors. They work with two types of stone – natural cut stone, such as marble, granite, and limestone, and artificial stone made from concrete, marble chips, or other masonry materials. Stonemasons usually work on nonresidential structures, such as houses of worship, hotels, and office buildings.

Working Conditions: Brickmasons, blockmasons, and stonemasons usually work outdoors and are exposed to the elements. They stand, kneel, and bend for long periods and often have to lift heavy materials. Common hazards include injuries from tools and falls from scaffolds, but these can often be avoided when proper safety equipment is used and safety practices are followed.

Education, Training, Qualifications: Most brickmasons, blockmasons, and stonemasons pick up their skills informally, observing and learning from experienced workers. Many others receive training in vocational education schools or from industry-based programs that are common throughout the country. Another way to learn these skills is through an apprenticeship program, which generally provides the most thorough training. Individuals who learn the trade on the job usually start as helpers, laborers, or mason tenders. These workers carry materials, move scaffolds, and mix mortar.

Earnings: Median hourly earnings of brickmasons and blockmasons in 2002 were $20.11 (around $41,800 in annual earnings). The middle 50 percent earned between $15.36 and $25.32. Median hourly earnings in the industries employing the largest number of brickmasons in 2002 were:

- Nonresidential building construction $22.12
- Foundation, structure, and building
  exterior contractors $20.26

Median hourly earnings of stonemasons in 2002 were $16.36. The middle 50 percent earned between $12.06 and $20.76.

Earnings for workers in these trades can be reduced on occasion because poor weather and downturns in construction activity limit the time they can work.

Key Contacts: For information on the work of brickmasons, blockmasons, or stonemasions, contact:

- **Associated Builders and Contractors:** Workforce Development Department, 4250 N. Fairfax Drive, 9th Floor, Arlington, VA 22203. Website: www.abc.org.

- **International Masonry Institute:** Apprenticeship and Training, The James Brice House, 42 East Street, Annapolis, MD 21401. Website: www.imiweb.org.

- **Associated General Contractors of America, Inc.:** 333 John Carlyle Street, Suite 200, Alexandria, VA 22314. Website: www.agc.org.

- **Brick Industry Association:** 11490 Commerce Park Drive, Reston, VA 20191-1525. Website: www.brickinfo.org.

- **National Association of Home Builders:** 1201 15th Street NW, Washington, DC 20005. Website: www.nahb.org.

- **National Concrete Masonry Association:** 13750 Sunrise Valley Drive, Herndon, VA 20171-4662. Website: www.ncma.org.

Carpenters

▷ **Annual Earnings:** $34,200
▷ **Education/Training:** On-the-job training
▷ **Outlook:** Excellent

Employment Outlook: Job opportunities for carpenters are expected to be excellent in the coming decade, largely due to the numerous openings arising each year as experienced carpenters leave this large occupation. Because there are no strict training requirements for entry, many people with limited skills take jobs as carpenters but eventually leave the occupation because they dislike the work or cannot find steady employment. Employment of carpenters is expected to grow about as fast as average for all occupations. Construction activity should increase in response to new housing and commercial and industrial plants and the need to renovate and modernize existing structures. The demand for larger homes with more amenities and for second homes will continue to rise, especially as the baby boomers reach their peak earning years and can afford to spend more on housing. Carpenters can experience periods of unemployment because of the short-term nature of many construction projects and the cyclical nature of the construction industry.

Nature of Work: Carpenters are involved in many different kinds of construction activity. They cut, fit, and assemble wood and other materials for the construction of buildings, highways, bridges, docks, industrial plants, boats, and many other structures. Carpenters' duties vary by type of employer. Builders increasingly are using specialty trade contractors who, in turn, hire carpenters who specialize in just one or two activities. Such activities include setting forms for concrete construction, erecting scaffolding, or doing finishing work, such as interior and exterior trim. However, a carpenter directly employed by a general building contractor often must perform a variety of the tasks associated with new construction, such as framing walls and partitions, putting in doors and windows, building stairs, laying hardwood floors, and hanging kitchen cabinets. Carpenters employed outside the construction industry perform a variety of installation and maintenance work. They may replace panes of glass, ceiling tiles, and doors, as well as repair decks, cabinets, and other furniture.

Working Conditions: As is true of other building trades, carpentry work is sometimes strenuous. Prolonged standing, climbing, bending, and kneeling often are necessary. Carpenters risk injury working with sharp or rough materials, using sharp tools and power equipment, and working in situations where they might slip or fall. Additionally, many carpenters work outdoors. Some carpenters change employers each time they finish a construction job. Others alternate between working for a contractor and working as contractors themselves on small jobs.

Education, Training, Qualifications: Carpenters learn their trade through on-the-job training, as well as formal training programs. Most pick up skills informally by working under the supervision of experienced workers. Many acquire skills through vocational education. Others participate in employer training programs or apprenticeships. Most employers recommend an apprenticeship as the best way to learn carpentry. Apprenticeship programs are administered by local point union-management committees of the United Brotherhood of Carpenters and Joiners of America, the Associated General Contractors of America, Inc., and the National Association of Home Builders.

Earnings: Median hourly earnings of carpenters were $16.44 ($34,200 in annual earnings). The middle 50 percent earned between $12.59 and $21.91 an hours. Median hourly earnings in the industries employing the largest numbers of carpenters in 2002 were:

- Nonresidential building construction $18.31
- Building finishing contractors $17.30
- Residential building construction $16.02
- Foundation, structure, and building exterior
  contractors $16.01

Earnings can be reduced on occasion, because carpenters lose work time in bad weather and during recessions when jobs are unavailable. Some carpenters are members of the United Brotherhood of Carpenters and Joiners of America.

Key Contacts: For information on training opportunities and carpentry in general, contact:

- **Associated Builders and Contractors:** Workforce Development Department, 4250 N. Fairfax Drive, 9th Floor, Arlington, VA 22203. Website: www.abc.org.

- **Associated General Contractors of America, Inc.:** 333 John Carlyle Street, Suite 200, Alexandria, VA 22314. Website: www. agc.org.

- National Association of Home Builders: 1201 15th Street NW, Washington, DC 20005. Website: www.nahb.org.

- United Brotherhood of Carpenters and Joiners of America: 50 F Street NW, Washington, DC 20001. Website: www.carpenters. org.

Construction and Building Inspectors

⇨ **Annual Earnings:** $41,620
⇨ **Education/Training:** Experience, certificate, associate degree
⇨ **Outlook:** Good

Employment Outlook: Employment of construction and building inspectors is expected to grow about as fast as the average for all occupations in the coming decade. Growing concern for public safety and improvements in the quality of construction should continue to stimulate demand for construction and building inspectors. In addition to the expected employment growth, some job openings will arise from the need to replace inspectors who transfer to other occupations or leave the labor force. Inspectors are involved in all phases of construction, including maintenance and repair work, and are therefore less likely to lose jobs when new construction slows during recessions. As the population grows and the volume of real estate transactions increases, greater emphasis on home inspections should result in strong demand for home inspectors.

Nature of Work: There are many types of specialized inspectors related to the construction and repair processes: building, plan, electrical, elevator, mechanical, plumbing, public works, specification, and home inspectors. Construction and building inspectors examine the construction, alteration, or repair of buildings, highways and streets, sewer and water systems, dams, bridges, and other structures to ensure compliance with building codes and ordinances, zoning regulations, and contract specifications. Building codes and standards are the primary means by which building construction is regulated in the United States for health and safety of the general public. Building inspectors inspect the structural quality and general safety of buildings. Some specialize in such areas as structural steel or reinforced concrete structures. Home inspectors conduct inspections of newly built or previously owned homes. Home inspection has become a standard practice in the home purchasing process. Although inspections are primarily visual, inspectors may use tape measures, survey instruments, metering devices, and test equipment such as concrete strength measurers. They keep a log of their work, take photographs, file reports, and, if necessary, act on their findings. Many inspectors also investigate construction or alterations being done without proper permits.

Working Conditions: Construction and building inspectors usually work alone. However, several may be assigned to large, complex projects, particularly because inspectors tend to specialize in different areas of construction. Although they spend considerable time inspecting construction worksites, inspectors also spend time in a field office reviewing blueprints, answering letters or telephone calls, writing reports, and scheduling inspections. Inspection sites are dirty and may be cluttered with tools, materials, or debris. Inspectors may have to climb ladders or many flights of stairs, or crawl around in tight spaces. Although their work generally is not considered hazardous, inspectors, like other construction workers, wear hard hats and adhere to other safety requirements while at a construction site. Inspectors normally work regular hours. However, they may work additional hours during periods when a lot of construction is taking place.

Education, Training, Qualifications: Although requirements very considerably depending upon where one is employed, construction and building inspectors should have a thorough knowledge of construction materials and practices in either a general area, such as structural or heavy construction, or in a specialized area, such as electrical or plumbing systems, reinforced concrete, or structural steel. Applicants for construction or building inspection jobs need several years of experience as a construction manager, supervisor, or craftworker. Many inspectors previously worked as carpenters, electricians, plumbers, or pipefitters. Because inspectors must possess the right mix of technical knowledge, experience, and education, employers prefer applicants who have formal training as well as experience. Most employers require at least a high school diploma or equivalent, even for workers with considerable experience. Construction and building inspectors usually receive much of their training on the job, although they must learn building codes and standards on their own. Most states and cities require some type of certification for employment. To become certified, inspectors with substantial experience and education must pass stringent examinations on code requirements, construction techniques, and materials.

Earnings: Median annual earnings for construction and building inspectors were $41,620 in 2002. The median hourly earnings were $20.01. The middle 50 percent earned between $15.81 and $25.05. Median annual earnings in the industries employing the largest numbers of construction and building inspectors in 2002 were:

- Local government $42,260
- Architectural, engineering, and related services $40,770
- State government $39,610

Generally, building inspectors, including plan examiners, earn the highest salaries. Salaries in large metropolitan areas are substantially higher than those in small jurisdictions.

Key Contacts: For information on careers and certification, contact the following organizations:

- **International Code Council:** 5203 Leesburg Pike, Suite 600, Falls Church, VA 22041. Website: www.iccsafe.org.

- **Association of Construction Inspectors:** 1224 North Nokomis NE, Alexandria, MN 56308. Website: www.iami.org/aci.

- **International Association of Electrical Inspectors:** 901 Waterfall Way, Suite 602, Richardson, TX 75080-7702. Website: www.iaei. com.

- **American Society of Home Inspectors:** 932 Lee Street, Suite 101, Des Plaines, IL 60016. Website: www.ashi.org.

- **National Association of Certified Home Inspectors:** 1220 Valley Forge Road, Building 47, P.O. Box 987, Valley Forge, PA 19482-0987. Website: www.nachi.org.

- **National Association of Home Inspectors:** 4248 Park Glen Road, Minneapolis, MN 55416. Website: www.nahi.org.

Drywall Installers, Ceiling Tile Installers, and Tapers

⇨ **Annual Earnings:** $33,700
⇨ **Education/Training:** Experience and apprenticeships
⇨ **Outlook:** Good

Employment Outlook: Job opportunities for drywall installers, ceiling tile installers, and tapers are expected to be good in the decade ahead – to grow faster than the average for all occupations, reflecting increases in new construction and remodeling projects. In addition to jobs involving traditional interior work, drywall workers will find employment opportunities in the installation of insulated exterior wall systems, which are becoming increasingly popular. Many jobs will open up each year because of the need to replace workers who transfer to other occupations or leave the labor force. Some drywall installers, ceiling title installers, and tapers with limited skills leave the occupation when they find that they dislike the work or fail to attain steady employment. Since most of their work is done indoors, these workers lose less work time because of inclement weather than do some other construction workers. Nevertheless, they may be unemployed between construction projects and during downturns in construction activity.

Nature of Work: There are two kinds of drywall workers – installers and tapers – although many workers do both types of work. Installers, also called applicators or hangers, fasten drywall panels to the inside framework of residential houses and other buildings. Tapers, or finishers, prepare these panels for painting by taping and finishing joints and imperfections. Ceiling tile installers, or acoustical carpenters, apply or mount acoustical tiles or blocks, strips, or sheets of shock-absorbing materials to ceilings and walls of buildings to reduce reflection of sound or to decorate rooms. Lathers fasten metal or rockboard lath to walls, ceilings, and partitions of buildings. Lath forms the support base for plaster, fireproofing, or acoustical materials.

Working Conditions: As in many other construction trades, the work sometimes is strenuous. Drywall installers, ceiling tile installers, and tapers spend most of the day on their feet, either standing, bending, or kneeling. Some tapers use stilts to tape and finish ceiling and angle joints. Installers have to lift and maneuver heavy panels. Hazards include falls from ladders and scaffolds and injuries from power tools and from working with sharp materials. Because sanding a joint compound to a smooth finish creates a great deal of dust, some finishers wear masks for protection.

Education, Training, Qualifications: Most drywall installers, ceiling tile installers, and tapers start as helpers and learn their skills on the job. Installer helpers start by carrying materials, lifting and holding panels, and cleaning up debris. Within a few weeks they learn to measure, cut, and install materials. Eventually they become fully experienced workers. Some drywall installers, ceiling tile installers, and tapers learn their trade in an apprenticeship program. The United Brotherhood of Carpenters and Joiners of America, in cooperation with local contractors, administers an apprenticeship program both in drywall installation and finishing and in acoustical carpentry. Apprenticeship programs consist of at least three years, or 6,000 hours, of on-the-job training and 144 hours a year of related classroom instruction. In addition, local affiliates of the Associated Builders and Contractors and the National Association of Home Builders conduct training programs for nonunion workers. The International Union of Painters and Allied Trades conducts an apprenticeship program in drywall finishing that lasts two to three years. Employers prefer high school graduates who are in good physical condition, but they frequently hire applicants with less education. High school or vocational school courses in carpentry provide a helpful background for drywall work. Drywall installers, ceiling tile installers, and tapers with a few years of experience and with leadership ability may become supervisors. Some workers start their own contracting businesses.

Earnings: In 2002, the median hourly earnings of drywall and ceiling tile installers were $16.21 (annual earnings of $33,700). The middle 50 percent earned between $12.43 and $21.50. The median hourly earnings in the industries employing the largest numbers of drywall and ceiling tile installers in 2002 were:

- Building finishing contractors $16.50
- Nonresidential building construction $14.66

In 2002, median hourly earnings of tapers were $18.75. The middle 50 percent earned between $14.57 and $24.68 an hour. Trainees usually started at about half the rate paid to experienced workers and received wage increases as they became more highly skilled.

Key Contacts: For information about work opportunities in drywall application and finishing and ceiling tile installation, contact local drywall installation and ceiling tile installation contractors, a local of the building unions, a local joint union-management apprenticeship committee, a state or local chapter of the Associated Builders and Contractors, or the nearest office of the state employment service or apprenticeship agency.

For details about job qualifications and training programs in drywall application and finishing and ceiling tile installation, contact:

- **Associated Builders and Contractors:** 4250 N. Fairfax Drive, 9th Floor, Arlington, VA 22203. Website: www.abc.org.

- **National Association of Home Builders:** 1201 15th Street NW, Washington, DC 20005. Website: www.nahb.org.

- **Home Builders Institute:** 1201 15th Street NW, 6th Floor, Washington, DC 20005. Website: www.hbi.org.

- **International Union of Painters and Allied Trades:** 1750 New York Avenue NW, Washington, DC 20006. Website: www.iupat.org.

- United Brotherhood of Carpenters and Joiners of America: 50 F Street NW, Washington, DC 20001. Website: www.carpenters. org.

Glaziers

⇨ **Annual Earnings:** $31,600
⇨ **Education/Training:** Experience and apprenticeship programs
⇨ **Outlook:** Excellent

Employment Outlook: Job opportunities are expected to be excellent for glaziers, largely due to the numerous openings arising each year as experienced glaziers leave the occupation. In addition, many potential workers may choose not to enter this occupation because they prefer work that is less strenuous and has more comfortable working conditions. Employment of glaziers is expected to grow about as fast as the average for all occupations in the coming decade, as a result of growth in residential and commercial construction. Demand for glaziers will be spurred by the continuing need to modernize and repair existing structures and the popularity of glass in bathroom and kitchen design. The need to improve glass performance related to insulation, privacy, safety, condensation control, and noise reduction also is expected to contribute to the demand for glaziers in both residential and nonresidential remodeling. Glaziers held 49,000 jobs in 2002.

Nature of Work: Glaziers are responsible for selecting, cutting, installing, replacing, and removing glass. They generally work on one of several types of projects. Residential glazing involves work such as replacing glass in home windows; installing glass mirrors, shower doors, and bathtub enclosures; and fitting glass for tabletops and display cases. On commercial interior projects, glaziers install items such as heavy, often etched, decorative room dividers or security windows. Glazing projects also may involve replacement of streetfront windows for establishments such as supermarkets, auto dealerships, or banks. In the construction of large commercial buildings, glaziers build metal framework extrusions and install glass panels or curtain walls.

Working Conditions: Glaziers often work outdoors, sometimes in inclement weather. At times, they work on scaffolds at great heights. They do a considerable amount of bending, kneeling, lifting, and standing. Glaziers may be injured by broken glass or cutting tools, by falls from scaffolds, or by improperly lifting heavy glass panels.

Education, Training, Qualifications: Many glaziers learn the trade informally on the job. They usually start as helpers, carrying glass and cleaning up debris in glass shops. They often practice cutting on discarded glass. After a while, they are given an opportunity to cut glass for a job. Eventually, helpers assist experienced workers on simple installation jobs. By working with experienced glaziers, they eventually acquire the skills of a fully qualified glazier. Employers recommend that glaziers learn the trade through a formal apprenticeship program that lasts three to four years. Apprenticeship programs, which are administered by the National Glass Apprenticeship and local union-management committees or local contractors' associations, consist of on-the-job training and a minimum of 144 hours of classroom instruction or home study each year. On the job, apprentices learn to use the tools and equipment of the trade; handle, measure, cut, and install glass and metal framing; cut and fit moldings; and install and balance glass doors.

Earnings: In 2002, median hourly earnings of glaziers were $15.20 ($31,600 per year). The middle 50 percent earned between $11.56 and $20.53. Median hourly earnings in the industries employing the largest numbers of glaziers in 2002 were:

- Advertising and related services $48,070
- Local government $42,000
- Business, professional, labor, political,
  and similar organizations $39,330
- Colleges, universities, and professional schools $36,820

Glaziers covered by union contracts generally earn more than their nonunion counterparts. Apprentice wage rates usually start at between 40 and 50 percent of the rate paid to experienced glaziers and increase as apprentices gain experience in the field.

Key Contacts: For more information about glazier apprenticeships or work opportunities, contact local glazing or general contractors, a local of the International Union of Painters and Allied Trades, a local joint union-management apprenticeship agency, or the nearest office of the state employment service or state apprenticeship agency. For information about the work and training of glaziers, contact:

- **International Union of Painters and Allied Trades:** 1750 New York Ave. NW, Washington, DC 20006. Website: www.iupat. org.

- **National Glass Association:** Education and Training Department, 8200 Greensboro Drive, Suite 302, McLean, VA 22102-3881. Website: www.glass.org.

- **Associated Builders and Contractors:** Workforce Development Department, 4250 N. Fairfax Drive, 9th Floor, Arlington, VA 22203. Website: www.abc.org.

Hazardous Materials Removal Workers

▷ **Annual Earnings:** $32,500
▷ **Education/Training:** High school diploma and training
▷ **Outlook:** Good

Employment Outlook: Job opportunities are expected to be good for hazardous materials removal workers. The occupation is characterized by a relatively high rate of turnover, resulting in a number of job openings each year. Many potential workers are not attracted to this occupation, because they prefer work that is less strenuous and under safer working conditions. Employment of hazardous materials removal workers is expected to grow much faster than the average for all occupations in the decade ahead, reflecting increasing concern for a safe and clean environment. Special-trade contractors will have strong demand for the largest segment of these workers, namely, asbestos abatement and lead abatement workers; lead abatement should offer particularly good opportunities. Mold remediation is an especially rapidly growing part of the occupation at the present time, but it is unclear whether its rapid growth will continue. Employment of decontamination technicians, radiation safety technicians, and decommissioning and decontamination workers is expected to grow in response to increased pressure for safer and cleaner nuclear and electric generator facilities.

Nature of Work: Hazardous materials workers identify, remove, package, transport, and dispose of various hazardous materials, including asbestos, lead, and radioactive and nuclear materials. The removal of hazardous materials, or "hazmats," from public places and the environment also is called abatement, remediation, and decontamination. Hazardous materials removal workers use a variety of tools and equipment, depending on the work at hand. Equipment ranges form brooms to personal protective suits that completely isolate workers from the hazardous materials. The equipment required varies with the threat of contamination and can include disposable or reusable coveralls, gloves, hard hats, shoe covers, safety glasses or goggles, chemical-resistant clothing, face shields, and devices to protect one's hearing. Most workers also are required to wear respirators while working, to protect them from airborne particles. Asbestos abatement workers and lead abatement workers remove asbestos, lead, and other materials from buildings scheduled to be renovated or demolished. Using a variety of hand and power tools, such as vacuums and scrapers, these workers remove the asbestos and lead from surfaces. Emergency and disaster response workers clean up hazardous materials after train derailments and trucking accidents. These workers also are needed when an immediate cleanup is required, as would be the case after an attack by biological or chemical weapons. Decommissioning and decontamination workers remove and treat radioactive materials generated by nuclear facilities and power plants. Treatment, storage, and disposal workers transport and prepare materials for treatment or disposal. Nearly 38,000 hazardous materials removal workers held jobs in 2002.

Working Conditions: Hazardous materials removal workers function in a highly structured environment, to minimize the danger they face. Each phase of an operation is planned in advance, and workers are trained to deal with safety breaches and hazardous situations. Crews and supervisors take every precaution to ensure that the worksite is safe. Whether they work in asbestos, mold, or lead abatement or in radioactive decontamination, hazardous materials removal workers must stand, stoop, and kneel for long periods. Some must wear fully enclosed personal protective suits for several hours at a time. These workers face different working conditions, depending on their area of expertise. Although many work a standard 40-hour week, overtime and shift work are common, especially in asbestos and lead abatement. Hazardous materials removal workers may be required to travel outside their normal working areas in order to respond to emergencies.

Education, Training, Qualifications: No formal education beyond a high school diploma is required for a person to become a hazardous materials removal worker. Federal regulations require an individual to have a license to work in the occupation, although, at present, there are few laws regulating mold removal. Most employers provide technical training on the job, but a formal 32- to 40-hour training program must be completed if one is to be licensed as an asbestos abatement and lead abatement worker or a treatment, storage, and disposal worker. For decommissioning and decontamination workers employed at nuclear facilities, training is more extensive. Workers in all fields are required to take refresher courses every year in order to maintain their license. Because much of the work is done in buildings, a background in construction is helpful.

Earnings: In 2002, median hourly earnings of hazardous materials removal workers were $15.61 ($32,500 per year). The middle 50 percent earned between $12.37 and $22.18 per hour. The median hourly earnings in remediation and other waste management services, the largest industries employing hazardous materials removal workers, were $14.92 in 2002. Treatment, storage, and disposal workers usually earn slightly more than asbestos abatement and lead abatement workers. Decontamination and decommissioning workers and radiation protection technicians, though constituting the smallest group, tend to earn the highest wages.

Key Contacts: For more information on hazardous materials removal workers, including information on training, contact:

- **Laborers-AGC Education and Training Fund:** 37 Deerfield Road, P.O. Box 37, Pomfret, CT 06259. Website: www.laborerslearn.org.

Insulation Workers

- ↺ **Annual Earnings:** $28,900
- ↻ **Education/Training:** Experience and apprenticeships
- ↻ **Outlook:** Excellent

Employment Outlook: Job opportunities are expected to be excellent for insulation workers. Because there are no strict training requirements for entry, many people with limited skills work as insulation workers for a short time and then move on to other types of work, creating many job openings. Employment of insulation workers should grow as fast as average for all occupations in the coming decade, due to growth in residential and commercial construction. Demand for efficient use of energy to heat and cool buildings will create an increased demand for these workers in the construction of new residential, industrial, and commercial buildings. Insulation workers in the construction industry may experience periods of unemployment because of the short duration of many construction projects.

Nature of Work: Insulation workers cement, staple, wire, tape, or spray insulation. When covering a steam pipe, for example, insulation workers measure and cut sections of insulation to the proper length, stretch it open along a cut that runs the length of the material, and slip it over the pipe. They fasten the insulation with adhesive, staples, tape, or wire bands. When covering a wall or other flat surface, workers may use a hose to spray foam insulation onto a wire mesh that provides a rough surface to which the foam can cling and which adds strength to the finished surface. In attics or exterior walls of uninsulated buildings, workers blow in loose-fill insulation. In new construction or on major renovations, insulation workers staple fiberglass or rock-wool batts to exterior walls and ceilings before drywall, paneling, or plaster walls are put in place. Insulation workers use common hand tools – trowels, brushes, knives, scissors, saws, pliers, and stapling guns. They use power saws to cut insulating materials, welding machines to join sheet metal or secure clamps, and compressors to blow or spray insulation.

Working Conditions: Insulation workers generally work indoors. They spend most of the workday on their feet, either standing, bending, or kneeling. Sometimes they work from ladders or in tight spaces. The work requires more coordination than strength. Insulation work often is dusty and dirty, and the summer heat can make the insulation worker very uncomfortable. Minute particles from insulation materials, especially when blown, can irritate the eyes, skin, and respiratory system. Workers must follow strict safety guidelines to protect themselves from the dangers of insulating irritants. They keep work areas well ventilated; wear protective suites, masks, and respirators; and take decontamination showers when necessary.

Education, Training, Qualifications: Most insulation workers learn their trade informally on the job, although some complete formal apprenticeship programs. For entry-level jobs, insulation contractors prefer high school graduates who are in good physical condition and licensed to drive. Applicants seeking apprenticeship positions should have a high school diploma or its equivalent and be at least 18 years old. Trainees who learn on the job receive instruction and supervision from experienced insulation workers. Trainees begin with simple tasks, such as carrying insulation or holding material while it is fastened in place. On-the-job training can take up to two years, depending on the nature of the work.

Earnings: In 2002, median hourly earnings of insulation workers were $13.91 ($28,900 per year). The middle 50 percent earned between $10.58 and $18.36 per hour.

Key Contacts: For information on training programs or other work opportunities in this trade, contact a local insulation contractor, the nearest office of the state employment service or apprenticeship agency, or the following organizations:

- **National Insulation Association:** 99 Canal Center Plaza, Suite 222, Alexandria, VA 22314. Website: www.insulation.org.

- **Insulation Contractors Association of America:** 1321 Duke Street, Suite 303, Alexandria, VA 22314. Website: www.insulate. org.

Painters and Paperhangers

⇨ **Annual Earnings:** $29,100
⇨ **Education/Training:** Experience and apprenticeships
⇨ **Outlook:** Good

Employment Outlook: Job prospects should be good as thousands of painters and paperhangers transfer to other occupations or leave the labor force each year. Because there are no strict training requirements for entry, many people with limited skills work as painters or paperhangers for a short time and then move on to other types of work. Employment of painters and paperhangers is expected to grow about as fast as average for all occupations in the decade ahead, reflecting increases in the level of new construction and in the supply of buildings and others structures that require maintenance and renovation.

Nature of Work: Painters apply paint, stain, varnish, and other finishes to buildings and other structures. They choose the right paint or finish for the surface to be covered, taking into account durability, ease of handling, method of applications, and customers' wishes. Painters first prepare the surfaces to be covered. This may require removing the old coat of paint by stripping, sanding, wire brushing, burning, or water and abrasive blasting. Painters also wash walls and trim to remove dirt and grease, fill nail holes and cracks, sandpaper rough spots, and brush off dust. When working on tall buildings, painters erect scaffolding, including "swing stages," scaffolds suspended by ropes, or cables attached to the roof hood.

Paperhangers cover walls and ceilings with decorative wall coverings made of paper, vinyl, or fabric. They first prepare the surface to be covered by applying "sizing," which seals the surface and makes the covering stick better. When redecorating, they may first remove the old covering by soaking, steaming, or applying solvents. When necessary, they patch holes and take care of other imperfections before hanging the new wall covering. After the surface has been prepared, paperhangers must prepare the paste or other adhesive. Then they measure the area to be covered, check the covering for flaws, cut the covering into strips of the proper size, and closely examine the pattern in order to match it when the strips are hung. The next step is to brush or roll the adhesive onto the back of the covering and then place the strips on the wall or ceiling, making sure the pattern is matched, the strips are hung straight, and the edges are butted together to make tight, closed seams. They finally smooth the strips to remove bubbles and wrinkles, trim the top and bottom with a razor knife, and wipe off any excess adhesive.

Working Conditions: Most painters and paperhangers work 40 hours a week or less; about one-quarter have variable schedules or work part time. Painters and paperhangers must stand for long periods. Their jobs also require a considerable amount of climbing and bending. These workers must have stamina, because much of the work is done with their arms raised overhead. Painters often work outdoors but seldom in wet, cold, or inclement weather. These workers risk injury from slipping or falling off ladders and scaffolds. They sometimes may work with materials that can be hazardous if masks are not worn or if ventilation is poor. Some painting jobs can leave a worker covered with paint. In some cases, painters may work in a sealed self-contained suit to prevent inhalation of, or contact with, hazardous materials.

Education, Training, Qualifications: Painting and paperhanging are learned through apprenticeships or informal, on-the-job instruction. Although training authorities recommend completion of an apprenticeship program as the best way to become a painter or paperhanger, most painters learn the trade informally on the job as a helper to an experienced painter. Limited opportunities for informal training exist for paperhangers because few paperhangers need helpers. The apprenticeships for painters and paperhangers consists of two to four years of on-the-job training, in addition to 144 hours of related classroom instruction each year. Apprentices receive instruction in color harmony, use and care of tools and equipment, surface preparation, application techniques, paint mixing and matching, characteristics of different finishes, blueprint reading, wood finishing, and safety. Painters and paperhangers may advance to supervisory or estimating jobs with painting and decorating contractors. Many establish their own painting and decorating businesses.

Earnings: The median annual earnings of painters (construction and maintenance) were $13.98 ($29,100 annually). The middle 50 percent earned between $11.08 and $18.00 an hour. Median hourly earnings in the industries employing the largest numbers of painters in 2002 were:

- Local government $17.46
- Residential building construction $14.01
- Building finishing contractors $14.00
- Lessors of real estate $11.62

In 2002, median earnings for paperhangers were $15.22. The middle 50 percent earned between $11.52 and $20.38.

Earnings for painters may be reduced on occasion because of bad weather and the short-term nature of many construction jobs. Hourly wage rates for apprentices usually start at 40 to 50 percent of the rate for experienced workers and increase periodically.

Key Contacts: For information about the work of painters and paperhangers, contact local painting and decorating contractors, a local of the International Union of Painters and Allied Trades, a local joint union-management apprenticeship committee, or an office of the state apprenticeship agency or employment services:

- **International Union of Painters and Allied Trades:** 1750 New York Avenue NW, Washington, DC 20006. Website: www.iupat. org.

- **Associated Builders and Contractors:** Workforce Development Department, 4250 N. Fairfax Drive, 9th Floor, Arlington, VA 22203. Website: www.abc.org.

- **Painting and Decorating Contractors of America:** 11960 Westline Industrial Drive, Suite 201, St. Louis, MO 63146-3209. Website: www.pdca.org.

Pipelayers, Plumbers, Pipefitters, and Steamfitters

⇨ **Annual Earnings:** $28,500 and $40,200
⇨ **Education/Training:** Apprenticeship
⇨ **Outlook:** Excellent

Employment Outlook: Job opportunities are expected to be excellent, as demand for skilled pipelayers, plumbers, pipefitters, and steamfitters is expected to outpace the supply of workers trained in these crafts. Many potential workers may prefer work that is less strenuous and has more comfortable working conditions. Employment of individuals in these trades is expected to grow about as fast as the average for all occupations in the coming decade. Demand for plumbers will stem from building renovation, including the growing use of sprinkler systems; repair and maintenance of existing residential systems; and maintenance activities for places having extensive systems of pipes, such as power plants, water and wastewater treatment plants, pipelines, office buildings, and factories. Employment of pipelayers, plumbers, pipefitters, and steamfitters generally is less sensitive to changes in economic conditions than is employment of some other construction trades. Even when construction activity declines, maintenance, rehabilitation, and replacement of existing piping systems, as well as the increasing installation of fire sprinkler systems, provide many jobs for pipelayers, plumbers, pipefitters, and steamfitters.

Nature of Work: Although pipelaying, plumbing, pipefitting, and steam-fitting sometimes are considered a single trade, workers generally specialize in one of the four areas. Pipelayers lay clay, concrete, plastic, or cast-iron pipe for drains, sewers, water mains, and oil or gas lines. Before laying the pipe, pipelayers prepare and grade the trenches either manually or with machines. Plumbers install and repair the water, waste disposal, drainage, and gas systems in homes and commercial and industrial buildings. Plumbers also install plumbing fixtures – bathtubs, showers, sinks, and toilets – and appliances such as dishwashers and water heaters. Pipefitters install and repair both high- and low-pressure pipe systems used in manufacturing, in the generation of electricity, and in heating and cooling buildings. They also install automatic controls that are increasingly being used to regulate these systems. Some pipefitters specialize in only one type of system. Steamfitters, for example, install pipe systems that move liquids or gases under high pressure. Sprinkler fitters install automatic fire sprinkler systems in buildings.

Working Conditions: Because pipelayers, plumbers, pipefitters, and steamfitters frequently must lift heavy pipes, stand for long periods, and sometimes work in uncomfortable or cramped positions, they need physical strength as well as stamina. They also may have to work outdoors in inclement weather. In addition, they are subject to possible falls from ladders, cuts from sharp tools, and burns from hot pipes or soldering equipment. Pipelayers, plumbers, pipefitters, and steamfitters engaged in construction generally work a standard 40-hour week. Those involved in maintenance services under contract may have to work evening or weekend shifts, as well as be on call. These maintenance workers may spend quite a bit of time traveling to and from worksites.

Education, Training, Qualifications: Virtually all pipelayers, pipefitters, plumbers, and steamfitters undergo some type of apprenticeship training. Many apprenticeship programs are administered by local union-management committees made up of members of the United Association of Journeymen and Apprentices of the Plumbing and Pipefitting Industry of the United States and Canada, and local employers who are members of either the Mechanical Contractors Association of America, the National Association of Plumbing-Heating-Cooling Contractors, or the National Fire Sprinkler Association. Nonunion training and apprenticeship programs are administered by local chapters of the Associated Builders and Contractors, the National Association of Plumbing-Heating-Cooling Contractors, the American Fire Sprinkler Association, or the Home Builders Institute of the National Association of Home Builders. Apprenticeships – both union and nonunion – consist of four or five years of on-the-job training, in addition to at least 144 hours per year of related classroom instruction. As apprentices gain experience, they learn how to work with various types of pipe and how to install different piping systems and plumbing fixtures.

Earnings: Pipelayers, plumbers, pipefitters, and steamfitters are among the highest paid construction occupations. In 2002, median annual earnings of pipelayers were $13.70 ($28,500 per year). The middle 50 percent earned between $10.96 and $13.70. Also, in 2002, median hourly earnings of plumbers, pipefitters, and steamfitters were $19.31 ($40,200 per year). The middle 50 percent earned between $14.68 and $25.87. Median hourly earnings in the industries employing the largest numbers of plumbers, pipefitters, and steamfitters in 2002 were:

- Nonresidential building construction $19.65
- Building equipment contractors $19.52
- Utility system construction $17.81
- Ship and boat building $16.62
- Local government $16.21

Apprentices usually are paid about 50 percent of the wage rate paid to experienced pipelayers, plumbers, pipefitters, and steamfitters.

Key Contacts: For information on apprenticeship opportunities for pipelayers, plumbers, pipefitters, and steamfitters, contact:

- **United Association of Journeymen and Apprentices of the Plumbing, Pipefitting, Sprinkler Fitting Industry of the United States and Canada:** 901 Massachusetts Avenue NW, Washington, DC 20001. Website: www.ua.org.

For more informaton about training programs for pipelayers, plumbers, pipefitters, and steamfitters, contact:

- **Associated Builders and Contractors:** Workforce Development Department, 4250 North Fairfax Drive, 9th Floor, Arlington, VA 22203. Website: www.abc.org.

- **National Association of Home Builders:** 1201 15th Street NW, Washington, DC 20005. Website: www.nahb.org.

- **Home Builders Institute:** 1201 15th Street NW, 6th Floor, Washington, DC 20005. Website: www.hbi.org.

For general information about the work of pipelayers, plumbers, and pipefitters, contact:

- Mechanical Contractors Association of America: 1385 Piccard Drive, Rockville, MD 20850. Website: www.mcaa.org.

- National Association of Plumbing-Heating-Cooling Contractors: 180 S. Washington Street, P.O. Box 6808, Falls Church, VA 22040. Website: www.phccweb.org.

For general information about the work of sprinkler fitters, contact:

- American Fire Sprinkler Association, Inc.: 9696 Skillman Street, Suite 300, Dallas, TX 75243-8264. Website: www.firesprinkler.org.

- National Fire Sprinkler Association: P.O. Box 1000, Patterson, NY 12563. Website: www.nfsa.org.

Sheet Metal Workers

⇨ **Annual Earnings:** $35,600
⇨ **Education/Training:** Apprenticeship
⇨ **Outlook:** Good

Employment Outlook: Employment opportunities are expected to be good for sheet metal workers in the construction industry and in construction-related sheet metal fabrication, reflecting both employment growth and openings arising each year as experienced sheet metal workers leave the occupation. In addition, many potential workers may prefer work that is less strenuous and that has more comfortable working conditions, thus limiting the number of applicants for sheet metal jobs. Opportunities should be particularly good for individuals who acquire apprenticeship training.

Employment of sheet metal workers in construction is expected to grow about as fast as the average for all occupations in the decade ahead. This will be in response to growth in the demand for sheet metal installations as more industrial, commercial, and residential structures are built. The need to install energy-efficient air-conditioning, heating, and ventilation systems in the increasing numbers of old buildings and to perform other types of renovation and maintenance work also should boost employment.

Nature of Work: Sheet metal workers make, install, and maintain heating, ventilation, and air-conditioning duct systems; roofs; siding; rain gutters; downspouts; skylights; restaurant equipment; outdoor signs; railroad cars; tailgates; customized precision equipment; and many other products made from metal sheets. They also may work with fiberglass and plastic materials. Although some workers specialize in fabrication, installation, or maintenance, most do all three jobs. Sheet metal workers do both construction-related sheet metal work and mass production of sheet metal products in manufacturing. Sheet metal workers held about 205,000 jobs in 2002. Nearly two-thirds of all sheet metal workers were found in the construction industry. Of those employed in construction, almost half worked for plumbing, heating, and air-conditioning contractors; most of the rest worked for roofing and sheet metal contractors.

Working Conditions: Sheet metal workers usually work a 40-hour week. Those who fabricate sheet metal products work in shops that are well-lighted and well-ventilated. However, they stand for long periods and lift heavy materials and finished pieces. Sheet metal workers must follow safety practices because working around high-speed machines can be dangerous. They also are subject to cuts from sharp metal, burns from soldering and welding, and falls from ladders and scaffolds. They usually wear safety glasses but must not wear jewelry or loose-fitting clothing that could easily be caught in a machine. Those performing installation work do considerable bending, lifting, standing, climbing, and squatting, sometimes in close quarters or in awkward positions.

Education, Training, Qualifications: Apprenticeship generally is considered to be the best way to learn this trade. The apprenticeship program consists of four to five years of on-the-job training and an average of 200 hours per year of classroom instruction. Apprenticeship programs may be administered by local joint committees composed of the Sheet Metal Workers' International Association and local chapters of the Sheet Metal and Air-Conditioning Contractors National Association. On the job, apprentices learn the basics of pattern layout and how to cut, bend, fabricate, and install sheet metal. In the classroom, apprentices learn drafting, plan and specification reading, trigonometry and geometry applicable to layout work, the use of computerized equipment, welding, and the principles of heating, air-conditioning, and ventilating systems.

Some people pick up the trade informally, usually by working as helpers to experienced sheet metal workers. Most sheet metal workers in large-scale manufacturing receive on-the-job training, with additional classwork or in-house training when necessary.

Earnings: In 2002, median hourly earnings of sheet metal workers were $16.62 ($35,600 per year). The middle 50 percent earned between $12.15 and $23.03. The median hourly earnings of the largest industries employing sheet metal workers in 2002 were:

- Federal government $19.73
- Building equipment contractors $17.47
- Building finishing contractors $16.77
- Foundation, structure, and building exterior
  contractors $15.48
- Architectural and structural metals
  manufacturing $14.60

Apprentices normally start at about 40 to 50 percent of the rate paid to experienced workers.

Key Contacts: For more information on apprenticeships or other work opportunities, contact local sheet metal contractors or heating, refrigeration, and air-conditioning contractors; a local of the Sheet Metal Workers International Association; a local of the Sheet Metal and Air-Conditioning Contractors National Association; a local joint union-management apprenticeship committee; or the nearest office of your state employment service or apprenticeship agency.

For general and training information about sheet metal workers, contact:

- **International Training Institute for the Sheet Metal and Air Conditioning Industry:** 601 N. Fairfax Street, Suite 240, Alexandria, VA 22314. Website: www.sheetmetal-iti.org.

- **Sheet Metal and Air Conditioning Contractors National Association:** 4201 Lafayette Center Drive, Chantilly, VA 20151-1209. Website: www.smacna.org.

- **Sheet Metal Workers International Association:** 1750 New York Avenue NW, Washington, DC 20006. Website: www.smwia. org.

Structural and Reinforcing Iron and Metal Workers

- ⇨ **Annual Earnings:** $40,700
- ⇨ **Education/Training:** Apprenticeships
- ⇨ **Outlook:** Good to excellent

Employment Outlook: Employment of structural and reinforcing iron and metal workers is expected to grow about as fast as the average for all occupations in the decade ahead, largely on the basis of continued growth in industrial and commercial construction. The rehabilitation, maintenance, and replacement of a growing number of older buildings, factories, power plants, highways, and bridges is expected to create employment opportunities. The number of job openings fluctuates from year to year with economic conditions and the level of construction activity.

Nature of Work: Structural and reinforcing iron and metal workers place and install iron or steel girders, columns, and other construction materials to form buildings, bridges, and other structures. They also position and secure steel bars or mesh in concrete forms in order to reinforce the concrete used in highways, buildings, bridges, tunnels, and other structures. In addition, they repair and renovate older buildings and structures. Even though the primary metal involved in this work is steel, these workers often are known as ironworkers.

Working Conditions: Structural and reinforcing iron and metal workers usually work outside in all kinds of weather. However, those who work at great heights do not work during wet, icy, or extremely windy conditions. Because the danger of injuries due to falls is great, ironworkers use safety devices such as safety belts, scaffolding, and nets to reduce risk. Some ironworkers fabricate structural metal in fabricating shops, which usually are located away from the construction site. These workers usually work a 40-hour week. They held about 107,000 jobs in 2002.

Education, Training, Qualifications: Most employers recommend a three- or four-year apprenticeship consisting of on-the-job training and evening classroom instruction as the best way to learn this trade. Apprentice-ship programs usually are administered by committees made up of representatives of local unions of the International Association of Bridge, Structural, Ornamental and Reinforcing Iron Workers or the local chapters of contractors' associations. Ironworkers must be at least 18 years old. A high school diploma is preferred by employers and local apprenticeship committees.

Earnings: In 2002, median hourly earnings of structural iron and steel workers in all industries were $19.55 ($40,700 per year). The middle 50 percent earned between $14.45 and $26.00. In 2002, median hourly earnings of reinforcing iron and rebar workers in all industries were $17.66. Median hourly earnings of structural iron and steel workers in 2002 employed by foundation, structure, and building exterior contractors were $21.35, and in nonresidential building construction, $16.98. According to the International Association of Bridge, Structural, Ornamental, and Reinforcing Iron Workers, average hourly earnings, including benefits, for structural and reinforcing metal workers who belonged to a union and worked full time were 34 percent higher than the hourly earnings of nonunion workers.

Key Contacts: For information on apprenticeships or other work opportunities, contact local general contractors; a local of the International Association of Bridge, Structural, Ornamental, and Reinforcing Iron Workers Union; a local iron workers' joint union-management apprenticeship committee; a local or state chapter of the Associated Builders and Contractors or the Associated General Contractors of America; or the nearest office of your state employment service or apprenticeship agency.

For apprenticeship information, contact:

- **International Association of Bridge, Structural, Ornamental, and Reinforcing Iron Workers:** Apprenticeship Department, 1750 New York Avenue NW, Suite 400, Washington, DC 20006. Website: www.ironworkers.org.

For general information about ironworkers, contact either of the following sources:

- **Associated Builders and Contractors:** Workforce Development Department, 4250 N. Fairfax Drive, 9th Floor, Arlington, VA 22203. Website: www.abc.org.

- **Associated General Contractors of America:** 333 John Carlyle Street, Suite 200, Alexandria, VA 22314. Website: www.agc.org.

9

Installation, Maintenance, and Repair Occupations

T HE INCREASED USE OF TECHNOLOGY and machinery requires more and more workers who are experts at installing, maintaining, and repairing equipment. Most of these jobs require some postsecondary education and training, such as attending specialized trade school classes, receiving on-the-job training, and acquiring certification. Individuals entering these fields can expect to regularly acquire additional education and training in order to keep up with the latest developments in their respective fields.

Most of the jobs profiled in this chapter are expected to grow substantially in the decade ahead as well as generate high median earnings for their workers. Many are attractive alternatives for installation- and repair-oriented individuals who are entering the job market but who do not have the requisite education credentials to enter other occupational fields. These also are some of the safest jobs – relatively recession-proof and impossible to offshore. Entry into one of these jobs should lead to a relatively comfortable and secure employment future.

Aircraft and Avionics Equipment Mechanics and Service Technicians

⇨ **Annual Earnings:** $20.71 hourly
⇨ **Education/Training:** Trade school, on-the-job training, and certificate
⇨ **Outlook:** Excellent

Employment Outlook: Opportunities for aircraft and avionics equipment mechanics and service technician jobs should be excellent for persons who have completed aircraft mechanic training programs. Employment of aircraft mechanics is expected to increase about as fast as average for all occupations through 2012, and large numbers of additional job openings should arise from the need to replace experienced mechanics who retire. Avionics technicians are projected to increase at a slower than average rate. Contributing to favorable future job opportunities for mechanics is the long-term trend towards fewer students entering technical schools to learn maintenance and repair trades. Many of the students who have the ability and aptitude to work on planes are choosing to go to college, work in computer-related fields, or go to other repair and maintenance occupations with better working conditions. If the trend continues, the supply of trained aviation mechanics will not be able to keep up with air transportation industry needs when growth resumes in the industry.

Job opportunities are likely to be best at small commuter and regional airlines, at FAA repair stations, and in general aviation. Commuter and regional airlines are the fastest growing segment of the air transportation industry, but wages in these companies tend to be lower than those in the major airlines, so they attract fewer job applicants. In general, prospects will be best for applicants with experience. Mechanics who keep abreast of technological advances in electronics, composite materials, and other areas will be in greatest demand. The number of job openings for aircraft mechanics in the federal government should decline as the government increasingly contracts out service and repair functions to private repair companies.

Nature of Work: Aircraft and avionics equipment mechanics and service technicians perform scheduled maintenance, make repairs, and complete inspections required by the Federal Aviation Administration (FAA). Many aircraft mechanics specialize in preventive maintenance. They inspect engines, landing gear, instruments, pressurized sections, accessories – brakes, valves, pumps, and air-conditioning systems, for example – and other parts of the aircraft, and do the necessary maintenance and replacement of parts. Inspections take place following a schedule based on the number of hours the aircraft has flown, calendar days since the last inspection, cycles of operation, or a combination of these factors.

To examine an engine, aircraft mechanics work through specially designed openings while standing on ladders or scaffolds, or use hoists or lifts to remove the entire engine from the aircraft. After taking an engine apart, mechanics use precision instruments to measure parts for wear and use x-ray and magnetic inspection equipment to check for invisible cracks. Worn or defective parts are repaired or replaced. After completing all repairs, they must test the equipment to ensure that it works properly. Mechanics work as fast as safety permits so that the aircraft can be put back into service quickly. Some mechanics work on one or many different types of aircraft, such as jets, propeller-driven airplanes, and helicopters.

Avionics systems are now an integral part of aircraft design and have vastly increased aircraft capability. Avionics technicians repair and maintain components used for aircraft navigation and radio communications, weather radar systems, and other instruments and computers that control flight, engine, and other primary functions. These duties may require additional licenses issued by the Federal Communications Commission (FCC). Because of technological advances, an increasing amount of time is spent repairing electronic systems, such as computerized controls. Technicians also may be required to analyze and develop solutions to complex electronic problems.

Working Conditions: Mechanics usually work in hangars or in other indoor areas, although they can work outdoors – sometimes in unpleasant weather – when hangars are full or when repairs must be made quickly. Mechanics often work under time pressure to maintain flight schedules or, in general aviation, to keep from inconveniencing customers. At the same time, mechanics have a tremendous responsibility to maintain safety standards, and this can cause the job to be stressful.

Frequently, mechanics must lift or pull objects weighing as much as 70 pounds. They often stand, lie, or kneel in awkward positions and occasionally must work in precarious positions on scaffolds or ladders. Noise and vibration are common when engines are being tested, so ear protection is necessary. Aircraft mechanics usually work 40 hours a week on eight-hour shifts around the clock. Overtime work is frequent.

Education, Training, Qualifications: The majority of mechanics who work on civilian aircraft are certificated by the FAA as an "airframe mechanic," "powerplant mechanic," or "avionics repair specialist." Mechanics who also have an inspector's authorization can certify work completed by other mechanics and perform required inspections. Uncertified mechanics are supervised by those with certificates.

The FAA requires at least 18 months of work experience for an airframe, powerplant, or avionics repairer's certificate. Completion of a program at an FAA-certified mechanic school can substitute for the work experience requirement. Applicants for all certificates also must pass written and oral tests and demonstrate that they can do the work authorized by the certificate. Few people become mechanics through on-the-job training. Most learn their job in one of about 200 trade schools certified by the FAA. About one-third of these schools award two- and four-year degrees in avionics, aviation technology, or aviation maintenance management. Some aircraft mechanics in the military acquire enough general experience to satisfy the work experience requirements for the FAA certificate. With additional study they may pass the certifying exam. In general, however, jobs in the military services are too specialized to provide the broad experience required by the FAA. In any case, military experience is a great advantage when seeking employment; employers consider trade school graduates who have this experience to be the most desirable applicants.

Aircraft mechanics must do careful and thorough work that requires a high degree of mechanical aptitude. Employers seek applicants who are self-motivated, hard-working, enthusiastic, and able to diagnose and solve complex mechanical problems. Agility is important for the reaching and climbing necessary to do the job. Because they may work on the tops of wings and fuselages on large jet planes, aircraft mechanics must not be afraid of heights.

Earnings: Median hourly earnings of aircraft mechanics and service technicians were about $20.71 in 2002. Some earned less than $13.16, while the highest 10 percent earned more than $28.92. Median hourly earnings of avionics technicians were about $20.21 in 2002. While some earned less than $14.01, the highest 10 percent earned more than $27.00. Mechanics who work on jets for the major airlines generally earn more than those working on other aircraft. Airline mechanics and their immediate families receive reduced-fare transportation on their own and most other airlines. Almost four in 10 aircraft and avionics equipment mechanics and service technicians are members of, or covered, by union agreements.

Key Contacts: Information about jobs with a particular airline can be obtained by contacting the personnel manager of the company. For general information about aircraft and avionics equipment mechanics and service technicians, contact:

- **Professional Aviation Maintenance Association:** 717 Princess Street, Alexandria, VA 22314. Website: www.pama.org.

Automotive Service Technicians and Mechanics

⇨ **Annual Earnings:** $30,600
⇨ **Education/Training:** High school and training
⇨ **Outlook:** Good

Employment Outlook: Automotive service technicians and mechanics held about 818,000 jobs in 2002. Employment of automotive service technicians and mechanics is expected to increase about as fast as average in the decade ahead. Population growth will boost demand for motor vehicles, which will require regular maintenance and service. Growth of the labor force and in the number of families in which both spouses need vehicles to commute to work will contribute to increased vehicle sales and employment in this industry. Growth of personal income will also contribute to families owning multiple vehicles. Employment growth will continue to be concentrated in automobile dealerships and independent automotive repair shops. Many new jobs also will be created in small retail operations that offer after-warranty repairs, such as oil changes, brake repair, air-conditioner service, and other minor repairs. Most persons who enter the occupation can expect steady work, because changes in general economic conditions and developments in other industries have little effect on the automotive repair business.

Nature of Work: The ability to diagnose the source of a problem quickly and accurately requires good reasoning ability and a thorough knowledge of automobiles. The work of automotive service technicians and mechanics has evolved from mechanical repair to a high-tech job. Today, integrated electronic systems and complex computers run vehicles and measure their performance while on the road. Technicians must have the ability to work with electronic diagnostic equipment and computer-based technical reference materials.

Automotive service technicians and mechanics use their high-tech skills to inspect, maintain, and repair automobiles and light trucks that have gasoline engines. The increasing sophistication of automotive technology, including new hybrid vehicles, now requires workers who can use computerized shop equipment and work with electronic components while maintaining their skills with traditional hand tools. Service technicians use a variety of tools in their work – power tools such as pneumatic wrenches to remove bolts quickly; machine tools like lathes and grinding machines to rebuild brakes; welding and flame-cutting equipment to remove and repair exhaust systems; and jacks and hoists to lift cars and engines. They also use common hand tools, such as screwdrivers, pliers, and wrenches, to work on small parts and in hard-to-reach places. Automotive service technicians in large shops have increasingly become specialized.

Working Conditions: About half of automotive service technicians work a standard 40-hour week, but almost 30 percent work more than 40 hours a week. Many of those working extended hours are self-employed technicians. To satisfy customer service needs, some service shops offer evening and weekend service. Generally, service technicians work indoors in well-ventilated and -lighted repair shops. However, some shops are drafty and noisy. Although they fix some problems with simple computerized adjustments, technicians frequently work with dirty and greasy parts, and in awkward positions. They often lift heavy parts and tools. Minor cuts, burns, and bruises are common, but technicians usually avoid serious accidents when the shop is kept clean and orderly and safety practices are observed.

Education, Training, Qualifications: Automotive technology is rapidly increasing in sophistication, and most training authorities strongly recommend that persons seeking automotive service technician and mechanic jobs complete a formal training program in high school or in a postsecondary vocational school. However, some service technicians still learn the trade solely by assisting and learning from experienced workers.

Many high schools, community colleges, and public and private vocational and technical schools offer automotive service technician training programs. The traditional postsecondary programs usually provide a thorough career preparation that expands upon the student's high school repair experience. Postsecondary automotive technician training programs vary greatly in format, but normally provide intensive career preparation through a combination of classroom instruction and hands-on practice. Some trade and technical school programs provide concentrated training for six months to a year, depending on how many hours the student attends each week. Community college programs normally spread the training over two years; supplement the automotive training with instruction in English, basic mathematics, computers, and other subjects; and award an associate degree or certificate. Some students earn repair certificates and opt to leave the program to begin their career before graduation. Recently, some programs have added to their curricula training on employability skills such as customer service and stress management. Employers find that these skills help technicians handle the additional responsibilities of dealing with the customers and parts vendors.

Most employers regard the successful completion of a vocational training program in automotive service technology as the best preparation for trainee positions. Experience working on motor vehicles in the Armed Forces or as a hobby also is valuable. A growing number of employers require the completion of high school and additional postsecondary training.

Earnings: Median hourly earnings of automotive service technicians and mechanics, including those on commission, were $14.71 in 2002. The highest 10 percent earned more than $25.21. Median annual earnings in the industries employing the largest number of service technicians in 2002 were: local government, $18.04; automobile dealers, $17.66; gasoline stations, $13.04; automotive repair and maintenance, $12.77; and automotive parts, accessories, and tire stores, $12.60. Many experienced technicians employed by automobile dealers and independent repair shops receive a commission related to the labor cost charged to the customer. Employers frequently guarantee commissioned mechanics and technicians a minimum weekly salary. Some automotive service technicians are members of labor unions.

Key Contacts: For more details about work opportunities, contact local automobile dealers and repair shops or local offices of the state employment service. The state employment service may also have information about training programs. A list of certified automotive service technician training programs can be obtained from:

- **National Automotive Technicians Education Foundation:** 101 Blue Seal Drive, Suite 101, Leesburg, VA 20175. Website: www. natef.org.

For a directory of accredited private trade and technical schools that offer programs in automotive service technician training, contact:

- **Accrediting Commission of Career Schools and Colleges of Technology:** 2101 Wilson Blvd., Suite 302, Arlington, VA 22201. Website: www.accsct.org.

For a list of public automotive service technician training programs, contact:

- **SkillsUSA-VICA:** P.O. Box 3000, Leesburg, VA 20177-0300. Website: www.skillsusa.org.

Information on automobile manufacturer-sponsored programs in automotive service technology can be obtained from:

- **Automotive Youth Educational Systems (AYES):** 100 W. Big Beaver, Suite 300, Troy, MI 48084. Website: www.ayes.org.

Information on how to become a certified automotive service technician is available from:

- **National Institute for Automotive Service Excellence (ASE):** 101 Blue Seal Drive SE, Suite 101, Leesburg, VA 20175. Website: www.asecert.org.

For general information about a career as an automotive service technician, contact:

- **National Automobile Dealers Association:** 8400 Westpark Drive, McLean, VA 22102. Website: www.nada.org.

- **Automotive Retailing Today:** 8400 Westpark Drive, MS#2, McLean, VA 22102. Website: www.autoretailing.org.

Coin, Vending, and Amusement Machine Servicers and Repairers

⇨ **Annual Earnings:** $13.16 hourly
⇨ **Education/Training:** Prefer high school graduates/ on-the-job training
⇨ **Outlook:** Average growth

Employment Outlook: Employment of coin, vending, and amusement machine servicers and repairers is expected to grow about as fast as average for all occupations through 2012, primarily because of the increasing number of vending and amusement machines in operation. Job openings will arise from employment growth and from the need to replace experienced workers who transfer to other occupations or leave the labor force.

Businesses are expected to install additional vending machines to meet the public demand for snacks and other food items. The range of products dispensed by vending machines is expected to increase as vending machines continue to become increasingly automated and begin to incorporate microwave ovens, mini-refrigerators, and freezers. Government-sponsored lotteries are increasingly using coin-operated machines to sell scratch-off tickets in grocery stores and other public places.

Opportunities should be especially good for persons with some knowledge of electronics, because electronic circuitry is an important component of vending and amusement machines. If firms cannot find trained or experienced workers for these jobs, they are likely to train qualified route drivers or hire inexperienced people who have acquired some mechanical, electrical, or electronics training by taking high school or vocational courses. However, improved technology in newer machines will moderate employment growth because these machines require less frequent maintenance than do older ones.

New machines will need restocking less often, and they contain computers that record sales and inventory data, reducing the amount of time-consuming paperwork that otherwise would have to be filled out. The Internet is beginning to play a large role in the monitoring of vending machines from remote locations. Some new machines use wireless transmitters to signal the vending machine company when the machine needs restocking or repairing. This allows servicers and repairers to be dispatched only when needed, instead of having to check each machine on a regular schedule.

Nature of Work: Coin, vending, and amusement machine servicers and repairers install, service, and stock the machines and keep them in good working order. Vending machine servicers, often called route drivers, visit machines that dispense soft drinks, candy, and snacks, and other items. They collect money from the machines, restock merchandise, and change labels to indicate new selections. They also keep machines clean and appealing. Vending machine repairers, often called mechanics or technicians, make sure that the machines operate correctly. When checking complicated electrical and electronic machines, such as beverage dispensers, they ascertain whether the machines mix drinks properly and whether the refrigeration and heating units work correctly. If the machines are not in good working order, the mechanics repair them. Because many vending machines dispense food, these workers must comply with state and local public health and sanitation standards.

Amusement machine servicers and repairers work on jukeboxes, video games, pinball machines, and slot machines. They make sure the various mechanisms function properly so that the games remain fair and the jukebox selections are accurate. Those who work in the gaming industry must adhere to strict guidelines, because federal and state agencies regulate many gaming machines.

Vending machine servicers and repairers employed by small companies may both fill and fix machines on a regular basis. These combination servicers-repairers stock machines, collect money, fill coin and currency changers, and repair machines when necessary. Servicers and repairers also do some paperwork, such as filing reports, preparing repair cost estimates, ordering parts, and keeping daily records of merchandise distributed and money collected. Newer machines with computerized inventory controls reduce the paperwork a servicer must complete.

Working Conditions: Some vending and amusement machine repairers work primarily in company repair shops, but many spend substantial time on the road, visiting machines wherever they have been placed. Repairers generally work a total of 40 hours a week. However, vending and amusement machines operate around the clock, so repairers may be on call to work at night and on weekends and holidays.

Vending and amusement machine repair shops generally are quiet, are well lighted, and have adequate workspace. However, when machines are serviced on location, the work may be done where pedestrian traffic is heavy, such as in busy supermarkets, industrial complexes, offices, casinos, or arcades. Repair work is relatively safe, although workers must take care to avoid hazards such as electrical shocks and cuts from sharp tools and other metal objects. At times they may be expected to move (or assist with moving) heavy vending and amusement machines.

Education, Training, Qualifications: Although most workers learn their skills on the job, employers prefer to hire high school graduates. High school or vocational school courses in electricity, refrigeration, and machine repair are an advantage in qualifying for entry-level jobs. . Employers usually require applicants to demonstrate mechanical ability, either through work experience or by scoring well on mechanical aptitude tests.

Because coin, vending, and amusement machine servicers and repairers sometimes handle thousands of dollars in merchandise and cash, employers hire persons who seem to have a record of honesty. The ability to deal tactfully with people is also important, because the servicers and repairers play a significant role in relaying customers' requests and concerns. A driver's license and a good driving record are essential for most vending and amusement servicer and repairer jobs. Some employers require their servicers to be bonded.

To learn about new machines, repairers and servicers sometimes attend training sessions sponsored by manufacturers and distributors that may last from a few days to several weeks. Both trainees and experienced workers sometimes take evening courses in basic electricity, electronics, microwave ovens, refrigeration, and other related subjects to stay on top of new techniques and equipment. Skilled servicers and repairers may be promoted to supervisory jobs or go into business for themselves.

Earnings: Median hourly earnings of coin, vending, and amusement machine servicers and repairers were $13.16 in 2002. Many earned less than $8.07 an hour, and the highest 10 percent more than $20.12 an hour. Typically, states with some form of legalized gaming have the highest wages. Most coin, vending, and amusement machine servicers and repairers work eight hours a day, five days a week, and receive premium pay for overtime. Some union contracts stipulate higher pay for night work and for emergency repair jobs on weekends and holidays than for regular hours.

Key Contacts: Information on job opportunities in this field can be obtained from local vending machine firms and local offices of each state employment service. For general information on vending machine repair, contact:

- **National Automatic Merchandising Association**: 20 N. Wacker Dr., Suite 3500, Chicago, IL 60606-3102. Website: www.vending. org.

- **Automatic Merchandiser Vending Group**: Cygnus Business Media, P.O. Box 803, 1233 Janesville Ave., Fort Atkinson, WI 53538-0803.

Heating, Air-Conditioning, and Refrigeration Mechanics and Installers

⇨ **Annual Earnings:** $16.78 hourly
⇨ **Education/Training:** Technical school or apprenticeship training preferred
⇨ **Outlook:** Faster than average growth

Employment Outlook: Employment of heating, air-conditioning, and refrigeration mechanics and installers is expected to grow faster than the average for all occupations through the year 2012. Job prospects are expected to be good, especially for those with technical school or formal apprenticeship training.

As the population and economy grow, so does the demand for new residential, commercial, and industrial climate-control systems. Technicians who specialize in installation work may experience periods of unemployment when the level of new construction activity declines, but maintenance and repair work usually remains stable. In addition, the continuing focus on improving indoor air quality should contribute to the creation of more jobs for heating, air-conditioning, and refrigeration technicians. The growth of businesses that use refrigerated equipment – such as supermarkets and convenience stores – will also contribute to a growing need for technicians. In addition to openings created by employment growth, thousands of openings will result from the need to replace workers who transfer to other occupations or leave the labor force.

Nature of Work: Heating, air-conditioning, and refrigeration systems consist of many mechanical, electrical, and electronic components, such as motors, compressors, pumps, fans, ducts, pipes, thermostats, and switches. Technicians must be able to maintain, diagnose, and correct problems throughout the entire system. To do this, they adjust system controls to recommended settings and test the performance of the entire system using special tools and test equipment. Although they are trained to do both, technicians often specialize in either installation or maintenance and repair. Some specialize in one type of equipment – for example, oil burners, solar panels, or commercial refrigerators. Technicians may work for large or small contracting companies or directly for a manufacturer or wholesaler. Those working for smaller operations tend to do both installation and servicing, and work with heating, cooling, and refrigeration equipment. Depending on the size of the company, technicians may work solely on residential or commercial projects, although typically they service both. Service contracts – which involve work for particular customers on a regular basis – are becoming more common. Service agreements help to reduce the seasonal fluctuations of this work.

HVACR (heating, ventilation, air-conditioning, and refrigeration) mechanics and installers are adept at using a variety of tools, including hammers, wrenches, metal snips, electric drills, pipe cutters and benders, measurement gauges, and acetylene torches, to work with refrigerant lines and air ducts. They use voltmeters, thermometers, pressure gauges, manometers, and other testing devices to check airflow, refrigerant pressure, electrical circuits, burners, and other components.

Other craftworkers sometimes install or repair cooling and heating systems. For example, on a large air-conditioning installation job, especially where workers are covered by union contracts, ductwork might be done by sheet metal workers and duct installers; electrical work by electricians; and installation of piping, condensers, and other components by pipelayers, plumbers, pipefitters, and steamfitters.

Working Conditions: Heating, air-conditioning, and refrigeration mechanics and installers work in homes, stores, hospitals, office buildings, and factories – anywhere there is climate-control equipment. They may be assigned to specific jobsites at the beginning of each day, or if they are making service calls, they may be dispatched to jobs by radio, telephone, or pager. Increasingly, employers are using cell phones to coordinate technicians' schedules.

Technicians may work outside in cold or hot weather or in buildings that are uncomfortable because the air-conditioning or heating equipment is broken. Technicians might have to work in awkward or cramped positions and sometimes are required to work in high places. Hazards include electrical shock, burns, muscle strains, and other injuries from handling heavy equipment. Appropriate safety equipment is necessary when handling refrigerants because contact can cause skin damage, frostbite, or blindness. Inhalation of refrigerants when working in confined spaces also is a possible hazard.

The majority of mechanics and installers work at least a 40-hour week. During peak seasons they often work overtime or irregular hours. Maintenance workers, including those who provide maintenance services under contract, often work evening or weekend shifts and are on call. Most employers try to provide a full workweek year-round by scheduling both installation and maintenance work, and many manufacturers and contractors now provide or even require service contracts. In most shops that service both heating and air-conditioning equipment, employment is stable throughout the year.

Education, Training, Qualifications: Because of the increasing sophistication of heating, air-conditioning, and refrigeration systems, employers prefer to hire those with technical school or apprenticeship training. Many mechanics and installers, however, still learn the trade informally on the job. Those who acquire their skills on the job usually begin by assisting experienced technicians.

Many secondary and postsecondary technical and trade schools, junior and community colleges, and the military offer month-long to two-year programs in heating, air-conditioning, and refrigeration. Students study theory, design, and equipment construction, as well as electronics. They also learn the basics of installation, maintenance, and repair. Courses in shop math, mechanical drawing, applied physics and chemistry, blueprint reading, and computer applications provide a good background for those interested in entering this occupation. Some knowledge of plumbing or electrical work also is helpful. A basic understanding of electronics is becoming more important because of the increasing use of this technology in equipment controls. Because technicians frequently deal directly with the public, they should be courteous and tactful, especially when dealing with an aggravated customer. They should also be in good physical condition because they sometimes have to lift and move heavy equipment.

Earnings: Median hourly earnings of heating, air-conditioning, and refrigeration mechanics and installers were $16.78 in 2002. Some earned less than $10.34 an hour, whereas the top 10 percent earned more than $26.20. Apprentices usually begin at about 50 percent of the wage rate paid to experienced workers. In addition to typical benefits such as health insurance and pension plans, some employers pay for work-related training and provide uniforms, company vans, and tools. About 20 percent of workers are members of a union.

Key Contacts: For more information about opportunities for training and employment in this trade, contact local vocational and technical schools; local heating, air-conditioning, and refrigeration contractors; or the nearest office of the state employment service. For information on career opportunities, training, and technician certification, contact:

- **Air Conditioning Contractors of America**: (ACCA) 2800 Shirlington Road, Suite 300, Arlington, VA 22206. Website: www.acca. org.

- **Refrigeration Service Engineers Society**: (RSES) 1666 Rand Rd., Des Plaines, IL 60016-3552. Website: www.rses.org

- **Plumbing-Heating-Cooling Contractors**: (PHCC) 180 S. Washington St., P.O. Box 6808, Falls Church, VA 22040. Website: www. phccweb.org.

- **Sheet Metal and Air Conditioning Contractors' National Association**: 4201 Lafayette Center Dr., Chantilly, VA 20151-1209. Website: www.smacna.org.

- **North American Technician Excellence**: (NATE) 4100 North Fairfax Dr., Suite 210, Arlington, VA 22203. Website: www.natex. org.

Home Appliance Repairers

⇨ **Annual Earnings:** $30,390
⇨ **Education/Training:** High school diploma
⇨ **Outlook:** Average growth

Employment Outlook: Good job prospects are expected as job openings will continue to outnumber job seekers. Although employment of self-employed home appliance repairers is projected to decline, employment of wage and salary workers will increase about as fast as average. The number of home appliances in use is expected to increase with growth in the numbers of households and businesses. Appliances are also becoming more technologically advanced and will increasingly require a skilled technician to diagnose and fix problems.

In recent years, many consumers have tended to purchase new appliances when existing warranties expired rather than invest in repairs on old appliances. However, over the next decade, as more consumers purchase higher priced appliances designed to have much longer lives, they will be more likely to use repair services than to purchase new appliances. Employment is relatively steady during economic downturns because there is still demand for appliance repair services. In addition to new jobs created over the 2002-12 period, openings will arise as home appliance repairers retire or transfer to other occupations.

Self-employment of home appliance repairers will continue to decline due to the availability of manufacturer-sponsored training programs. Manufacturers often make these programs available only to large equipment dealers, thereby discouraging repairers from becoming self-employed or working for small shops. Many self-employed repairers are forced to join larger shops so that they can stay abreast of developments in the industry. Jobs are expected to be increasingly concentrated in larger companies as the numbers of smaller shops and family-owned businesses decline. However, repairers who maintain strong industry relationships may still go into business for themselves.

Nature of Work: Home appliance repairers, often called service technicians, keep home appliances working and help prevent unwanted breakdowns. Some repairers work specifically on small appliances such as microwave and vacuum cleaners; others specialize in major appliances such as refrigerators, dishwashers, washers, and dryers.

Home appliance repairers visually inspect appliances and check for unusual noises, excessive vibration, fluid leaks, or loose parts to determine why the appliances fail to operate properly. They use service manuals, troubleshooting guides, and experience to diagnose particularly difficult problems. Repairers disassemble the appliance to examine its internal parts for signs of wear or corrosion. They follow wiring diagrams and use testing devices to check electrical systems for shorts and faulty connections.

After identifying problems, home appliance repairers replace or repair defective belts, motors, heating elements, switches, gears, or other items. They tighten, align, clean, and lubricate parts as necessary. When repairing appliances with electronic parts, they may replace circuit boards or other electronic components. Home appliance repairers generally install household durable goods such as refrigerators, washing machines, and cooking products. Repairers also answer customers' questions about the care and use of appliances. Repairers write up estimates of the cost of repairs for customers, keep records of parts used and hours worked, prepare bills, and collect payments. Self-employed repairers also deal with the appliance manufacturers to recoup monetary claims for work performed on appliances still under warranty.

Working Conditions: Home appliance repairers who handle portable appliances usually work in repair shops that are generally quiet and adequately lighted and ventilated. Those who repair major appliances usually make service calls to customers' homes. They carry their tools and a number of commonly used parts with them in a truck or van for use on service calls. Repairers may spend several hours a day driving to and from appointments and emergency calls. They may work in clean comfortable rooms such as kitchens, or in damp, dirty, or dusty areas of a home. Repairers sometimes work in cramped and uncomfortable positions when they are replacing parts in hard-to-reach areas of appliances. Repairer jobs are generally not hazardous, but workers must exercise care and follow safety precautions to avoid electrical shocks and injuries when lifting and moving large appliances. When repairing gas appliances and microwave ovens, repairers must be aware of the dangers of gas and radio frequency energy leaks.

Home appliance repairers usually work with little or no direct supervision, a feature of the job that is appealing to many people. Many home appliance repairers work a standard 40-hour week, but they may work overtime and weekend hours in the summer months when they are in high demand to fix air-conditioners and refrigerators. Some repairers work early morning, evening, and weekend shifts and may remain on call in case of emergency.

Education, Training, Qualifications: Employers generally require a high school diploma for home appliance repairer jobs. Repairers of small appliances commonly learn the trade on the job; repairers of large household appliances often receive training in a formal trade school, community college, or directly from the appliance manufacturer. Mechanical and electrical aptitudes are desirable, and those who work in customers' homes must be courteous and tactful.

Employers prefer to hire people with formal training in appliance repair and electronics. Many repairers complete one- or two-year formal training programs in appliance repair and related subjects in high school, private vocational schools, and community colleges. Courses in basic electricity and electronics are increasingly important as more manufacturers install circuit boards and other electronic control systems in home appliances.

The U.S. Environmental Protection Agency (EPA) has mandated that all repairers who buy or work with refrigerants must be certified in their proper handling; a technician must pass a written examination to become certified. Exams are administered by organizations approved by the EPA, such as trade schools, unions, and employer associations. Though no formal training is required for certification, many of these organizations offer training programs designed to prepare workers for the certification examination.

Repairers in large shops or service centers may be promoted to supervisor, assistant service manager, or service manager. Some repairers advance to managerial positions such as regional service manager or parts manager for appliance or tool manufacturers. Experienced repairers who have sufficient funds and knowledge of small-business management may open their own repair shop.

Earnings: Median annual earnings, including commission, of home appliance repairers were $30, 390 in 2002. Some earned less than $18,210; the highest 10 percent earned more than $48,170 a year. Median annual earnings of home appliance repairers working for electronics and appliance stores, which employ the largest number of these workers was $27,340.

Earnings of home appliance repairers vary according to the skill level required to fix equipment, geographic location, and the type of equipment repaired. Because many repairers receive commissions along with their salary, earnings increase along with the number of jobs a repairer can complete in a day. Many larger dealers, manufacturers, and service stores offer typical benefits such as health insurance, sick leave, and retirement and pension programs. Some home appliance repairers belong to the International Brotherhood of Electrical Workers.

Key Contacts: For general information about the work of home appliance repairers, contact any of the following:

- **North American Retail Dealers Association:** 10 E. 22nd Street, Suite 310, Lombard, IL 60148. Website: www.narda.com.

- **National Appliance Service Association:** P.O. Box 2514, Kokomo, IN 46904. Website: http://nasa1.org.

- **United Servicers Association, Inc.:** 6428 Coldwater Canyon Ave., North Hollywood, CA 91606. Website: www.unitedservicers.com.

For information on the NASTeC certification program, contact:

- **International Society of Certified Electronics Technicians:** 3608 Pershing Ave., Fort Worth, TX 76107. Website: www.iscet.org.

Line Installers and Repairers

- ➪ **Annual Earnings:** $23.33 hourly
- ➪ **Education/Training:** High school diploma
- ➪ **Outlook:** Average growth

Employment Outlook: Overall employment of line installers and repairers is expected to grow about as fast as average for all occupations through 2012. Much of this increase will result from growth in the construction and telecommunications industries. With the increasing competition in electrical distribution, many companies are contracting out construction of new lines. The introduction of new technologies, especially fiber-optic cable, has increased the transmission capacity of telephone and cable television networks. Job growth also will stem from the maintenance and modernization of telecommunications networks. Jobs will be generated as telephone and cable television companies expand and improve networks that provide customers with high-speed access to data, video, and graphics. Line installers and repairers will be needed not only to construct and install networks, but also to maintain the ever-growing systems of wires and cables. Besides those due to employment growth, many job openings will result from the need to replace the large number of older workers reaching retirement age.

Little or no growth in employment of electrical powerline installers and repairers is expected through 2012. The demand for electricity has been consistently rising, driving the expansion of powerline networks, which tends to increase employment. However, industry deregulation is pushing companies to cut costs and maintenance, which tends to reduce employment. Because electrical power companies have reduced hiring and training in past years, opportunities are best for workers who possess experience and training.

Nature of Work: Vast networks of wires and cables provide customers with electrical power and communication services. Networks of electrical powerlines deliver electricity from generating plants to customers. Communication networks of telephone and cable television lines provide voice, video, and other communication services. These networks are constructed and maintained by line installers and repairers.

Line installers install new lines by constructing utility poles, towers, and underground trenches to carry the wires and cables. They use a variety of construction equipment, including digger derricks, trenchers, cable plows, and borers. When construction is complete, line installers string cable along the poles, towers, tunnels, and trenches. Other installation duties include setting up service for customers and installing network equipment.

In addition to installation, line installers and repairers also are responsible for maintenance of electrical, telecommunications, and cable television lines. Workers periodically travel in trucks, helicopters, and airplanes to visually inspect the wires and cables. Sensitive monitoring equipment can automatically detect malfunctions on the network, such as loss of current flow. When line repairers identify a problem, they travel to the location of the malfunction and repair or replace defective cables or equipment. Bad weather or natural disasters can cause extensive damage to networks. Line installers and repairers must respond quickly to these emergencies to restore critical utility and communication services. This can often involve working outdoors in adverse weather conditions.

Installation and repair work may require splicing, or joining together, separate pieces of cable. Many communication networks now use fiber-optic cables instead of conventional wire or metal cables. Splicing fiber-optic cable requires specialized equipment that carefully slices, matches, and aligns individual glass fibers. The fibers are joined by either electrical fusion (welding) or a mechanical fixture and gel (glue).

Working Conditions: Line installers and repairers must climb and maintain their balance while working on poles and towers. They lift equipment and work in a variety of positions, such as stooping or kneeling. Their work often requires that they drive utility vehicles, travel long distances, and work outdoors under a variety of weather conditions. Many line installers and repairers work a 40-hour week; however, emergencies may require overtime work. For example, when severe weather damages electrical and communication lines, line installers and repairers may work long and irregular hours to restore service.

Line installers and repairers encounter serious hazards on their jobs and must follow safety procedures to minimize potential danger. They wear safety equipment when entering utility holes and test for the presence of gas before going underground. Electric powerline workers have the most hazardous jobs. High-voltage powerlines can cause electrocution, and line installers and repairers must consequently use electrically insulated protective devices and tools when working with live cables. Powerlines are typically higher than telephone and cable television lines, increasing the risk of severe injury due to falls. To prevent these injuries, line installers and repairers must use fall-protection equipment when working on poles or towers.

Education, Training, Qualifications: Line installers and repairers are trained on the job, and employers require at least a high school diploma. Employers also prefer a technical knowledge of electricity, electronics, and experience obtained through vocational/technical programs, community colleges, or the Armed Forces. Prospective employees should possess a basic knowledge of algebra and trigonometry, and mechanical ability. Customer service and interpersonal skills also are important. Because the work entails lifting heavy objects (many employers require applicants to be able to lift at least 50 pounds), climbing, and other physical activity, applicants should have stamina, strength, and coordination, and must be unafraid of heights. The ability to distinguish colors is necessary because wires and cables may be color-coded.

Many community or technical colleges offer programs in telecommunications, electronics, and/or electricity. Some schools, working with local companies, offer one-year certificate programs that emphasize hands-on field work; graduates get preferential treatment in the hiring process at companies participating in the program. More advanced two-year associate degree programs provide students with a broader knowledge of telecommunications and electrical utilities through courses in electricity, electronics, fiber-optics, and microwave transmission.

Electrical line installers and repairers complete formal apprenticeships or employer training programs. These are sometimes administered jointly by the employer and the union representing the workers. Government safety regulations strictly define the training and education requirements for apprentice electrical line installers.

Line installers and repairers in telephone and cable television companies receive several years of on-the-job training. They also may attend training or take courses provided by equipment manufacturers, schools, unions, or industry training organizations.

Entry-level line installers may be hired as ground workers, helpers, or tree trimmers, who clear branches from telephone and power lines. These workers may advance to positions stringing cable and performing service installations. With experience, they may advance to more sophisticated maintenance and repair positions responsible for increasingly larger portions of the network. Promotion to supervisory or training positions also is possible, but more advanced supervisory positions often require a college diploma.

Earnings: Earnings for line installers and repairers are higher than those in most other occupations that do not require postsecondary education. Median hourly earnings for electrical powerline installers and repairers were $23.33 in 2002. Some earned less than $13.22, and the highest 10 percent earned more than $32.08. Median hourly earnings for telecommunications line installers and repairers were $19.06 in 2002. The lowest 10 percent earned less than $10.31, and the highest 10 percent earned more than $27.70.

Most line installers and repairers belong to unions, principally the Communications Workers of America, the International Brotherhood of Electrical Workers, and the Utility Workers Union of America. For these workers, union contracts set wage rates, wage increases, and the time needed to advance from one job level to the next.

Key Contacts: For more details about employment opportunities, contact the telephone, cable television, or electrical power companies in your community. For general information and some educational resources on line installer and repairer jobs, contact:

- **Communication Workers of America:** 501 3ʳᵈ Street NW, Washington, DC 20001. Website: www.cwa-union.org.

- **International Brotherhood of Electrical Workers:** Telecommunications Department, 1125 15ᵗʰ Street NW, Washington, DC 20005. Website: www.ibew.org.

Maintenance and Repair Workers

↪ **Annual Earnings:** $29,400
↪ **Education/Training:** High school and training
↪ **Outlook:** Excellent

Employment Outlook: General maintenance and repair workers held 1.3 million jobs in 2002. They were employed in almost every industry. About one in five worked in manufacturing industries, almost evenly distributed through all sectors. About 17 percent worked for different government bodies. Others worked for wholesale and retail firms and for real-estate firms that operate office and apartment buildings. Employment of general maintenance and repair workers is expected to grow about as fast as average for all occupations in the decade ahead. However, job openings should be plentiful. Maintenance and repair is a large occupation with significant turnover, and many job openings should result from the need to replace workers who transfer to other occupations or stop working for other reasons.

Employment is related to the number of buildings – for example, office and apartment buildings, stores, schools, hospitals, hotels, and factories – and the amount of equipment needing repair. However, as machinery becomes more advanced and requires less maintenance, the need for general maintenance and repair workers diminishes.

Nature of Work: Most craft workers specialize in one kind of work, such as plumbing or carpentry. General maintenance and repair workers, however, have skills in many different crafts. They repair and maintain machines, mechanical equipment, and buildings, and work on plumbing, electrical, and air-conditioning and heating systems. They build partitions, make plaster or drywall repairs, and fix or paint roofs, windows, doors, floors, woodwork, and other parts of building structures. They also maintain and repair specialized equipment and machinery found in cafeterias, laundries, hospitals, stores, offices, and factories. Typical duties include troubleshooting and fixing faulty electrical switches, repairing air-conditioning motors, and unclogging drains. New buildings sometimes have computer-controlled systems, requiring workers to acquire basic computer skills.

General maintenance and repair workers inspect and diagnose problems and determine the best way to correct them, frequently checking blueprints, repair manuals, and parts catalogs. They replace or fix work or broken parts, where necessary, or make adjustments to correct malfunctioning equipment and machines. General maintenance and repair workers also perform preventive maintenance and ensure that machines continue to run smoothly, building systems operate efficiently, and the physical condition of buildings does not deteriorate. Employees in small establishments, where they are often the only maintenance worker, make all repairs, except for very large or difficult jobs. In larger establishments, their duties may be limited to the general maintenance of everything in a workshop or a particular area.

Working Conditions: General maintenance and repair workers often carry out several different tasks in a single day, at any number of locations. They may work inside a single building or in several different buildings. They may have to stand for long periods, lift heavy objects, and work in uncomfortably hot or cold environments, in awkward and cramped positions, or on ladders. They are subject to electrical shock, burns, falls, cuts, and bruises. Most general maintenance workers work a 40-hour week. Some work evening, night, or weekend shifts, or are on call for emergency repairs. Those employed in small establishments often operate with only limited supervision. Those working in larger establishments frequently are under the direct supervision of an experienced worker.

Education, Training, Qualifications: Many general maintenance and repair workers learn their skills informally on the job. They start as helpers, watching and learning from skilled maintenance workers. Some learn their skills by working as helpers to other repair or construction workers, including carpenters, electricians, or machinery repairers. Necessary skills also can be learned in high school shop classes and postsecondary trade or vocational schools. It generally takes from one to four years of on-the-job training or school, or a combination of both, to become fully qualified – depending on the skill level.

Graduation from high school is preferred for entry into this occupation. High school courses in mechanical drawing, electricity, woodworking, blueprint reading, science, mathematics, and computers are useful. Mechanical aptitude, the ability to use shop mathematics, and manual dexterity are important. Good health is necessary because the job involves a great of walking, standing, reaching, and heavy lifting. Many positions require the ability to work without direct supervision. Many general maintenance and repair workers in large organizations advance to maintenance supervisor or become a craftworker such as an electrician, a heating and air-conditioning mechanic, or a plumber. Within small organizations, promotion opportunities are limited.

Earnings: Median hourly earnings of general maintenance and repair workers were $14.12 in 2002. The highest 10 percent earned more than $22.78. Median hourly earnings in the industries employing the largest numbers of general maintenance and repair workers in 2002 were: local government, $14.83; elementary and secondary schools, $14.01; activities related to real estate, $11.79; lessors of real estate, $11.54; traveler accommodations, $10.58. Some general maintenance and repair workers are members of unions.

Key Contacts: Information about job opportunities may be obtained from local employers and local offices of the state employment service.

Small Engine Mechanics

> ⇨ **Annual Earnings:** $13.03 hourly
> ⇨ **Education/Training:** Vocational training program/ on-the-job training
> ⇨ **Outlook:** Average

Employment Outlook: Employment of small engine mechanics is expected to grow about as fast as the average for all occupations through the year 2012. Most of the job openings are expected to be replacement jobs, because many experienced small engine mechanics are expected to transfer to other occupations, retire, or stop working for other reasons. Job prospects should be especially favorable for persons who complete mechanic training programs.

Growth of personal disposal income should provide consumers with more discretionary dollars to buy motorboats, lawn and garden power equipment, and motorcycles. While advancements in technology will lengthen the interval between routine maintenance, the need for qualified mechanics to perform this service will increase. Employment of motorcycle mechanics should increase as the popularity of motorcycles continues to grow. Greater numbers of people will be entering the 40-and-older age group, the group responsible for the largest segment of marine craft purchases. These potential buyers will expand the market for motorboats, maintaining the demand for qualified mechanics. The building boom will result in an increase in the sales of lawn and garden equipment, increasing the need for mechanics. However, equipment growth may be slowed by trends toward smaller lawns and the contracting out of maintenance to lawn service firms, as well as the tendency of many consumers to dispose of and replace relatively inexpensive items rather than have them repaired.

Nature of Work: Small engine repair mechanics repair and service power equipment ranging from racing motorcycles to chain saws. Like large engines, small engines require periodic service to minimize the chance of breakdowns and keep them operating at peak performance. When a piece of equipment breaks down, mechanics use various techniques to diagnose the source and extent of the problem. The mark of a skilled mechanic is the ability to diagnose mechanical, fuel, and electrical problems and to make repairs in a minimal amount of time. Quick and accurate diagnosis requires problem-solving ability and a thorough knowledge of the equipment's operation.

In larger repair shops, mechanics may use special computerized diagnostic testing equipment as a preliminary tool in analyzing equipment. After pinpointing the problem, the mechanic makes the needed adjustments, repairs, or replacements. Some jobs require minor adjustments. A complete engine overhaul, on the other hand, requires a number of hours to disassemble the engine and replace worn valves, pistons, bearings, and other internal parts.

Small engine mechanics use common hand tools, such as wrenches, pliers, and screwdrivers. They also utilize power tools, such as drills and grinders, when customized repairs warrant their use. Computerized engine analyzers, compression gauges, ammeters and voltmeters, and other testing devices help mechanics locate faulty parts and tune engines. Hoists may be used to lift heavy equipment such as motorcycles, snowmobiles, or motorboats. Mechanics often refer to service manuals for detailed directions and specifications while performing repairs.

Working Conditions: Small engine mechanics usually work in repair shops that are well lighted and ventilated, but are sometimes noisy when engines are tested. Motorboat mechanics may work outdoors at docks or marinas, as well as in all weather conditions, when making repairs aboard boats. They may work in cramped or awkward positions to reach a boat's engine.

During the winter months in the northern United States, mechanics may work fewer than 40 hours a week, because the amount of repair and service work declines when lawnmowers, motorboats, and motorcycles are not in use. Many mechanics work only during the busy spring and summer seasons. However, many schedule time-consuming engine overhauls or work on snowmobiles and snow-blowers during winter downtime. Mechanics may work considerably more than 40 hours a week when demand is strong.

Education, Training, Qualifications: Due to the increasing complexity of motorcycles and motorboats, most employers prefer to hire mechanics who graduate from formal training programs for small engine mechanics. Because the number of these specialized postsecondary programs is limited, most mechanics learn their skills on the job or while working in related occupations. For trainee jobs, employers hire persons with mechanical aptitude who are knowledgeable about the fundamentals of small two- and four-stroke engines. Many trainees develop an interest in mechanics and acquire some basic skills through working on automobiles, motorcycles, motorboats, or outdoor power equipment as a hobby. Others may be introduced to mechanics through vocational automotive training in high school or one of many postsecondary institutions.

Most employers prefer to hire high school graduates for trainee mechanic positions, but will accept applicants with less education if they possess adequate reading, writing, and arithmetic skills. Helpful high school courses include small engine repair, automobile mechanics, science, and business arithmetic.

Knowledge of basic electronics is essential for small engine mechanics, because electronic components control an engine's performance, the vehicle's instruments displays, and a variety of other functions of motorcycles, motorboats, and outdoor power equipment. The skills used as a small engine mechanic generally transfer to other occupations, such as automobile, diesel, or heavy vehicle and mobile equipment mechanics, Experienced mechanics with leadership ability may advance to shop supervisor or service manager jobs. Mechanics with sales ability sometimes become sales representatives or open their own repair shops.

Earnings: Median hourly earnings of motorcycle mechanics were $13.03 in 2002. Median earnings of motorboat mechanics were $13.97, and for outdoor power equipment mechanics median earnings were $11.93. The lowest 10 percent averaged $8.15, and the highest paid earned more than $21.20.

Key Contacts: General information about motorcycle mechanic careers may be obtained from:

- **American Motorcycle Institute**: 3042 West International Speedway Blvd., Daytona Beach, FL 32124. Tel. 800-881-2264. Website: www.amiwrench.com.

- **Motorcycle Mechanics Institute**: 2844 West Deer Valley Rd., Phoenix, AZ 85027. Tel. 800-528-7995.

For general information about motorboat mechanic careers contact:

- **American Marine and Watercraft Institute**: 3042 West International Speedway Blvd., Daytona Beach, FL 32124. Tel. 800-881-2264.

- **Marine Mechanics Institute**: 9751 Delegates Dr., Orlando, FL 32827. Tel. 800-342-9253.

10

Production Occupations

I N THIS CHAPTER WE OUTLINE a few production jobs for people re-entering the workforce. Most of these jobs require some post-secondary education and training. Some are best entered through on-the-job training and apprenticeships. Most are skilled occupations that pay modest wages.

Since most of our production jobs are plentiful, you should have little difficulty finding and changing jobs in these fields. Similar to the jobs outlined in Chapter 9, the jobs profiled here are relatively safe from offshoring. Most of these jobs also are becoming increasingly technical and automated. Technology will continue to transform these workplaces, and workers will be required to learn new skills through on-the-job training programs.

Computer-Control Programmers and Operators

⇨ **Annual Earnings:** $16.00 hourly
⇨ **Education/Training:** Prefer technical and vocational school training
⇨ **Outlook:** Average growth/excellent opportunities

Employment Outlook: Computer-control programmers and operators should have excellent job opportunities. Due to the limited number of people entering training programs, employers are expected to continue to have difficulty finding workers with the necessary skills and knowledge, which means good job opportunities for those with the necessary skills. Employment of computer-controlled machine tool operators is projected to grow more slowly than the average for all occupations through 2012, but employment of numerical tool and process control programmers is expected to grow about as fast as average for all occupations through 2012. Job growth in both occupations will be driven by the increasing use of computer numerically controlled (CNC) machine tools. Advances in CNC machine tools and manufacturing technology will further automate production, boosting CNC operator productivity and limiting employment growth.

Nature of Work: Computer-control programmers and operators use numerically controlled (CNC) machines to cut and shape precision products, such as automobile parts, machine parts, and compressors. CNC machines include machining tools such as lathes, multiaxis spindles, milling machines, and electrical discharge machines (EDM), but the functions formerly performed by human operators are performed by a computer-control module. CNC machines cut away material from a solid block of metal, plastic, or glass – known as a workpiece – to form a finished part. Computer-control programmers and operators normally produce large quantities of one part, although they may produce small batches or one-of-a-kind items.

Before CNC programmers machine a part, they must carefully plan and prepare the operation. First, these workers review three-dimensional computer aided/automated design (CAD) blueprints of the part. Next, they calculate where to cut or bore into the workpiece, how fast to feed the metal into the machine, and how much metal to remove. They then select tools and materials for the job and plan the sequence of cutting and finishing operations.

Next, CNC programmers turn the planned machining operations into a set of instructions. These instructions are translated into a computer aided/automated manufacturing (CAM) program containing a set of commands for the machine to follow. These commands normally are a series of numbers (hence, numerical control) that describes where cuts should occur, what type of cut should be used, and the speed of the cut. CNC programmers and operators check new programs to ensure that the machinery will function properly and that the output will meet specifications. Because a problem with the program could damage costly machinery and cutting tools, computer simulations may be used to check the program instead of a trial run.

After the programming work is completed, CNC operators perform the necessary machining operations. CNC operators position the metal stock on the CNC machine tool – spindle, lathe, milling machine, or other – set the controls, and let the computer make the cuts. Heavier objects may be loaded with the assistance of other workers, autoloaders, a crane, or a forklift. CNC operators detect some problems by listening for specific sounds – for example, a dull cutting tool or excessive vibration. Dull cutting tools are removed and replaced. Operators listen for vibrations and then adjust the cutting speed to compensate. CNC operators also ensure that the workpiece is being properly lubricated and cooled, because the machining of metal products generates a significant amount of heat.

Working Conditions: Most machine shops are clean, well lit, and ventilated. Most modern CNC machines are partially or totally enclosed, minimizing the exposure of workers to noise, debris, and the lubricants used to cool workpieces during machining. Nevertheless, working around high-speed machine tools presents certain dangers, and workers must follow safety precautions. The job requires stamina because operators stand most of the day and, at times, may need to lift moderately heavy workpieces.

Numerical tool and process control programmers work on desktop computers in offices that typically are near, but separate from, the shop floor. These work areas usually are clean, well-lit, and free of machine noise. Numerical tool and process control programmers occasionally need to enter the shop floor to monitor CNC machining operations. On the shop floor, CNC programmers encounter the same hazards and exercise the same safety precautions as do CNC operators.

Most computer-control programmers and operators work a 40-hour week. CNC operators increasingly work evening and weekend shifts as companies justify investments in more expensive machinery by extending hours of operation. Overtime is common during peak production periods.

Education, Training, Qualifications: Computer-control programmers and operators train in various ways – in apprenticeship programs, informally on the job, and in secondary, vocational, or postsecondary schools. Due to a shortage of qualified applicants, many employers teach introductory courses, which provide a basic understanding of metalworking machines, safety, and blueprint reading. A basic knowledge of computers and electronics also is helpful. Experience with machine tools is extremely important. In fact, many entrants to these occupations have previously worked as machinists or machine setters, operators, and tenders. Persons interested in becoming computer-control programmers or operators should be mechanically inclined and able to work independently and do accurate work.

High school courses or vocational school courses in mathematics (algebra and trigonometry), blueprint reading, computer programming, metalworking, and drafting are recommended. Apprenticeship programs consist of shop training and related classroom instruction. In shop training, apprentices learn filing, handtapping, and dowel fitting, as well as the operation of various machine tools. Classroom instruction includes math, physics, programming, blueprint reading, CAD software, safety, and shop practices. All skilled computer-control programmers and operators need an undestanding of the machining process, including the complex physics that occur at the cutting point. Thus, most training programs teach CNC operations on manual machines prior to operating CNC machines. A growing number of computer-control programmers and operators receive most of their formal training from community or technical colleges. Less skilled CNC operators may need only a couple of weeks of on-the-job training. Qualifications for CNC programmers vary widely depending on the complexity of the job. Employers often prefer skilled machinists or those with technical school training.

Earnings: Median hourly earnings of computer-controlled machine tool operators, metal and plastic, were $13.97 in 2002. Some earned less than $9.14, whereas the top 10 percent earned more than $21.27. Median hourly earnings of numerical tool and process control programmers were $18.04 in 2002. The lowest 10 percent earned less than $11.53, while the top 10 percent earned more than $27.37.

Key Contacts: For general information about computer-control program-mers and operators, contact:

- **Precision Machined Products Association:** 6700 West Snowville Road, Brecksville, OH 44141-3292. Website: www.pmpa.org.

For a list of training centers and apprenticeship programs, contact:

- **National Tooling and Machining Association:** 9300 Livingston Road, Fort Washington, MD 20744. Website: www.ntma.org.

For occupational information, including a list of training programs, contact:

- **Precision Metalforming Association Educational Foundation:** 6363 Oak Tree Blvd., Independence, OH 44131-2500. Website: www.pmaef.org.

Food-Processing Occupations

⇨ **Annual Earnings:** $25,500
⇨ **Education/Training:** Education/on-the-job training
⇨ **Outlook:** Average growth

Employment Outlook: Overall employment in the food-processing occupations is expected to grow as fast as average for all occupations through 2012. Increasingly, cheaper meats from abroad will have a negative effect on domestic employment in many food-processing occupations. Job growth will be concentrated at the manufacturing level, as more cutting and processing of meat shifts from retail stores to food-processing plants. Nevertheless, job opportunities should be available at all levels of the occupation due to the need to replace experienced workers who transfer to other occupations or leave the labor force.

As the nation's population grows, the demand for meat, poultry, and seafood should continue to increase. Marketing by the poultry industry is likely to increase the demand for chicken and ready-to-heat products. Similarly the development of prepared food products that are lower in fat and more nutritious is likely to stimulate the consumption of red meat. The trend toward preparing case-ready meat at the processing level also should contribute to demand for animal slaughterers and meatpackers. Employment growth of lesser skilled meat, poultry, and fish cutters and trimmers – who work primarily in animal slaughtering and processing plants – is expected to increase about as fast as the average for all occupations in coming years. Fish cutters will be in demand, as the task of preparing ready-to-heat fish goods gradually shifts from retail stores to processing plants. Advances in fish farming, or "aquaculture," should help meet the growing demand for fish and produce opportunities for fish cutters.

Employment of more highly skilled butchers and meatcutters, who work primarily in retail stores, is expected to decline. Automation and the consolidation of the animal slaughtering and processing industries are enabling employers to transfer employment from higher paid butchers to lower-wage slaughterers and meatpackers in meatpacking plants. At present, most red meat arrives at grocery stores partially cut up, but a growing share of meat is being delivered prepackaged, with additional fat removed, to wholesalers and retailers. This trend is resulting in less work and, thus, fewer jobs for retail butchers.

While high-volume production equipment limits the demand for bakers in manufacturing, overall employment of bakers is expected to increase about as fast as average due to growing numbers of large wholesale bakers, in-store and specialty shops, and traditional bakeries. The numbers of specialty bread and bagel shops have been growing, spurring demand for bread and pastry bakers.

Employment of food batchmakers, food and tobacco cooking and roasting machine operators and tenders is expected to grow more slowly than average. As more of this work is being done at the manufacturing level rather than at the retail level, potential gains will be offset by productivity gains from automated cooking and roasting equipment. All other food processing workers should experience average growth in their occupational field.

Nature of Work: Food-processing occupations include many different types of workers who process raw food products into the finished goods sold by grocers or wholesalers, restaurants, or institutional food services. Butchers and meat, poultry and fish cutters and trimmers are employed at different stages in the process by which animal carcasses are converted into manageable pieces of meat, known as boxed meat, that are suitable for sale to wholesalers and retailers. Meat, poultry, and fish cutters and trimmers commonly work in animal slaughtering and processing plants, while butchers and meatcutters usually are employed at the retail level. As a result, the nature of these jobs varies significantly.

In animal slaughtering and processing plants, slaughterers and meatpackers slaughter cattle, hogs, goats, and sheep and cut the carcasses into large wholesale cuts, such as rounds, loins, ribs, and chucks, to facilitate the handling, distribution, and marketing of meat. In some plants, slaughterers and meatpackers also further process the large parts into cuts that are ready for retail use. These workers also produce hamburger meat and meat trimmings which are used to prepare sausages, luncheon meats, and other fabricated meat products. Slaughterers and meatpackers usually work on assembly lines, with each individual responsible for only a few of the many cuts needed to process a carcass.

In grocery stores, butchers and meatcutters separate wholesale cuts of meat into retail cuts or individually sized servings. They cut meat into steaks and chops, shape and tie roasts, and grind beef for sale as chopped meat. Butchers and meatcutters in retail food stores may also weigh, wrap, and label the cuts of meat, arrange them in refrigerated cases for display, and prepare special cuts to fill unique orders.

Poultry cutters and trimmers slaughter and cut up chickens, turkeys, and other types of poultry. Although the poultry-processing industry is becoming increasingly automated, many jobs, such as trimming, packing, and deboning, are still done manually. Most perform routine cuts on poultry as it moves along production lines. Fish cutters and trimmers are likely to be employed in both manufacturing and retail establishments. These workers primarily scale, cut, and dress fish by removing the head, scales, and other inedible portions and cutting the fish into steaks or fillets.

Bakers mix and bake ingredients in accordance with recipes to produce varying quantities of breads, pastries, and other baked goods. Bakers are commonly employed in grocery stores and specialty shops and produce small quantities of breads, pastries, and other baked goods for consumption on premises or for sale as specialty baked goods. In manufacturing, bakers produce goods in large quantities, using high-volume mixing machines, ovens, and other equipment. Goods produced in large quantities usually are available for sale through distributors, grocery stores, or manufacturers' outlets.

Working Conditions: Working conditions vary by type and size of establishment. In animal slaughtering and processing plants and large retail food establishments, butchers and meatcutters work in large meatcutting rooms equipped with power machines and conveyors. In small retail markets, the butcher or fish cleaner may work in a cramped space behind the meat or fish counter. To prevent viral and bacterial infections, work areas must be kept clean and sanitary.

Butchers and meatcutters, poultry and fish cutters and trimmers, and slaughterer and meatpackers often work in cold, damp rooms, which are refrigerated to prevent meat from spoiling and are damp because meat cutting generates large amounts of blood, condensation, and fat. Cool, damp floors increase the likelihood of slips and falls. In addition, cool temperatures, long periods of standing, and repetitive physical tasks make the work tiring. As a result, butchers and meat, poultry, and fish cutters are more susceptible to injury than are most other workers. Meatpacking plants had one of the highest incidences of work-related injury and illness of any industry in 2002. Injuries include cuts and occasional amputations, which occur when knives, cleavers, or power tools are used improperly. Also, repetitive slicing and lifting often lead to cumulative trauma injuries, such as carpal tunnel syndrome. Employers promote ways to reduce injury, but workers in this occupation still face the serious threat of disabling injuries.

Most traditional bakers work in bakeries, cake shops, hot-bread shops, hotels, restaurants, and cafeterias. They also may work in the bakery departments of supermarkets and cruise ships. Bakers may work under hot and noisy conditions. Also, bakers typically work under strict order deadlines and critical time-sensitive baking requirements, both of which can induce stress. Bakers usually work in shifts and may work early mornings, evenings, weekends, and holidays, While many bakers often work as part of a team, they also may work alone when baking particular items. Bakers in retail establishments may be required to serve customers.

Other food processing workers, such as food batchmakers, food and tobacco roasting, baking, and drying machine operators, and food cooking machine operators and tenders, typically work in production areas that are specially designed for food preservation or processing. Food batchmakers, in particular, work in kitchen-type, assembly-line production facilities. Because this work involves food, work areas must meet governmental sanitation regulations. The ovens, as well as the motors of blenders, mixers, and other equipment, often make work areas very warm and noisy. There are some hazards, such as burns, created by the equipment that these workers use. Food batchmakers; food and tobacco roasting, baking, and drying machine operators; and food cooking machine operators and tenders spend a great deal of time on their feet and generally work a regular 40-hour week that may include evening and night shifts.

Education, Training, Qualifications: Training varies widely among food-processing occupations. However, most manual food-processing workers require little or no training prior to being hired.

Most butchers and poultry and fish cutters and trimmers acquire their skills on the job through formal and informal training programs. The length of training varies significantly. Simple cutting operations require a few days to learn, while more complicated tasks, such as eviscerating slaughtered animals, generally require several months to learn. The training period for highly skilled butchers at the retail level may be one or two years.

Generally, on-the-job trainees begin by doing less difficult jobs, such as making simple cuts or removing bones. After demonstrating skill with various meatcutting tools, trainees learn to divide carcasses into wholesale cuts and wholesale cuts into retail and individual portions. Trainees may also learn to roll and tie roasts, prepare sausage, and cure meat. Those employed in retail food establishments often are taught operations such as inventory control, meat buying, and record keeping. In addition, growing concern about the safety of meats has led employers to offer their employees numerous safety seminars and extensive training in food safety.

Skills that are important to meat, poultry, and fish cutters and trimmers include manual dexterity, good depth perception, color discrimination, and good hand-eye coordination. Physical strength often is needed to lift and move heavy pieces of meat. Butchers and fish cleaners who wait on customers should have a pleasant personality, a neat appearance, and the ability to communicate clearly. In some states, a health certificate is required for employment.

Bakers often start as apprentices or trainees. Apprentice bakers usually start in craft bakeries, while in-store bakeries, such as those in supermarkets, often employ trainees. Bakers need to be skilled in baking, icing, and decorating. They also need to be able to follow instructions, have an eye for detail, and communicate well with others. Knowledge of bakery products and ingredients, as well as mechanical mixing equipment, is important. Many apprentice bakers participate in correspondence study and may work towards a certificate in baking. The complexity of skills required for certification as a baker is often underestimated. Bakers need to know about applied chemistry, ingredients and nutrition, government health and sanitation regulations, business concepts, and production processes, including how to operate and maintain machinery. Modern food plants typically use high-speed, automated equipment that often is operated by computers.

Food-machine operators and tenders usually are trained on the job, a process that can last anywhere from a month to a year, depending on the complexity of the tasks and the number of products involved. A degree in the appropriate area – dairy processing for those working in dairy product operations, for example – is helpful for advancement to lead worker or a supervisory role. Most food batchmakers participate in on-the-job training, usually from about a month to a year. Some food batchmakers learn their trade through an approved apprenticeship program.

Food-processing workers in retail or wholesale operations may progress to supervisory jobs, such as department managers or team leaders in supermarkets. A few of these workers may become buyers for wholesalers or supermarket chains. Some may open their own markets or bakeries. In processing plants, workers may advance to supervisory positions or become team leaders.

Earnings: Earnings vary by industry, skill, geographic region, and educational level. Median annual earnings of butchers and meatcutters were $25,500 in 2002. Some earned less than $15,490 and the highest-paid 10 percent earned more than $42,330 annually. Butchers and meatcutters employed at the retail level typically earn more than those employed in manufacturing.

Meat, poultry, and fish cutters and trimmers typically earn less than butchers and meatcutters. In 2002, median annual earnings for these lower skilled workers were $17,820. The highest 10 percent earned more than $24,840, while the lowest 10 percent earned less than $14,270.

Median annual earnings of bakers were $20,580 in 2002. The highest paid earned more than $33,470 and the lowest 10 percent earned less than $13,930. Median annual earnings of food batchmakers were $21,920 in 2002. Median annual earnings for slaughterers and meatpackers were $20,370; for food cooking machine operators, $21,860; and for food and tobacco roasting, baking, and drying machine operators and tenders, $23,260.

Food-processing workers generally received typical benefits, including pension plans for union members or those employed by grocery stores. However, poultry workers rarely earned substantial benefits. In 2002, 25 percent of all butchers and other meat, poultry, and fish processing workers were union members or were covered by a union contract. Sixteen percent of all bakers and 18 percent of all food batchmakers also were union members or were covered by a union contract.

Key Contacts: State employment service offices can provide information about job openings for food-processing occupations.

Machinists

⬦ **Annual Earnings:** $15.66
⬦ **Education/Training:** Apprenticeship program/high school, community, or technical program
⬦ **Outlook:** Slower than average growth /good job opportunities

Employment Outlook: Despite projected slower-than-average employment growth, job opportunities for machinists should continue to be excellent. The number of workers obtaining the skills and knowledge necessary to fill machinist jobs is expected to be less than the number of job openings arising each year from employment growth and from the need to replace machinists who transfer to other occupations or retire.

Employment of machinists is expected to grow more slowly than the average for all occupations over the 2002-12 period because of rising productivity among these workers. Machinists will become more efficient as a result of the expanded use of, and improvements in, technologies such as CNC machine tools, autoloaders, and high-speed machining. This allows fewer machinists to accomplish the same amount of work previously performed by more workers. Technology is not expected to affect the employment of machinists as significantly as that of most other production occupations because machinists monitor and maintain many automated systems. Due to modern production techniques, employers prefer workers, such as machinists, who have a wide range of skills and are capable of performing almost any task in a machine shop.

Employment levels are influenced by economic cycles – as the demand for machined goods falls, machinists involved in production may be laid off or forced to work fewer hours.

Nature of Work: Machinists use machine tools, such as lathes, milling machines, and machining centers, to produce precision metal parts. They use their knowledge of the working properties of metals and their skill with machine tools to plan and carry out the operations needed to make machined products that meet precise specifications.

Before they machine a part, machinists must carefully plan and prepare the operation. These workers first review blueprints or written specifications for the job. They calculate where to cut or bore into the piece of metal being shaped, select the tools and materials for the job, plan the sequence of operations, and mark the metal to show where cuts should be made. After this layout work is completed, machinists perform the necessary machining operations. After the work is completed, machinists use both simple and highly sophisticated measuring tools to check the accuracy of their work against blueprints.

Some machinists may produce large quantities of one part, especially parts requiring the use of complex operations and great precision. Many modern machine tools are computer numerically controlled (CNC). Because most machinists train in CNC programming, they may write basic programs themselves and often modify programs in response to problems encountered during test runs.

Working Conditions: Today, most machine shops are relatively clean, well lit, and ventilated. Many computer-controlled machines are partially or totally enclosed, minimizing the exposure of workers to noise, debris, and the lubricants used to cool workpieces during machining. Nevertheless, working around machine tools presents certain dangers, and workers must follow safety precautions. Machinists wear protective equipment, such as safety glasses to shield against bits of flying metal and earplugs to reduce machinery noise. The job requires stamina, because machinists stand most of the day and, at times, may need to lift moderately heavy workpieces. Modern factories extensively employ autoloaders and overhead cranes, reducing heavy lifting.

Most machinists work a 40-hour week. Evening and weekend shifts are becoming more common as companies justify investments in more expensive machinery by extending hours of operation. Overtime is common during peak production periods.

Education, Training, Qualifications: Machinists train in apprenticeship programs, informally on the job, and in high schools, vocational schools, or community or technical colleges. Experience with machine tools is helpful. Many entrants previously have worked as machine setters, operators, or tenders. Persons interested in becoming machinists should be mechanically inclined, have good problem-solving abilities, be able to work independently, and be able to do highly accurate work (tolerances may reach 1/10,000th of an inch) that requires concentration and physical effort.

High school or vocational school courses in mathematics (especially trigonometry), blueprint reading, metalworking, and drafting are highly recommended. Apprenticeship programs consist of shop training and related classroom instruction lasting up to four years. In shop training, apprentices work almost full time and are supervised by an experienced machinist while learning to operate various machine tools. Classroom instruction includes math, physics, materials science, blueprint reading, mechanical drawing, and quality and safety practices. In addition, as machine shops have increased their use of computer-controlled equipment, training in the operation and programming of CNC machine tools has become essential.

Apprenticeship classes are taught in cooperation with local community or vocational colleges. A growing number of machinists learn the trade through two-year associate degree programs at community or technical colleges.

Graduates of these programs still need significant on-the-job experience before they are fully qualified. As new automation is introduced, machinists normally receive additional training to update their skills. This training usually is provided by a representative of the equipment manufacturer or a local technical school.

Earnings: Median hourly earnings of machinists were $15.66 in 2002. Some earned less than $9.57, while the top 10 percent earned more than $23.17. Median hourly earnings in the manufacturing industries employing the largest number of machinists in 2002 ranged from $16.75 in metalworking machinery manufacturing to $15.18 in motor vehicle parts manufacturing.

Key Contacts: For general information about machinists, contact:

- **Precision Machined Products Association**: 6700 West Snowville Road, Brecksville, OH 44141-3292. Website: www.pmpa.org.

For a list of training centers and apprenticeship programs, contact:

- **National Tooling and Machining Association**: 9300 Livingston Rd., Fort Washington, MD 20744. Website: www.ntma.org.

For general occupational information and a list of training programs, contact:

- **Precision Metalforming Association Educational Foundation**: 6363 Oak Tree Blvd., Independence, OH 44131-2500. Website: www.pmaef.org.

Tool and Die Makers

- ⇨ **Annual Earnings:** $20.54 hourly
- ⇨ **Education/Training:** Apprenticeship/postsecondary program
- ⇨ **Outlook:** Little growth/good job opportunities

Employment Outlook: Applicants with the appropriate skills and background should enjoy excellent opportunities for tool and die maker jobs. The number of workers receiving training in this field is expected to continue to be fewer than the number of openings created each year by workers who retire or transfer to other occupations.

Despite expected excellent employment opportunities, little or no growth in employment of tool and die makers is projected over the 2002-12 period because advancements in automation, including CNC machine tools and computer-aided design, should improve worker productivity, thus limiting employment. On the other hand, tool and die makers play a key role in building and maintaining advanced automated manufacturing equipment. As firms invest in new equipment, modify production techniques, and implement product design changes more rapidly, they will continue to rely heavily on skilled tool and die makers for retooling.

Nature of Work: Tool and die makers are among the most highly skilled workers in manufacturing. These workers produce tools, dies, and special guiding and holding devices that enable machines to manufacture a variety of products we use daily – from clothing and furniture to heavy equipment and parts for aircraft. Toolmakers craft precision tools and machines that are used to cut, shape, and form metal and other materials. They also produce jigs and fixtures (devices that hold metal while it is bored, stamped, or drilled) and gauges and other measuring devices. Die makers construct metal forms (dies) that are used to shape metal in stamping and forging operations. They also make metal molds for diecasting and for molding plastics, ceramics, and composite materials.

To perform these functions, tool and die makers employ many types of machine tools and precision measuring instruments. As a result, tool and die makers are knowledgeable in machining operations, mathematics, and blueprint reading. In fact, tool and die makers often are considered highly specialized machinists. The main difference between tool and die makers and machinists is that machinists normally make a single part during the production process, while tool and die makers make parts and machines used in the production process.

Working from blueprints, tool and die makers first must plan the sequence of operations necessary to manufacture the tool or die. Next, they measure and mark the pieces of metal that will be cut to form parts of the final product. At this point, tool and die makers cut, drill, or bore the part as required, checking to ensure that the final product meets specifications. Finally, these workers assemble the parts and perform finishing jobs such as filing, grinding, and polishing surfaces. Modern technology has changed the ways in which tool and die makers perform their jobs. These works often use computer-aided design (CAD) to develop products and parts. Specifications entered into computer programs can be used to electronically develop drawings for the required tools and dies. Numerical tool and process control programmers use computer aided manufacturing (CAM) programs to convert electronic drawings into computer programs that contain instructions for a sequence of cutting tool operations.

After machining the parts, tool and die makers carefully check the accuracy of the parts using many tools, including coordinate measuring machines (CMM), which use software and sensor arms to compare dimensions of the part to the electronic blueprints. Next, they assemble the different parts into a functioning machine. Finally, they set up a test run using the tools or dies they have made to make sure the manufactured parts meet specifications. If problems occur, they compensate by adjusting the tools or dies.

Working Conditions: Tool and die makers usually work in toolrooms. These areas are quieter than the production floor because there are fewer machines in use at one time. They are also generally kept clean and cool to minimize heat-related expansion of metal workpieces and to accommodate the growing number of computer-operated machines. To minimize the exposure of workers to moving parts, machines have guards and shields. Most computer-controlled machines are totally enclosed, minimizing the exposure of workers to noise, dust, and the lubricants used to cool workpieces during machining. Tool and die makers also must follow safety rules and wear protective equipment, such as safety glasses to shield against bits of flying metal, earplugs to protect against noise, and gloves and masks to reduce exposure to hazardous lubricants and cleaners. These workers also need stamina because they often spend much of their day on their feet and may do moderately heavy lifting.

Companies employing tool and die makers have traditionally operated only one shift per day. Overtime and weekend work are common, especially during peak production periods.

Education, Training, Qualifications: Most tool and die makers learn their trade through four or five years of education and training in formal apprenticeships or postsecondary programs. Apprenticeship programs include a mix of classroom instruction and job experience and often require 10,400 hours, or about five years to complete. According to most employers, these apprenticeship programs are the best way to learn all aspects of tool and die making. A growing number of tool and die makers receive most of their formal classroom training from community and technical colleges, sometimes in conjunction with an apprenticeship program. Even after completing their apprenticeship, tool and die makers still need years of experience to become highly skilled. Most specialize in making certain types of tools, molds, or dies.

Tool and die makers learn to operate a variety of machines and hand tools. Classroom training usually consists of mechanical drawing, tool designing, tool programming, blueprint reading, and mathematics courses, including algebra, geometry, trigonometry, and basic statistics. Tool and die makers increasingly must have good computer skills to work with CAD technology, CNC machine tools, and computerized measuring machines.

Workers who become tool and die makers without completing formal apprenticeships generally acquire their skills through a combination of informal on-the-job training and classroom instruction at a vocational school or junior college. They often begin as machine operators and gradually take on more difficult assignments. Many machinists become tool and die makers.

Because tools and dies must meet strict specifications – precision to 1/10,000th of an inch is common – the work of tool and die makers requires skill with precision measuring devices and a high degree of patience and attention to detail. Good eyesight is essential. Persons entering this occupation also should be mechanically inclined, able to work and solve problems independently, and capable of doing work that requires concentration and physical effort.

Earnings: Median hourly earnings of tool and die makers were $20.54 in 2002. The lowest 10 percent had earnings of less than $12.97, while the top 10 percent earned more than $30.74. Those working in motor vehicle parts manufacturing averaged the highest earnings at $25.64.

Key Contacts: For career information and to have inquiries on training and employment referred to member companies, contact:

- **Precision Machined Products Association:** 6700 West Snowville Road, Bresckville, OH 44141-3292. Website: www.pmpa.org.

For lists of schools and employers with tool and die apprenticeship and training programs, contact:

- **National Tooling and Machining Association:** 9300 Livingston Road, Ft. Washington, MD 20744. Website: www.ntma.org.

For information on careers, education and training, earnings, and apprenticeship opportunities in metalworking, contact:

- **Precision Metalforming Association Educational Foundation:** 6363 Oak Tree Blvd., Independence, OH 44131-2500. Website: www.pmaef.org.

Welding, Soldering, and Brazing Workers

⇨ **Annual Earnings:** $14.02 hourly
⇨ **Education/Training:** On-the-job training/high school/ vocational school
⇨ **Outlook:** Average growth/excellent job opportunities

Employment Outlook: Employment of welding, soldering, and brazing workers is expected to grow about as fast as the average for all occupations through 2012. However, job prospects should be excellent, as many potential entrants who could be welders may prefer to attend college or do work that has more comfortable working conditions. In addition, many openings will occur as workers retire or leave the occupation for other reasons.

The major factor affecting employment of welders is the economic health of the industries in which they work. Because almost every manufacturing industry uses welding at some stage of manufacturing or in the repair and maintenance of equipment, a strong economy will keep demand for welders high. A downturn affecting industries such as auto manufacturing, construction, or petroleum, however, would have a negative impact on the employment of welders in those areas, and could cause some layoffs. Levels of government funding for shipbuilding as well as for infrastructure repairs and improvements are expected to be another important determinant of the future number of welding jobs.

Regardless of the state of the economy, the pressures to improve productivity and hold down labor costs are leading many companies to invest more in automation, especially computer-controlled and robotically controlled welding machinery. This will reduce the demand for some low-skilled welders, solderers, and brazers because these simple, repetitive jobs are being automated. The growing use of automation, however, should increase demand for higher skilled welding, soldering, and brazing machine setters, operators, and tenders. Welders working on construction projects or in equipment repair will not be affected by technology change to the same extent, because their jobs are not as easily automated.

Nature of Work: Welding is the most common way of permanently joining metal parts. In this process, heat is applied to metal pieces, melting and fusing them to form a permanent bond. Because of its strength, welding is used in shipbuilding, automobile manufacturing and repair, aerospace applications, and thousands of other manufacturing activities. Welding is also used to join beams when constructing buildings, bridges, and other structures, and to join pipes in pipelines, power plants, and refineries.

Welders use many types of welding equipment set up in a variety of positions, such as flat, vertical, horizontal, and overhead. They may perform manual welding, in which the work is entirely controlled by the welder, or semiautomatic welding, in which the welder uses machinery, such as a wire feeder, to perform welding tasks. Skilled welding, soldering, and brazing workers generally plan their work from drawings or specifications or use their knowledge of fluxes and base metals to analyze the parts to be joined. These workers then select and set up welding equipment, execute the planned welds, and examine welds to ensure that they meet standards or specifications. Highly skilled welders often are trained to work with a wide variety of materials in addition to steel, such as titanium, aluminum, or plastics. Some welders have more limited duties. They perform routine jobs that already have been planned and laid out and do not require extensive knowledge or welding techniques.

Working Conditions: Welding, soldering, and brazing workers often are exposed to a number of hazards, including the intense light created, poisonous fumes, and very hot materials. They wear safety shoes, goggles, hoods with protective lenses, and other devices designed to prevent burns and eye injuries and to protect them from falling objects. They normally work in well-ventilated areas to limit their exposure to fumes. Automated welding, soldering, and brazing machine operators are not exposed to as many dangers, however, and a face shield or goggles provide adequate protection for these workers.

Welders and cutters may work outdoors, often in inclement weather, or indoors, sometimes in a confined area designed to contain sparks and glare. Outdoors, they may work on a scaffold or platform high off the ground. In addition, they may be required to lift heavy objects and work in a variety of awkward positions, while bending, stooping, or standing to perform work overhead.

Although about 55 percent of welders, solderers, and brazers work a 40-hour week, overtime is common, and some welders work up to 70 hours per week. Welders also may work in shifts as long as 12 hours. Some welders, solderers, brazers, and machine operators work in factories that operate around the clock, necessitating shift work.

Education, Training, Qualifications: Training for welding, soldering, and brazing workers can range from a few weeks of school or on-the-job training for low-skilled positions to several years of combined school and on-the-job training for highly skilled jobs. Formal training is available in high schools, vocational schools, and postsecondary institutions, such as vocational-technical institutes, community colleges, and private welding schools. The military services operate welding schools as well. Some employers provide training. Courses in blueprint reading, shop mathematics, mechanical drawing, physics, chemistry, and metallurgy are helpful. Knowledge of computers is gaining importance, especially for welding, soldering, and brazing machine operators, who are becoming responsible for the programming of computer-controlled machines, including robots.

Welding, soldering, and brazing workers need good eyesight, hand-eye coordination, and manual dexterity. They should be able to concentrate on detailed work for long periods and be able to bend, stoop, and work in awkward positions. In addition, welders increasingly need to be willing to receive training and perform tasks in other production jobs.

Earnings: Median hourly earnings of welders, solderers, and brazers were $14.02 in 2002. Some workers earned less than $9.41 while the highest 10 percent earned over $21.79. Median hourly earnings of welding, soldering, and brazing machine setters, operators, and tenders were $13.90. The lowest 10 percent earned less than $9.36 while the highest 10 percent earned more than $24.60. Median hourly earnings in motor vehicle parts manufacturing, the industry employing the largest numbers of welding machine operators in 2002, were $18.29.

Key Contacts: For information on training opportunities and jobs for welding, soldering, and brazing workers, contact local employers, the local office of the state employment service, or schools providing welding, soldering, and brazing training. Information on careers and educational opportunities in welding is available from:

- **American Welding Society**: 550 NW Lejeune Road, Miami, FL 33126-5699. Website: www.aws.org.

11

Transportation and
Material Moving Occupations

I F MANY OF YOUR INTERESTS and skills relate to transportation and material moving occupations, be sure to survey the jobs outlined in this final chapter. Many job and career opportunities are available for those who enjoy these lines of work. While these are not high paying jobs, they are plentiful and can lead to long-term job security. Similar to the jobs profiled in the previous two chapters, our transportation and material moving occupations are some of today's safest jobs – relatively recession-proof and difficult to offshore.

Since most to the following jobs require a basic education and a limited amount of training, they are especially attractive for individuals re-entering the job market who need to quickly find a job but who may have limited work experience. Most of these jobs require a high school diploma and some specialized training. A few jobs, especially bus, truck, and taxi drivers, require a license and a good driving record.

If you are re-entering the job market with little work experience, few marketable skills, or some red flags in your background, consider getting started in one of the jobs profiled in this chapter. They may provide an important first step for your new work life.

Bus Drivers

⇨ **Annual Earnings:** $14.22 hourly
⇨ **Education/Training:** Commercial driver's license
⇨ **Outlook:** Average growth

Employment Outlook: Persons seeking jobs as bus drivers should encounter good opportunities. Individuals who have good driving records and who are willing to work part time or an irregular schedule should have the best job prospects. School bus driving jobs, particularly in rapidly growing suburban areas, should be the easiest to acquire because most are part-time positions with high turnover and minimal training requirements. Those seeking higher paying intercity and public transit bus driver positions may encounter competition. Employment prospects for motorcoach drivers will fluctuate with the cyclical nature of the economy, as demand for motorcoach services is very dependent on tourism.

Employment of bus drivers is expected to increase about as fast as the average for all occupations through the year 2012, primarily to meet the transportation needs of the growing general population and the school-age population. Many additional job openings are expected to occur each year because of the need to replace workers who take jobs in other occupations or who retire.

Nature of Work: Bus drivers are essential in providing passengers with an alternative to their automobiles or other forms of transportation. Intercity bus drivers transport people between regions of a state or of the country; local-transit bus drivers do so within a metropolitan area or county; motor coach drivers take clients on charter excursions and tours; and school bus drivers take youngsters to and from school and related events. Drivers pick up and drop off passengers at bus stops, stations, or, in the case of students, at regularly scheduled neighborhood locations based on strict time schedules. Drivers must operate vehicles safely, especially when traffic is heavier than normal. However, they cannot let light traffic put them ahead of schedule so that they miss passengers.

Local-transit and intercity bus drivers report to their assigned terminal or garage where they stock up on tickets or transfers and prepare trip report forms. In some transportation firms, maintenance departments are responsible for keeping vehicles in good condition. In other firms, drivers may be responsible for keeping their vehicles in good condition. During their shift these drivers collect fares; answer questions about schedules, routes, and transfer points; and sometimes announce stops.

Motorcoach drivers transport passengers on charter trips and sightseeing tours. Drivers routinely interact with clients and tour guides to make the trip as comfortable and informative as possible. They are responsible for keeping to strict schedules, adhering to the guidelines of the tours' itinerary, and ensuring the overall success of the trip. These drivers act as a customer service representative, tour guide, program director, and safety guide. Trips frequently last more than one day. The driver may be away for more than a week if assigned to an extended tour.

School bus drivers usually drive the same routes each day, stopping to pick up pupils in the morning and return them to their homes in the afternoon. Some school bus drivers also transport students and teachers on field trips or to sporting events. In addition to driving, some school bus drivers work part-time in the school system as janitors, mechanics, or classroom assistants when not driving buses.

Working Conditions: Driving a bus through heavy traffic while dealing with passengers is more stressful and fatiguing than physically strenuous. Intercity bus drivers may work nights, weekends, and holidays and often spend nights away from home, during which they stay in hotels at company expense. Drivers with seniority and regular routes have routine weekly work schedules, but others do not have regular schedules and must be prepared to work on short notice. They report for work only when called for a charter assignment or to drive extra buses on a regular route.

School bus drivers work only when school is in session. Many work 20 hours a week or less, driving one or two routes in the morning and afternoon. Drivers taking field or athletic trips, or who also have midday kindergarten routes, may work more hours a week.

Regular local-transit bus drivers usually have a five-day workweek; Saturdays and Sundays are considered regular workdays. Some drivers work evenings and after midnight. To accommodate commuters, many work "split shifts," for example, 6am to 10am and 3pm to 7pm, with time off in between. Tour and charter bus drivers may work any day and all hours of the day, including weekends and holidays. Their hours are dictated by the charter trips booked and the scheduled prearranged itinerary of tours. However, all bus drivers must comply with the limits placed on drivers by the Department of Transportation's rules and regulations concerning hours of service.

Education, Training, Qualifications: Qualifications and standards for bus drivers are established by state and federal regulations. Federal regulations require drivers who operate commercial vehicles to hold a commercial driver's license (CDL) from the state in which they live. To qualify for a commercial driver's license, applicants must pass a written test on rules and regulations and then demonstrate that they can operate a bus safely. A national databank permanently records all driving violations incurred by persons who hold commercial licenses. A state may not issue a CDL to a driver who has already had a license suspended or revoked in another state. A driver with a CDL must accompany trainees until the trainees get their own CDL. There are physical requirements mandated for bus drivers as well. Age requirements may vary by state and employer.

All drivers must be able to read and speak English well enough to read road signs, prepare reports, and communicate with law enforcement officials and the public. Many employers prefer high school graduates and require a written test of ability to follow complex bus schedules. Because bus drivers deal with passengers, they must be courteous. They need an even temperament and emotional stability because driving in heavy, fast-moving, or stop-and-go traffic and dealing with passengers can be stressful.

Many companies and school systems give driver trainees instruction in Department of Transportation and company work rules, safety regulations, state and municipal driving regulations, and safe driving practices. During training, drivers practice driving on set courses.

Opportunities for promotion are generally limited. However, experienced drivers may become supervisors or dispatchers, assigning buses to drivers, checking whether drivers are on schedule, rerouting buses to avoid blocked streets or other problems, and dispatching extra vehicles and service crews to scenes of accidents and breakdowns. A few drivers may become managers. Promotion in publicly owned bus systems is often by competitive civil service examination. Some motorcoach drivers purchase their own equipment and open their own business.

Earnings: Median hourly earnings of transit and intercity bus drivers were $14.22 in 2002. Some earned less than $8.37 an hour, while the highest 10 percent earned more than $22.51 an hour. The median hourly earnings of school bus drivers were $10.77 in 2002. Some earned less than $6.24 an hour, while the highest 10 percent earned more than $16.44 an hour.

The benefits bus drivers receive from their employers vary greatly. Most intercity and local-transit bus drivers receive paid health and life insurance, sick leave, vacation leave, and free bus rides on any of the regular routes of their line or system. School bus drivers receive sick leave, and many are covered by health and life insurance and pension plans. Because they do not generally work when school is not in session, they do not get vacation leave. Most intercity and many local transit bus drivers are members of the Amalgamated Transit Union.

Key Contacts: For information on employment opportunities, contact local transit systems, intercity bus lines, school systems, or the local office of the state employment service. General information on school bus driving is available from:

- **National School Transportation Association:** 43 South West Street, 4th Floor, Alexandria, VA 22314. Tel. 800-222-NSTA. Website: www.schooltrans.com.

General information on local-transit bus driving is available from:

- **American Public Transportation Association:** 1666 K Street NW, Suite 1100, Washington, DC 20006. Website: www.apta. com.

General information on motorcoach driving is available from:

- **United Motorcoach Association:** 113 S. West Street, 4th Floor, Alexandria, VA 22314. Website: www.uma.org.

Cargo and Freight Agents

- ➪ **Annual Earnings:** $31,400
- ➪ **Education/Training:** High school diploma
- ➪ **Outlook:** Good

Employment Outlook: Employment of cargo and freight agents is expected to grow about as fast as the average for all occupations in the decade ahead in response to the continuing growth of cargo traffic and next-day shipping services.

Nature of Work: Cargo and freight agents arrange for and track incoming and outgoing cargo and freight shipments in airline, train, or trucking terminals or on shipping docks. The expedite the movement of shipments by determining the route that shipments are to take and by preparing all necessary shipping documents.

Working Conditions: Cargo and freight agents work in a variety of settings. Some work in warehouses, stockrooms, or shipping and receiving rooms while others may spend time in cold storage rooms or outside on loading platforms, where they are exposed to the weather.

Education, Training, Qualifications: A high school diploma is usually sufficient for entry in these positions.

Earnings: The median hourly earnings in 2002 for cargo and freight agents were $15.10 ($31,400 per year).

Key Contacts: Information on job opportunities for cargo and freight agents is available from local employers and local offices of the state employment service.

Material Moving Occupations

⇨ **Annual Earnings:** $19,718
⇨ **Education/Training:** Prefer high school diploma
⇨ **Outlook:** Employment opportunities excellent

Employment Outlook: Job openings should be numerous because the occupation is very large and the turnover is relatively high – characteristic of occupations requiring little formal training. Many openings will arise from the need to replace workers who transfer to other occupations, retire, or leave the labor force for other reasons. However, overall employment in material moving occupations will increase more slowly than average for all occupations through 2012. Employment growth will stem from an expanding economy and increased spending on the nation's infrastructure, such as highways and bridges. However, equipment improvements, including the growing automation of material handling in factories and warehouses, will continue to raise productivity and moderate demand for material movers.

Job growth for material movers largely depends on growth in the industries employing them and the type of equipment the workers operate or the materials they handle. For example, employment of operators in manufacturing will decline due to increased automation and efficiency in the production process. On the other hand, employment will grow rapidly in temporary help organizations as firms contract out material moving services. Employment will grow in warehousing and storage as more firms contract out their warehousing to firms that specialize in them. Both construction and manufacturing are sensitive to changes in economic conditions, so the number of job openings in these industries may fluctuate from year to year. Although increasing automation may eliminate some manual tasks, new jobs will be created to operate and maintain material moving equipment.

Nature of Work: Material moving workers are categorized into two groups – operators and laborers. Operators use machinery to move construction materials, earth, petroleum products, and other heavy materials. Generally, they move materials over short distances – around a construction site, factory, or warehouse. Some move materials onto or off of trucks and ships. Operators control equipment by moving levers or foot pedals, operating switches, or turning dials. They may also set up and inspect equipment, make adjustments, and perform minor repairs when needed. Laborers and hand material movers manually handle freight, stock, or other materials; clean vehicles, machinery, and other equipment; and pack or package products and materials. Material moving occupations are classified by the type of equipment they operate or goods they handle. Each piece of equipment requires different skills to move different types of loads.

Working Conditions: Many material moving workers work outdoors in every type of climate and weather condition. The work tends to be repetitive and physically demanding. They may lift and carry heavy objects, and stoop, kneel, crouch, or crawl in awkward positions. Some work at great heights, or outdoors in all weather conditions. Some jobs expose workers to harmful materials or chemicals, fumes, odors, loud noise, or dangerous machinery. To avoid injury, these workers wear safety clothing, such as gloves and hard hats, and devices to protect their eyes, mouth, or hearing. These jobs have become much safer as safety equipment such as overhead guards on forklift trucks has become common.

Material movers generally work eight-hour shifts, though longer shifts also are common. In many industries that work around the clock, material movers work evening or "graveyard" shifts. Some may work at night because the establishment may not want to disturb customers during normal business hours. Refuse and recyclable material collectors often work shifts starting at 5 or 6 am. Some material movers work only during certain seasons, such as when the weather permits construction activity.

Education, Training, Qualifications: Most material moving jobs require little work experience or specific training. Some employers prefer applicants with a high school diploma, but most simply require workers to be at least 18 years old and physically able to do the work. For those jobs requiring physical exertion, employers may require that applicants pass a physical exam. Some employers also require drug testing or background checks before employment. Workers often are younger than workers in other occupations – reflecting the limited training but significant physical requirements of many of these jobs.

Material movers generally learn skills informally, on the job, from more experienced workers or supervisors. However, workers who use industrial trucks, other dangerous equipment, or handle toxic chemicals must receive specialized training in safety awareness and procedures. This training is usually provided by the employer. Employers must also certify that each operator has received the training and evaluate each operator at least once every three years. Material moving equipment operators need a good sense of balance, distance judgment, and eye-hand-foot coordination. Most jobs require reading and basic math skills to read procedure manuals and billing and other documents. Mechanical aptitude and high school training in automobile or diesel mechanics are helpful because workers may perform some maintenance on their equipment. Experience operating mobile equipment, such as tractors on farms or heavy equipment in the military, is an asset. As material moving equipment becomes more automated, many workers will need basic computer and technical knowledge to operate the equipment.

Earnings: Median hourly earnings of material moving workers in 2002 were relatively low. These earnings averaged $12.95 across the wide variety of fields encompassed by this broad category of workers. But since the largest number of workers tend to be found in the lower paying positions, the average wage was actually closer to $9.48 hourly. Pay rates vary according to experience and job responsibilities. Pay usually is higher in metropolitan areas. The seasonality of work may reduce earnings.

Key Contacts: For information about job opportunities and training programs, contact local state employment service offices, building or construction contractors, manufacturers, and wholesale and retail establishments. Information on safety and training requirements is available from:

- **U.S. Department of Labor**: Occupational Safety and Health Administration (OSHA), 200 Constitution Ave. NW., Washington, DC 20210. Website: www.osha.gov.

Information on industrial truck and tractor operators is available from:

- **Industrial Truck Association**: 1750 K Street NW, Suite 460, Washington, DC 20006. Website: www.indtrk.org.

Taxi Drivers and Chauffeurs

⇨ **Annual Earnings:** $8.91 hourly
⇨ **Education/Training:** Chauffeur/taxi driver's license
⇨ **Outlook:** Faster than average growth

Employment Outlook: Persons seeking jobs as taxi drivers and chauffeurs should encounter good opportunities, because of the need to replace the many people who work in this occupation for short periods and then transfer to other occupations or leave the labor force. Opportunities should be best for persons with good driving records and the ability to work flexible schedules. Employment of taxi drivers and chauffeurs is expected to grow faster than average for all occupations through the year 2012, as local and suburban travel increases with population growth. Employment growth also will stem from federal legislation requiring services for persons with disabilities. Rapidly growing metropolitan areas should offer the best job opportunities. The number of job openings can fluctuate with the cycle of the overall economy because the demand for taxi and limousine transportation depends on travel and tourism. Extra drivers may be hired during holiday seasons and peak travel and tourist times.

Nature of Work: Taxi drivers help passengers get to and from their homes, workplaces, and recreational pursuits such as dining, entertainment, and shopping. At the start of their driving shift, taxi drivers usually report to a taxicab service or garage where they are assigned an automobile modified for commercial passenger use. Taxi drivers pick up passengers in one of three ways: "cruising" the streets to pick up random passengers; prearranged pickups; and picking up passengers from taxi stands established in highly trafficked areas.

Drivers should be familiar with the streets in the areas they serve so they can use the most efficient route to destinations. They should know the location of frequently requested destinations, such as airports, bus and railroad terminals, convention centers, hotels, and other points of interest. In case of emergency, the driver should also know the location of fire and police stations and hospitals. Upon reaching the destination, drivers determine the fare and announce it to the rider. Fares often consist of many parts which may included a surcharge for additional passengers, a fee for handling luggage, or a drop charge. Each jurisdiction determines the rate and structure of the fare system of zones through which the taxi passes during a trip. Passengers usually add a tip to the fare.

Chauffeurs operate limousines, vans and private cars for limousine companies, private businesses, government agencies, and wealthy individuals. Chauffeur service differs from taxi service in that all trips are prearranged. Many chauffeurs transport customers in large vans between hotels and airports, bus, or train terminals. Others drive luxury vehicles such as limousines, to business events, entertainment venues, and social events. Still others provide full-time personal transportation for wealthy families and private companies. Chauffeurs cater to passengers with attentive customer service and a special regard for detail. They help riders into the car by holding open doors, holding umbrellas when it is raining, and loading packages and luggage into the trunk of the car. A growing number of chauffeurs work as full-service executive assistants, simultaneously acting as driver, secretary, and itinerary planner.

Working Conditions: Taxi drivers and chauffeurs occasionally have to load and unload heavy luggage and packages. Driving for long periods can be tiring and uncomfortable, especially in densely populated urban areas. Drivers must be alert to conditions on the road, especially in heavy and congested traffic or in bad weather. Taxi drivers also risk robbery because they work alone and often carry large amounts of cash.

Work hours vary greatly. Some jobs offer full-time or part-time employment with work hours that can change from day to day or remain the same every day. It is often necessary for drivers to report to work on short notice. Chauffeurs who work for a single employer may be on call much of the time. Evening and weekend work are common for limousine and taxicab services. The needs of the client or employer dictate the work schedule for chauffeurs. The work of taxi drivers is much less structured. Working free of supervision, they may break for a meal or a rest whenever their vehicle is unoccupied. Many taxi drivers and chauffeurs like the independent, unsupervised work of driving their automobile. This occupation is attractive to individuals seeking flexible work schedules, such as college and postgraduate students, and to anyone seeking a second source of income.

Full-time taxi drivers usually work one shift a day, which may last from eight to 12 hours. Part-time drivers may work half a shift each day, or work a full shift once or twice a week. Drivers may work shifts at all times of the day and night, because most taxi companies offer services 24 hours a day. Early morning and late night shifts are common. Drivers work long hours during holidays, weekends, and other special times during which demand for their services may be heavier. Independent drivers, however, often set their own hours and schedules.

Design improvements in newer cabs have reduced some of the stress and increased the comfort and efficiency of drivers. Many regulatory bodies overseeing taxi and chauffeur services require standard amenities such as air-conditioning and general upkeep of the vehicles. Modern taxicabs also are equipped with sophisticated tracking devices, fare meters, and dispatching equipment. Satellites and tracking systems link many of these state-of-the-art vehicles with company headquarters. In a matter of seconds, dispatchers can deliver directions, traffic advisories, weather reports, and other important communication to drivers anywhere in the transporting area. The satellite link also allows dispatchers to track vehicle location, fuel consumption, and engine performance. Drivers can easily communicate with dispatchers to discuss delivery schedules and courses of action should there be mechanical problems. For instance, automated dispatch systems help dispatchers locate the closest driver to a customer in order to maximize efficiency and quality of service. When threatened with crime or violence, drivers may have special "trouble lights" to alert authorities of emergencies and ensure that help arrives quickly.

Taxi drivers and chauffeurs meet many different types of people. Dealing with rude customers and waiting for passengers requires patience.

Education, Training, Qualifications: Persons interested in driving a limousine or taxicab must first have a regular automobile driver's license. They also must acquire a chauffeur or taxi driver's license, commonly called a "hack" license. Local governments set license standards and requirements for taxi drivers and chauffeurs that include minimum qualifications for driving experience and training. Local authorities generally require applicants for a hack license to pass a written exam or complete a training program that may require up to 80 hours of classroom instruction. To qualify through either an exam or training program, applicants must know local geography, motor vehicle laws, safe driving practices, regulations governing taxicabs, and display some aptitude for customer service. Many taxi and limousine companies set higher standards than required by law. It is common for companies to review applicants' medical, credit, criminal, and driving records. In addition, many companies require a higher minimum age than that which is legally required and prefer that drivers be high school graduates.

In small and medium-sized communities, drivers are sometimes able to buy their taxi, limousine, or other type of automobile and go into business for themselves. These independent owner-drivers require an additional permit allowing them to operate their vehicle as a company. Some big cities limit the number of operating permits. In these cities, drivers become owner-drivers by buying permits from owner-drivers who leave the business. Although many owner-drivers are successful, some fail to cover expenses and eventually lose their permit and automobile. Good business sense and courses in accounting, business, and business arithmetic can help an owner-driver to become successful. Knowledge of mechanics enables owner-drivers to perform their own routine maintenance and minor repairs to cut expenses.

Earnings: Earnings of taxi drivers and chauffeurs vary greatly, depending upon such factors as the number of hours worked, customers' tips, and geographic location. Median hourly earnings of salaried taxi drivers and chauffeurs, including tips, were $8.91 in 2002. Some earned less than $6.31 an hour, and the highest 10 percent earned more than $15.18 an hour.

Key Contacts: Information on licensing and registration of taxi drivers and chauffeurs is available from local government agencies that regulate taxicabs. For information about work opportunities as a taxi driver or chauffeur, contact local taxi or limousine companies or state employment service offices. For general information about the work of limousine drivers, contact:

- **National Limousine Association:** 49 South Maple Ave., Marlton, NJ 08053. Website: www.limo.org.

Truck Drivers

↪ **Annual Earnings:** $33,210
↪ **Education/Training:** Training and license
↪ **Outlook:** Good

Employment Outlook: Employment is expected to grow about as fast as average for all occupations in the decade ahead. Job opportunities in this large occupation should be plentiful because of the growing demand for truck transportation services and the need to replace drivers who leave the occupation. The increased use of rail, air, and ship transportation requires truck drivers to pick up and deliver shipments. Demand for long-distance drivers will remain strong because these drivers transport perishable and time-sensitive goods more efficiently than do alternative modes of transportation.

Nature of Work: The work of truck drivers varies. Long-distance drivers may make short "turnaround" hauls where they deliver a load to a nearby city, pick up another loaded trailer, and drive back to their home base in one day. Other runs take an entire day or longer, and drivers remain away from home overnight. Local truck drivers may pick up a loaded truck in the morning and spend the rest of the day making deliveries or may make several trips between their dispatch point and customers to make deliveries.

Working Conditions: Truck driving has become less physically demanding because most trucks now have more comfortable seats, better ventilation, and improved cab designs. However, driving for many hours at a stretch, unloading cargo, and making deliveries can be tiring. Driving in bad weather, heavy traffic, or over mountains can be nerve-racking. Some self-employed long- distance truck drivers who own as well as operate their trucks spend over 240 days a year away from home. Local truck drivers frequently work 48 hours or more a week. Many who handle food for chain grocery stores, produce markets, or bakeries drive at night or early in the morning. Many load and unload their own trucks, which requires considerable lifting, carrying, and walking.

Education, Training, Qualifications: Qualifications are established by state and federal regulations. All truck drivers must have a driver's license issued by the state in which they live, and most employers strongly prefer a good driving record. All drivers of trucks designed to carry at least 26,000 pounds are required to obtain a special commercial driver's license. Many firms require that drivers be at least 25 years old, be able to lift heavy objects, and have driven trucks for three to five years. Many prefer to hire high school graduates and require annual physical examinations. Since drivers often deal directly with the company's customers, they must get along well with people they encounter.

Earnings: As a rule, local truck drivers are paid by the hour and receive extra pay for working overtime – usually after 40 hours. Long-distance drivers are generally paid by the mile and their rate per mile can vary greatly. In 2002, truck drivers had average straight-time hourly earnings of $15.97. The middle 50 percent earned between $12.51 and $20.01 an hour.

Median hourly earnings in the industries employing the largest numbers of heavy truck and tractor-trailer drivers in 2002 were as follows:

- General freight trucking $17.56
- Grocery and related product wholesalers $16.90
- Specialized freight trucking $15.79
- Other specialty trade contractors $14.25
- Cement and concrete product manufacturing $14.14

Median hourly earnings of light or delivery services truck drivers were $11.48 in 2002. The middle 50 percent earned between $8.75 and $15.58 an hour. Median hourly earnings in the industries employing the largest numbers of light or delivery service truck drivers in 2002 were as follows:

- Couriers $17.48
- General freight trucking $14.92
- Grocery and related product wholesalers $12.26
- Building material and supplies dealers $10.83
- Automotive parts, accessories, and tire stores $7.82

Median hourly earnings of driver/sales workers, including commission, were $9.92 in 2002. The middle 50 percent earned between $6.98 and $14.70 an hour. Median hourly earnings in the industries employing the largest numbers of driver/sales workers in 2002 were as follows:

- Specialty food stores $14.98
- Drycleaning and laundry services $14.74
- Grocery and related product wholesalers $12.66
- Limited-service eating places $6.78
- Full-service restaurants $6.47

Most long-distance drivers operate tractor-trailers, and their earnings vary from as little as $24,000 annually to over $50,000. Most self-employed truck drivers are primarily engaged in long-distance hauling, and earnings of $26,000 to $32,000 a year are common after deducting living expenses and the costs associated with operating their trucks.

Key Contacts: Information on career opportunities in truck driving may be obtained from:

- American Trucking Associations, Inc.: 2200 Mill Road, Alexandria, VA 22314. Website: www.truckline.org.

- **International Brotherhood of Teamsters:** 25 Louisiana Avenue, NW, Washington, DC 20001. Website: www.teamster.org.

A list of certified tractor-trailer driver training courses may be obtained from:

- **Professional Truck Driver Institute:** 2200 Mill Road, Alexandria, VA 22314. Website: www.ptdi.org.

Index to Jobs

The Authors

FOR MORE THAN TWO DECADES Ron and Caryl Krannich, Ph.Ds, have pursued a passion – assisting hundreds of thousands of individuals, from students, the unemployed, and ex-offenders to military personnel, international job seekers, and CEOs, in making critical job and career transitions. Focusing on key job search skills, career changes, and employment fields, their impressive body of work has helped shape career thinking and behavior both in the United States and abroad. Their sound advice has changed numerous lives, including their own!

Ron and Caryl are two of America's leading career and travel writers who have authored, co-authored, or ghost-written more than 70 books. A former Peace Corps Volunteer and Fulbright Scholar, Ron received his Ph.D. in Political Science from Northern Illinois University. Caryl received her Ph.D. in Speech Communication from Penn State University. Together they operate Development Concepts Incorporated, a training, consulting, and publishing firm in Virginia.

The Krannichs are both former university professors, high school teachers, management trainers, and consultants. As trainers and consultants, they have completed numerous projects on management, career development, local government, population planning, and rural development in the United States and abroad. Their career books focus on key job search skills, military and civilian career transitions, government and international careers, travel jobs, and nonprofit organizations and include such classics as *High Impact Resumes and Letters*, *Interview for Success*, and *Change Your Job, Change Your Life*. Their books represent one of today's most comprehensive collections of career writing. With nearly 3 million copies in print, their publications are widely available in bookstores, libraries, and career centers. No strangers to the Internet world, they have written *America's Top Internet Job Sites* and *The Directory of Websites for International Jobs* and published several Internet recruitment and job search books. They also have developed career-related websites: www.impactpublications.com, www.winningthejob.com, www.exoffender reentry.com, www.contentforcareers.com, and www.veteransworld.com. Many of their career tips have appeared on such major websites as www.monster.com, www.careerbuilder.com, www.employmentguide.com, www.washingtonpost.com, and www.campuscareercenter.com.

Ron and Caryl live a double life with travel being their best kept *"do what you love"* career secret. Authors of over 20 travel-shopping guidebooks on various destinations around the world, they continue to pursue their international and travel interests through their innovative *Treasures and Pleasures of...Best of the Best* travel-shopping series and related websites: www.ishoparoundtheworld.com, www.contentfortravel.com, and www. travel-smarter.com. When not found at their home and business in Virginia, they are probably somewhere in Europe, Asia, Africa, the Middle East, the South Pacific, the Caribbean, or the Americas following their other passion – researching and writing about quality antiques, arts, crafts, jewelry, hotels, and restaurants as well as adhering to the career advice they give to others: *"Pursue a passion that enables you to do what you really love to do."*

As both career and travel experts, the Krannichs' work is frequently featured in major newspapers, magazines, and newsletters as well as on radio, television, and the Internet. Available for interviews, consultation, and presentations, they can be contacted as follows:

Ron and Caryl Krannich
krannich@impactpublications.com

Career Resources

THE FOLLOWING CAREER RESOURCES are available directly from Impact Publications. Full descriptions of each title, as well as several downloadable catalogs and specialty flyers, can be found on our website: www.impactpublications.com. Complete the following form or list the titles, include shipping (see formula at the end), enclose payment, and send your order to:

IMPACT PUBLICATIONS
9104 Manassas Drive, Suite N
Manassas Park, VA 20111-5211 USA
1-800-361-1055 (orders only)
Tel. 703-361-7300 or Fax 703-335-9486
Email address: info@impactpublications.com
Quick & easy online ordering: www.impactpublications.com

Orders from individuals must be prepaid by check, money order, or major credit card. We accept telephone, fax, and email orders.

Qty.	TITLES	Price	TOTAL
Featured Title			
____	America's Top Jobs for People Re-Entering the Workforce	$19.95	____
Other Titles By Authors			
____	101 Secrets of Highly Effective Speakers	$15.95	____
____	201 Dynamite Job Search Letters	$19.95	____
____	America's Top Internet Job Sites	$19.95	____
____	America's Top 100 Jobs for People Without a Four-Year Degree	$19.95	____
____	Best Jobs for the 21st Century	$19.95	____
____	Best Resumes and CVs for International Jobs	$24.95	____
____	Change Your Job, Change Your Life	$21.95	____
____	Complete Guide to Public Employment	$19.95	____

_____ Directory of Websites for International Jobs $19.95 _____
_____ Discover the Best Jobs for You $15.95 _____
_____ Dynamite Salary Negotiations $15.95 _____
_____ The Ex-Offender's Job Hunting Guide $17.95 _____
_____ Find a Federal Job Fast $15.95 _____
_____ Get a Raise in 7 Days $14.95 _____
_____ Haldane's Best Cover Letters for Professionals $15.95 _____
_____ Haldane's Best Resumes for Professionals $15.95 _____
_____ Haldane's Best Answers to Tough Interview Questions $15.95 _____
_____ High Impact Resumes and Letters $19.95 _____
_____ I Want to Do Something Else, But I'm Not Sure
       What It Is $15.95 _____
_____ Interview for Success $15.95 _____
_____ The Job Hunting Guide: College to Career $14.95 _____
_____ Job Hunting Tips for People With Hot
       and Not-So-Hot Backgrounds $17.95 _____
_____ Job Interview Tips for People With
       Not-So-Hot Backgrounds $14.95 _____
_____ Jobs for Travel Lovers $19.95 _____
_____ Military Resumes and Cover Letters $21.95 _____
_____ Nail the Cover Letter $17.95 _____
_____ Nail the Job Interview $13.95 _____
_____ Nail the Resume $17.95 _____
_____ No One Will Hire Me! $13.95 _____
_____ Salary Negotiation Tips for Professionals $16.95 _____
_____ Savvy Interviewing: The Nonverbal Advantage $10.95 _____
_____ The Savvy Networker $13.95 _____
_____ The Savvy Resume Writer $12.95 _____

Testing and Assessment

_____ Aptitude, Personality, and Motivation Tests $17.95 _____
_____ Career Tests $12.95 _____
_____ Discover the Best Jobs for You $15.95 _____
_____ Discover What You're Best At $14.00 _____
_____ Do What You Are $18.95 _____
_____ Finding Your Perfect Work $16.95 _____
_____ Gifts Differing $16.95 _____
_____ I Could Do Anything If Only I Knew What It Was $14.95 _____
_____ I Don't Know What I Want, But I Know It's Not This $14.00 _____
_____ I Want to Do Something Else, But I'm Not Sure
       What It Is $15.95 _____
_____ I'm Not Crazy, I'm Just Not You $16.95 _____
_____ Now, Discover Your Strengths $28.00 _____
_____ The Pathfinder $15.00 _____
_____ What Should I Do With My Life? $14.95 _____
_____ What Type Am I? $14.95 _____
_____ What's Your Type of Career? $18.95 _____

Attitude and Motivation

_____ 100 Ways to Motivate Yourself $14.99 _____
_____ Attitude Is Everything $14.95 _____
_____ Change Your Attitude $15.99 _____
_____ Reinventing Yourself $18.99 _____

Inspiration and Empowerment

_____	7 Habits of Highly Effective People (2nd Edition)	$15.00 _____
_____	7 Habits of Highly Effective Teens	$14.00 _____
_____	The 8th Habit: From Effectiveness to Greatness	$26.00 _____
_____	101 Secrets of Highly Effective Speakers	$15.95 _____
_____	Awaken the Giant Within	$15.00 _____
_____	Change Your Thinking, Change Your Life	$24.95 _____
_____	Do What You Love for the Rest of Your Life	$24.95 _____
_____	Dream It Do It	$16.95 _____
_____	Eat That Frog	$19.95 _____
_____	Finding Your Own North Star	$14.95 _____
_____	Goals	$14.95 _____
_____	It's Only Too Late If You Don't Start Now	$15.00 _____
_____	Live the Life Your Love	$12.95 _____
_____	Life Strategies	$13.95 _____
_____	Magic of Thinking Big	$13.00 _____
_____	Maximum Achievement	$14.00 _____
_____	Power of Positive Thinking	$12.95 _____
_____	Power of Purpose	$20.00 _____
_____	Practical Dreamer's Handbook	$13.95 _____
_____	Purpose-Driven Life	$19.99 _____
_____	Self Matters	$14.00 _____
_____	Who Moved My Cheese?	$19.95 _____

Career Exploration and Job Strategies

_____	5 Patterns of Extraordinary Careers	$17.95 _____
_____	25 Jobs That Have It All	$12.95 _____
_____	50 Best Jobs for Your Personality	$16.95 _____
_____	50 Cutting Edge Jobs	$15.95 _____
_____	95 Mistakes Job Seekers Make & How to Avoid Them	$13.95 _____
_____	100 Great Jobs and How to Get Them	$17.95 _____
_____	101 Ways to Recession-Proof Your Career	$14.95 _____
_____	150 Jobs You Can Start Today	$12.95 _____
_____	200 Best Jobs for College Grads	$16.95 _____
_____	250 Best Jobs Through Apprenticeships	$24.95 _____
_____	300 Best Jobs Without a Four-Year Degree	$16.95 _____
_____	America's Top 100 Jobs for People Without a Four-Year Degree	$19.95 _____
_____	Best Entry-Level Jobs	$16.95 _____
_____	Best Jobs for the 21st Century	$19.95 _____
_____	Career Change	$14.95 _____
_____	Change Your Job, Change Your Life (9th Edition)	$21.95 _____
_____	Cool Careers for Dummies	$19.99 _____
_____	Directory of Executive Recruiters	$49.95 _____
_____	Five Secrets to Finding a Job	$12.95 _____
_____	A Fork in the Road: A Career Planning Guide for Young Adults	$14.95 _____
_____	Great Careers in Two Years	$19.95 _____
_____	High-Tech Careers for Low-Tech People	$14.95 _____
_____	How to Get a Job and Keep It	$16.95 _____
_____	How to Get Interviews From Classified Job Ads	$14.95 _____
_____	How to Succeed Without a Career Path	$13.95 _____
_____	Job Hunting Guide: College to Career	$14.95 _____

_____	Job Search Handbook for People With Disabilities	$17.95 _____
_____	Knock 'Em Dead	$14.95 _____
_____	Me, Myself, and I, Inc.	$17.95 _____
_____	Monster Careers	$18.00 _____
_____	Occupational Outlook Handbook	$16.90 _____
_____	O*NET Dictionary of Occupational Titles	$39.95 _____
_____	Quick Guide to Career Training in Two Years or Less	$16.95 _____
_____	Quick Prep Careers	$18.95 _____
_____	Quit Your Job and Grow Some Hair	$15.95 _____
_____	Rites of Passage at $100,000 to $1 Million+	$29.95 _____
_____	Suddenly Unemployed	$14.95 _____
_____	What Color Is Your Parachute?	$17.95 _____

Career Directories

_____	Almanac of American Employers	$199.95 _____
_____	Associations USA	$75.00 _____
_____	Enhanced Occupational Outlook Handbook	$39.95 _____
_____	Job Hunter's Sourcebook	$160.00 _____
_____	Occupational Outlook Handbook	$16.90 _____
_____	O*NET Dictionary of Occupational Titles	$39.95 _____
_____	Professional Careers Sourcebook	$150.00 _____
_____	Vocational Careers Sourcebook	$150.00 _____

Internet Job Search

_____	100 Top Internet Job Sites	$12.95 _____
_____	America's Top Internet Job Sites	$19.95 _____
_____	Career Exploration On the Internet	$24.95 _____
_____	Cyberspace Job Search Kit	$18.95 _____
_____	Directory of Websites for International Jobs	$19.95 _____
_____	Guide to Internet Job Searching	$14.95 _____

Resumes and Letters

_____	101 Great Tips for a Dynamite Resume	$13.95 _____
_____	175 Best Cover Letters	$14.95 _____
_____	201 Dynamite Job Search Letters	$19.95 _____
_____	Best KeyWords for Resumes, Cover Letters, & Interviews	$17.95 _____
_____	Best Resumes and CVs for International Jobs	$24.95 _____
_____	Best Resumes for $75,000+ Executive Jobs	$16.95 _____
_____	Best Resumes for $100,000+ Jobs	$24.95 _____
_____	Best Resumes for People Without a Four-Year Degree	$19.95 _____
_____	Best Cover Letters for $100,000+ Jobs	$24.95 _____
_____	Blue Collar Resumes	$11.99 _____
_____	College Grad Resumes to Land $75,000+ Jobs	$24.95 _____
_____	Competency-Based Resumes	$13.99 _____
_____	Cover Letters for Dummies	$16.99 _____
_____	Cover Letters That Knock 'Em Dead	$12.95 _____
_____	Cyberspace Resume Kit	$18.95 _____
_____	e-Resumes	$11.95 _____
_____	Executive Resumes	$34.95 _____
_____	Expert Resumes for People Returning to Work	$16.95 _____
_____	Gallery of Best Cover Letters	$18.95 _____
_____	Gallery of Best Resumes	$18.95 _____

_____	Haldane's Best Cover Letters for Professionals	$15.95 _____
_____	Haldane's Best Resumes for Professionals	$15.95 _____
_____	High Impact Resumes and Letters	$19.95 _____
_____	Military Resumes and Cover Letters	$21.95 _____
_____	Resume Shortcuts	$14.95 _____
_____	Resumes for Dummies	$16.99 _____
_____	Resumes in Cyberspace	$14.95 _____
_____	Resumes That Knock 'Em Dead	$12.95 _____
_____	The Savvy Resume Writer	$12.95 _____

Networking

_____	A Foot in the Door	$14.95 _____
_____	Great Connections	$11.95 _____
_____	How to Work a Room	$14.00 _____
_____	Masters of Networking	$16.95 _____
_____	Networking for Job Search and Career Success	$16.95 _____
_____	Power Networking	$14.95 _____
_____	The Savvy Networker	$13.95 _____

Dress, Image, and Etiquette

_____	Dressing Smart for Men	$16.95 _____
_____	Dressing Smart for Women	$16.95 _____
_____	Power Etiquette	$14.95 _____

Interviews

_____	101 Dynamite Questions to Ask At Your Job Interview	$13.95 _____
_____	Haldane's Best Answers to Tough Interview Questions	$15.95 _____
_____	Interview for Success	$15.95 _____
_____	Job Interview Tips for People With Not-So-Hot Backgrounds	$14.95 _____
_____	Job Interviews for Dummies	$16.99 _____
_____	KeyWords to Nail Your Job Interview	$17.95 _____
_____	Nail the Job Interview!	$13.95 _____
_____	The Savvy Interviewer	$10.95 _____
_____	Sweaty Palms	$13.95 _____

Salary Negotiations

_____	Better Than Money	$18.95 _____
_____	Dynamite Salary Negotiations	$15.95 _____
_____	Get More Money On Your Next Job	$17.95 _____
_____	Get a Raise in 7 Days	$14.95 _____
_____	Salary Negotiation Tips for Professionals	$16.95 _____

Ex-Offenders in Transition

_____	9 to 5 Beats Ten to Life	$15.00 _____
_____	99 Days and a Get Up	$9.95 _____
_____	Ex-Offender's Job Hunting Guide	$17.95 _____
_____	Man, I Need a Job	$7.95 _____
_____	Putting the Bars Behind You (6 books)	$57.95 _____

Government Jobs

____	Book of U.S. Government Jobs	$21.95 ____
____	FBI Careers	$18.95 ____
____	Find a Federal Job Fast!	$15.95 ____
____	Post Office Jobs	$19.95 ____
____	Ten Steps to a Federal Job	$39.95 ____

International and Travel Jobs

____	Careers in International Affairs	$24.95 ____
____	Directory of Websites for International Jobs	$19.95 ____
____	International Job Finder	$19.95 ____
____	Jobs for Travel Lovers	$19.95 ____

VIDEOS

Interview, Networking, and Salary Videos

____	Best 10¼ Tips for People With a Not-So-Hot Past	$98.00 ____
____	Build a Network for Work and Life	$99.00 ____
____	Common Mistakes People Make in Interviews	$79.95 ____
____	Exceptional Interviewing Tips	$79.00 ____
____	Extraordinary Answers to Interview Questions	$79.95 ____
____	Extreme Interview	$69.00 ____
____	Make a First Good Impression	$129.00 ____
____	Seizing the Job Interview	$79.00 ____
____	Quick Salary Negotiations Video	$149.00 ____
____	Why Should I Hire You?	$99.00 ____

Dress and Image Videos

____	Head to Toe	$98.00 ____
____	Tips and Techniques to Improve Your Total Image	$98.00 ____

Resumes, Applications, and Cover Letter Videos

____	The Complete Job Application	$99.00 ____
____	Effective Resumes	$79.95 ____
____	Quick Cover Letter Video	$149.00 ____
____	Quick Resume Video	$149.00 ____
____	Resumes, Cover Letters, and Portfolios	$98.00 ____

Assessment and Goal Setting Videos

____	Career Path Interest Inventory	$149.00 ____
____	Career S.E.L.F. Assessment	$89.00 ____
____	Skills Identification	$129.00 ____
____	You DO Have Experience	$149.00 ____

Attitude, Motivation, and Empowerment Videos

____	Down But Not Out	$129.00 ____
____	Gumby Attitude	$69.00 ____
____	Looking for Work With Attitude Plus	$129.00 ____

SOFTWARE

____	Job Browser Pro 1.4	$359.00 ____
____	Multimedia Career Center	$385.00 ____
____	Multimedia Career Pathway	$199.00 ____
____	OOH Career Center	$349.95 ____

SPECIAL VALUE KITS FEATURED ON PAGES 260-261

____	Discover What You're Best At Kit	$389.95 ____
____	Interview and Salary Smarts Kit	$359.95 ____
____	Resumes and Letters for Re-Entry Kit	$599.95 ____

SUBTOTAL ____

Virginia residents add 5% sales tax ____

POSTAGE/HANDLING ($5 for first
product and 8% of SUBTOTAL) $5.00

8% of SUBTOTAL -- ____

TOTAL ENCLOSED ------------------------- ____

SHIP TO:

NAME _____

ADDRESS: _____

_____

_____

PAYMENT METHOD:

❑ I enclose check/money order for $ _____ made payable to
IMPACT PUBLICATIONS.

❑ Please charge $ _____ to my credit card:

❑ Visa   ❑ MasterCard   ❑ American Express   ❑ Discover

Card # _____ Expiration date: ____/____

Signature _____

Job Search Resources

Resumes and Letters for Re-Entry Kit

Make sure your career resource center includes this terrific set of resume and cover letter books for college students and graduates. Jam-packed with resume writing, production, and distribution advice as well as hundreds of examples of winning resumes and letters. Can purchase separately. **SPECIAL:** $599.95 for all 38 guides.

- *101 Best Resumes* ($12.95)
- *101 More Best Resumes* ($11.95)
- *101 Quick Tips for a Dynamite Resume* ($13.95)
- *201 Dynamite Job Search Letters* ($19.95)
- *America's Top Resumes for America's Top Jobs* ($19.95)
- *Best KeyWords for Resumes, Cover Letters, and Interviews* ($17.95)
- *Best Cover Letters for $100,000+ Jobs* ($24.95)
- *Best Resumes for $75,000+ Executive Jobs* ($16.95)
- *Best Resumes for $100,000+ Jobs* ($24.95)
- *Best Resumes and CVs for International Jobs* ($24.95)
- *Best Resumes for College Students and New Grads* ($12.95)
- *Best Resumes for Grads* ($11.95)
- *Best Resumes for People Without a Four-Year Degree* ($19.95)
- *Blue Collar Resumes* ($11.99)
- *College Grad Resumes to Land $75,000+ Jobs* ($24.95)
- *Complete Resume and Job Search Book for College Students* ($12.95)
- *Competency-Based Resumes* ($13.99)
- *Cover Letter Magic* ($16.95)
- *Cover Letters for Dummies* ($16.99)
- *Cyberspace Resume Kit* ($18.95)
- *Developing a Professional Vita or Resume* ($10.95)
- *e-Resumes* ($11.95)
- *Expert Resumes for People Returning to Work* ($16.95)
- *Expert Resumes for Teachers and Educators* ($16.95)
- *Gallery of Best Cover Letters* ($18.95)
- *Gallery of Best Resumes* ($18.95)
- *Haldane's Best Cover Letters for Professionals* ($15.95)
- *Haldane's Best Resumes for Professionals* ($15.95)
- *How to Prepare Your Curriculum Vitae* ($15.95)
- *High Impact Resumes and Letters* ($19.95)
- *Military Resumes and Cover Letters* ($21.95)
- *Resume Magic* ($18.95)
- *Resume Shortcuts* ($14.95)
- *Resumes for Dummies* ($16.99)
- *Resumes in Cyberspace* ($14.95)
- *Resumes That Knock 'em Dead* ($12.95)
- *The Savvy Resume Writer* ($12.95)
- *Top Secret Executive Resumes* ($15.99)

For Re-Entry

Discover What You're Best At Kit

Finding the right job and career path requires the correct assessment of interests before all else. These resources are jam-packed with the tools to help you get in touch with your inner strengths. **SPECIAL:** $389.95 for the complete kit!

- *Career Tests* ($12.95)
- *Dictionary of Holland Occupational Codes* ($58.00)
- *Discover the Best Jobs for You* ($15.95)
- *Discover What You're Best At* ($14.00)
- *Do What You Are* ($18.95)
- *Finding Your Perfect Work* ($17.95)
- *Gifts Differing* ($16.95)
- *I Could Do Anything If I Only Knew What It Was* ($16.00)
- *I Don't Know What I Want, But I Know It's Not This* ($14.00)
- *I Want to Do Something Else, But I'm Not Sure What It Is* ($15.95)
- *I'm Not Crazy, I'm Just Not You* ($16.95)
- *Pathfinder* ($15.00)

- *The P.I.E. Method for Career Success* ($14.95)
- *Real People, Real Jobs* ($15.95)
- *What Color Is Your Parachute Workbook* ($9.95)
- *What Should I Do With My Life?* ($14.95)
- *What Type Am I?* ($14.95)
- *What's Your Type of Career?* ($18.95)

INSTRUMENTS

- *Barriers to Employment Success Inventory Kit* (Set of 25, $39.95)
- *Career Interests to Jobs Chart* (Set of 10, $19.95)
- *Guide to Occupational Exploration Inventory* (Set of 25, $29.95)

Interview and Salary Smarts Kit

The job interview is the most important step in a job search. Here's the ultimate collection of inexpensive job interview and salary negotiation books. "Must" resources for all career libraries. $359.95 for complete kit of 28 books.

- *101 Dynamite Questions to Ask at Your Job Interview* ($13.95)
- *101 Great Answers to the Toughest Interview Questions* ($11.99)
- *101 Salary Secrets* ($12.95)
- *250 Job Interview Questions You'll Most Likely Be Asked* ($9.95)
- *Best Answers to 201 Most Frequently Asked Interview Questions* ($10.95)
- *Better Than Money* ($18.95)
- *Complete Q&A Job Interview Book* ($14.95)
- *Dynamite Salary Negotiations* ($15.95)
- *Essential Book of Interviewing* ($15.00)
- *Get More Money On Your Next Job* ($14.95)
- *Haldane's Best Answers to Tough Interview Questions* ($15.95)

- *Haldane's Best Salary Tips for Professionals* ($15.95)
- *Interview for Success* ($15.95)
- *Interview Kit* ($14.95)
- *Interview Power* ($14.95)
- *Interview Rehearsal Book* ($12.00)
- *Interview Strategies That Will Get You the Job You Want* ($12.95)
- *Job Interviews for Dummies* ($16.99)
- *Killer Interviews* ($10.95)
- *Nail the Job Interview* ($13.95)
- *Naked at the Interview* ($14.95)
- *Negotiate Your Job Offer* ($17.95)
- *Perfect Interview* ($17.95)
- *Power Interviews* ($12.95)
- *Preparing for the Behavior-Based Interview* ($13.95)
- *Quick Interview and Salary Negotiation Book* ($12.95)
- *Savvy Interviewing* ($10.95)
- *Sweaty Palms* ($13.95)

ORDER: 1-800-361-1055, 703-361-7300 or fax 703-335-9486
9104-N Manassas Drive, Manassas Park, VA 20111
www.impactpublications.com

Keep in Touch . . .
On the Web!

www.impactpublications.com
www.exoffenderreentry.com
www.ishoparoundtheworld.com
www.travel-smarter.com
www.winningthejob.com
www.veteransworld.com

Writing Themes About Literature

Writing Themes

About Literature

BRIEF EDITION

Edgar V. Roberts

Herbert H. Lehman College
of
The City University of New York

Prentice-Hall, Inc., Englewood Cliffs, New Jersey   07632

ₐₙg in Publication Data

ₐ v.
₆ themes about literature.

Includes index.
1. English language—Rhetoric. 2. Literature—Study
and teaching. I. Title.
PE1408.R593 1982   808′.0668021   81-15880
ISBN 0-13-970566-X   AACR2

Design and editorial/
    production supervision by
    Chrys Chrzanowski
Cover design by 20/20 Services, Inc.
    Mark Berghash, designer
Manufacturing buyer: Harry P. Baisley

ISBN 0-13-970566-X

PRENTICE-HALL INTERNATIONAL, INC., *London*
PRENTICE-HALL OF AUSTRALIA PTY., LIMITED, *Sydney*
PRENTICE-HALL OF CANADA, LTD., *Toronto*
PRENTICE-HALL OF INDIA PRIVATE LIMITED, *New Delhi*
PRENTICE-HALL OF JAPAN, INC., *Tokyo*
PRENTICE-HALL OF SOUTHEAST ASIA PTE. LTD., *Singapore*
WHITEHALL BOOKS LIMITED, *Wellington, New Zealand*

Contents

chapter 1

The Précis Theme, or Abstract 35

chapter 2

The Summary Theme 41

chapter 3

The Theme About Likes or Dislikes 47

chapter 4

The Theme of Character Analysis 54

chapter 5

*The Theme About
Point of View* 63

chapter 6

*The Theme About
Setting* 72

chapter 7

*The Theme About
a Major Idea* 79

chapter 8

The Theme on a Problem   87

chapter 9

Themes on (I) Imagery, and (II) Symbolism and Allegory   96

chapter 10

*The Themes of
Comparison-Contrast
and Extended
Comparison-Contrast*   112

appendix a

*Taking Examinations
on Literature*   126

appendix b

A Note on Documentation   139

appendix c

Works Used
for the Sample Themes   150

To the Instructor

I am presenting this shorter version of *Writing Themes About Literature* after many years of deliberation. Advisers have pointed out the need for just such a book designed for the one-semester composition course based on literary subject matter. At the same time they have indicated that the full edition of *Writing Themes About Literature* is too comprehensive for such a course. This shorter version has been designed to meet this need. Containing ten chapters from the forthcoming fifth edition, it is short enough to fit the one-semester composition course but still lengthy enough to provide for a wide variety of theme-writing topics.

This selection, slightly more than half of the full version, represents a balanced blend of topics. Some are general, some more literary in scope. Chapters 3, 4, 5, 6, and 9 are grounded specifically in the study of literature, while 1, 2, 7, 8, and 10 are of a general nature. All the assignments are designed to develop writing skills that may be carried over to any course in the college curriculum. The more general techniques, such as the study of ideas and problems, can be used directly. The more literary techniques have various special applications for topics in other disciplines (e.g., the use of point of view in the analysis of political speeches; the study of imagery, such as Plato's cave, in philosophy). An additional value is that students handling them may go to other disciplines with confidence in their developing writing strengths.

In offering this shorter edition of *Writing Themes About Literature*, I have tried to keep and strengthen those qualities that have occasioned so much support from so many of you over the years. As always, my approach is not based on genres from which theme assignments are to be somehow determined, but instead each chapter is designed to produce full-length student themes on any assigned work, regardless of genre. The chapters, naturally, may also be used as the basis for study and classroom discussions about the various approaches. In addition, they may be used for paragraph-length assignments. The result is that the book offers great scope and variety—with the possibility of complete or close-to-complete use—for a one-semester composition course.

The chapters are still arranged in an order of difficulty, going from simpler to more complex matters as students progress. With the précis theme in Chapter 1, students may begin with the simplest form of writing about any of the genres. The first three themes become broader in scope, with Chapter 3, on likes or dislikes, being new in this edition. The next three are designed primarily for narrative (both prose and poetry) and drama. Applicable to any of the genres are the final four chapters (including one about imagery, a "literary" subject that is essential to the study of just about all writing). These provide a number of reading and writing techniques that build to the comparison-contrast theme. This theme could suitably employ any analytic technique that students have acquired up to that point in the course. The theme of extended comparison could be an assignment that might be made as the long theme for the one-semester course.

Although you might wish to assign the chapters in order throughout the course, you are at liberty to assign them as you choose, in any order you wish. One instructor, for example, might choose to omit the first two chapters and repeat certain assignments such as those on character and setting. Another might prefer not to use the longer comparison-contrast theme, but might repeat the shorter one for a number of separate assignments such as comparative studies of imagery, character, personal likes, or point of view. Still another might wish to use just a few of the chapters, assigning them two or more times until it seems clear that the students have overcome all problems with the materials. The book offers the possibility for such uses according to your needs.

As in each past edition of *Writing Themes About Literature*, the chapters are composed of two parts. The first is a discussion of the problems raised by a particular literary approach, and the second is a sample theme (or two) showing how the problems may be treated in a theme.

I have designed all changes in the descriptive sections to emphasize the process of writing itself. Most of these sections are extensively revised; some have been almost entirely rewritten. I had always planned these sections as instruction in the process of understanding literary concepts, preparing materials for a theme, and writing the theme. My changes bring this process into even stronger focus. All discussions of analytical concepts have the thrust of enabling students to know what to look for and what to do in the invention-prewriting stages of their themes. I have minimized references to critical problems that are of interest mainly to the student of literature. Generally, I have cut discussions of exceptions, qualifications, and "pitfalls" in favor of including these at the appropriate places in the Instructor's Manual.

The sample themes are presented in the belief that the word *imitation* does not have to be preceded by adjectives like *slavish* or *mere*. The purpose is to give students a concrete visualization of what might be done on particular assignments. Such examples, I believe, help them in their composing and writing. With the sample in mind, they have a construction that gives them something to aim for. Without such an example, they must add the task of creating their own form of expression to the already formidable need for understanding new concepts and interpreting a new work of literature. Although some students will follow the samples closely, others will wish to adapt the discussions and samples to their own needs or wishes. The samples thus encourage students to write at a more advanced level than they otherwise might be able to do.

Because the sample themes are guides, they represent a full treatment of each of the various topics. Nevertheless, in this edition they have been held within the approximate length of most assignments in freshman classes. If students are writing outside of class, they can readily create themes as full as the samples. Even though the samples treat an average of three aspects of particular topics (making for the traditional five-paragraph theme), there is nothing to prevent assigning only one aspect, either for an impromptu or for an outside-class theme. For example, using the chapter on setting, you might assign a paragraph about the use of setting in only the first scene of a story, or you might require a paragraph about interior settings, or about references to a particular color, or about the use of light and darkness. With such variations, not only the entire sample theme, but separate parts, may be used as a guide.

To make the sample themes more accessible to students, in this shorter version I have based them on the pieces included in Appendix C (many of the discussions are also based on these). This practice (except for longer works) was adopted in the second edition of *Writing Themes About Literature*, but critical response did not warrant its continuance in the third and fourth editions. Now, because of renewed recommendations, it is adopted systematically here. Thus the student studying point of view can compare the sample theme on that topic with the complete text of Frank O'Connor's "First Confession," which is printed in Appendix C. This story is also used in the two comparison-contrast themes in Chapter 10, and in the sample theme on character developed extensively in the preliminary chapter on the writing process. It is my hope that the reliance on these anthologized works will give this shorter version a unity and coherence that will help students in understanding the nature of their assignments.

Following each sample theme is a commentary—a feature new in the fourth edition and continued in this one—presented to help students make the connection between the precepts in the first part of the chapter and the example in the second.

My hope is that all revisions and changes will be readable and clear. Throughout, I have tried to use an easy, "plain" style, to borrow a description from classical rhetoric. This has meant a general shortening of sentences and paragraphs and a preference for concrete words of the least number of syllables that correctness will allow. The success of my attempts will have to await the responses of students as expressed in their themes.

This shorter version brings into focus something that has always been true of *Writing Themes About Literature*. The book is to be used in the classroom as a practical guide for writing. It is also a guide to a number of literary approaches that are clarified for students because of the reinforcement of writing. The chapters are writing assignments and the goal is to improve student writing. The reading of literary works is introduced as the means of developing support for ideas during the invention-prewriting stage of themes. In short, the stress throughout the book is on the process of writing.

This method, which has been constant in my book since its first edition appeared in 1964, is designed to equip students to face the situations encountered in college. There, they are required to write about problems in other departments like psychology, economics, sociology, biology, and political science. Instructors in these departments present texts or ask their students to develop raw data, and they assign writing on this basis. Writing is on external, written materials, not on descriptions of the student's own experiences or on opinions. Writing is about reading.

Yet we instructors of composition face the problem we have always faced. On the one hand the needs of other departments have caused a wide diversification of subject matter, creating both a strain on the general knowledge of the staff and also a certain thematic disunity. On the other, in programs where personal experiences or offhand topic materials are the subject matter, the course has little bearing on writing for other courses. As an institutional matter, recent emphasis on writing-across-the-curriculum has created a greater awareness of the disciplinary writing needs of other departments. But coordinators and instructors of composition still face the problem of content in the basic writing courses. With a background in literature, the English faculty has the task of meeting the service needs of the institution without compromising their own disciplinary commitment.

The approach in this book deals with this problem. Teachers can work with their own discipline—literature—while also fulfilling their primary responsibility of teaching writing. Thus the book keeps all these problems in perspective:

The requirement of the institution for composition.

The need of students to develop writing skills based on written texts.

The responsibility of English faculty to teach writing while still working within their own area of expertise.

It is gratifying to claim that the approach in *Writing Themes About Literature* has been tested for many years. It is no longer new, but it is still novel. It works. It gives coherence to the sometimes fragmented composition course. It also provides for adaptation and, as I have stressed, variety. Using the book, you can develop a virtually endless number of new topics for themes. One obvious benefit is the possibility of entirely eliminating not only the traditional "theme barrels" of infamous memory in fraternity and sorority houses, but also the newer interference from business "enterprises" that provide themes to order.

While *Writing Themes About Literature* is designed as a rhetoric of practical criticism for students, it is based on profoundly held convictions. I believe that true liberation in a liberal arts curriculum is achieved only through clearly defined goals. Just to make assignments and to let students do with them what they can is to encourage them to continue in a state of frustration and mental enslavement. But if students can develop a deep knowledge of specific approaches to subject material, they can begin to develop some of that expertness which is essential to freedom. As Pope said:

True ease in writing comes from art, not chance,
As those move easiest who have learned to dance.

It is almost axiomatic that the development of writing skill in one area—in this instance the interpretation of literature—can have an enabling effect on the development of skill in other areas. The search for information with a particular goal in mind, the asking of pointed questions, the testing, rephrasing, and developing of ideas—all these and more are transferable skills on which students can build throughout their college years and beyond.

I have one concluding article of faith. Those of us whose careers have been established in the study of literature have made commitments to our belief in its value. The study of literature is valid in and for itself. But literature as an art form employs techniques and creates problems for readers that can be dealt with only through analysis, and analysis means work. Thus, the immediate aim of *Writing Themes About Literature* is to help students to do their work and to write about it. But the ultimate objective (in the past I wrote *"primary* objective") is to promote the pleasurable study and, finally, the love of literature.

—**Edgar V. Roberts**

Acknowledgments

The decision to develop this Brief Edition of *Writing Themes About Literature* was based on the thoughts and comments of many instructors over the past years. A developing consensus was that a shorter version might suit their needs in some of their courses better than the full text. Thus, as in all past editions of *Writing Themes About Literature,* I am not only deeply grateful, but deeply indebted, to those who have used and thoughtfully responded to the book. I should also like to extend my thanks to Professors Douglas Buttress, Peter DeBlois, Kathleen Dubs, George Hayhoe, Henry Jacobs, and John Ramsey, all of whom offered detailed suggestions for improving this edition of *Writing Themes About Literature.* Their expertise and insights were the causes of many important additions, excisions, and revisions. To Bill Oliver, Bud Therien, and Bruce Kennan of Prentice-Hall, I am particularly grateful. I shall long remember their kindness, concern, intelligence, and helpfulness. Chrys Chrzanowski of Prentice-Hall designed the Brief Edition, and for her skill and hard work I am thankful. Finally, I should like to thank Ilene McGrath, who copyedited the manuscript and who offered many, many improvements.

Edgar V. Roberts

The chapters that follow are theme assignments based on a number of analytical approaches important to the study of literature. The assignments are designed to fulfill two goals of composition and English courses: (1) to write good themes, and (2) to assimilate great works of literature into the imagination. On the negative side, the chapters aim to help you avoid writing themes that are no more than retellings of a story, vague statements of like or dislike, or biographies of an author. On the positive side, the book aims to help you improve your writing skills through the use of literature as subject matter. Integral to your writing is your standard of literary judgment and the knowledge you need to distinguish good literature from bad. The book aims to encourage the development of these abilities by requiring you to apply, in well-prepared themes, specific approaches to good reading.

No educational process is complete until you have applied what you have studied. That is, you have not really learned something until you can talk or write about it or until you can apply it to some question or problem. The need for application requires you to recognize where your learning is incomplete, so that you may strengthen your knowledge. Thus, it is easy for you to read the chapter on *point of view* (the position from which details are seen, described, and considered), and it is presumably easy to read, say, Frank O'Connor's story "First Confession." But your grasp of point of view as a concept will not be complete—nor will your appreciation of at least one aspect of the technical artistry of O'Connor's story be complete—until you have written about point of view in the story. (Please see Chapter 5.) As you write, you may discover that you need to go back to the work, to study your notes on it, and to compare them with what you understand about the problem itself. In writing, you must check facts, grasp their relationship to your topic, develop insights into the value and artistry of the work, and express your understanding in a well-organized and well-developed theme. After you have finished a number of such themes, you should be able to approach other literary works with more certainty and skill. The more you know and the more you can apply, the more expert and demanding you will be.

General Reading Habits

The need to write themes on specific topics of literary analysis should help you improve your general reading and study habits. The principle of being a good reader is to derive a factual basis for emotional responses and intelligent interpretation. Obviously, everyone goes about reading in his or her own way, but it stands to reason that casual readers may often read so superficially that their responses are uncertain and unreliable. Preparing and writing a number of separate analytical themes should enable you to develop habits that you can use long after you have left your writing class. Here are some of the general habits that you should have as a long-range goal:

1. Study each word carefully. Look up all words you do not know.
2. Consider your thoughts and responses as you read. Did you laugh, smile, worry, get scared, feel a thrill, learn a great deal, feel proud, find a lot to think about? Try to describe how the various parts of the work caused your reactions.
3. Make notes on interesting characterizations, events, techniques, and ideas. If you like a character, try to describe what you like. If you dislike an idea, try to describe what you dislike.
4. Try to see patterns developing. Make an outline or scheme for the story or main idea. What are the conflicts in the story? How are these resolved? Is one force, idea, or side the winner? Why? How do you respond to the winner, or the loser?
5. Is there anything you do not understand? Make a note of the difficulty and ask your instructor about it in class.
6. For further study, underline what seem to be key passages. Write some of these on cards, and carry the cards with you. When you are riding or walking to class, or at other times, try to memorize phrases, sentences, or lines of poetry.

What Is Literature?

Technically, anything spoken or written is literature. This includes every-thing from a grocery list to Shakespeare's sonnets. It seems clear, however, that a grocery list, though written, should be excluded as "literature" be-cause it does not do those things that we expect from literature. That is, it does not interest, entertain, stimulate, broaden, or ennoble the reader. Even though the list may be structured according to the places in a su-permarket (dairy areas, frozen food areas, produce areas, and so on) it is not designed to engage the reader's imagination. A grocery list, in short, is simply useful. It is not literature. Rather, it is to works that invite emo-tional and intellectual engagement that we confine our definition of liter-ature.

The literature that is studied in introductory college courses is most often in a written form. This form offers certain advantages, although they may not seem immediately clear. Written literature gives great flexibility. You can choose to read a work according to your mood at any time you wish. Compared with a television show, for example, which you can see only when it is scheduled, literature offers freedom. When you read, you depend only on your own effort and imagination. There are no actors, no settings, no photographic or musical techniques to supersede your own reconstruc-tion of the author's ideas. If you wish, you may reread a passage once or many times. You may stop reading and think for a while about what you have just read. Or you may get up to do something else if you need to. When you return you may pick up your book and continue it just where you left it. The book will always wait for you and will not change during the time you are gone. By contrast, any such interruptions with a film or television show are virtually permanent losses; you must wait for the re-peats or else must see the picture again to pick up where you left off. In short, with a book you gain freedom and adaptability, whereas with a television show or movie you must force yourself to conform to demands of other people.

This is not to denigrate the "warmer" media of television and film, but only to contrast them with written forms of literature. All literature, in whatever form, has many things to offer you. The study of literature should help you develop what William Hazlitt, in a work entitled "Advice to a Patriot," called "long views." This term is idealistic and somewhat broad in meaning, yet it describes the value of literary study and humanistic study generally. The idea is that none of us can learn a great deal about the world if we rely only on our own limited experiences in the small areas around us. However, if we read extensively, we can build up our thoughts and our insights. Reading satisfies curiosity and stimulates imagination. It provides knowledge about our own times, and it also teaches us about the lives and concerns of people at other times and in other cultures. Writers of imaginative literature do not write works of psychology, politics, morality, philosophy, and religion, yet we learn about these topics as we read. Literature accelerates growth and transforms our perceptions of life in ways that we can never predict, or ever even know for sure. It makes us human. William Wordsworth, in his "Tintern Abbey" poem, described such an effect:

> . . . thy mind
> Shall be a mansion for all lovely forms,
> Thy memory be as a dwelling-place
> For all sweet sounds and harmonies;
>
> (lines 139–142)

It is from a base such as this that you can see your own life and the obligations that you face as a human being living in the 1980s. Without such a base you can be a follower. With such a base, however, with "long views" like those that literature can encourage, you may develop those capacities that can help you become a leader.

Types of Literature: The Four Genres

In practice, works of literature fall into four categories or *genres:* (1) narrative, (2) drama, (3) poetry, and (4) nonfiction prose. All these forms have many common characteristics. While the major purpose of nonfiction prose, for example, is to inform, the other genres also provide information (although informing is incidental to the others). All the genres are art forms, each with its own internal requirements of structure and style. In varying degrees, all the forms are dramatic and imaginative. Even a work of nonfiction prose designed to instruct will be unsuccessful unless it makes at least some appeal to the imagination.

NARRATIVE FICTION

A narrative is an account of a series of events, usually fictional, although sometimes fictional events may be tied to events that are genuinely historical. The two kinds of narrative fiction you will read most often are *short stories* and *novels. Myths, parables, romances,* and *epics* are also part of the genre. A short story is usually about one or two characters undergoing some sort of difficulty or facing some sort of problem. The characters may go uphill or downhill, but they almost never remain the same, for even staying the same may usually be interpreted as either downhill or uphill. Although the characters will interact with other characters and with the circumstances surrounding them, usually these relationships are described fairly briefly, for the shortened form of the story does not permit a great deal of development about how human character changes in response to human beings and environment. The novel, on the other hand, permits a full development of these interactions, and its length is caused by this fullness of development. Like the short story, the novel usually focuses on a small number of characters, although the cast of secondary characters is often large and the number of incidents is multiplied.

DRAMA

A drama or play is designed to be performed on a stage by live actors. It therefore consists of dialogue together with directions for action. Like narrative fiction, it focuses on a single character or a small number of characters. Drama does not rely on narration, however, but presents you with speech and action which actually *render* the interactions that cause change in the characters and that resolve the conflicts in which the characters are engaged. Drama shows you people talking and doing, whereas narrative tells you about these activities. (To the degree that short stories and novels actually include dialogue, they use the technique of drama.) A *film script* is like drama although films often require much unspoken action, therefore verging on *pantomime*. It is often difficult to read a dramatic text because you miss a good deal of what real actors could bring to their parts by way of interpretation. Reading a play therefore requires a good deal of imaginative reconstruction on your part.

The dramatic types are *tragedy, comedy,* and *farce*. In the face of human disasters, tragedy attempts to elevate human values. Comedy treats people as they are, laughing at them or sympathizing with them, but showing them to be successful nevertheless. Farce exaggerates human foolishness, gets the characters into improbable and lunatic situations, and laughs at everyone in sight.

POETRY

Poetry is a broad term that includes many subtypes, such as *sonnet, lyric, pastoral, ballad, song, ode, drama* (which may be in either prose or poetry), *epic, mock epic,* and *dramatic monologue*. Essentially, poetry is a compressed and often highly emotional form of expression. Each word counts for more than in prose, and the basic arrangement is separate lines rather than paragraphs, although *stanzas* correspond to paragraphs, and *cantos* sometimes correspond to chapters. Poetry relies more heavily than prose on *imagery*, that is, on a comparative, allusive, suggestive form of expression that is applicable to a wide number of human situations. It is this compactness of expression, combined with the broadness of application, that makes poetry unique. Because poetry is so compact, the *rhythms* of poetic speech become as vital as the emotions and ideas. Sometimes these rhythms are called the *music* of poetry. Some poetic forms are fairly free, particularly poetry written since the time of the American poet Walt Whitman. Other forms are carefully arranged and measured into definite, countable units, and often employ *rhymes* to affect the minds of the readers and listeners.

The topic material of poetry can be just about anything. Love, personal meditations, psychological studies, reviews of folklore, attacks on conspicuous consumption, religious worship, friendship, funerary occasions, celebrations of the seasons, observations on life in the streets or in the home—these are just a few of the topics found. While writers of narrative and drama confine themselves exclusively to their respective forms, the poet is free to select any form he or she wishes. Thus some of the best poetry is dramatic (for example, Shakespeare's plays) and narrative (Milton's epic poem *Paradise Lost*).

NONFICTION PROSE

This is a broad term referring to short forms like *essays* and *articles* and to longer nonfictional and nondramatic works. The essay or article is a form designed primarily to express ideas, interpretations, and descriptions. The topics of essays are unlimited; they may be on social, political, artistic, scientific, and other subjects. In an essay an author focuses on one topic such as the influence of diet on health or the contrast between envy and ambition. The writer usually develops a single topic fully but not exhaustively. When exhaustiveness is the aim, the writer expands the essay into the form of an entire book, which retains the same centralized focus as the essay but permits a wide examination and application of the entire subject.

The *article* is a form closely related to the essay. It is designed to explore and draw conclusions from facts and sometimes is exclusively factual. Therefore the article is used in all scholarly areas, such as economics, chemistry, physics, geology, anthropology, and history. When an article is used exclusively for the reporting of research findings, it is distant from the essay in style, but when a writer combines factual material with conclusions and interpretations, the article comes close to the essay. When the scope of the article is enlarged, it grows into a complete book.

What Is Literary Analysis?

Literary analysis is no different from any other kind of analysis: it attempts to find truth. The process of analysis begins with dividing a problem into parts. Once the parts are separated and considered singly, it is easier to study their natures, functions, and interrelationships. For example, if you have a problem in chemical qualitative analysis of finding the elements in a solution, you can make only one test at a time. If you tried to make all your tests at once, you would not be able to control or distinguish your results.

In very much the same way, you cannot talk about everything in a literary work at once, even though the work is an entirety. It is better to narrow the scope of your discussion by dealing with separate topics like point of view, character, or imagery. (These are a few of the chapter assignments in this book.) Your topics will then be small enough so that you can go deeply into them.

As you develop materials for your themes, please remember that literary analysis is a way of deepening your understanding and appreciation of the work. To this end, there are four broad areas of analysis: (1) meaning, (2) form, (3) technique, and (4) background. These are not distinct classes, but overlap. For example, if your write about point of view, you will need to stress its connection to ideas (meaning). Similarly, a discussion of ideas (meaning) often extends to the origin of the ideas (background). It is always wise, in fact, to emphasize the connection of your topic to other elements in the work. In this way you are really demonstrating the relationship of literary analysis to literary appreciation, which is the aim, though sometimes unacknowledged, of all intelligent discourse about literature.

THE USE OF IMAGINATION IN WRITING ABOUT LITERATURE

One of the major problems in literary analysis is that you will somehow remain outside the work and only with difficulty see the work as the author saw it. The goal is to try to recreate to some degree the way in which the author looked at the work, to see the blank page the author originally saw and to try to reconstruct the choices and ideas the author had. Thus you should exert a good deal of imagination when you read a work. If you had an idea about rendering a personality that is insecure and fearful, as Franz Kafka did in his story-fantasy "A Country Doctor," you might try to create such a story yourself. A clinician, for example, might give a straightforward report of a character suffering from a deep-rooted sense of inadequacy. But Kafka chose to represent this story from the point of view of the country doctor himself, describing his fears in the form of a fantasy, a dream in which mysterious horses appear to carry him off to a sickroom where a young man is ill of a disease that cannot be diagnosed. In considering this story you would serve yourself well if you tried to visualize in what other ways this story could be told, what other organization could be used. In short, you should face the story as an open situation which offers innumerable possibilities.

If you can develop a capacity to look at works in this way, you can then understand better what the author has actually done. You will be in a position both of looking at the work as a finished product and determining what the work is actually like, and of seeing it as a developing product that comes into being as a result of many artistic, conscious choices. The questions to ask as you prepare your themes are: How else could this be done? What would be the possible effects of some other method? In what way or ways is the method the author chose superior to these other ways? In answering these questions you are developing the objectivity necessary to evaluate works, while preserving your sense of the work that is actually there. You may never need to include the answers to these questions, but the fact that you raised them will sharpen your own observations and interpretations.

Writing Themes About Literature

THE NEED FOR A POINT

Writing is not like classroom discussion and ordinary conversation, because writing must stick with great determination to a specific point. Classroom discussion is a form of organized talk, but there may be digressions that are sometimes not relevant. Thus classroom discussion, while formal, is free and spontaneous. Ordinary conversation is usually random and disorganized. It shifts frequently—sometimes without clear cause—from topic to topic, and it is sometimes needlessly repetitive. Writing, by contrast, is the most concise and highly organized form of expression that will ever be required of you.

WHAT IS A THEME?

It needs to be emphasized again and again that writing demands tight organization and control. The first requirement of the finished theme—although it is *not* the first requirement in the writing process—is that it have a *central idea*. The word *theme* is defined by the presence of this idea, for to be a theme, a piece of writing must have the central idea as its core. Everything in the theme should be directly related to this idea or should contribute to the reader's understanding of the idea.

Let us consider this thought as it relates to themes about literature. Such a theme should be a brief "mind's full," not an exhaustive treatment, on a particular subject; it might be a character study, an analysis of point of view, or a comparison-contrast, for example. This "mind's full" is achieved by the consistent reference to the central idea throughout the theme. That is, typical central ideas might be (1) that a character is strong and tenacious,

(2) that the point of view makes the action seem personalized, or (3) that one work is better than the other. Everything in the themes written with these central ideas is to be related to these ideas. Thus (1) the fact that the character works like a slave for ten years shows her strength and tenacity, (2) the fact that details such as a brother-sister conversation are reported is a sign of the personal quality, and (3) the fact that one work tells more about its characters than the other is a sign of superiority.

In the finished theme, all these principles should hold. When planning and writing your theme, you should have them as your goal. Here they are again:

1. The theme should cover the assigned topic (for example, character, point of view, etc.).
2. The theme should have a central idea that governs its development.
3. The theme should be organized so that every part contributes something to the reader's understanding of the central idea.

"WRITER'S BLOCK"

This is not the same as saying that themes just organize themselves magically as they are being written. When students look at a finished, polished, well-formed essay written by someone else, they may at first believe that it was perfect as it flowed from the writer's pen or typewriter. Realizing that their own beginning work does not come out so well, they often despair and go into "writer's block." That is, they may sit for hours facing their blank sheets of paper, waiting for the perfect, polished theme to "arrive." Because it does not appear, they are able to write nothing at all, they are blocked.

This cause of writer's block—the belief that the theme must be perfect the first time it is written—is false. The fact is that everyone has to work hard to produce a good piece of writing. If you could see the early drafts of some of the writing you admire, you would be surprised—and encouraged—to see how tentative they are. In final drafts, early ideas are discarded and others added; new facts are introduced; early paragraphs are cut in half and assembled elsewhere with parts of other early paragraphs; words are changed (and misspellings sometimes corrected); sentences are revised or completely written over; and new writing is added to flesh out the reassembled materials.

All of this is a normal process. In fact, for your own purposes, you should use finished themes as goals at which you should aim. How you reach the goal is up to you, because everyone has unique work habits. But you should emphasize for yourself that writing is a process in which you have to overcome not only the difficulties of reading and interpreting the literary work, but also the obstacles offered by your own mind. While they are trying to write, many people find that their minds wander. They think about something else, look out the window, turn on the radio or television set, go to sleep, get something to eat, go out to find a little action, or do anything else to delay the moment of composition.

Many of these difficulties can be overcome by the realization that things do not need to be perfect the first time. It is important just to start writing, no matter how bad the first products seem, to create a beginning. You are not committed to anything you do. You may throw it out and write something else that you believe is better. But if you keep it locked in your mind you will have nothing to work with, and then your frustration will be justified.

The Process of Writing a Theme

Despite what has just been said, there are a number of things you can do systematically in the process of writing a theme about literature. These have been entitled *invention* and *prewriting*. Invention is the process by which you discover or create the things you want to say. Prewriting is that process by which you study, think, raise and answer questions, plan, develop tentative ideas and first drafts, cross out, erase, change, rearrange, and add. In a way, prewriting and invention are merely different words for the same processes of planning and thinking. They both acknowledge the sometimes uncertain way in which the mind works and also the fact that ideas are often not known until they get written down. Writing, at any stage, should always be thought of as a process of discovery and creation. There is always something more to develop.

The following description of the writing process is presented as an approximation of what you should be doing in planning and writing your themes. You may change the order or omit some steps. In the entire process, however, you will probably not vary the steps widely.

Not every single step in the writing process can be detailed here. There is not enough space to illustrate the development of separate drafts before the final draft. If you compare the original notes with early drafts of observations and paragraphs, however, you can see that many changes take place and that one step really merges with another.

1. *Read the work through at least once for general understanding.* It is important that you have a general knowledge of the work before you try to start developing materials for your theme. Be sure, in this reading, to follow all the general principles outlined above (p. 2).

2. *Take notes with your specific assignment in mind.* If you are to write about a character, for example, take notes on things done, said, and thought about by that character. The same applies if your assignment is on imagery, or ideas, and so on. By concentrating your notes in this way, and by excluding other elements of the work, you are already focusing on your writing assignment.

3. *Use a pen or a pencil as an extension of your mind.* Writing, together with actually *seeing* the things written, is for most people a vital part of thinking. Therefore you must get any thoughts down on paper so that you have a concrete form of your thoughts. Your hand is a psychological necessity in this process. Let your ideas flow through your hand so that you will have something visible to work with later.

In addition, at some advanced part of the composing process, prepare a complete draft of what you have written. A clean, readable draft gives you the chance to see everything together and to make even more improvements. Sight is vital.

4. *Use the questions provided in the chapter on which the assignment is based.* Your answers to these questions, together with your notes and ideas, will be the basis of your theme.

5. *For all your preliminary materials, use cards or only one side of the paper.* In this way, you may spread out everything and get an overview as you plan and write your theme. Do not write on both sides of the paper, for ideas that are out of sight are often "out of mind."

6. *Once you have put everything together in this way, try to develop a central idea.* This will serve as the focus of your planning and writing.

FINDING A CENTRAL IDEA

You cannot find a central idea in a hat. It comes about as a result of the steps just described. In a way, you might think of discovering a central idea as the climax of your initial note-taking and invention. Once you have the idea, you have a guide for accepting some of your materials, rejecting others, rearranging, changing, and rewording. It is therefore necessary to see how the central idea may be developed and how it may be used.

Let us assume that your assignment is a theme about the character Jackie, in Frank O'Connor's story "First Confession." (For the complete story, please see Appendix C, pp. 174–180). The following is a collection of notes and observations that you might write when reading the story for this assignment (Chapter 4: Character Analysis). Notice that page numbers are noted, so that you can easily go back to the story at any time to refresh your memory on any details.

> Jackie the narrator blames others, mainly his grandmother, for his troubles. He hates her bare feet and her eating and drinking habits. He dislikes his sister, Nora, for "sucking up" to the grandmother. Also, Nora tells on him. He is ashamed to bring a friend home to play because of grandmother. (p. 174)

> He likes money rather than Mrs. Ryan's talk of hell.
> He is shocked by the story about the "fellow" who "made a bad confession." (p. 175)

After learning to examine his conscience, he believes that he has broken all ten commandments because of the grandmother.
He lies about a toothache to avoid confession. A kid's lie. (p. 175)

He believes his sister is a "raging malicious devil." He remembers her "throwing" him through the church door. (p. 176)
Very imaginative. Believes that he will make a "bad confession and then die in the night and be continually coming back and burning people's furniture." This is funny, and also childish. He thinks women are hypocrites. (p. 176)
He is frightened by the dark confessional. (p. 177)

Curious and adventurous. He gets up on the shelf and kneels.
He is also frightened by the tone of the priest's voice. He falls out on the church floor and gets whacked by his sister. (p. 177)

Note: All the things about Jackie as a child are told by Jackie as an older person. The man is sort of telling a joke on himself.

Jackie is smart, can think about himself as a sinner once the priest gives him a clue. He likes the kind words of the priest, is impressed with him. He begins reacting against the words of Mrs. Ryan and Nora, calling them "cackling." (p. 178)

He has sympathy for his mother. Calls her "poor soul." Seems to fear his father, who has given him the "flaking." (p. 174)

Note: Jackie is a child, and easily swayed. He says some things that are particularly childish and cute, such as coming back to burn furniture. His fears show that he is childish and naive. He is gullible. His memory of his anger against his sister shows a typical attitude of brother and sister.

Writing Observations from Your Notes: "Brainstorming"

Once you have a set of notes like these, your job is to make something out of them. They are by no means a theme, but you can begin working them into one by studying them closely and making observations about them. For the assignment we are considering here, you should try to establish traits of character. If you were studying a comparable set of notes on, say, a main idea in the work, you would try to concentrate on thoughts or ideas. The same technique would apply if you were discussing likes, point of view, imagery, and so on.

With this in mind, you can write a set of single-sentence observations. The following are all based on the previous set of notes, and they are all on character traits rather than actions. As you will see, some of them are phrased not as positive statements, but as questions to be explored further.

> Jackie likes thinking about money (the half crown) rather than hell. Is he irreligious, or does this show his childish nature?

> He has a dislike for his sister that seems to be normal brother-and-sister rivalry.

> He tells a fib about the toothache, but he tells everything else to the priest. He is not a liar.

> He blames his gran for his troubles. Is he irresponsible? No, he is just behaving like a child.

> He is curious and adventurous, as much as a seven-year-old can be.

> He is easily scared and impressed (see his response to the bad confession story, and his first response to the priest).

> He says cute things, the sort of things a child would say (the old man in the pew, coming back to burn the furniture). He seems real as a child.

These are all observations that might or might not turn out to be worth much in your theme. It is not possible to tell until you do some further thinking about them. These basic ideas, however, are worth working up further, along with some more substantiating details.

Developing Your Observations as Paragraphs

That, then, is the next step. As you develop these ideas, you should be consulting the original set of notes and also looking at the text to make sure that all your facts are correct. As you write, you should bring in any new details that seem relevant. Here are some paragraphs written in expansion of the observations presented above. You might consider this paragraph-writing phase a "second step" in the brainstorming needed for the theme:

1. Jackie comes to life. He seems real. His experiences are those that a child might have, and his reactions are lifelike. All brothers and sisters fight. All kids are "heart scalded" when they get a "flaking."

2. Jackie shows a great amount of anger. He kicks his grandmother on the shin and won't eat her cooking. He is mad at Nora for the penny that she gets from grandmother, and he "lashes out" at Nora with the bread knife. He blames his troubles on his grandmother. He talks about the "hypocrisy of women." He thinks that the stories of Mrs. Ryan and the religion of his sister are the "cackle of old women and girls" (p. 176).

3. Everything about Jackie as a child that we get in the story is told by Jackie when he is older, probably a grown man. The story is comic, and part of the comedy comes because the man is telling a joke-like story about himself.

4. Jackie's main characteristic is that he is a child and does many childish things. He remembers his anger with his sister. He also remembers being shocked by Mrs. Ryan's stories about hell. He crawls onto the ledge in the confessional. He is so impressed with the bad confession story that he says twice that he fears burning furniture. Some of these things are charming and cute, such as the observation about the old man having a grandmother and his thinking about the money when Mrs. Ryan offers the coin to the first boy who holds his finger in the candle flame.

Determining Your Central Idea

Once you have reached this stage in your thinking, you are ready to assemble all your materials and see how well they might fit a theme. You should now be searching hard for a central idea, for once you have that, you can shape your thoughts into a form for development as a theme.

If we study the notes, brainstorming observations, and paragraphs, we can find an idea that is common to them all: Jackie has many childlike characteristics. The anger, the sibling rivalry, the attraction to the coin, the fear of burning someone's furniture, the fib about the toothache—all these can be seen as childlike. Once we have found this common bond (and it could easily have been some other point, such as Jackie's anger, or his attitude toward the females around him), we can use it as the central idea for our developing theme.

Because the central idea is so vital in shaping the theme, it should be written as a complete sentence. Just the word "childishness" would not give us as much as any of the following sentences:

1. The main trait of Jackie is his childishness.
2. Jackie is bright and sensitive, but above all childlike.
3. Jackie is no more than a typical child.
4. Jackie is above all a child, with all the beauties of childhood.

Each one of these ideas would make a different kind of theme. The first would promote a theme showing that Jackie's actions and thoughts are childlike. The third would do much the same thing, but would also stress Jackie's limitations as a child. The second would try to show Jackie's better qualities, and would show how they are limited by his age. The fourth might try to emphasize the charm and "cuteness" that were pointed out in some of the notes and observations.

The point here is this: Because the central idea is so important in shaping materials for the theme, it should be phrased carefully as a sentence. You should try out as many different ways of phrasing as you can. You may ultimately decide on the first sentence you write, but in trying different shapes for your central idea, you may get new thoughts about where you want your theme to go.

Once you have the central idea (let us use the first one), you will be able to bring materials into focus with it. Let's take paragraph two in the brainstorming phase, the one about Jackie's anger. With childishness as our central idea, we can use the topic of anger as a way of illustrating Jackie's childlike character. Is his anger adult or childish? Is it normal or psychotic? Is it sudden or deliberate? In the light of these questions, we may conclude that all the examples of angry action and thought can be seen as normal childlike responses or reflections. With the material thus "arranged" in this way, we can reshape the second paragraph as follows:

Original Paragraph	Reshaped Paragraph
Jackie shows a great amount of anger. He kicks his grandmother on the shin and won't eat her cooking. He is mad at Nora for the penny that she gets from grandmother, and he "lashes out" at Nora with the bread knife. He blames his troubles on his grandmother. He talks about the "hypocrisy of women." He thinks the stories of Mrs. Ryan and the religion of his sister are the "cackle of old women and girls" (p. 178).	Jackie's great amount of anger is child-like. Kicking his grandmother, refusing to eat her cooking, and lashing out at Nora with the bread knife are the re-flexive actions of childish anger. His jealousy of Nora and his distrust of women (as hypocrites) are the results of thought, but immature, childish thought. His religious anger, still child-like, is his claim that the fears of Mrs. Ryan and Nora are the "cackle of old women and girls" (p. 178).

Notice here that the materials in each paragraph are substantially the same but that the central idea has shaped the right-hand paragraph. The left-hand column describes Jackie's anger, while the one on the right makes the claim that all the examples of angry action and thought are childlike and immature. Once our paragraph has been shaped in this way, it is almost ready for placement into the developing theme.

THE THESIS SENTENCE

Using the central idea as a guide, we can now go back to the earlier materials for arrangement. The goal is to establish a number of points to be developed as paragraphs in support of the central idea. The paragraphs written during the brainstorming will serve us well. Paragraph two, the one we have just "shaped," discusses childish anger. Paragraph three has material that could be used in an introduction (since it does not directly discuss any precise characteristics, but instead describes how the reader gets the information about Jackie). Paragraph one has material that might be good in a conclusion. Paragraph four has two topics (it is not a unified paragraph), which may be labeled "responses" and "outlook." We may put these points into a list:

1. Responses
2. Outlook
3. Anger

Once we have established this list, we may use it as the basic order for the development of our theme.

For the benefit of the reader, however, we should also use this ordering for the writing of our *thesis sentence*. This sentence is the operative sentence in the first part of the following general plan for most themes:

Tell what you are going to say.

Say it.

Tell what you've said.

The thesis sentence tells your reader what to expect. It is a plan for your theme: it connects the central idea and the list of topics in the order you plan to present them. Thus, if we put the central idea at the left and our list of topics at the right, we have the shape of a thesis sentence:

Central idea	Topics
The main trait of Jackie is his childish-ness.	1. Responses 2. Outlook 3. Anger

From this arrangement we can write the following thesis sentence, which should usually be the concluding sentence before the body of the theme (that section in which you "say it," that is, in which you develop your central idea):

> The childishness is emphasized in his responses, outlook, and anger.

With any changes made necessary by the context of your final theme, this thesis sentence and your central idea can go directly into your introduction. The central idea, as we have seen, is the glue of the theme. The thesis sentence shows the parts that are to be fastened together, that is, the topics in which the central idea will be demonstrated.

THE BODY OF THE THEME: TOPIC SENTENCES

The term regularly used in this book for the development of the central idea is *body*. The body is the section where you present the materials you have been working up in your planning. You may rearrange or even reject some of what you have developed, as you wish, as long as you change your thesis sentence to account for the changes. Since in our thesis sentence we have three topics, we will use these. Most of your themes will require that you write from 400 to 600 words. If we allow about 100 words for each of the points, that means you will most often write three 100-word paragraphs in the body of your theme. There may be more or fewer, and they may be longer or shorter, depending on how much supporting detail you are able to bring to your points.

Just as the organization of the entire theme is based on the thesis sentence, the organization of each paragraph is based on its *topic sentence*. The topic sentence is made up of one of the topics listed in the thesis sentence, combined with some assertion about how the topic will support the central idea. The first topic in our example is Jackie's responses, and the topic sentence should show how these responses illustrate a phase of Jackie's childishness. Suppose we choose the phase of the child's gullibility or impressionability. We can put together the topic and the phase, to get the following topic sentence:

> Jackie's responses show childish impressionability.

The details that will be used to develop the paragraph will then show how Jackie's responses exactly illustrate the impressionability and gullibility associated with children.

You should follow the same process in forming your other topic sentences, so that when you finish them you can use them in writing your theme.

THE OUTLINE

All along we have actually been developing an *outline* to give our finished theme an easily followed plan. Some writers never use a formal outline at all, whereas others find the outline to be quite helpful to them as they write. Still other writers insist that they cannot produce an outline until they have finished their themes. All of these views can be reconciled if you realize that finished themes should have a tight structure. At some point, therefore, you should create an outline as a guide. It may be early in your prewriting, or it may be late. What is important is that your final theme follows an outline form.

The kind of outline we have been developing here is the "analytical sentence outline." This type is easier to create than it sounds, for it is nothing more than a graphic form, a skeleton, of your theme. It consists of the following:

1. Title
2. Introduction
    a. Central idea
    b. Thesis sentence
3. Body
    a.
    b.   } points predicted in the thesis sentence
    c. etc.
4. Conclusion

The conclusion is optional in this scheme. Because the topic of the conclusion is a separate item, it is technically independent of the body, but it is part of the thematic organization and hence should be closely tied to the central idea. It may be a summary of the main points in the theme ("tell what you've said"). It may also be an evaluation or criticism of the ideas, or it may suggest further points of analysis that you did not write about in the body. In each of the following chapters, suggestions will help you in developing materials for your conclusions.

Remember that your outline should be a guide for organizing many thoughts and already completed paragraphs. Throughout our discussion of the process of writing the theme, we have seen that writing is discovery. At the right point, your outline can help you in this discovery. That is, the need to make your theme conform to the plan of the outline may help you to reshape, reposition, and reword some of your ideas.

When completed, the outline should have the following appearance (using the character study of Jackie in "First Confession"):

1. Title: "Jackie's Childish Character in O'Connor's 'First Confession' "
2. Introduction. Paragraph 1
    a. Central idea: The main trait of Jackie is his childishness.
    b. Thesis sentence: This childishness is emphasized in his responses, outlook, and anger.
3. Body: Topic sentences for paragraphs 2–4
    a. Jackie's responses show childish impressionability.
    b. His outlook reflects the simplicity of a child.
    c. His anger is also that of a child.
4. Conclusion. Paragraph 5
    Topic sentence: Jackie seems real as a child.

By the time you have created an outline like this one, you will have been planning and drafting your theme for quite some time. The outline will thus be a guide for *finishing* and *polishing* your theme, not for actually developing it. Usually you will have completed the main parts of the body and will use the outline for the introduction and conclusion.

Briefly, here is the way to use the outline:

1. Include both the central idea and the thesis sentence in your introduction. (Some instructors require a fusion of the two in the final draft of the theme. Therefore, make sure you know what your instructor expects.) Use the suggestions in the chapter assignment to determine what else might be included in the introduction.

2. Include the various topic sentences at the beginning of your paragraphs, changing them as necessary to provide transitions or qualifications. Throughout this book the various topics are confined to separate paragraphs. However, it is also acceptable to divide the topic into two or more paragraphs, particularly if the topic is difficult or highly detailed. Should you make this division, your topic then is really a *section*, and your second and third paragraphs should each have their own topic sentences.

Usually, in paragraphs of demonstration your topic sentence should go first in the paragraph. The details then "illustrate" or "show" the truth of the assertion in the topic sentence. (Details about the use of evidence will follow below, pp. 23–25.) It is also acceptable to have the topic sentence elsewhere in the paragraph, particularly if your paragraph is a "thought paragraph," in which you use details to lead up to your topic idea.

Throughout this book, for illustrative purposes, all the central ideas, thesis sentences, and topic sentences are underlined so that you may distinguish them clearly as guides for your own writing.

THE SAMPLE THEME

The following theme is a sample of the finished product of the process we have been illustrating. You will recognize the various organizing sentences because they are underlined. These are the sentences from the outline, with changes made to incorporate them into the theme. You will also see that some of the paragraphs and thoughts have been taken from the prewriting stages, with necessary changes to bring them into tune with the central idea. (Please see the illustration of this change on p. 15.)

In each of the chapters in this book there are one or two similar sample themes. It would be impossible to show the complete writing process for each of these themes, but you may assume that each one was completed more or less as the one that has been described and illustrated here. There were many good starts, and many false ones. Much was changed and rearranged, and much was redone once the outline for the theme was established. The materials for each theme were developed in the light of the issues introduced and exemplified in the first parts of each of the chapters. The plan for each theme corresponds to an outline, and its length is within the limits of most of the themes you will be assigned to write.

Jackie's Childish Character in O'Connor's "First Confession"

[1] Jackie, the main character in O'Connor's "First Confession," is a child at the time of the action. All the things we learn about him, however, are told by him as a man, or at least as an older person. The story is funny, and part of the comedy comes because the narrator is telling what amounts to a joke on himself. For this reason he brings out his own childhood childishness. That is, if Jackie were mature, the joke would not work because so much depends on his being young, powerless, and gullible. The main thing about Jackie, then, is his childishness.* This quality is emphasized in his responses, outlook, and anger.†

[2] Jackie's responses show the ease with which a child may be impressed. His grandmother embarrasses him with her drinking, eating, and unpleasant habits. He is so "shocked" by the story about the bad confession that twice he states his fear of saying a bad confession and coming back to burn furniture. He is quickly impressed by the priest and is able to change his mind about his sins (to his own favor) after no more than a few words with this man.

[3] His outlook above all reflects the limitations and the simplicity of a child. He is not old enough to know anything about the outside world, and therefore he supposes that the old man next to him at confession has also had problems with a grandmother. This same limited view causes him to think only about the half crown when Mrs. Ryan talks about punishment. It is just like a child to see everything in personal terms, without the detached, broad views of an experienced adult.

[4] His anger is also that of a child, although an intelligent one. Kicking his grandmother and lashing out against Nora with the bread knife are the reflexive actions of childish anger. He also has anger that he thinks about. His jealousy of Nora and his claim that women are hypocrites are the results of thought, even though it is immature and childish. His thinking about religion after first speaking to the priest makes him claim that the fears of Mrs. Ryan and Nora are the "cackle of old women and girls" (p. 178). He is intelligent, but he is also childish.

Jackie therefore seems real as a child. His reactions are the right ones for

*Central idea
†Thesis sentence
For the text of this story, please see Appendix C, pp. 174–180.

[5] a child to have. All brothers and sisters fight, and all children are "heart scalded" when they get a "flaking." The end of life and eternal punishment are remote for a child, whose first concern is the pleasure that money can buy. Therefore, Jackie's thoughts about the half crown are truly those of a child, as are all his thoughts and actions. The strength of "First Confession" is the reality of Jackie's childlike nature.

Theme Commentaries

Throughout this book, short commentaries follow each of the sample themes. Each discussion points out how the assignment is handled and how the instruction provided in the first part of the chapter is incorporated into the theme. For themes in which several approaches are suggested, the commentary points out which one is employed. When a sample theme uses two or more approaches, the commentary makes this fact clear. It is hoped that the commentaries will help you develop the insight necessary to use the sample themes as aids in your own writing.

Some Common Problems in Writing Themes About Literature

The fact that you understand the writing process and can apply the principles of developing a central idea and organizing with an outline and thesis sentence does not mean that you will have no problems in writing well. It is not hard to recognize good writing when you see it, but it is usually harder to explain why it is superior.

The most difficult and perplexing questions you will ask as you write are: (1) "How can I improve my writing?" (2) "If I got a C on my last theme, why wasn't the grade a *B* or an *A*? How can I get higher grades?" These are really the same question, but each has a different emphasis. Another way to ask this question is: "When I first read a work, I have a hard time following it. Yet when my instructor explains it, my understanding is greatly increased. I would like to develop the ability to understand the work and write about it well without my instructor's help. How can I succeed in this aim? How can I become an independent, confident reader and writer?"

The theme assignments in this book are designed to help you do just that. One of the major flaws in many themes about literature is that, despite the writer's best intentions and plans, they do no more than retell a story or describe an idea. Retelling the story shows only that you have read the work, not that you have thought about it. Writing a good theme, however, shows that you have digested the material and have been able to put it into a pattern of thought. In only one of the following chapters are you asked to retell a story or rephrase factual material. This is the *précis theme* (Chapter 1), and even here a major purpose is to help you make the distinction between retelling a story and making an analysis for a theme. All other chapters require and illustrate analytical processes that show your thought and understanding.

ESTABLISHING AN ORDER
IN MAKING REFERENCES

There are a number of ways in which you may set up patterns of development to show your understanding. One is to refer to events or passages in your own order. You may reverse things, or even mix them around, as long as they fit into your own thematic plans. Rarely, if ever, should you begin your theme by describing the opening of the work; it is better to talk about the conclusion or the middle of the work first. Beginning the body of your theme by referring to later parts of the work will almost force you to discuss your own central idea rather than to retell events. If you look back at paragraph three of the sample theme on "First Confession," you will see that this technique has been used. The two references there are presented in reverse order from the story. This reversal shows the theme writer's own organization, not the organization of the work being analyzed.

YOUR MYTHICAL READER:
A STUDENT WHO HAS READ
BUT NOT THOUGHT

Another important idea is to consider the "mythical reader" for whom you are writing your theme. Imagine that you are writing to other students like yourself. They have read the assigned work, just as you have, but they have not thought about it. You can immediately see what you would write for such mythical readers. They know the events or have followed the thread of the argument. They know who says what and when it is said. As a result, you do not need to tell these readers about everything in the work, but should think of your role as that of an *explainer* or *interpreter*. Tell them what things mean in relationship to your central idea. *Do not, however, tell them the things that happen.*

To look at the situation in still another way, you may have read stories about Sherlock Holmes and Dr. Watson. Holmes always points out to Watson that all the facts are available to both of them, but that, though Watson *sees*, he does not *observe*. Your role is like that of Holmes, explaining and interpreting facts, and drawing conclusions that Dr. Watson has been unable to draw for himself. Once again, if you look back at the sample theme on "First Confession," you will notice that everywhere *the assumption has been made that the reader has read the story already*. References to the story are thus made primarily to remind the reader of something he or she already knows, but *the principal emphasis of the theme is to draw conclusions and develop arguments*.

USING LITERARY MATERIAL
AS EVIDENCE

The analogy with Sherlock Holmes should remind you that whenever you write on any topic, your position is much like that of a detective using clues as evidence for building a case, or of a lawyer using evidence as support for arguments. If you argued in favor of securing a greater voice for students in college government, for example, you would introduce such evidence as past successes with student government, increased maturity of modern-day students, the constitutional amendment granting 18-year-olds the right to vote, and so on.

Writing about literature requires evidence as well. *For practical purposes only*, when you are writing a theme, you may conveniently regard the work assigned as evidence for your arguments. You should make references to the work only as a part of the logical development of your discourse. Your objective is to convince your reader of your own knowledge and reasonableness, just as lawyers attempt to convince a jury of the reasonableness of their arguments.

The whole question of the use of evidence is a far-reaching one. Students of law spend years studying proper uses of evidence. Logicians have devised the system of syllogisms and inductive reasoning to regulate the use of evidence. It would not be logical, for example, to conclude from Shakespeare's play *Macbeth* that Macbeth behaves like a true friend and great king. His murders, his rages, and his pangs of guilty conscience form evidence that makes this conclusion absurd.

To see how material from the work may become supporting evidence in a theme, let us refer again to the sample theme on "First Confession." The fourth paragraph is about Jackie's anger being an aspect of his childlike nature. Four separate details from the story are introduced in support. If you will also look again at how this paragraph was first developed in the light of the central idea (p. 15), you will see that the details are not introduced to tell the story. Two of them specifically show the reflexive nature of childhood anger, and the other two show Jackie's immature, childish thought, despite his obvious intelligence. Use this way of introducing detail as a model for your own themes.

It is vital to use evidence correctly in order for your reader to follow your idea. Let us look briefly at two examples to see how writing may be made better by the evidential use of details. These are from themes analyzing Thomas Hardy's story "The Three Strangers."

1

After a short lapse of time, the second stranger enters to seek shelter from the rain. He is a rather full-fleshed man dressed in gray, with signs on his face of drinking too much. He tells the guests that he is en route to Caster-bridge. He likes to drink, exhausting the large mug full of mead that is offered to him, and quickly demanding more, which makes Shepherd Fennel's wife extremely angry. With the mead going to his head and making him drunk, he relates his occupation by singing a song in the form of a riddle. This second stranger is a hangman who is supposed to hang a man in Casterbridge for stealing a sheep. As he reveals his occupation, stanza by stanza, an increasing air of dismay is cast over the guests. They are horrified by the hangman's description of his job, but he makes a big joke about all the grim details, such as making a mark on the necks of his "customers" and sending them to a "far countree."

2

Hardy uses the second stranger—the hangman—to produce sympathy for the shepherds and distrust of the law. By giving the hangman a selfish thirst for mead, which drains some of the Fennels' meager supply, Hardy justifies Mrs. Fennel's anger and anxiety. An even greater cause for anxiety than this personal arrogance is the harsh legal oppression that the hangman represents to the shepherds. Indeed, the shepherds were already sympathetic to the plight of Summers, the first stranger (whose crime seems reward-able, not punishable), but the domineering manner of the hangman clearly makes them go beyond just sympathy. They silently decide to oppose the law by hiding Summers. Hardy thus makes their obstructionism during the later manhunt seem right and reasonable. Perhaps he has stacked the deck against the law here, but he does so to make the reader admire the shepherd folk. In this plan, the hangman's obnoxiousness is essential.

Although the first example has more words than the second (174 words in column 1, 151 in column 2), it is not adequate, for it shows that the writer felt only the obligation to retell the story. The paragraph is cluttered with details and it contains no conclusions and no observations. If you had read the story, the paragraph would not provide you with a single piece of new information, and absolutely no help at all in understanding the story. The writer did not have to think much in order to write the paragraph. On the other hand, the second column is responsive to the reader's needs, and it required a good deal of thought to write. Phrases like "Hardy thus makes" and "In this plan" show that the writer of the second theme has assumed that the reader knows the details of the story and now wants help in interpretation. Column 2 therefore leads readers into a pattern of thought that may not have occurred to them when they were reading the story. In effect, column 2 brings evidence to bear on a point and excludes all irrelevant details; column 1 provides nothing more than raw, undirected evidence.

The answer to that difficult question about how to turn *C* writing into *A* writing is to be found in the comparison of the two columns. Besides using English correctly, superior writers always allow their minds to play upon the materials. They always try to give readers the results of their thoughts. They dare to trust their responses and are not afraid to make judgments about the literary work they are considering. Their principal aim in referring to events in a work is to develop their own thematic pattern. Observe this quality again by comparing two sentences which deal with the same details from the story:

1	2
He likes to drink, exhausting the large mug full of mead that is offered to him, and quickly demanding more, which makes Shepherd Fennel's wife extremely angry.	By giving the hangman a selfish thirst for mead, which drains some of the Fennels' meager supply, Hardy justifies Mrs. Fennel's anger and anxiety.

Sentence 1 is detailed but no more. Sentence 2 links the details as a pattern of cause and effect within the author's artistic purpose. Notice the words "By giving" and "Hardy justifies." These indicate the writer's *use* of the facts. There are many qualities in good writing, but perhaps the most important is the way in which the writer uses known facts as evidence in a pattern of thought that is original. Always try to achieve this quality in all your writing about literature.

KEEPING TO YOUR POINT

Whenever you write a theme about literature, then, you must pay great attention to the proper organization and to the proper use of references to the work assigned. As you write, you should try constantly to keep your material unified, for should you go off on a tangent, you are following the material rather than leading it. It is all too easy to start with your point but then wander off into a retelling of events or ideas. Once again, resist the tendency to be a narrator rather than an interpreter.

Let us look at another example. The following paragraph is taken from a theme on the "Idea of Personal Responsibility in Homer's *The Odyssey*." This is the third paragraph; the writer has stated the thematic purposes in the first paragraph, and in the second has shown that various characters in *The Odyssey* believe that human beings are responsible for their actions and must bear the consequences.

More forcefully significant than these statements of the idea is the way it is demonstrated in the actions of the characters in the epic. Odysseus, the hero, is the prime example. Entrapped by Polyphemus (the son of Poseidon the Earth-Shaker by the nymph Thoosa) and threatened with death, Odysseus in desperation puts out the eye of his captor, who then begs his father Poseidon for vengeance. Answering his son's anguished curse, Poseidon frustrates Odysseus at every turn in the voyage back to Ithaca, and forces him to wander for ten years before reaching home.

This paragraph shows how easily writers may be diverted from their objective in writing. The first sentence rightly states that the idea is to be demonstrated in the actions of the epic. That the remainder of the paragraph concentrates on Odysseus is no flaw, because the writer concentrates on other characters in following paragraphs. The flaw is that the material about Odysseus does not go beyond the story itself; it does not come to grips with the topic of personal responsibility; it does not indicate understanding. The material may be relevant to the topic, but the writer does not point out its relevance. Remember always that in expository writing you should not rely on making your meaning clear simply by implication; you must make all relationships *explicitly* clear.

Let us see how this problem can be solved. If the ideal paragraph could be schematized with line drawings, we might say that the paragraph's topic should be a straight line, moving toward and reaching a specific goal (explicit meaning), with an exemplifying line moving away from the straight line briefly in order to bring in evidence, but returning to the line after each new fact in order to demonstrate the relevance of this fact. Thus, the ideal scheme would look like this:

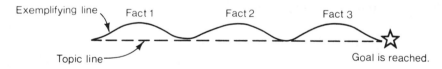

Notice that the exemplifying line, or the example or the documenting line, always returns to the topic line. A scheme for the above paragraph on *The Odyssey*, however, would look like this:

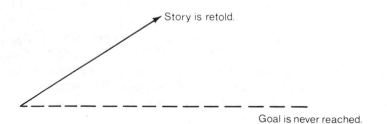

How might this paragraph be improved? The best way is to reintroduce the topic again and again throughout the paragraph to keep reminding the reader of the relevance of the exemplifying material. Each time you mention the topic you are bringing yourself back to the line, and this practice should prevail no matter what the topic. If you are analyzing point of view, for example, you should keep pointing out the relevance of your material to the point of view of the work, and the same applies to *character* or whatever aspect of literature you are studying. According to this principle, we might revise the paragraph on *The Odyssey* as follows, keeping as much of the original wording as we can. (Parts of sentences stressing the relationship of the examples to the topic of the paragraph are underlined.)

> More forcefully significant than these statements of the idea is the way it is demonstrated in the actions of the characters in the epic. Odysseus, the hero, is the prime example. When he is entrapped and threatened with death by Polyphemus (the son of Poseidon the Earth-Shaker by the nymph Thoosa), Odysseus in desperation puts out the eye of his captor. Though his action is justifiable on grounds of self-preservation, <u>he must, according to the main idea, suffer the consequences.</u> Polyphemus begs his father Poseidon for vengeance. Poseidon hears, <u>and accordingly this god becomes the means of enforcing Odysseus'</u> punishment, since Odysseus, in injuring the god's son, has insulted the god. The Ithacan king's ten years of frustration and exile are therefore not caused by whimsy; <u>they are punishment for his own action. Here the idea of personal responsibility is shown with a vengeance;</u> despite the extenuating circumstances, <u>the epic makes clear that characters must answer for their acts.</u>

The paragraph has been lengthened and improved. You might object that if all your paragraphs were lengthened in this way your theme would grow too long. The answer to this objection is that *it is better to develop a few topics fully than many scantily.* Such revision might require you to throw away some of your topics or else to incorporate them as subpoints in the topics you keep. This process can only improve your theme. But the result of greater length here is that the exemplifying detail points toward the topic, and the paragraph reaches its goal.

The same need for sticking to your point is true of your entire theme, for you will not be successful unless you have thoroughly convinced your reader that your central idea is valid. The two following themes should illustrate this truth. The theme on the left is only rudimentary. The writer begins by indicating a concern for the harm the parents cause their children in the two plays being compared. Although occasionally the theme gets back to this point, it rarely gets above the level of a précis. The theme in the right-hand column is superior because the writer announces a central idea and pursues it throughout. As in the earlier paragraph, those parts of the following themes that emphasize the central idea will be underlined.

The type of theme is *comparison-contrast* (Chapter 10), and the assignment was made specifically on Arthur Miller's *All My Sons* and Tennessee Williams's *The Glass Menagerie*.

Theme 1
A Comparison of
Two Plays

Miller's *All My Sons* and Williams's *The Glass Menagerie* are the two plays being compared. Both plays have the family as the center around which the characters revolve. In both families, <u>the parents hurt the children.</u> Miller writes of a well-off, factory-owning family; Williams of a low-class family.

The comparison of the families may start with the fathers. Joe Keller of *All My Sons* is an ambitious, conniving, and good businessman. He allows a defective shipment to go through because, as he says, he could not let forty years' work go down the drain. He also says to Chris that he did what he did because he wanted Chris to have something for his future, a business. Not much is mentioned of the father in *The Glass Menagerie,* but from what is given the reader, we picture him as a worthless drunkard. He had no purpose in life and consequently was a poor provider for his family. One should not condone Keller for what he did, but at least Keller had some initiative and

Theme 2
The Destruction of
Children by Parents
in Two Plays

In both Miller's *All My Sons* and Williams's *The Glass Menagerie,* the family is the center of the action. Miller's family is well off; Williams's is lower class. This difference is not material in view of the fact that both dramatists demonstrate the <u>destructive effects of parents upon children,</u> regardless of class. It is true that these parents were once children themselves, and that presumably they were recipients of <u>equally destructive effects from their parents.</u> This element gives both plays direct, universal appeal: that is, both plays dramatize the process by which our society is <u>generally hurt by what,</u> to the dramatists, <u>are outmoded economic and social values, transmitted by parents to children.</u> The fathers, mothers, and children will be discussed in that order.

The fathers in both plays seem to be the ones <u>first to do hurt. Both are irresponsible. Joe's unscrupulousness causes the death of twenty-one boys who flew in airplanes made defective by his deliberate negligence.</u> The Wingfield father simply <u>abandons his family.</u> Joe's defense of his action makes good sense. <u>His motives are not bad</u> from a short-term point of view. He really did not want to let forty years of work go down the drain, and he really did want to give Chris (and Larry) a thriving business. His means, however, <u>were selfish and hurtful—primarily economic rather than human and loving—</u>just as the Wingfield father causes his family <u>untold damage</u> by abandoning foresight whereas the Wingfield father had nothing. <u>Both fathers hurt their children.</u>

Next we can compare the mothers in the two works. In Miller's play the mother is a sensitive, unyielding, and loving person. It is she who stands firm in her belief that Larry is still living. By doing this she prevents her other son, Chris, from marrying Ann. In a sense, she is looking out for her son's interest because if Larry was ever to return, chaos would result. Amanda, the mother of *The Glass Menagerie*, is a very sociable person. Her daughter is unbelievably shy. The mother attempts to help her daughter. She does, also, what she thinks will be in the interests of her daughter. Therefore she concludes that marriage is the answer to Laura's problems. We can see how two different mothers with the same goals—happiness for their children—<u>achieve the opposite results because they fail to attend to the needs and desires of their children.</u>

Lastly, the children will be compared. Chris is both an idealistic as well as realistic person. He tries to think the best of people, as he does with his father. When he finds out otherwise, he <u>is terribly shocked and disappointed.</u> Much the same thing happens when Laura finds out that Jim is going to get married; her reaction is one of <u>disappointment and withdrawal.</u> Just when she has finally gotten socially involved with someone, he leaves. So we see how both children have to put up with <u>disappointments;</u> one finds out his father is a murderer, while the other loses the first person she ever loved.

them for a life that to many might seem very pleasant.

While less <u>creators of hurt</u> than <u>agents of it,</u> the mothers in both families also <u>cause much damage.</u> Kate Keller, while sensitive and unyielding, is nevertheless loving. Her firm belief that her son Larry is still alive is caused by a defense against her awareness of Joe's great crime, but <u>the end result is the unhappiness of her son Chris.</u> Her love is mixed with a <u>deliberately unreal outlook.</u> While superficially different from Kate, <u>Amanda is similarly destructive.</u> Attempting to look out for the interests of her daughter, she tries to make a carbon copy of herself, even though her background is dead, as far as her daughter is concerned. Her failure is that she does not see her daughter as an individual with distinct needs. Laura's reaction to her mother's manipulation is <u>withdrawal,</u> but Amanda cannot see any <u>harmful effect.</u> Both mothers, desiring to make their children happy, <u>produce the same unhappy results.</u>

The full effects of <u>these destructive parents are felt by the children.</u> Larry, we learn, <u>has killed himself because of shame for his father's deed.</u> Chris, we see demonstrated, <u>is shocked, angered, and embittered by it.</u> Laura is <u>disappointed,</u> ostensibly by hearing that Jim is going to marry another, but ultimately by having been brought up <u>without a father and with her mentally disjointed mother.</u> Tom simply leaves, but he remembers his mother objectively and his father condescendingly. Thus the effects of the parents on the children, and beyond that, of the society on its members, are the same—<u>destruction and decay.</u>

Through comparing and contrasting the members of each family we have been able to see how these families are different and how they are similar. In both families, however, the children are hurt by well-intentioned but foolish parents.

Comparing and contrasting the two families in this way brings out their similarities. The parents in both families are interesting and not abnormal. They have values which hurt their children. In the Kellers it is money against humanity. In the Wingfields it is social position against individuality. In both families everyone loses, because neither family is committed to the idea of humanity and individuality. Though the relevance of this theme to society at large has been only mentioned, the implication in both plays is that society must make a commitment to human and individual values if it is to survive. If people do not make this commitment, the destructive patterns in the Keller and Wingfield families will continue.

GROWTH: DEVELOPMENT

There is another reason why the theme on the right is superior. In addition to sticking to the point, the writer in a number of spots suggests that the harmful influences of the parents are related to impractical or unjust economic values. At the end, the writer interprets the central idea by stating that society at large needs to commit itself to human values. In short, the writer has made the idea *grow,* not simply by exemplifying it, but by considering a number of its implications.

The idea of growth or development deserves special treatment. Let us take another example, the eighteenth-century novel *Tom Jones* (1749) by Henry Fielding. This novel is about the childhood and early manhood of Tom Jones, who is apparently a bastard (a shocking topic at the time), but who is eventually recognized as the son of Bridget Allworthy and therefore as a legitimate heir of his uncle, the wealthy Squire Allworthy. Tom is raised and educated with his half-brother Blifil, and during most of the novel Blifil, a hypocritical sort, is seemingly in great favor while Tom is not. Tom experiences many difficulties as he moves toward gaining his birthright and marrying his lifelong sweetheart, Sophia Western. In the end, however, everything turns out well for him, and Blifil is discredited.

Let us assume that a student with an assignment on *Tom Jones* decides on this central idea: "Fielding's exposure of hypocrisy in *Tom Jones* is made most evident in the person of Blifil." This much is good, but the problem is that many students will do no more with this idea than cite a number of instances in the novel which illustrate Blifil's hypocrisy. Such a line of development gets some of the point across, but it does not lead readers toward any new understanding of Fielding's artistic or moral purposes in *Tom Jones*. Something more needs to be done; the writer needs to exert an imaginative effort to interest and arouse potential readers.

As an analogy, let us suppose that we see a pencil and a knife on a table and are asked to describe them. Many people might do no more than simply describe these things, but an imaginative person will write something more. For example, one writer might say that people can use a pencil to create ideas that might change the world or ideas that might strengthen human thought for centuries to come. The first drafts of the Declaration of Independence were probably made with a pencil. Another imaginative writer might say that a knife is a basic tool that has unlocked the previously closed doors of technology and enabled human beings to hunt, to carve, to create, and to make civilization. Before there was modern technology, there was the primitive and useful knife. Both developments of such common subjects promise something interesting; they lead readers imaginatively into new and previously unconsidered areas of perception.

The developing of an idea is hence vital in good writing. The writer should make the subject grow from the initial statement of the central idea. In the case of Blifil's hypocrisy, it is not enough simply to establish that Blifil is a hypocrite, but one must show that this hypocrisy leads to important areas in *Tom Jones* and also to important ideas that Fielding was considering about human nature. In considering the development of the hypocrisy of Blifil, a writer might include the following thoughts:

> Blifil's hypocrisy leads both to serious problems for Tom and Sophia and to the destruction of Blifil himself.

> For example, by refusing to tell Allworthy that Bridget, before her death, had acknowledged Tom as her son, Blifil makes it possible for Tom to be disowned by Allworthy and to be cast adrift in the countryside. In despair because of being disowned, Tom has no concern for what happens to him, and in this mood he is self-destructive, as any person might naturally be in such circumstances. He thus commits the sexual indiscretions that give him trouble with Sophia but that also give him pangs of conscience. It is the development of conscience and his concern to raise himself in the esteem of Sophia and Allworthy that make Tom a

developing character worthy of being the center of interest in the novel. Thus, in one respect Tom is hurt by Blifil, but in another, Blifil becomes the cause of Tom's moral growth.

Also, because of his own hypocrisy, Blifil is finally unable to detect his own faults, and to this degree he cuts himself away from common human morality. His fear of Allworthy's anger at the end of the novel does not result from introspective pangs of conscience, but rather from the fear of Allworthy's disfavor and the consequent loss of money that this disfavor will bring. At the end of the work Blifil is nothing more than a money-grubbing hypocrite, to be contrasted with Tom.

As you can see from these examples, the writer has gone from a basic, central idea—that Blifil is a hypocrite—toward a development of that idea in terms of how the hypocrisy is important in the novel *Tom Jones*. Details from the book are naturally included, but they are not mere illustration. Instead, they are used as parts of a process of reasoning or argumentation. In other words, the central idea has been developed; growth has taken place. Without such growth, there is no totally successful writing, just as there is no successful thinking.

It should be clear that whenever you write, an important goal should be the development of your central idea. You should try to go somewhere with your idea, to give your readers insights about the literary materials that they did not have before they started reading. To the degree that you can learn to develop your ideas, you will receive recognition for increasingly superior writing achievements.

Admittedly, in a short theme you will be able to move only a short distance with an idea, but you should never be satisfied to leave the idea exactly where you found it. Nurture it and make it grow. Constantly adhere to your topic and constantly develop it.

USING ACCURATE AND FORCEFUL LANGUAGE

The best writing has a quality of accuracy, force, and insight. Quite often the first products of our minds are rather weak, and they need to be rethought, recast, and reworded. Sometimes this process cannot be carried out immediately, for it may take days or even weeks for us to gain objectivity about what we say. As a student you usually do not have that kind of time, and thus you must acquire the habit of challenging your own statements almost as soon as you write them. Ask yourself whether they really mean what you want, or if you can make a stronger statement than you have.

As an example, consider the following statement, a central idea about E. M. Forster's short story "The Machine Stops," an allegory about a future

world in which people are completely dependent on machinery but perish
when the machinery breaks down.

> The central idea of this story is that because of the machine and its
> marvelous powers, the people place their total dependence on it.

This central idea could not carry you very far if you were writing a theme
based on it. But try to restate and strengthen the essential material in the
sentence. Two possibilities are as follows:

> 1. Forster shows that human beings, by accepting the machine and by
>   becoming hostile to Nature, have alienated themselves from their
>   environment and are therefore responsible for their own destruction.
> 2. Forster shows that the pursuit of ideas and technology to the exclusion
>   of Nature has led human beings to destroy themselves.

Either of these two sentences would be more helpful as a statement of a
central idea than the first example.

Sometimes, in seeking to say something, we wind up saying nothing.
Here are two sentences from themes about Robert Frost's "Stopping by
Woods on a Snowy Evening."

> 1. It seems as though the author's anticipation of meeting with death
>   causes him to respond as he does in the poem.
> 2. This incident, although it may seem trivial or unimportant, has sub-
>   stantial significance in the creation of his poem; by this I mean the
>   incident which occurred is essentially what the poem is all about.

The vagueness of sentences like these must be resisted. A sentence should
not end up in limbo the way these do. The first sentence is satisfactory
enough up to the verb "causes," but then it falls apart. If Frost has created
a response for the speaker in the poem, it is best to describe *what* that
response is rather than to state simply that there *is* a response. A more
forceful restatement of the first sentence may thus be, "It seems as though
the author's anticipation of meeting with death causes him to think about
the need to meet his present responsibilities." With this revision, the writer
could go on to a consideration of the meaning of Frost's final stanza and
could relate the ideas there to the events and ideas described in the first
part of the poem. Without the revision, it is not clear where the writer
would go.

The second sentence is so vague that it confuses rather than informs.
Essentially, such sentences hint at an idea and claim importance for it, but
they never directly define what that idea is. If we adopt the principle that
it is always better to name the specific things we are talking about, perhaps
the second sentence could be revised as follows:

> Although stopping by the woods to watch the snow fall may seem trivial
> or insignificant, the incident causes the poet to meditate on beauty and

responsibility; the important thoughts in the poem thus grow from the simplest of events.

When you write your own sentences, you might test them in a similar way. Are you referring to an idea? State the idea directly. Are you mentioning a response or impression? Do not say simply, "The poem left me with a definite impression," but describe the impression: "The poem left me with an impression of sympathy," or "of understanding the hard lot of the migrant farmer." Similarly, do not rest with a statement such as "I found this story interesting," but try to describe what was interesting and why it was interesting. If you always confront your impressions and responses by trying to name them and to pin them down, your sentences should take on exactness and force. Naturally, your instructor will probably tell you whatever you have accomplished or failed to accomplish. Good writing habits that you develop from these criticisms of your work, and from discussions with your instructor, will help you to write more forcefully and accurately.

Whenever you write a theme, then, keep these ideas in mind. Keep returning to the point you wish to make; regard the material of the work you have read as evidence to substantiate your arguments, not as material to be described. Keep demonstrating that all exemplifying detail is relevant to your main point. Keep trying to develop your topic; make it bigger than it was when you began writing. Constantly keep trying to make your statements accurate and forceful. If you observe these precepts, you should be well on the way toward handling any of the following theme assignments successfully.

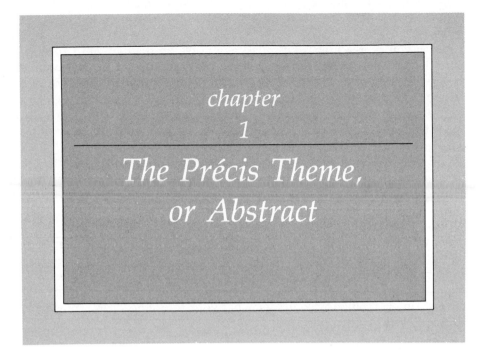

chapter

1

The Précis Theme, or Abstract

A précis is a shortening, in your own words, of the text of a written work. In writing a précis you describe, as accurately as possible, what happens in a story or play, or you briefly restate, abridge, digest, or encapsulate the substance or main ideas in an essay, article, or poem. Other words that describe the précis or abstract are *paraphrase, condensation, and epitome*. All these words suggest a shortening or a highlighting of only the most significant details and sections of a work.

The length of your précis depends on the extent of the original work and the approximate length of your assignment. Thus, a 3,000-word story might be condensed into 100 or 1,000 words. The amount of detail to include naturally depends on the desired length of the précis. The 1,000-word précis would contain much detail, whereas the 100-word précis would not have much more than the main headings.

Uses of the Précis

The précis is important in the service of study, research, and speaking and writing. One of the best ways to study any work is to write a précis of it, for by so doing you force yourself to grasp each of the parts. Also, referring later to your précis helps to bring the entire work back to your memory. There are few better ways to begin careful study.

When you do research, you must take notes on the material you find. Here the ability to shorten and paraphrase is essential, for it is impossible to reproduce everything in your notes. The better you are able to write a précis, the better will be your research.

In discussions, you will improve your arguments if you refer briefly but accurately to sections of the work being discussed. When you are writing a theme, particularly a longer one, it is often necessary to remind your reader of the events or facts in the work. Here the need is not to tell *everything*, but just enough so that your conclusions will be self-sustaining. In an argumentative or persuasive speech or theme, when you are trying to convince your listener or reader, it is necessary to get the facts straight in order to eliminate objections that may arise about your use of detail.

For all these occasions you will profit from being able to paraphrase or abstract. Although you will sometimes need to condense an entire story or epitomize an entire argument, most often you will need to refer only to parts of works, because your arguments will depend on a number of separate interpretations. No matter what your future needs are, however, your ability to write a précis will be helpful to you.

Problems in Writing a Précis

1. ACCURACY. Just as the précis is important in establishing a "handle" on the facts, one of the first problems in writing a précis is to be sure that you get the facts straight. You should make no unsupported statements. Let us suppose that you are writing about so simple and well-remembered a story as "Hansel and Gretel." Suppose you write that "the children eventually overcome the witch by thrusting her into the oven." This statement is only partially true. It is not *both* children who defeat the witch, but Gretel alone, for Hansel is locked up in a cage at the time the witch and Gretel are preparing the oven. If you think only casually about what to write, however, it would be natural to say that "the children" are both agents of victory. It is important to go over your précis carefully to make sure that all you say is factually correct.

2. USING YOUR OWN WORDS. Another problem is the difficulty you may find in using *your own* words in your précis to replace the words and ideas in the original. The best way is to read the work carefully at least three times. Then put the work away, out of sight, and do your writing. In this way you force yourself to use your own words, without the temptation of borrowing directly from the original.

If you find, however, that you have used some words and phrases from your source, be careful to underline, star, or otherwise mark these borrowed words, and then try to use your own words when you revise. If it seems impossible to make changes of some words, you may preserve a small number of the originals, but be sure to include them within quotation marks in your final draft.

3. **SELECTING DETAILS.** A third problem is deciding what details to select. Try to pick out only those that are of greatest significance. A writer may tell about two people who, in a restaurant, order a wide variety of dishes and engage in lengthy conversation. Obviously, in a précis you do not want to mention each item of food and drink. If one of the characters gets drunk, however, it might be important to state that the character drank too much. Similarly, you would not need to report all the conversation, but only that part which contained the important details, such as that a character was happy or unhappy. The reporting of detail is critical in the way your précis will be judged. Some things are more important than others, and you must choose details according to this scale of importance.

4. **AVOIDING CONCLUSIONS.** Surprisingly, a major problem in a précis is to avoid making conclusions. It is true that your understanding of the work determines those details which you think are important and that a précis thus represents the factual basis for most of your conclusions. But in the précis itself you should avoid these conclusions and concentrate only on facts. Report them accurately and impartially. The following columns show the difference between good and bad methods:

Theme A *with* conclusions: wrong	Theme B *without* conclusions: right
Gretel fulfills her plan to overcome the witch by pretending ignorance. Thus she confesses her inability to open the door, in this way leading the witch to doom. Angered by Gretel, the witch demonstrates the proper way to open the door. Gretel, having seen the success of her plan, quickly pushes the witch into the fire and rescues Hansel.	Because Gretel states that she is unable to manage the oven, the witch angrily goes to the door and demonstrates the proper way to open it. Gretel then quickly pushes the witch into the fire and rescues Hansel.

Often, of course, it is necesssary to generalize about parts of the work. Let us suppose that a story contains many details showing that a character is cheerful. It is *proper* to state generally that the character is cheerful, for you may make that statement fairly and it is important to make your theme as brief and as comprehensive as possible. However, it is *improper* here to add your own conclusions, such as "this cheerfulness shows the character's courage in the face of danger." The conclusion may be the right one, but you should not offer interpretations of this type in a précis. Stick to the details.

5. AVOIDING CHOPPY SENTENCES. Although you concentrate on essentials in your précis, you should avoid short, choppy sentences. Here is an example:

> It is December, just before Christmas. Phoenix Jackson is beginning to walk to Natchez. She is a black woman. She is old but cheerful. She walks with a cane. She has walked this way many times.

Here there are six sentences, all very short and beginning with the subject followed immediately by the verb. Sentences like these are almost impossible to read for an entire paper. A revision should reduce the number of sentences but keep the same details, as in the following:

> Just before Christmas, Phoenix Jackson begins her familiar walk through the country from her home to Natchez. She is a poor and old black woman, who needs a cane for support, but she is cheerful.

Your Theme

Your task is to make a reduction of the original with the least possible distortion. Thus you should select things only as they come in the work. In her story "A Worn Path," for example, Eudora Welty reveals in the last page that the main character has gone into town to get medicine for her infirm grandchild. It would be helpful to introduce that detail at the start of the précis, but because the author has included it only at the end of the story, it is proper to bring it in only at the comparable stage of the précis.

If your précis is to be very short, 100 to 150 words, for example, you might confine everything to only one paragraph. If you have a longer word limit, like 200 to 500 words, it is good to arrange your paragraphs according to the natural divisions in the original work. Thus, if the work has parts or sections, you might devote a paragraph to each of these divisions. If an undivided story moves from place to place, as in the sample theme below, you might provide a paragraph for events occurring at each place. Or if the story takes place in only one location, you might use paragraphs to describe (1) the events leading up to the main action, (2) the action itself, and (3) the consequences of the action. If you are writing a précis of an essay or article, you might organize according to the author's main divisions, such as the background of the problem, possible solutions, and consequences. Whether you are writing about fiction, drama, poetry, essay, or article, however, follow the general principle of letting the work itself be your guide about paragraphing.

Sample Theme
A Précis of Eudora Welty's "A Worn Path"

[1] Just before Christmas, Phoenix Jackson begins her familiar walk through the country from her home to Natchez. She is a poor and old black woman, who needs a cane for support, but she is cheerful. She releases herself from a thorny bush, climbs a high hill, and finds her way through areas with no marked path. She is attacked by a large dog and falls into a ditch, but soon is assisted by a young white hunter, who frightens off the dog. Phoenix sees the man drop a nickel before he chases the dog; she recovers it and hides it. Though the man advises her to go back home, Phoenix resolutely continues on her way toward Natchez.

[2] As she enters town, she is successful in getting a white lady on the street to tie her shoes, for she states that neatly tied shoes are essential for going to an important building. Almost without thinking about where she is going, she climbs many stairs to find the medical office in the building, and then she sits down there, blankly.

[3] While an attendant asks her about her business, a nurse enters and reveals to the attendant that Phoenix has come to get medicine for her grandson, who two or three years earlier had drunk lye and is now totally disabled. Phoenix receives the free medicine, and the attendant gives her a nickel. With these, together with the nickel she had recovered earlier, Phoenix states that she will buy a little paper windmill for her grandson. She then leaves the office.

Commentary on the Theme

Though many details from the story must necessarily be eliminated, each paragraph concentrates on the major actions that occur in each of the main locations in the story. The sample theme is about 250 words long, and therefore it is possible to include some of the details about Phoenix when she first reaches Natchez. With a shorter word limit it would be necessary to eliminate these details and instead concentrate on the events in the medical office, for these concluding details are more important than what happens to Phoenix on the Natchez streets.

The précis is successful as a précis for the foregoing reasons and also because it includes most of the details that in the story itself are the basis

For the text of this story, please see Appendix C, pp. 181–187.

for Eudora Welty's portrait of Phoenix. She is cheerful even though she has suffered great sorrow and poverty, and her lot in life will not change. She is dependent, forgetful, kind, and trusting, with a harmless trace of larceny. She is both strong and simple. Eudora Welty uses the events in the story to bring out all these traits, and the précis, by the presentation of the same events, could be used as the basis for such conclusions about the character of Phoenix.

chapter
2

The Summary Theme

The summary theme is a step beyond the précis. Like the précis, it concentrates on the details in a work, but unlike the précis, it requires the thematic structure of a central idea, a thesis sentence, and topic sentences. Because of these requirements, the summary theme demands that you make judgments. To this degree, you are beginning to write criticism.

This criticism is not just "literary," however; it is characteristic of the mental processes that you must employ in any of your college courses. For example, in a history course you will rarely be requested simply to present a list of facts and dates; you will be required to show how the facts are related to a dominating idea or "tendency" in history. Here is a short paragraph showing how historical details can be placed in the context of an idea; the technique is that of the summary theme:

> The major fault of the British government—and one of the major causes of the Revolutionary War—was not that it imposed taxes, but that it did so without consulting the Colonials. This was true of the Stamp Act, which the British withdrew in 1766 after fierce riots in the colonies. It was also true of the commodities taxes, like those on glass, paint, and tea, which were imposed late in the 1760's. There was a need for these taxes, but the Colonials did not share in making the laws which imposed them, and it was resentment over this, rather than taxation itself, which led to the Boston Tea Party in 1773.

Notice here that the major idea—that there was no consultation—controls the presentation of the facts. This idea is stressed throughout the paragraph. The need for relating facts to a main thought is important in good writing. Writing a summary theme thus should provide you with a basic technique you can apply in your other college courses where extensive writing is required.

What Do You Summarize?

The summary theme assumes that you are able to write a précis of the work assigned, whether it is a story, a play, a longer poem, an essay, or an article. Once you have reached this level, you will be faced with the major problem of organization; that is, of relating your materials to a main idea. This main idea is your description of the plot or idea of the work.

PLOT

If your work is a drama or a narrative, you should try to discover the plot. There is a difference between a plot and a story. The story is the set of events, details, or speeches in the work as they appear in chronological or act-by-act order. It is the story that you condense as you write a précis. The plot is something more. It is the reasons or the logic underlying the story and causing it to take the form in which it appears. The essence of plot is the existence of a *conflict* between opposing forces—human beings against themselves, against other human beings, or against some natural or supernatural force. The conflict produces those actions and interactions that are resolved in a *climax*, in which one person, force, or idea wins out.

There is little question, of course, about what happens in the story, since all the events are before you. But there is room for interpretation of the plot, because the reasons why characters do things are not always clear.

If you can make a brief description of the plot, you can use it as the central idea of your theme. In a summary theme about Eudora Welty's "A Worn Path," for example, you might find two possible main thoughts. One is that the life of the rural poor is miserable; the other is that the main character, Phoenix, has strength that rises above this misery. A glance ahead at the first paragraph in the sample theme shows how this second idea can be used as a central idea:

> Welty shows that Phoenix has great personal strength and cheerfulness despite the grimness of her life.

There could be other central ideas, for good plays and stories, like most literary works, are as complex as life itself. There will always be a chance for endless debate about any interpretation, no matter how good or complete it seems. Do not worry about the "rightness" of your interpretation, therefore; just use it to unify your theme.

IDEA

If you have been assigned a nonnarrative work such as a poem, essay, or article, you may look for the same sort of help in the work itself. You have, first, the details in the work—similar to the events in a story—and second, the author's main idea, such as "My love for you goes beyond time" (Shakespeare's Sonnet No. 18) or "Death cruelly cuts short the best and leaves the world to the worst" (Milton's "Lycidas"). The author's ideas here are like the plot in a story or play, and you may use them as your own central idea in a summary theme.

Planning the Theme

The first thing to do is to study your notes. Try to determine how the events or details fit into a pattern that you can describe as a central idea. In the famous ancient Greek play *Oedipus the King* by Sophocles, for example, it is possible to determine that the events occur as illustrations of the *pride* of Oedipus. That is, the events are caused by his belief that he was superior to his fate. Thus, he killed a stranger on the road when he knew that he was foredoomed to kill his own father, and he married a widowed queen when he knew that he was fated to marry his own mother. Somehow he believed that he was above these deeds and could avoid them. But he could not, and the ancient play shows how Oedipus learns that he, like everyone else, cannot change his fate. In a theme on this play it would be necessary to show how during most of the action Oedipus tries to avoid this realization, thus preserving for a time, at least, his sense of his own importance—his pride. In this manner, for any work, look at the details carefully and try to find a common denominator that will help you launch your theme.

Choosing and Limiting Details

You need include only enough detail to bring out your central idea. Let us suppose that you are writing about Mark Twain's novel *Huckleberry Finn*, and you establish a central idea that the book is about "the growth of the individual to maturity." You develop the following thesis sentence: "This growth is shown by Huck's experiences under the care of the Widow Douglas and by his trip on a raft with the runaway slave Jim." In developing a theme from this thesis sentence, you would not have to include all the details from the early part of the book, but only those that seem to have an influence on Huck's judgment and developing maturity, such as being told by Tom that a Sunday-school picnic was really a meeting of Arabs. Similarly, you would need to include only those incidents on the river which helped Huck grow; thus you would emphasize details that show his increasing sense of obligation to Jim. You might claim that there is a great deal in the novel that you would be leaving out. *That is exactly the point.* You should include in a summary theme only enough detail to make clear your central idea, and no more. Your job is to write a well-organized theme to give your readers a sense of what to notice on their own reading of the work.

Organizing Your Theme

Usually there will be two parts in a summary theme, the introduction and the summary itself.

PART I: INTRODUCTION

The introduction identifies the work, the most significant character or characters, and the general situation; it is the place for your central idea and thesis sentence. In the introduction you should also describe the most noticeable physical characteristics of the work—that it is a play, story, poem, essay, article, or novel; that the work is mainly in dialogue, or narration; that the narration of events is accompanied by descriptions of the hero's thoughts; that the story is told by the hero himself or herself; that the description of present events is augmented by reminiscences of past events; that the reader must infer the relationships among the characters; that much of the story is in dialect; that the author relies on the research of others, and so on.

PART II: THE SUMMARY

The summary itself grows out of your thesis sentence. The development of your theme should follow the form of the work that you are summarizing. That is, you should present the main events as they occur in the story, even if much of the story is related by a flashback method; you should try to recreate the actual movement of the story itself. Remember, however, that what characterizes your theme *as a theme* is your central idea—your general interpretation of the work—and your guiding topic sentences that give unity to each of your paragraphs. Remind yourself as you write that (1) you should closely follow the work you summarize, (2) you should write accurately, precisely, and vividly, and (3) you should use an occasional word, phrase, or passage from the work to give your reader a taste of the original.

Sample Theme

A Summary of Eudora Welty's "A Worn Path"

[1] In "A Worn Path," a story of about 3,500 words, Eudora Welty describes a brief incident in the life of an old but almost timeless black woman, Phoenix Jackson. Welty shows that Phoenix possesses great personal strength and cheerfulness despite the grimness of her life.* The story is mostly narrative, with dialogue when characters other than Phoenix appear, and with monologue as Phoenix herself addresses animals, a thornbush, birds, a scarecrow, and herself. Her spiritual strength and optimism are shown in her walk through the countryside, her experience on the streets, and her meeting with the medical personnel.†

[2] Her walk to Natchez, by far the longest section of the story, demonstrates Phoenix's strong determination. Just before Christmas she is walking on a way through the countryside that she obviously knows well. This is the "worn path." She conquers a long hill, gets loose from a prickly thornbush, balances on a log across a creek, and crawls through a barbed wire fence. Having no one to speak to, she carries on a cheerful monologue with the creatures and objects around her, thus overcoming her loneliness. When she is attacked by a large black dog she falls in a ditch, from which she is pulled by a young white hunter. He is impressed with her single-mindedness and bravery, although he advises her to go back home. A trace of minor larceny is shown by Phoenix when she steals a nickel the young man had dropped as he left her to scare away the dog, but she is honest enough with herself to realize that this "theft" is a violation of her integrity.

[3] Once Phoenix reaches Natchez, she has left the danger of the countryside and expects only friendliness on the streets. She sees a white woman carrying Christmas bundles, and persuades this woman to tie her shoelaces, a task which the woman obligingly performs. Phoenix's confidence in this instance is rewarded.

[4] After Phoenix finds the building that marks her destination, the perspective of the story changes to make plain the grim facts of her daily life. This section is mainly dialogue between the attendant and the nurse. The nurse has known Phoenix for a long time and reveals to the attendant that Phoenix's grandson had drunk lye two or three years before and is now an invalid in the sole care of Phoenix. Phoenix has come for a soothing syrup, which the nurse gives her, while the attendant gives her a nickel. Phoenix decides to buy a paper windmill and take it to her grandson. On this note of confidence and resolution the story ends.

---

*Central idea
†Thesis sentence
For the text of this story, please see Appendix C, pp. 181–187.

Commentary on the Theme

To clarify the distinction between a summary theme and a précis, this summary theme is about the same story that is discussed in the sample theme in Chapter 1. The summary theme contains a paragraph of introduction, in which details about the physical appearance of the story are included. The first paragraph also contains a central idea and a thesis sentence. A précis contains none of this material.

The second paragraph begins with a topic sentence about Phoenix's determination, and all the details in the paragraph are related to her character. The paragraph thus shows that she *conquers* a hill, that she *overcomes* loneliness by speaking to her surroundings, that she is *single-minded* in her discussion with the hunter, and even after stealing the nickel that she is aware of a breach in her *integrity*.

In each of the remaining paragraphs the details are similarly related to positive aspects of Phoenix's character. The theme is therefore unified by means not expected of a précis. A summary theme, like any fully developed theme, will be unsuccessful unless the central idea is emphasized throughout.

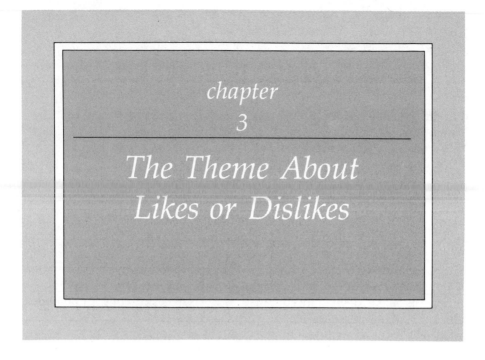

chapter

3

The Theme About Likes or Dislikes

Generally, you will like a literary work for one or more of the following reasons:

> You like and admire the characters and approve of what they do and stand for.
> You learn more about topics very important to you.
> You learn something you had never known or thought before.
> You gain new or fresh insights into things you had already known.
> You learn about characters from different ways of life.
> You are involved and interested in the outcome of the action or ideas, and you do not want to put the work down until you have finished it.
> You feel happy because of reading the work.
> You are amused and laugh often as you read.
> You like the author's presentation.
> You find that some of the ideas and expressions are beautiful and worth remembering.

Obviously, if you find none of these things in the work, or find something that is distasteful, you will not like the work.

Keep a Notebook for Your First Responses

No one can tell you what you should or should not like. Liking is your own concern. For this reason, in preparing a theme about your likes you should build on your own responses. The best way to do this is to keep a notebook in which you record your thoughts immediately after finishing a work, or even while you are reading it. Be absolutely frank in your opinion. Write about what you like and what you do not like. Try to explain the reasons for your response, even if these reasons are brief. If, on later thought, you change or modify your first impression, record that too. Here is such a notebook entry, about Guy de Maupassant's story "The Necklace" (this story is included in Appendix C, pp. 167–173):

> I liked "The Necklace" because of the surprise ending. It isn't that I liked Mathilde's bad luck, but I liked the way De Maupassant hid the most important fact in the story until the end. Mathilde thus did all that work and sacrifice for no real reason, and the surprise ending makes this point strongly.

This paragraph could easily be developed for a theme. The virtue of it is that it is a clear statement of the writer's liking, followed by an explanation of the major reasons for this response. This pattern, which can best be phrased as "I like [dislike] this because . . . ," is necessary in your notebook entries.

The challenge in writing a theme about likes or dislikes is that, to create a full thematic development, you must explore some of the "because" areas. For this reason it is important to try to pinpoint some of the specific things you liked or disliked while your first impressions of the work are fresh in your mind. If at first you cannot write your reasons fully, at least list the particular things that you liked or disliked. Once you start drafting your theme, you can fill in details and try to phrase your reasons fully and more clearly. If you allow yourself to lose your responses, however, your later task will be that much more difficult.

What Do You Do with Dislikes?

It is important to know that disliking a work is acceptable and that you do not need to hide this response. Here are two short notebook responses expressing dislike for "The Necklace":

1. I didn't like "The Necklace" because Mathilde seems spoiled, and I didn't think she was worth reading about.
2. "The Necklace" is not an adventure story, and I like reading only adventure stories.

These are both legitimate responses. The first is based on a distaste for the major character, the second on a preference for stories with rapid action which evoke interest in the dangers faced and overcome by the main characters.

Here is a paragraph expanded from the first response. What is important here is that the reasons for dislike are explained; they would need only slightly more development for an entire theme:

I did not like "The Necklace" because Mathilde seems spoiled and I didn't think she was worth reading about. She is a phony. She nags her husband because he is not rich. She never tells the truth. I especially dislike her hurrying away from the party because she is afraid of being seen in her shabby coat. It is foolish and dishonest of her not to tell Jeanne Forrestier about losing the necklace. It is true that she works hard to pay the debt, but she also puts her husband through ten years of misery that are unnecessary. If Mathilde had faced facts, she might have had a better life. I do not like her and cannot like the story because of her.

As long as your reasons for dislike are clearly stated, as they are in this paragraph, you can confidently base your theme on a dislike. It is better to write directly about your own response than to force yourself into a positive central idea which you do not really believe.

Putting Dislikes into a Larger Context

If one can give an honest opinion, however, it is also necessary to expand one's taste. For example, the dislike based on a preference for only adventure stories, if it is applied generally, would cause a person to dislike most great works of literature. This seems unnecessarily self-limiting.

If a person can put negative responses into a larger context, it is possible to expand his or her likes in line with very personal responses. A young woman might be deeply involved in personal concerns and therefore be uninterested in seemingly remote literary figures. However, if by reading about literary characters she can gain insight into general problems of life, and therefore her own concerns, she can like just about any work of literature. A young man might like sports events and therefore not care for reading anything but sports magazines. But what interests him in sports is the competition. If he can find competition, or conflict, in a work of literature, he can like that work. The principle here is that already established reasons for liking something may be stimulated by works which at first did not seem to bring them out.

As an example, let us consider the dislike based on a preference for adventure stories again, and see if this preference can be analyzed. Here are some reasons for liking adventure:

1. Adventure has fast action.
2. Adventure has danger.
3. Adventure has daring, active characters.
4. Adventure has obstacles which the characters work hard to overcome.

Not much can be done for "The Necklace" with the first three points, but the last point is promising. In looking at Mathilde Loisel, we can see that she works hard to overcome an obstacle—paying off a large debt. If our student likes adventure because the characters try to gain a worthy goal, perhaps he or she can also like "The Necklace" because of Mathilde's efforts. A comparison like this one can become the basis for a thoughtful favorable response.

The following paragraph shows how the comparison may be expanded to form the basis for an entire theme on liking. (The sample theme is also developed along these lines.)

> I like only adventure stories, and therefore I disliked "The Necklace" because it is not adventure. But I see that one reason for liking adventure is that the characters work hard to overcome difficult obstacles like finding buried treasure or exploring new places. Mathilde also works hard to overcome an obstacle—helping to pay back the money, with interest, borrowed to buy the replacement necklace. I like adventure characters because they stick to things and win out. I see the same toughness in Mathilde. Her problems therefore become interesting as the story moves on after a slow beginning. I can truthfully say that I came to like the story.

This example shows the ability to apply an accepted principle of liking to another work where it also applies. A person who applies principles in this open-minded way can, no matter how slowly, redefine dislikes and expand the ability to like and appreciate many kinds of literature.

Another, equally open-minded way to develop understanding and appreciation is to try to put dislikes in the following light: An author's creation of an unlikable character or repulsive event may be deliberate; your dislike results from the author's *intentions*. A first task of writing therefore becomes the attempt to explain the intention or plan. As you put the plan into your own words, you may find that you can like a work with unlikable things in it. Here is a paragraph showing this pattern:

> De Maupassant apparently wanted the reader to dislike Mathilde, and I do. He shows her as unrealistic and spoiled. She lies to everyone and nags her husband. Her rushing away from the party so that no one can see her shabby coat is a form of lying. But I can like the story itself because De Maupassant makes another kind of point. He does not hide her bad qualities, but makes me see that she herself is the cause of her trouble. If people like Mathilde never face the truth, they will get into bad situations. This is a good point, and I like the way De Maupassant makes it. The entire story is therefore worth liking even though I still do not like Mathilde.

Please observe that neither of the two ways shown of broadening the contexts of dislike is dishonest to the original expressions of dislike. In the first paragraph, the writer applies one of his principles of liking to include "The Necklace." In the second the writer considers her initial dislike in the context of the work, and discovers a basis for liking the story as a whole while still disliking the main character. The main concern is to keep an open mind despite initial dislike, and then to see if this response can be modified.

However, if, after consideration, you decide that your dislike overbalances any reasons you can find for liking, then you should go ahead to write about your dislike of the work. The central idea of such a theme would be the expression of dislike, and the body would develop the major reasons for this response. Thus, a theme on "The Necklace" in line with the earlier paragraph (p. 49), might develop Mathilde's "spoiled" character and her untruthfulness.

Organizing Your Theme

INTRODUCTION

You should open by describing briefly the conditions that influenced your response. Your central idea should be whether you liked or disliked the work. The thesis sentence should list the major causes of your response, to be developed in the body of your theme.

BODY

1. One approach is to consider the thing or things about the work that you liked or disliked (for a list of possible reasons for liking a work, see the beginning of this chapter, p. 47). You may like a particular character, or maybe you got so interested in the story that you could not put it down. Also, it may be that a major idea, a new or fresh insight, or a particular outcome is the major point that you wish to develop. A sample paragraph earlier in this chapter (p. 48) shows how a "surprise ending" can be the cause of a favorable response.

2. Another approach is to give details about how your responses developed in your reading of the work. This approach requires that you pinpoint, in order, the various good parts of the work (or the bad) and how you responded to them. Your aim here should not be to retell the story, but to discuss those details which caused your like or dislike.

3. Two additional types of response are described in some detail above (pp. 49–51). The first is attempting to show how a principle for liking one type of literature may be applied to the assigned work. The second is beginning with an initial dislike but finding a larger context which may permit a favorable response.

CONCLUSION

Here you might briefly summarize the reasons for your major response. You might also try to face any issues brought up by a change in your responses. That is, if you have always held certain assumptions about your taste but liked the work despite these assumptions, you may wish to talk about your own change or development. This topic is personal, but in a theme about likes or dislikes, discovery about yourself is not undesirable.

Sample Theme

Some Reasons for Liking
Guy de Maupassant's "The Necklace"

---

[1]   To me, the most likable kind of reading or entertainment is adventure. Although there are many reasons for my preference, an important one is that adventure characters work hard to overcome obstacles. Because "The Necklace" is not adventure, I did not like it at first. But in one respect the story is like adventure. Mathilde, with her husband, works hard for ten years to overcome a difficult obstacle. Thus, because Mathilde does what adventure characters also do, the story is likable.* Mathilde's appeal results from her hard work, strong character, and sad fate.†

[2]   Mathilde's hard work makes her seem good. Once she and her husband are faced with the huge debt of 36,000 francs with interest, she works like a slave to pay it back. She gives up her servant and moves to a cheaper place. She does the household drudgery, wears cheap clothes, and bargains with shopkeepers for low prices. Just like the characters in adventure stories, who sometimes must do hard and unpleasant things, she does what she has to, and this makes her admirable.

[3]   Her strong character makes her endure, a likable trait. To do the bad jobs, she needs toughness. At first she is a nagging, spoiled person, always dreaming about wealth and telling lies, but she changes for the better. She sees her responsibility for losing the necklace, and she has enough sense of self-sacrifice to pay for restoring it. She sacrifices "heroically" (de Maupassant's word) not only her position, but also her youth and beauty. Her jobs are not the exotic and glamorous ones of adventure stories, but her force of character makes her as likable as an adventure heroine.

[4]   Her sad fate also makes her likable. In adventure stories the characters often suffer as they do their jobs. Mathilde also suffers, but in a different way, because her suffering is permanent while the hardships of adventure characters are temporary. This fact makes her pitiable, and even more so because all her sacrifices are really not necessary. Thus there is a sense of injustice about her which makes the reader take her side.

Obviously "The Necklace" is not an adventure story, but some of the good

---

*Central idea
†Thesis sentence
For the text of this story, please see Appendix C, pp. 167–173.

qualities of adventure characters can also be seen in Mathilde. Also, the surprise revelation that the lost necklace was false is an unforgettable twist [5] which makes her more deserving than she seems at first. De Maupassant has arranged the story so that the reader finally admires Mathilde. "The Necklace" is a skillful and likable story.

Commentary on the Theme

The argument in this theme is that "The Necklace," which at first was not liked, can be liked because Mathilde, the major character, has qualities that evoke liking for characters in works of adventure. Each of the reasons brought out for liking Mathilde is also a reason for liking adventure characters. Although the liking for adventure is thus a bridge which the writer crosses on the way to liking "The Necklace," some other reasons are brought out in the conclusion.

In the introduction the connection is made between adventure characters and Mathilde. The thesis sentence lists three topics for development in the body of the theme.

Paragraph two gives instances of Mathilde's hard work as a cause for liking, and concludes by comparing Mathilde and adventure characters as workers. The third paragraph gives examples of Mathilde's toughness of character and also compares her strength with that of adventure characters. In paragraph four a comparison on the basis of suffering and hardship is made, and the pity and sympathy felt for Mathilde are claimed as causes for liking her. The conclusion restates the comparison, and also lists the surprise ending and the development of the story as reasons for liking "The Necklace."

chapter

4

The Theme of Character Analysis

Character in literature is an extended verbal representation of a human being, specifically the inner self that determines thought, speech, and behavior. Through dialogue, action, and commentary, literature captures some of the interactions of character and circumstance. Literature makes these interactions interesting by portraying characters who are worth caring about, rooting for, and even loving, although there are also characters at whom you may laugh or whom you may dislike or even hate.

Choice and Character

The choices that people make indicate their characters, if we assume that they have freedom of choice. We always make silent comparisons with the choices made or rejected. Thus, if you know that John works twelve hours a day, while Tom puts in five, and Jim sleeps under a tree, you have a number of separate facts, but you do not conclude anything about their characters unless you have a basis for comparison. This basis is easy: The usual, average number of working hours is eight. With no more than this knowledge for comparison, you might conclude that John is a workaholic, Tom lazy, and Jim either unwell or a dropout. To be fair, you would need to know much more about the lives and financial circumstances of each character before your conclusions would be final.

Character and Completeness

In literature you may expect such completeness of context. You may think of each action or speech, no matter how small or seemingly unusual, as an accumulating part of a total portrait. Whereas in life things may "just happen," in literature the actions, interactions, speeches, and observations are all arranged to give you the details you need for conclusions about character. Thus you read about important events like a first confession (O'Connor's "First Confession"), a long period of work and sacrifice (De Maupassant's "The Necklace"), the taking of a regular journey of mercy (Welty's "A Worn Path"), or a sudden change from anger to love (Chekhov's *The Bear*). From these happenings in their contexts you make inferences about the characters involved. In effect, you determine the "character" of the various characters.

Major Character Traits

In writing about a literary character, you should try to describe the character's major trait or traits. As in life, characters may be lazy or ambitious, anxious or serene, aggressive or fearful, assertive or bashful, confident or self-doubting, adventurous or timid, noisy or quiet, visionary or practical, reasonable or hotheaded, careful or careless, fair or partial, straightforward or underhanded, "winners" or "losers," and so on.

With this sort of list, to which you may add at will, you can analyze and write about character. For example, in studying Mathilde Loisel, the main character in De Maupassant's "The Necklace" (and the subject of the sample theme, pp. 60–61), you would note that she spends much time at the start in daydreaming about wealth she cannot have. She might be considered a dreamer. This is not unusual, but she is so swept up in her visions of ease that she is unhappy with the life that she has. It is fair to conclude that this conflict indicates a weakness or flaw, because her dream life hurts her real life. It is out of conflicts such as this that you can get a "handle" on characters for your theme.

Appearance, Action, and Character

When you study character, be sure to consider physical descriptions, but also be sure to relate the physical to the mental. Suppose your author stresses the neatness of one character and the sloppiness of another. Most likely, these descriptions can be related to your character study. The same also applies to your treatment of what a character *does*. Go beyond the actions themselves and try to indicate what they show *about* the character. Always try to get from the outside to the inside, for it is on the inside that character resides.

Change and Development

There is a great deal of interaction between character and the outcome of any story or drama. In some types of literature certain character traits are essential. In cowboy or detective stories, for example, it is essential that the main characters be strong, tough, steadfast, and clever so that they may overcome the obstacles before them or solve the crime. In Greek tragedy a fatal flaw of character is the cause of the hero's downfall. In these cases there are consequences that proceed logically and inevitably from character; the characters stay the same throughout the work and therefore cause their own success or failure.

In many works, however, you will see a change or growth of character, and therefore an outcome that might have seemed inevitable will alter. You may decide for yourself whether human character is capable of radical change, or whether change is really to be described as growth or development. If a person who as a child was very combative becomes successful and peaceful as an adult lawyer, he or she may simply have transferred youthful aggression into the acceptable arena of legal wrangles and tangles. Was there a change or was there development? Similarly, Shakespeare's Juliet is a young, impressionable girl at the start of *Romeo and Juliet*, but by the end of the play she is a determined, resolute woman. Does her character change, or does it develop? It is more important to observe and discuss such character modifications accurately than to take an arbitrary position on whether you have change or development. Of course some authors arrange their characterizations as an embodiment of either change or development. If the position of the author is clear to you, you must take this view into account in your analysis of the character.

How is Character Disclosed
in Literature?

In preparing your theme, you should look for the following four specific ways in which writers may give you information about character. Always remember that authors rely on you for the knowledge of ordinary behavior to make the comparisons spoken of earlier.

1. *What the characters themselves say (and think, if the author expresses their thoughts).* On the whole, speeches may be accepted at face value to indicate

the character of the speaker. Sometimes, however, a speech may be made offhand, or it may reflect a momentary emotional or intellectual state. Thus, if characters in deep despair say that life is worthless, you must balance this speech with what the same characters say when they are happy. You must also consider the situation or total context of a statement. Macbeth's despair at the end of *Macbeth* is voiced after he has been guilty of ruthless political suppression and assassination. His speech therefore reflects his own guilt and self-hatred. You should also consider whether speeches show change or development. A despairing character might say depressing things at the start but happy things at the end. Your analysis of such speeches should indicate how they show change in your character.

2. *What the characters do.* You have heard that "actions speak louder than words," and you should interpret actions freely as signs of character. Thus you might consider Phoenix's trip through the woods (Welty's "A Worn Path") as a sign of a loving, responsible character, even though Phoenix nowhere says that she is loving and responsible. The difficulty and hardship she goes through on the walk, however, justify such a conclusion.

Sometimes you may find that action is inconsistent with words. Here you might have hypocrisy, weakness, or an approaching change. Smirnov, in Chekhov's *The Bear*, would be crazy to teach Mrs. Popov how to use the dueling pistol properly, because she has threatened to kill him with it. But he is about ready to declare love for her, and this cooperative if potentially self-destructive act shows that his loving nature is even stronger than his sense of self-preservation.

3. *What other characters say about them.* In literature, as in life, people always talk about other people. If the speakers are shown as honest, you may usually accept their opinions as accurate descriptions of character. But sometimes a person's prejudices and interests distort what that person says. You know, for example, that the word of a person's enemy is usually slanted, unfair, or even untrue. Therefore an author may give you a good impression of characters by having a bad character say bad things about them. Similarly, the word of a close friend or political manager may be biased in favor of a particular character. You must always consider the context and source of all dramatic remarks before you use them in your analysis.

4. *What the author says about them, speaking as storyteller or observer.* What the author says about a character is usually to be accepted as truth. Naturally, authors must be accepted on matters of fact. But when they *interpret* the actions and characteristics of their characters, they themselves assume the critic's role, and their opinions may be either right or wrong. For this reason authors frequently avoid interpretations and devote their skill instead to arranging events and speeches so that their conclusions are obvious to the reader.

Reality and Probability

You are entitled to expect that characters in literature will be true to life. That is, their actions, statements, and thoughts must all be what human beings are *likely* to do, say, and think under given conditions. This is the standard of *probability*.

Probability does not rule out surprise or even exaggeration. Thus, in Chekhov's *The Bear*, the main characters, who are strangers when the short play opens, fall in love. This change might at first seem improbable, but it is only sudden. Chekhov shows that both Mrs. Popov and Smirnov have deeply loving and emotional natures, and that they are given to suddenness or whim. Under the emotional crisis of their threatened duel, it is therefore probable that they would turn directly to loving each other. The action, though surprising and exaggerated, meets the standard of probability.

There are, of course, many ways of rendering the probable in literature. Fiction attempting to mirror life—the realistic, naturalistic, or "slice of life" types of fiction—sets up conditions and raises expectations about the characters that are different from those of fiction attempting to portray a romantic, fanciful world. A character's behavior and speech in the "realistic" setting would be out of place in the romantic setting.

But the situation is more complex than this, for within the romantic setting a character might reasonably be *expected* to behave and speak in a fanciful, dreamlike way. Speech and action under both conditions are therefore *probable* as we understand the word, although different aspects of human character are presented in these two different types of works.

It is also possible that within the same work you might find some characters who are realistic but others who are not. In such works you have contrasting systems of reality. Shakespeare creates such a contrast in *Richard II*. Richard is a person with unrealistic expectations of himself and those around him; he lives in a dream world and is so out of touch with his surroundings that ultimately he is destroyed. You might also encounter works where there are mythical or supernatural figures who contrast with the realism of the other characters. In judging characters in works of this type, your only guide is that of probability.[1]

---

[1]You may reasonably wonder about how you should judge the character of gods, or devils, for that matter. Usually gods embody the qualities of the best, most moral human beings, although the ancient Greeks sometimes attributed to the gods some of the same follies and faults that beset humanity. To judge a devil, try thinking of the worst human qualities, but remember that the devil is often imagined as a character with many engaging traits, the easier to deceive poor sinners and lead them into hell.

Does the Character Come to Life?

With all these considerations in mind, you can see that literary characters should be true to life, under given circumstances and within certain literary specifications. The key to your study of character should always be to discover if the character—whether intended by the author to be a lifelike person or a romantic hero—does and says what you believe human beings might do and say under the exact conditions presented by the author. Do the characters ring true? Do they come to life? Do they illustrate many qualities that add up to accurate representations of human beings? Or do they seem to be one-dimensional or flat? The degree to which an author can make a character come alive is a mark of skill, and if you think that your author is successful in this regard, you should say so in your theme.

Organizing Your Theme

INTRODUCTION

Your theme should have a clearly stated central idea that runs throughout the entire character analysis. Your central idea will be whatever general statement you make to describe the character. The thesis sentence must be a brief statement of the main sections of your theme.

BODY

The organization is designed to illustrate and prove your central idea. You have much freedom in organizing your main points. Some possible methods are the following:

1. Organization around a central characteristic, like "kindness, gentleness, generosity, firmness," or "resoluteness of will frustrated by inopportune moments for action, resulting in despondency, doubt, and melancholy." A body containing this sort of material would demonstrate how the literary work brings out each of these qualities.

2. Organization around a development or change of character. Here you would attempt to show the character traits that a character possesses at the start of the work, and then describe the changes or developments that occur. Try to determine the author's view on such changes; that is, is the change genuine, or does the author establish hidden traits in the character which are brought out as the story progresses?

3. Organization around central incidents that reveal primary characteristics. Certain key incidents will stand out in a work, and you might create

an effective body by using three or four of these as guides for your discussion, taking care to show in your topic sentences that your purpose is to illuminate the character you have selected, not the incidents. In other words, you would regard the incidents only as they bring out truths about character. Naturally, with this arrangement, you would have to show how the incidents bring out the characteristics and also how they serve tó explain other things the character might do.

CONCLUSION

The conclusion should contain your statements about how the characteristics you have brought out are related to the work as a whole. If the person was good but came to a bad end, does this discrepancy elevate him or her to tragic stature? If the person was a nobody and came to a bad end, does this fact cause you to draw any conclusion about the class or type of which he or she was a part? Or does it illustrate the author's view of human life? Or both? Do the characteristics explain why the person helps or hinders other characters? Does your analysis help you to clear up any misunderstanding that your first reading of the work produced? Questions such as these should be raised and answered in your conclusion.

Sample Theme

*The Character of Mathilde Loisel
in Guy de Maupassant's "The Necklace"*

[1] Guy de Maupassant's character Mathilde Loisel, in "The Necklace," is above all a dreamer. Her dreams make her both weak and strong.* Her weakness is that her dream is not to have high ideals, but rather to have a life of ease and wealth. Her strength is her willingness to work to keep her dreams of honor. De Maupassant shows her qualities in the introduction, the cover-up, and the poverty she endures.†

[2] In the early part of the story Mathilde is a young housewife dreaming about wealth. She thinks money is everything, and her highest aim is ease and luxury, which she thinks that she was somehow born to have. Her husband, a lower-rank clerk, can afford only a small household. Mathilde gets angry at this gap between her dream and the reality of her life. The result is that she is not able

*Central idea
†Thesis sentence
For the text of this story, please see Appendix C, pp. 167-173.

to like anything that she has. She does not treat her husband with love and respect, but whines at him instead about their condition. Her borrowing of the necklace for the big party is, in a way, her attempt to escape her drab life and live out her dream, if only for a night.

[3] The cover-up of the loss of the necklace brings out the worst in Mathilde. She believes more strongly in the real value of the jewels than in her friendship with Jeanne Forrestier. If she had told the truth to Jeanne, she would never have had the trouble she faced. But her character is too weak to permit her to endure the embarrassment that the truth would bring. Thus, by covering up, she loses friendship, truth, and financial future all at the same time.

[4] But her life of poverty and sacrifice to pay back the money lenders brings out her strengths. She pitches in to work. She gives up her servant, her good address, and everything else connected with her dreams of good living. Although her character is excellent in this respect, her hard work makes her loud and coarse, just the opposite of the wealthy, refined person she dreamed of becoming.

[5] Thus Mathilde is a character whose dream life keeps her from seeing the truth until the truth hits her with a vengeance. It is this weakness, not her bad luck, that gives her all her pain. It is this same weakness that brings out her best quality of sharing the work to preserve her honor and good name. She may be dreamy, unlucky, and foolish, but she is not bad. On balance, she comes out looking good, getting a life that is much worse than she deserves.

Commentary on the Theme

This theme is representative of the first type of organization described above, organization around a central characteristic, (p. 59). The central characteristic described is Mathilde's dreaminess. The introduction asserts that this quality produces a character of both weakness and strength. The second paragraph develops her weakness inasmuch as Mathilde's dreams make her too unhappy to adjust to the life she has with her husband. This paragraph relies for its data on the author's descriptions of Mathilde's dreams and on her own complaints when her husband announces the party. The judgment on Mathilde is based on the theme writer's apparent belief that dream life should not have a negative effect on real life.

Paragraph three continues with the weak side of Mathilde, showing the disastrous effects of her false values. The data for this paragraph are taken from the description of the activities to hide the loss, together with a comparison of how a frank admission of the loss might have avoided the large debt.

The fourth paragraph emphasizes Mathilde's strengths, which result, like her weakness, from her character as a dreamer. The judgment is clearly based on the idea that hard work and cooperation are virtues.

The concluding paragraph attempts to weigh Mathilde's character (one might wish to dispute the assertion that the bad luck is not the major cause of her trouble), and states that her willingness to endure her hardship makes her seem worthy of a better fate than she received.

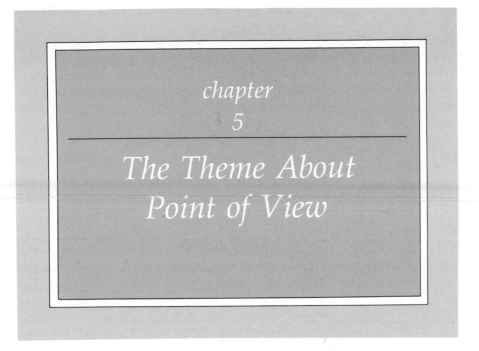

The Theme About Point of View

Point of view is the position from which details in a literary work are perceived, described, and interpreted. It is a method of rendering, a means by which authors create a centralizing intelligence, a narrative personality, an intellectual filter through which you receive the narration or argument. Other terms describing point of view are *viewpoint, unifying voice, perspective, persona, mask, center of attention,* and *focus.*

In practice, you can think of point of view as the character or speaker who does the talking. To write about point of view is to describe the effect of the speaker—his or her circumstances, traits, motives, and limitations—on the literary work.

You might respond that our definition means that authors do not use their own "voices" when they write, but somehow change themselves into another character, who may be a totally separate creation. This response is right. It is true that authors, as writers of their own works, are always in control of what gets written, but it does not follow that they always use their own voices. It is not easy to determine exactly what one's "own voice" is. Test yourself: When you speak to your instructor, to your friend, to a child, to a person you love, or to a distant relative, your voice always sounds the same. But the personality—or persona—that you employ changes according to the person you are talking to. Your point of view changes.

When writing about point of view, therefore, you should try to determine the nature of the speaker. It is not helpful to deal vaguely with "the author's point of view," as though you were talking about opinions. What you need is to analyze and describe the character and circumstances of the speaker.

Point of View and "Throwing the Voice"

A helpful way to think of point of view is that the speaker is a ventriloquist's dummy and the author is the ventriloquist. The author "throws" the voice into the dummy, whose words you actually read. Although the dummy or speaker is the one who is talking, the author is the one who makes the speaker believable and consistent. Often, of course, the speaker is the author in person, as nearly as that identity can be determined. But just as often the voice is separate and totally independent, a character who is completely imagined and consistently maintained by the author.

In short, the author creates not only stories and ideas, but also the speaker. To discuss point of view is to discuss the speaker.

It is most important to understand this fact. As an exercise, suppose for a moment that you are an author and are planning a set of stories. Try to imagine the speakers you would create for the following situations:

> A happy niece who has just inherited $25 million from an uncle recalls a childhood experience with the uncle years ago.
>
> A disappointed nephew who was cut off without a cent describes a childhood experience with the same uncle.
>
> A ship's captain who is filled with ideas of personal honor, integrity, and responsibility describes the life of a sailor who has committed a cowardly act.
>
> A person who has survived a youth of poverty and degradation describes a brother who has succumbed to drugs and crime.
>
> An economist looks at problems of unemployment.
>
> A person who has just lost a job looks at problems of unemployment.

In trying to create voices and stories for the various situations, you will recognize the importance of your *imagination* in the selection of point of view. You are always yourself, but your imagination can enable you to speak like someone else totally distinct from yourself. Point of view is hence an imaginative creation, just as much a part of the author's work as the events narrated or the ideas discussed.

Point of View as a
Physical Position

Thus far we have considered point of view as an interaction of personality and circumstance. There are also purely physical aspects, specifically (1) the actual place or position from which speakers or narrators see and hear the action, and (2) the capacities of the speakers as receivers of information from others. If narrators have been at the "scene" of an action, this position gives them credibility because they are reporting events they actually saw or heard. Some speakers may have been direct participants in the action; others may have been bystanders. It is possible that a speaker may have overheard a conversation, or may have witnessed a scene through a keyhole. If the speakers were not "on the spot," they must have gained their "facts" in a believable way. They could get them from someone else who was a witness or participant. They could receive letters, read newspaper articles, go through old papers in an attic or library, or hear things on a radio or television program. Sometimes the unidentified voice of the author comes from a person who seems to be hovering somehow right above the characters as they move and speak. Such a speaker, being present everywhere without being noticed, is a reliable source of all information presented in the narrative.

Kinds of Points of View

The kinds of points of view may be classified fairly easily. You may detect the point of view in any work by determining the grammatical voice of the speaker. Then, of course, you should go on to all the other considerations thus far discussed.

FIRST PERSON

If the story is told by an "I," the author is using the *first-person* point of view, usually a fictional narrator and not the author. First-person speakers report everything they see, hear, and think, and as they do so, they convey not only the action of the work, but also some of their own background, thinking, attitudes, and even prejudices. The speaker's particular type of speech will have a great effect on the language of the work itself. A sailor will use many nautical terms, and a sixteen-year-old boy may use much slang. For these reasons, the first-person speaker is often as much a subject of interest as the story itself. Nick Carraway in F. Scott Fitzgerald's *The Great Gatsby* is such a speaker. Nick is ostensibly a minor character in the action who tells what is happening in the lives of Gatsby and the Buchanans. Sometimes the "I" narrator is the major character in the book, like Mark Twain's Huckleberry Finn or Swift's Gulliver.

THIRD PERSON

If the narrator is not introduced as a character, and if everything in the work is described in the third person (that is, *he, she, it, they*), the author is using the *third-person* point of view. There are variants here.

The third-person point of view is called *omniscient* (all-knowing) when the speaker not only describes the action and dialogue of the work, but also seems to know everything that goes on in the minds of the characters. In the third-person omniscient point of view authors take great responsibility: by delving into the minds of their characters, they assume a stance that exceeds our ordinary experience with other persons. Like God, the omniscient speaker attempts to show the inner workings of a character's mind. If you encounter the omniscient point of view, you may be sure that the writer is displaying concern with psychological patterns and motivations. The omniscient point of view is characterized by phrases like "He thought . . ." and "As she approached the scene, she considered that . . ." and so on.

If an author uses the third person but confines the narration mainly to what one single character does, says, and sometimes thinks, then you have the third-person *limited* point of view. While the omniscient point of view takes in the thoughts of most of the characters, the limited focuses on only one. The limited viewpoint is thus midway between the first- and third-person points of view. In Guy de Maupassant's story "The Necklace," for example (see Appendix C, pp. 167–173), the character Mathilde Loisel is the major focus of the narration. Everything in the story is there because she would have experienced it, heard about it, or thought about it.

DRAMATIC

Writers using the *dramatic* point of view confine the work mainly to quotations and descriptions of actions. They avoid telling you that certain characters thought this or felt that, but instead allow the characters themselves to voice their thoughts and feelings. Often, too, an author using the dramatic point of view will allow certain characters to interpret the thoughts and feelings of other characters, but then attitudes and possible prejudices of these speakers enter into your evaluation of their interpretations. The key to the dramatic point of view is that the writer presents the reader with action and speech but does not overtly guide the reader toward any conclusions. Naturally, however, the conclusions may be readily drawn from the details presented. Guy de Maupassant is famous for creating stories rendered in the dramatic point of view, as are Hemingway and Sherwood Anderson.

It goes without saying that many novels, being long works, often have an intermingling of viewpoints. In a largely omniscient narrative, the writer may present a chapter consisting only of action and dialogue—the dramatic point of view—and another chapter that focuses entirely on one person— the limited. Writers of short stories, on the other hand, usually maintain a consistent and uniform point of view.

Point of View and "Evidence"

When you write a theme about point of view, you should try to consider all aspects that bear on the presentation of the material in the work you have read. You may imagine yourself somewhat like a member of a jury. Jury members cannot accept testimony uncritically, for some witnesses may have much to gain by misstatements, distortions, or outright lies. Before rendering a verdict, jury members must consider all these possibilities. Speakers in literary works are usually to be accepted as reliable witnesses, but it is true that their characters, interests, capacities, personal involvements, and positions to view action may have a bearing on the material they present. A classic example is the Japanese film, *Rashomon*, in which four separate persons tell a story as evidence in a court, and each presents a version that makes that person seem more honorable than he or she actually was. While most stories are not as complex as this, you should always consider the character of the speaker before you render your verdict on what the story is about.

Organizing Your Theme

In a theme on point of view, the areas of concern are language, selection of detail, characterization, interpretive commentaries, and narrative development. Your theme might be organized to include analysis of one, a few, or all of these elements. Generally you should determine how the point of view has contributed toward making the story uniquely as it is, and also toward your interpretation of the story. In what way has the author's voice entered into your response to the story? Are there any special qualities in the work that could not have been achieved if the author had used another point of view?

INTRODUCTION

In your introduction you should get at the matters that you plan to develop. Which point of view is used in the work? What is the major influence of this point of view on the work (for example—"The omniscient point of view causes full, leisurely insights into many shades of character," or "The first-person point of view enables the work to resemble an exposé of back-room political deals.")? To what extent does the selection of point of view make the work particularly interesting and effective, or uninteresting and ineffective? What particular aspects of the work (action, dialogue, characters, description, narration, analysis) do you wish to analyze in support of your central idea?

BODY

The questions you raise here will of course depend on the work you have studied. It would be impossible to answer all of the following questions in your analysis, but going through them should make you aware of the sorts of things you can include in the body of your theme.

If you have read a work with the first-person point of view, your analysis will necessarily involve the speaker. Who is she (if a woman)? Is she a major or a minor character? What is her background? What is her relationship to the person listening to her (if there is a listener)? Does she speak directly to you, the reader, in such a way that you are a listener or an eavesdropper? How does the speaker describe the various situations? Is her method uniquely a function of her character? Or (if a man), how reliable is he as an observer? How did he acquire the information he is presenting? How much does he disclose? How much does he hide? Does he ever rely on the information of others for his material? How reliable are these other witnesses? Does the speaker undergo any changes in the course of the work that have any bearing on the ways he presents the material? Does he notice one kind of thing (e.g., discussion) but miss others (e.g., natural scenery)? What might have escaped him, if anything? Does the author put the speaker into situations that he can describe but not understand? Why? Is the speaker ever confused? Is he close to the action, or distant from it? Does he show emotional involvement in any situations? Are you sympathetic to his concerns or are you put off by them? If the speaker makes any commentary, are his thoughts valid? To what extent, if any, is the speaker of as much interest as the material he presents?

If you encounter any of the third-person points of view, try to determine the characteristics of the voice employed by the author. Does it seem that the author is speaking in his or her own voice, or that the narrator has a special voice? You can approach this problem by answering many of the questions that are relevant to the first-person point of view. Also try to determine the distance of the narrator to the action. How is the action described? How is the dialogue recorded? Is there any background information given? Do the descriptions reveal any bias toward any of the characters? Are the descriptions full or bare? Does the author include descriptions or analyses of a character's thoughts? What are these like? Do you see evidence of the author's own philosophy? Does the choice of words direct you toward any particular interpretations? What limitations or freedoms devolve upon the story as a result of the point of view?

CONCLUSION

In your conclusion you should evaluate the success of the author's point of view: Was it consistent, effective, truthful? What did the writer gain (if anything) by the selection of point of view? What was lost (if anything)? How might a less skillful writer have handled similar material? After answering questions like these, you may end your theme.

Problems in Writing Your Theme

1. In considering point of view, you will encounter the problem of whether to discuss the author or the speaker as the originator of attitudes and ideas. If the author is employing the first-person point of view, there is no problem. Use the speaker's name, if he or she is given one (e.g., Nick Carraway, Huck Finn, Holden Caulfield), or else talk about the "speaker" or "persona" if there is no name. You face a greater problem with the third person points of view, but even here it is safe for you to discuss the "speaker" rather than the "author," remembering always that the author is manipulating the narrative voice. Sometimes authors emphasize a certain phase of their own personalities through their speakers. There are naturally many ideas common to both the author and the speaker, but your statements about these must be inferential, not absolute.

2. You may have a tendency to wander away from point of view into retelling the story or discussing the ideas. Emphasize the presentation of the events and ideas, and the causes for this presentation. Do not emphasize the subject material itself, but use it only as it bears on your consideration of point of view. Your object is not just to interpret the work, but also to show how the point of view enables you to interpret the work.

Obviously you must talk about the material in the work, but use it only to illustrate your assertions about point of view. Avoid the following pattern of statement, which will always lead you astray: "The speaker says this, which means this." Instead, adhere to the following pattern, which will keep your emphasis always on your central idea: "The speaker says this, which shows this about her and her attitudes." If a particular idea is difficult, you might need to explain it, but do not do so unless it illustrates your central idea.

3. Remember that you are dealing with point of view in the *entire* work and not simply in single narrations and conversations. For example, an individual character has her own way of seeing things when she states something, but in relation to the entire work her speech is a function of the dramatic point of view. Thus, you should not talk about Character *A*'s point of view, and Character *B*'s, but instead should state that "Using the dramatic point of view, Author *Z* allows the various characters to argue their cases, in their own words and with their own limitations."

4. Be particularly careful to distinguish between point of view and opinions or beliefs. Point of view refers to the total position from which things are seen, heard, and reported, whereas an opinion is a thought about something. In this theme, you are to describe not the ideas, but the method of narration of an author.

Sample Theme

Frank O'Connor's First-Person Point of View in "First Confession"

[1] In Frank O'Connor's "First Confession," a story based in early twentieth-century Ireland, the point of view is first person. The speaker is an adult named Jackie, who recalls the events leading up to and including his first confession as a boy of seven. Jackie has good recall and organizing ability, but has limited adult perspective.* These qualities make the story detailed, dramatic, and objective.†

[2] The detail of the story seems vivid and real because O'Connor presents Jackie as a person with strong recall. Events such as the knife scene, the drinking and eating by the barefoot grandmother, and the stories of Mrs. Ryan are colorful. They seem like high points of childhood that an adult would truly remember. The entire confession is presented as if it just happened, not as if it were an almost forgotten event of the past. Such vivid details, which give the story great interest, depend on their being still alive in the narrator's memory.

Beyond simple recall, O'Connor's drama rests on the organizing skills of the narrator. The story is made up of scenes that are unified and connected.

*Central idea
†Thesis sentence
For the text of this story, please see Appendix C, pp. 174–180.

[3] Thus the first part of the confession, ending with Jackie's falling out of the confessional and being whacked by Nora, is a short but complete farce. The burning handprints of the man of the bad confession become a theme in Jackie's mind as he waits for the priest. In the confession itself Jackie mentions even the dramatic pause before the priest responds to the confessed plan to kill the grandmother. The drama in all these scenes results from a good story-telling narrator.

[4] The objective quality of "First Confession," accounting for O'Connor's humor, is related to a flaw in the narrator. Jackie makes remarks about the action, but these are childish and not adult. A more mature narrator might comment about the fear the boy gains through his religious instruction, the difficulties of his family life, or the beauty of his first confession. But from the adult Jackie's point of view we get no such comments. O'Connor makes Jackie stick to the events, and therefore he keeps the story objective, simple, and funny.

[5] Thus O'Connor's selection of the first-person point of view gives the story strength and humor. Jackie the adult is faithful to his childhood feelings. We get everything from his side, and only his side. He never gives his father or his sister any credit. It is the consistent point of view that makes "First Confession" both comic and excellent. If Jackie showed more adult understanding, O'Connor's humor would be gone, and the story would not be such good entertainment.

Commentary on the Theme

This theme emphasizes both the abilities and the flaw of the narrator and attempts to relate these qualities to the nature of "First Confession." The introduction provides a brief background of the story, but gets right to the point of view. The qualification of Jackie as a first-person observer is mentioned, followed by the central idea and thesis sentence. The second paragraph states that the vivid detail of the story results from Jackie's powerful recall. The third paragraph connects the dramatic quality of the various scenes with his skill as a storyteller. In the fourth paragraph a flaw in Jackie's adult character—a lack of adult perceptiveness—is shown as the cause of the objectivity and humor in the story. The conclusion states that the point of view is consistent, even if it is immature. The last sentence goes back to paragraph four: The humor depends on the narrator's having a lack of sympathy for and understanding of childhood antagonists. Throughout the theme, therefore, certain qualities of the story are connected directly to the character, ability, and limited perspective of the point of view or centralizing mind.

chapter
6

The Theme About Setting

Setting refers to the natural and artificial scenery or environment in which characters in literature live and move. Things such as the time of day and the amount of light, the trees and animals, the sounds described, the smells, and the weather are part of the setting. Paint brushes, apples, pitchforks, rafts, six-shooters, watches, automobiles, horses and buggies, and many other items belong to the setting. References to clothing, descriptions of physical appearance, and spatial relationships among the characters are also part of setting. In short, the setting of a work is the sum total of references to physical and temporal objects and artifacts.

The setting of a story or novel is much like the sets and properties of the stage or the location for a motion picture. The dramatist writing for the stage is physically limited by what can be constructed and moved. Writers of nondramatic works, however, are limited only by their imaginations. It is possible for them to include details of many places without the slightest external restraint. For our purposes, the references to setting will be to literary works that establish a setting either in nature or in manufactured things.

The action of a story may occur in more than one place. In a novel, the locale may shift constantly. Although there may be several settings in a work, the term *setting* refers to all the places mentioned. If a story is short, all the scenes may be in one city or countryside, and so a theme about setting could include a discussion of all the locations within the story. If the story is longer, it is best to focus on the setting of only one major scene; otherwise you would be forced beyond the limits of a single theme.

Types of Settings

NATURAL

The setting for a great deal of literature is the out-of-doors, and, naturally enough, Nature herself is seen as a force that shapes character and action. A deep woods may make walking difficult or dangerous, or it may be a place where lovers meet at night. Long distances may keep characters apart and make them different; when they meet, they may have problems that were made by their separation. A barren desert at night may make travelers seek a shelter that turns out to be unsafe. The ocean may produce storms that threaten lives, or it may be so calm that sailing ships cannot move on it. Other natural places may be the location of a quest for identity or of a meditation about the vastness of God and the smallness of human beings.

MANUFACTURED

Manufactured things always reflect the people who made them. A building or a room tells about the people who build it and live in it, and ultimately about the social and political orders that maintain the conditions. A rich house shows the expensive tastes and resources of the characters owning it. A few cracks in the plaster and some chips in the paint may show the same persons declining in fortune and power. Ugly and impoverished surroundings may contribute to the weariness, insensitivity, negligence, or even hostility of the characters living in them.

Studying the Uses of Setting

In preparing to write about the setting of any work, your first concern should be to discover all the details that conceivably form a part of setting, and then to determine how the author has used these details. For example, as writers stress character, plot, or action, they may emphasize or minimize setting. At times a setting will be no more than a roughly sketched place where events occur. In other stories, the setting may be used as an active participant in the action. An instance of such "participation" is Eudora Welty's "A Worn Path," where the woods and roadway provide obstacles that are almost active antagonists against Phoenix as she pushes her way to Natchez.

You might also observe that setting may be a kind of pictorial language, a means by which the author makes statements. In the concluding scene of E. M. Forster's *A Passage to India*, a large rock divides the pathway along which the two major characters are riding. This rock is a direct barrier between them, but it is more than that. It is a visual way of asserting that there are profound cultural and political differences separating England and India and that these two cultures must go their separate ways.

Authors might also use setting as a means of organizing their works. It is often comic, for example, to move a character from one setting to another (provided that no harm is done in the process). Thus, Stephen Crane provokes smiles in the first part of "The Bride Comes to Yellow Sky" by shifting a backwoods town marshal into the plush setting of a Pullman railroad car. Crane's descriptions of the awkwardness of the marshal and the patronizing airs of the other characters is humorous.

Another organizational use of setting is the framing or enclosing method: An author frames a story by opening with a description of the setting, and then returns to the description at the end. Like a picture frame, the setting constantly influences the reader's response to the story. An example of this method is Hemingway's story "In Another Country," which is set in Milan, Italy, in World War I. The opening picture is one of windy, autumnal chill, with dusky light illuminating dead animals hanging in a butcher's shop. The twilight casts a pall over a hospital courtyard. At the story's end, one of the main characters gets the news that his wife has died. He has been wounded and is in the hospital, and the news of his wife's death leaves him despondently looking out the windows. What he sees is the same gloomy scene described at the opening of the story. By concluding in this way, Hemingway has enclosed the events in a setting of dusk, depression, and death.

Setting and Atmosphere

Setting also affects the *atmosphere* or *mood* of stories and poems. You might note that the description of an action requires no more than a functional description of setting. Thus, an action in a forest needs just the statement that the forest is there. However, if you read descriptions of the trees, the shapes, the light and shadows, the animals, the wind, and the sounds, you may be sure that the author is working to create an atmosphere or mood for the action. There are many ways of creating moods. Descriptions of "warm" colors (red, orange, yellow) may contribute to a mood of happiness. "Cooler" colors may suggest gloom. References to smells and sounds bring the setting even more to life by asking additional sensory responses from the reader. The setting of a story on a farm or in a city apartment may evoke a response to these habitats that may contribute to a story's atmosphere.

Organizing Your Theme

INTRODUCTION

In a theme on setting it is tempting to do no more than describe scenes and objects. You can correct this tendency by emphasizing the connection between setting and whatever aspect you choose. A central idea would thus be, "The setting is inseparable from the action." Throughout your theme, as long as you show how the setting is related to the action, you will be sticking to your central idea. Your thesis sentence should be a plan of the major paragraphs or sections of the theme (e.g., "This connection is made in the actions taking place in late afternoon, night, and morning," or "The closeness of setting and action is shown in details about the cabin and the ocean," and so on).

BODY

Following are four possible approaches to themes about setting. The one you choose is your decision, but you may find that some works almost invite you to pick one approach over the others. While each approach outlines a major emphasis in your theme, you may wish to bring in details from one of the others if they seem important at any point in your theme.

1. SETTING AND ACTION. Here you explore the use of setting in the various actions of the work. Among the questions to be answered are these: How detailed and extensive are the descriptions of the setting? Are the scenes related to the action? (Are they essential or incidental?) Does the setting serve as part of the action (places of flight or concealment; public places where people meet openly, out-of-the-way places where they meet privately; natural or environmental obstacles; sociological obstacles; seasonal conditions such as searing heat or numbing cold, etc.)? Do details of setting get used regularly, or are they mentioned only when they become necessary to an action? Do any physical objects figure into the story as causes of aspiration or conflict (e.g., a diamond necklace, a saddle, a doll, a revolver, a canary, a meal)?

2. SETTING AND ORGANIZATION. A closely related way of writing about setting is to connect it to the organization of the work. Some questions to help you get started with this approach are these: Is the setting a frame, an enclosure? Is it mentioned at various parts, or at shifts in the action? Does the setting undergo any expected or unexpected changes as the action changes? Do any parts of the setting have greater involvement in the action than other parts? Do any objects, such as money or property, figure into the developing or changing motivation of the characters? Do descriptions made at the start become important in the action later on? If so, in what order?

3. SETTING AND CHARACTER.   Your aim here is to pick those details that seem to have a bearing on character and to write about their effects. The major question is the degree to which the setting seems to interact with or influence character. You might get at this topic through additional questions: Are the characters happy or unhappy where they live? Do they express their feelings, or get into discussions or arguments about them? Do they seem adjusted? Do they want to stay or leave? Does the economic, cultural, or ethnic level of the setting make the characters think in any unique ways? What jobs do the characters perform because of their ways of life? What freedoms or restraints do these jobs cause? How does the setting influence their decisions, transportation, speech habits, eating habits, attitudes about love and honor, and general folkways?

4. SETTING AND ATMOSPHERE.   Here you should write about those aspects of setting that seem designed to evoke a mood. Some questions are: Does the detail of setting go beyond the minimum needed for action or character? Are the details clear or vague? Are words used essentially to "paint" verbal pictures? Does the author make references to colors, shapes, sounds, smells, or tastes? Does the setting seem to be used to comment on the story (e.g., a carnival scene in daylight as a complement to love, or at night as an ironic backdrop for murder; a scene among computers to reflect on numbered, unfolded, unspindled, computerized people)?

CONCLUSION

You always have the option of summarizing your major points as your conclusion, but you might also want to write about anything you neglected in the body of your theme. Thus, you might have been treating the relationship of the setting to the action and may wish to mention something about any ties the setting has with character or atmosphere. You might also wish to point out whether your central idea about the setting also applies to other major aspects of the work.

Sample Theme
De Maupassant's Use of Setting in "The Necklace" to Show the Character of Mathilde

In "The Necklace" De Maupassant does not give much detail about the setting. He does not describe even the necklace, which is the central object in the plot, but he says only that it is "superb." Rather he uses setting to reflect

[1] the character of the major figure, Mathilde Loisel.* He gives no more detail than is needed to explain her feelings. This carefully directed setting may be considered as the first apartment, the dream-life mansion rooms, and the attic flat.†

[2] Details about the first walkup apartment on the Street of Martyrs are presented to explain Mathilde's unhappiness. The walls are "drab," the furniture "threadbare," and the curtains "ugly." There is only a country girl to do housework. The tablecloth is not cleaned, and the best dinner dish is beef stew boiled in a kettle. Mathilde has no pretty dresses, but only a theatre dress which she does not like. These details show her dissatisfaction about life with her low-salaried husband.

[3] The dream-life, mansion-like setting is like the apartment, because it too makes her unhappy. In Mathilde's daydreams, the rooms are large, filled with expensive furniture and bric-a-brac, and draped in silk. She imagines private rooms for intimate talks, and big dinners with delicacies like trout and quail. With dreams of such a rich home, she feels even more despair about her modest apartment.

[4] Finally, the attic flat indicates the coarsening of her character. There is little detail about this flat except that it is cheap and that Mathilde must carry water up many stairs to reach it. De Maupassant emphasizes the drudgery that she must bear to keep up the flat, such as washing the floor using large pails of water. He indicates her loss of refinement by writing that she gives up caring for her hair and hands, wears cheap dresses, speaks loudly, and swears. In this setting, she no longer has her dreams of the mansion-like rooms. Thus the flat in the attic goes along with the loss of her youth and beauty.

[5] In summary, De Maupassant focuses everything, including the setting, on Mathilde. Anything extra is not needed, and he does not include it. Thus he says little about the big party scene, but emphasizes the necessary detail that Mathilde was a great "success." In "The Necklace," De Maupassant uses setting as a means to his end—the story of Mathilde and her needless misfortune.

Commentary on the Theme

This theme illustrates the approach of relating setting to character. The introduction makes the point that De Maupassant uses only as much detail as he needs, and no more. There is nothing to excess. The central idea is that the details of setting may be directly related to Mathilde's character and feelings. The thesis sentence does not indicate a plan to deal with all the aspects of setting in the story, but only two real ones and one imaginary one.

*Central idea
†Thesis sentence
For the text of this story, please see Appendix C, pp. 167–173.

Paragraphs two and three show how Mathilde's real-life apartment and dream-life mansion fill her with despair about her life. The fourth paragraph relates her flat in the attic in a cheaper neighborhood to the dulling and coarsening of her character. The idea here is that while better surroundings at the start fill her with despair, the ugly attic flat does not seem to affect her at all. At least, De Maupassant says nothing about her unhappiness with the poorer conditions.

The conclusion makes the assertion that, in the light of the general concentration in the story on the character of Mathilde, the setting is typical of De Maupassant's technique in "The Necklace."

The Theme About a Major Idea

An idea, narrowly defined, is a concept, belief, thought, proposition, principle, or assertion, but broadly speaking it is the product of any thinking process. In writing about an idea in a literary work, you may equate the word with *meaning*. In answering the question, "What does this, or that, mean?" your response will usually be in the form of a principle about human nature, conduct, or motivation. This is an idea.

Thus, you may state the following idea in writing about Phoenix Jackson from Welty's "A Worn Path": "She shows that human beings who are commited to care and nurture will suffer for this commitment." In discussing Mrs. Popov in Chekhov's *The Bear*, you might write that she "illustrates the idea that, even if a commitment to the dead is strong, the commitment to life is stronger."

How Do You Express Ideas?

Although an idea may be expressed in a phrase or single word, you will not give your reader much help unless you state ideas in complete sentences. Thus, "parental love" may be an idea in itself, but it is not specific as an idea for a theme. However, if you write, "Parental love is stronger than the love of country," that sentence could be used as the central idea for a theme about Luigi Pirandello's story "War." In this story, a major character, at the end, breaks down over grief for the loss of his dead son, despite his early claims that parents should be proud and glad to sacrifice children for the glory of their country. Similarly, the extension of parental commitment to one's grandchild could be shown as the idea underlying Phoenix's strength in enduring her hardships and disappointment. Whenever you select an idea for your theme, be sure to write it as a complete sentence.

Also be sure to phrase your sentence as an idea, not as a short description of the story. Thus, you might write, "O'Connor's 'First Confession' is a story about the family troubles a boy has before his first confession." This sentence describes the story fairly well, but it does not state an idea, and it would not be helpful for a theme. It would likely cause you to retell the story rather than discuss certain characters and events as they relate to an idea. A better sentence for an idea would be, "O'Connor's 'First Confession' shows the limitation of trying to instill religion through fear and punishment." This sentence would help you to concentrate on the behavior and advice of the sister, father, and Mrs. Ryan, and to show how their making Jackie confused illustrates the weakness of their threats of punishment. The end result would be a theme about an idea, not a retelling of the story.

Ideas and Values

As you write about an idea, you should know that ideas are tied closely to the values, or "value system," of your author. Unless an idea is abstract, say the idea of a geometric form, it usually carries with it some value judgment. Thus, an author may write a poem about the idea that warfare feeds on gullibility and destroys life. Here is a fragment from such a poem, Stephen Crane's "Do Not Weep, Maiden":

> Do not weep, maiden, for war is kind.
> Because your lover threw wild hands toward the sky
> And the affrighted steed ran on alone,
> Do not weep.
> War is kind.

—lines 1–5

Implicit in the poem are the values that life is a gift that should be treasured and not destroyed, and also that the power of persuasion—particularly the political persuasion in times of war that requires people to fight and be killed—is destructive and therefore bad. In talking about Crane's ideas in this poem, you would also discuss these values.

How Do You Find Ideas?

This is a key question. You read the work, consider the main characters and action, study the work some more, think, and express your judgment about the meaning in terms of an idea. As you study, you should know that there is latitude about the exact phrasing but that there should be agreement on the general outlines and extent of the idea. Thus, you might discover that Shakespeare's *Macbeth* illustrates a number of ideas, such as: (1) achieving ambition by ruthless means destroys innocent and guilty alike, (2) trusting the advice of the wrong person is self-destructive, and (3) using force to keep political control only causes rebellion. Although any one of these choices could be an idea for a theme about *Macbeth*, together with others that you might pick, they all have in common the danger or destructiveness of the means to which Macbeth resorts to gain and keep power. In other words, you have wide choice in deciding which idea you write about, but most of the ideas on a particular topic will have general similarities.

With this in mind, you may study your work for ideas. As you look, and think, you should realize that authors may express ideas in any or all of the following ways. You should also realize that the following classifications are for your convenience, because in a literary work all the methods may be occurring at the same time.

DIRECT STATEMENTS BY THE AUTHOR. Often an author states ideas directly, by way of commentary, to guide you or deepen your understanding. In the second paragraph of "The Necklace," for example, De Maupassant states the idea that women without strong family connections must rely on their charm and beauty to get on in the world. You might find this idea patronizing today, but it is nevertheless a true version of what De Maupassant says. In using it, and using other ideas directly from an author, you would likely wish to adapt it somewhat in line with your understanding of the story. Thus, a good idea for a theme would be this: " 'The Necklace' shows the idea that women, with no power except their charm and beauty, are helpless against chance or bad luck."

DIRECT STATEMENTS BY THE PERSONA. (Please see Chapter 5, about point of view, pp. 63–71.) Often personae state their own ideas. These may be the same as those of the author, or they may be totally the reverse. In addition, the author may cause the persona to make statements indicating a limited character. Thus the adult Jackie, in O'Connor's "First Confession," says things that show some of his ideas to be immature. You must be careful and use your ingenuity in deciding how closely the persona's ideas correspond with the author's.

DRAMATIC STATEMENTS MADE BY CHARACTERS. In many works, different characters state ideas that are in conflict. Authors may thus present thirteen ways of looking at a blackbird and leave the choice up to you. They may provide you with guides for your choice, however. For instance, they may create an admirable character whose ideas may be the same as their own. The reverse would be true for a bad character.

IMAGERY.   Authors often use figurative language for their ideas. As an example, here is a comparison from Chaucer's long poem *Troilus and Criseyde,* where Criseyde thinks about the harm that her love with Troilus will bring about:

> How that an eagle, feathered white as bone,
> Under her breast his long claws set
> And out her heart he rent [tore].
>
> —lines 926–28

This comparison suggests the idea that, granted the conditions of male supremacy, the act of falling in love for a woman without the power to protect herself may be self-destructive. Chaucer's story bears out this idea.

CHARACTERS WHO STAND FOR IDEAS.   Although characters are busy in the action of their respective works, they may also be shown to stand for ideas or values. Mathilde Loisel in "The Necklace" may be thought of as an embodiment of the idea that women of the nineteenth-century middle class, without the possibility of a career, are hurt by unrealizable dreams of wealth.

When you have two different characters, their ideas may be compared or contrasted. Mrs. Ryan and the priest in O'Connor's "First Confession," although they never meet and discuss things, represent totally opposing ideas about the true nature and function of religion.

In effect, characters who stand for ideas may be considered as symbols. Thus, in the stories of J. D. Salinger, the introduction of a bright, intuitive child is symbolic, for the child represents Salinger's idea that the insights of children, who are close to God in time, are evidence for the existence and nature of God. For this reason, children in Salinger's stories give an emotional and spiritual lift to jaded adults because they transmit traces of residual divine glory.

THE WORK ITSELF AS IT REPRESENTS IDEAS.   One of the most important ways in which authors express ideas is to render them as an inseparable part of the total impression of the work. All the events and characters may add up to an idea that is made effective by the impact of the story itself. Thus, although an idea may not be directly stated, it will be clear after you have finished reading. For example, in the novel *A Passage to India,* E. M. Forster dramatizes the idea that political, racial, and national barriers keep human beings apart when their greater interest is to unite. He does not use these words, but this idea is clearly rendered in the novel. Similarly, Shakespeare's *Hamlet* embodies the idea that a person doing an evil act sets strong forces in motion that cannot be stopped until everything in their path is destroyed.

When you write your theme, you should explore all these modes and use as many as you think will best provide you with the information you need. It may be that you rely most heavily on the author's direct statements, or on a combination of these and your interpretation of characters and actions. Or you might focus exclusively on a persona and use his or her ideas as a means of describing the author's.

As you write, you should make a point of stating the various sources of your facts. Thus, you might be writing sentences like these:

> Wordsworth describes a childhood theft of a boat to illustrate his idea that Nature is a corrective, moral force [author's statement].

> In one of his last speeches, Macbeth presents the idea that life is without purpose [dramatic statement by a character]. It would appear that Shakespeare creates this speech to support the idea that the use of illegal force leads to a moral dead end.

> Gulliver expresses the idea that religious controversy should be resolved by high authority [statement by a persona]. Because religion deals with mysteries and is potentially divisive, Gulliver's idea here seems close to Swift's.

> The priest's thoughtful, good-humored treatment of Jackie, contrasted with the harsh, punishing treatment by the others, shows the idea that religious incentive is best implanted by kindness and understanding, not by fear [idea embodied in the work as a whole].

Recognizing sources in this way keeps the lines of your conclusions clear. Thereby you will help your reader in following your arguments.

Organizing Your Theme

In developing and planning your theme, you can help yourself by answering questions like these: What is the best wording of the idea that you can make? What has the author done with the idea? How can the actions be related to the idea? Might any characters be measured according to whether they do or do not live up to the idea? What values does the idea seem to suggest? Does the author seem to be proposing a particular cause? Is this cause personal, social, economic, political, scientific, ethical, esthetic, or religious? Can the idea be shown to affect the organization of the work? How? Does imagery or symbolism develop or illustrate the idea?

INTRODUCTION

In your introduction you might state any special circumstances in the work that affect ideas generally or your idea specifically. Your statement of the idea will serve as the central idea for your theme. Your thesis sentence should indicate the particular parts or aspects of the work that you will examine.

BODY

The exact form of your theme will be controlled by your objective, which is (1) to define the idea, and (2) show its importance in the work. Each work will invite its own approach, but here are a number of areas that you might wish to include for your discussion:

1. **THE FORM OF THE WORK AS A PLAN, SCHEME, OR LOGICAL FORMAT.**
   Example: "The idea makes for a two-part work, the first showing religion as punishment, and the second showing religion as kindness and reward."
   Example: "Marvell's idea of the need to experience life in light of approaching death prompts the sequence of a condition, a negation of that condition, and a logical conclusion."

2. **A SPEECH OR SPEECHES.**
   Example: "The priest's conversation and responses to Jackie show in operation the idea that kindness and understanding are the best means to encourage religious commitment."

3. **A CHARACTER OR CHARACTERS.**
   Example: "Eliot's Prufrock is an embodiment of the idea that human beings in the twentieth century have been deprived of their identity and importance."

4. **AN ACTION OR ACTIONS.**
   Example: "The pursuit by the outlaws and the rescue by the rural police indicate Crane's optimistic idea that, on balance, the world furnishes protection and justice despite great danger."

5. **VARIOUS SHADES OR VARIATIONS OF THE IDEA.**
   Example: "The idea of punishment as a corrective is shown simply in the father, with spite in Nora, and with sadistic physical pain and cosmic torture in Mrs. Ryan."

6. **A COMBINATION OF THESE TOGETHER WITH ANY OTHER ASPECT RELEVANT TO THE WORK.**
   Example: "The idea that life is filled with ironies is shown in Hamlet's 'To be or not to be' soliloquy, his decision not to kill Claudius during the prayer scene, and his killing of Claudius after the death of his mother." [Here the idea would be applied to speech, character, and action.]

CONCLUSION

In your conclusion you might add your own thoughts. Here you would be considering the validity or force of the idea. If you are convinced, you might wish to say that the author has expressed the idea forcefully and convincingly, or else you might wish to show how the idea applies to current conditions. If you are not convinced, it is never enough just to say you disagree; you should try to show the reasons for your disagreement. If you would like to mention an idea related to the one you have discussed, you might introduce that here, being sure to stress the connection.

Sample Theme

The Idea of the Strength of Love in Chekhov's The Bear

---

[1] In the one-act farce *The Bear*, Anton Chekhov shows a man and woman, who have never met before, falling suddenly and helplessly in love. With such an unlikely main action, ideas may seem unimportant, but one can find a number of ideas in the play. A very important one is that love and desire are powerful enough to overcome the strongest obstacles.* This idea is shown as love conquers commitment to the dead, renunciation of womankind, and anger.†

[2] Commitment to her dead husband is the obstacle to love shown in Mrs. Popov. She states that she has made a vow never to see daylight because of her mourning, and she spends her time staring at her husband's picture and comforting herself with her faithfulness. Her devotion to the dead is so intense that she claims at the start that she is already in her grave. In her, Chekhov has created a strong obstacle to love so that he might illustrate his idea that love conquers all. By the play's end, Mrs. Popov is embracing Smirnov.

[3] Renunciation of women is the obstacle for Smirnov. He tells Mrs. Popov that his experience with women has made him bitter and that he no longer gives "a good goddamn" about women. His disillusioned words seem to make him an impossible candidate for love. But, in keeping with Chekhov's idea, Smirnov is the one who is soon confessing to the audience that he has fallen headlong for Mrs. Popov. For him, the force of love is so strong that he would even claim happiness at being shot by "those little velvet hands."

[4] Anger and the threat of violence make the greatest obstacle. The two characters become so mad over Smirnov's demand for payment that Smirnov challenges Mrs. Popov to a duel! Because of their individual obstacles, it would seem that the threat of the duel, even if poor Luka could forestall it, would cause the beginning of lifelong hatred between the two. And yet love knocks down all these obstacles, in line with Chekhov's idea that love's power is absolutely irresistible.

The idea, of course, is not new or surprising. It has been the cause of life

---

*Central idea
†Thesis sentence
For the text of this play, please see Appendix C, pp. 188–198.

[5] for all of us. What is surprising about Chekhov's use of the idea is that love in *The Bear* wins out suddenly against such bad conditions. These conditions bring up an interesting and closely related idea. Chekhov may be suggesting that the obstacles themselves, together with the intense involvement produced by anger, cause love. In the speeches of Smirnov and Mrs. Popov, one can see hurt, disappointment, regret, frustration, annoyance, anger, and rage. Yet at the high point of these negative feelings, the characters fall in love. Could Chekhov be saying that it is a mixture of such feelings that brings out love, in the way the Universe was created by God out of Chaos? Though *The Bear* is a farce, and a good one, Chekhov's use of the idea of love's power is anything but farcical.

Commentary on the Theme

This theme is based on the dialogue, soliloquies, and actions of the two major characters in Chekhov's play. Throughout, these sources are mentioned as the authority for the various conclusions. The idea about love's power is treated as it affects the organization of the play. There are thus three large structural units (which in fact are interwoven): the obstacles to love in (1) Mrs. Popov, (2) Smirnov, and (3) their anger.

The introduction notes the farcical action of the play but claims that a major serious idea, the theme's central idea, may be found in it nevertheless. The thesis sentence lists the three structural units just mentioned.

As an operative part of Chekhov's idea, paragraphs two through four detail the nature of the obstacles to be overcome by love. Note that in paragraph two the obstacle is characterized as "strong," in paragraph three as "impossible," and in paragraph four as "lifelong hatred." The concluding paragraph deals with a modest personal admission of the truth of the main idea and the surprise in Chekhov's use of it. The related idea about the closeness of love to all the other strong emotions is concluded with a tribute to Chekhov's use of the idea in the play.

chapter
8

The Theme on a Problem

A problem is any question that you cannot answer easily and correctly about a body of material that you know. The question, "Who is the major character in *Hamlet?*" is not a problem, because the obvious answer is Hamlet.

Let us, however, ask another question: "Why is it correct to say that Hamlet is the major character?" This question is not as easy as the first, and for this reason it is a problem. It requires that we think about our answer, even though we do not need to search very far. Hamlet is the title character. He is involved in most of the actions of the play. He is so much the center of our liking and concern that his death causes sadness and regret. To "solve" this problem has required a set of responses, all of which provide answers to the question "why?" With variations, most readers of Shakespeare's play would likely be satisfied with the answers.

More complex, however, and more typical of most problems, are questions like these: "Why does Hamlet talk of suicide in his first soliloquy?" "Why does he treat Ophelia so coarsely in the 'nunnery' scene?" "Why does he delay in avenging his father's death?" It is with questions like these that themes on a problem will normally be concerned. Simple factual responses do not answer such questions. A good deal of thought, together with a number of interpretations knitted together into a whole theme, is required.

The Usefulness of Problem Solving

The techniques of problem solving should be useful to you in most of your courses. In art, for example, you might need to write on the problem of representationalism as opposed to impressionism. In philosophy you may encounter the problem of whether reality is to be found in particulars or universals. You should know what to do with problems of this sort.

Without question, you have already had a good deal of experience in problem solving. The classroom method of questions and answers has caused you to put facts and conclusions together just as you need to do in a theme on a problem.

The process of solving problems is one of the most important experiences in the development of people's abilities as good readers and thinkers. Uncritical readers do not think about what they read. When they are questioned, they are embarrassed by what they do not remember or understand. However, if they try to answer their own questions as they read, they will have to search the material deeply and try to command it. In dealing with their questions, they must test a number of provisional solutions and organize and develop their responses. As they do these tasks, they become skilled as good, critical readers. In short, if they ask and answer their own questions as a matter of habit, they cannot lose.

Strategies for Your Theme About a Problem

The first purpose in a theme on a problem is to convince your reader that your solution is a good one. This you do by making sound conclusions from supporting evidence. In nonscientific subjects like literature you rarely will find absolute proofs, so your conclusions will not be *proved* in the way you can prove triangles congruent. But your organization, your use of facts from the text, your interpretations, and your application of general or specific knowledge should all be designed to make your conclusions *convincing*. Your basic strategy is thus persuasion.

Because problems and solutions change with the work being studied, each theme on a problem will be different from any other. Despite these differences, however, a number of common strategies might be adapted to whatever problem you face. You might wish to use one or more of these strategies throughout your theme. Always, you should be trying to solve the problem—to answer the question—and you should achieve this goal in the most direct, convenient way.

STRATEGY 1: THE DEMONSTRATION THAT CONDITIONS FOR A SOLUTION ARE FULFILLED.   In effect, this development is the most basic in writing, namely, illustration. In your theme, you first explain that certain conditions need to exist for your solution to be plausible. Your central idea—really a brief answer to the question—will be that the conditions do indeed exist. Your development will be to show how the conditions may be found in the work.

Let us suppose that you are writing on the problem of why Hamlet delays revenge against his uncle, Claudius (who before the play opens has murdered Hamlet's father, King Hamlet, and has become the new king of Denmark). Suppose that, in your introduction, you make the point that Hamlet delays because he is never completely sure that Claudius is guilty. This will be your "solution" to the problem. In the body of your theme you would support your answer by showing the flimsiness of the information Hamlet receives about the crime (i.e., the two visits from the Ghost and Claudius' distress at the play within the play). Once you have "attacked" these sources of data on the grounds that they are unreliable, you will have succeeded. You will have proposed a fair solution to the problem and will have shown that this solution is consistent with the facts of the play.

STRATEGY 2: THE ANALYSIS OF WORDS IN THE PHRASING OF THE PROBLEM. Another good approach is to explore the meaning and limits of important words or phrases in the question as it has been put to you. Your object should be to clarify the words and show how applicable they are. You may wish to define the words and to show whether they have any special meaning.

You will find that attention to words in this way might give you enough material for all or part of your theme. Thus the sample theme in this chapter briefly considers the meaning of the word "effective" when applied to Robert Frost's poem "Desert Places." Similarly, a theme on the problem of Hamlet's delay would benefit from a treatment of the word *delay*: What, really, does *delay* mean? What is the difference in Hamlet's case between reasonable and unreasonable delay? Does Hamlet in fact delay unreasonably? Is his delay the result of a psychological fault? Would speedy revenge be more or less reasonable than the delay? By the time you had devoted such attention to the word, you would have written a goodly amount of material that could be arranged into a full theme on the problem. Also, of course, you could use just a part of this material.

STRATEGY 3: THE REFERENCE TO LITERARY CONVENTIONS. Sometimes your best argument may be to establish that the problem can be solved by reference to the literary conventions of the work. Like people, literary works are not all the same; they reflect differences in stance and convention. Thus, the Greek tragedy *Oedipus the King* is different from Shakespeare's *Hamlet*, and Welty's "A Worn Path" is unlike O'Connor's "First Confession." What might appear to be a problem can often be treated as a normal characteristic, given the particular work you are studying. For example, a problem about the "artificiality" of the choruses in *Oedipus* may be resolved by reference to the fact that the choruses were normal features of Greek drama.

Similarly, you may find a problem about an "unreal" occurrence in a work. But if you can show that the work is laid out as a fantasy or as a dream, and not as a faithful representation of everyday reality, then you can also show that the "unreal" occurrence is normal *for that work*. A problem about the unnatural overreaction and bitterness of Goodman Brown in Hawthorne's "Young Goodman Brown" might be handled in this way. Suppose that the problem is the following: "Is Brown's bitterness unnaturally excessive inasmuch as it is caused by nothing more than a dream?" An answer to this question can be found in the demonstration that the entire story is dreamlike and symbolic and that Brown's reaction is made in what Hawthorne took to be an unreal, dehumanized system. Brown's entire existence, in other words, is unnatural, and his bitterness and suspicion are necessary consequences of this state. Here, the strategy is to resolve an apparent difficulty by trying to establish the context in which the difficulty vanishes. With variations, this method can work for many similar problems.

STRATEGY 4: THE ARGUMENT AGAINST POSSIBLE OBJECTIONS: PROCATALEPSIS. With this strategy, you raise an objection to your solution and then argue against this objection. This strategy, called *procatalepsis* or *anticipation*, is useful because it helps you to sharpen your own arguments. That is, the need to answer objections forces you to make analyses and use facts that you might ordinarily overlook. Although procatalepsis may be used point by point throughout your theme, you may find it most useful at the end. (Please see the last paragraph of the sample theme.) The situation you visualize is that someone might object to your arguments even after you have made your major points. If you can raise the objections first, before they are made by someone else, and then answer them, your theme will be that much more powerful and convincing.

Your aim with the strategy of procatalepsis should be to show that, compared with your solution, the objection (1) is not accurate or valid, (2) is not strong or convincing, or (3) is an exception, not a rule. Here are some examples of these approaches. The objections raised are underlined, so that you can easily distinguish them from the answers.

a. *The objection is not accurate or valid.* Here you reject the objection by showing that either the interpretation or the conclusions are wrong and also by emphasizing that the evidence supports your solution.

> Although Harnlet's delay is reasonable, <u>the claim might be made that his greater duty is to kill Claudius in revenge as soon as the Ghost accuses Claudius of his murder.</u> This claim is not persuasive because

it assumes that Hamlet knows everything the audience knows. The audience accepts the Ghost's word, right from the start, that Claudius is guilty, but from Hamlet's position there is every reason to doubt the Ghost and not to act. Would it not seem foolish and insane for Hamlet to kill Claudius, who is king legally, and then to claim that he did it because the Ghost told him to do so? The argument for speedy revenge is not good, because it is based on an incorrect view of the situation actually faced by Hamlet.

b. *The objection is not strong or convincing.* Here you *concede* that the objection has some truth or validity, but you then try to show that it is weak and that your own solution is stronger.

One might claim that Claudius' distress at the play within the play is evidence for his guilt and that therefore Hamlet should carry out his revenge right away. This argument has merit, and Hamlet's speech after Claudius has fled the scene ("I'll take the Ghost's word for a thousand pound") shows that the King's conscience has been caught. But this behavior is not a strong enough cause for killing him. One could justify a full investigation of Hamlet's father's death on these grounds, yes, but not killing for revenge. Claudius could not be convicted in any court on the strength of testimony that he was disturbed at seeing the Murder of Gonzago on stage. Even after the play within the play, the reasons for delay are stronger than those for action.

c. *The objection is an exception, not a rule.* Here you reject the objection on the grounds that it could be valid only if normal conditions were suspended. The objection depends on an exception, not a rule.

The case for quick action is simple: Hamlet should kill Claudius right after seeing the Ghost (I.3), or else after seeing the King's reaction to the stage murder of Gonzago (III.2) or the Ghost again (III.4). This argument wrongly assumes that due process does not exist in the Denmark of Hamlet and Claudius. Redress under these circumstances, goes the argument, must be both personal and extra-legal. The fact is, however, that the world of Hamlet is civilized, a place where legality and the rules of evidence are precious. Thus Hamlet cannot rush out to kill Claudius, because he knows that the King has not had anything close to due process. The argument for quick action is poor because it rests on an exemption being made from civilized law.

Organizing Your Theme

Writing a theme on a problem requires you to argue a position: Either there is a solution or there is not. To develop this position requires that you show the steps that have led you to your conclusion. The general form of your theme will thus be (1) a description of the conditions that need to be met for the solution you propose, and then (2) a demonstration that these conditions exist. If your position is that there is no solution, then your form would be the same for the first part, but your second part—the development—would show that these conditions have *not* been met.

As with most themes, you may assume that your reader is familiar with the work you have read. Your job is to arrange your materials convincingly around your main point. You should not use anything from the work that is not relevant to your central idea. You do not need to discuss things in their order of appearance in the work. You are in control and must make your decisions about order so that your solution to the problem may be brought out most effectively.

INTRODUCTION

Begin right away with a statement of the problem, and refer to the conditions that must be established for the problem to be solved. It is unnecessary to say anything about the author or the general nature of the work unless you plan to use this material as a part of your development. Your central idea will be your answer to the question, and your thesis sentence will indicate the main heads of your development.

BODY

The body should contain the main points of argument, arranged to convince your reader that your solution to the problem is sound. In each paragraph, the topic sentence will be an assertion that you believe is a major aspect of your answer, and this should be followed with enough detail to support the topic. Your goal should be to cause your reader to agree with you.

You might wish to use one or more of the strategies described in this chapter. These are, again, (1) the demonstration that conditions for a solution are fulfilled, (2) the analysis of words in the phrasing of the problem, (3) the reference to literary conventions, and (4) the argument against possible objections. You might combine these if a combination would help your argument. Thus, if we assume that you are writing to explain that Hamlet's delay is reasonable and not the result of a character flaw, you might begin by considering the word *delay* (strategy 2). Then you might use strategy 1 to explain the reasons for which Hamlet does delay. Finally, in order to answer objections to your argument, you might show that he is capable of action when he feels justified in acting (strategy 4). Whatever your topic, the important thing is to use the method or methods that best help you to make a good case for your solution to the problem.

CONCLUSION

In your conclusion you should affirm your belief in the validity of your solution in view of the supporting evidence. You might do this by reemphasizing those points that you believe are strongest. You might also summarize each of your main points. Or you might think of your argument as still continuing and thus might use the strategy of procatalepsis to raise and answer objections that could be made against your solution, as in the last paragraph of the sample theme.

Sample Theme

The Problem of Frost's Use of the Term "desert places" in the Poem "Desert Places"

---

[1]   In the last line of "Desert Places," the phrase "desert places" undergoes a shift of meaning. At the beginning it refers to the snowy scene of the first stanza, but at the last line it refers to a negative state of soul. The problem is this: Does the change happen too late to be effective? That is, does the new meaning come out of nowhere, or does it really work as a good closing thought? To solve this problem, one must say that the change cannot be effective if there is no preparation for it before the last line of the poem. But if there is preparation—that is, if Frost does show that the desert places of the natural world are like those within the speaker himself—then the shift is effective even though it comes at the very end. It is clear that Frost makes the preparation and therefore that the change is effective.* The preparation may be traced in Frost's references, word choices, and concluding sentences.†

[2]   In the first two stanzas Frost includes the speaker in his references to living things being overcome. The scene described in line 4 is "weeds and stubble showing last." Then come the hibernating animals "smothered in their lairs" in line 6. Finally the speaker includes himself. He states that he is "too absent-spirited to count," and that the "loneliness" of the scene "includes" him "unawares" (7, 8). This movement—from vegetable, to animal, to human—shows that everything alive is changed by the snow. Obviously the speaker will not die like the grass or hibernate like the animals, but he indicates that the "loneliness" overcomes him. Thus, these first eight lines connect the natural bleakness with the speaker.

    Word choices in the third stanza have human connotations and are therefore preparatory. The words *lonely* and *loneliness* (line 9), *more lonely* (10), *blanker*

*Central idea
†Thesis sentence
For the text of this poem, please see Appendix C, p. 155.

[3] and *benighted* (11), and *no expression, nothing to express* (12) all refer to human as well as natural conditions. The word *benighted* is most important, because it refers not only to night, but also to intellectual or moral ignorance. These words invite the reader to think of negative mental and emotional states. They provide a context in which the concluding shift of meaning will come naturally.

[4] Frost's concluding sentences form the climax of the preparation for the last two words. All along, the poet suggests that the speaker's soul is as bleak as the snowy field. This idea is focused in the last stanza, where in two sentences the speaker talks about himself:

> They cannot scare me with their empty spaces
> Between stars—on stars where no human race is.
> I have it in me so much nearer home
> To scare myself with my own desert places.

[5] In the context of the poem, therefore, the last words do not create a difficult problem of interpretation. They rather pull together the two parts of the comparison that Frost has been building from the very first line. Just as "desert places" refers to the snowy field, it also suggests human coldness, blankness, unconcern, insensitivity, and maybe even cruelty. The phrase does not spring out of nowhere, but is effective as the climax of the major idea of the poem.

[6] Although the conclusion is effective, a critic might still claim that it is weak because Frost does not develop the thought about the negative soul. He simply mentions "desert places" and stops. But the poem is not a long psychological study. To ask for more than Frost gives would be to expect more than sixteen lines can provide. A better claim against the effectiveness of the concluding phrase would be that "desert places" is trite and vague. If the phrase were taken away from the poem, this criticism might be acceptable. But in the poem it takes on the suggestions of the previous fifteen lines, and does so with freshness and surprise. Thus the shift of meaning is a major reason for Frost's success in "Desert Places."

Commentary on the Theme

The introductory paragraph states the problem about whether or not the shift of meaning at the end of Frost's poem is effective. Emphasis is on the condition that the poem must prepare the reader for this shift if effectiveness is to be claimed for it. The central idea indicates that the poem satisfies this requirement and that the shift is effective. The thesis sentence indicates three subjects for development.

The first half of paragraph two draws attention to three references to the snow's bleakness. These are considered in the second half, and thus the paragraph shows that there is preparation early in the poem for the shift. Paragraph three continues this line of development, illustrating the relationship of certain words in the third stanza to the human state, and thus to a shift in the poem from the vegetable to the human world. The fourth paragraph asserts that the concluding sentences build toward a climax of Frost's pattern of development.

Paragraphs five and six are a two-part conclusion. The fifth paragraph summarizes the arguments and offers an interpretation of the phrase. The last paragraph deals with two objections against the effectiveness of the phrase. The theme thus shows that a careful reading of the poem eliminates the grounds for claiming that there is any problem about the last line.

The general development of this theme illustrates strategy 1 described in this chapter (pp. 88–89). The attention to the word *effective* briefly illustrates the second strategy (p. 89). The concluding paragraph shows two approaches to the fourth strategy (pp. 90–91), using the arguments that the objections are not good because they are based on (1) an exception, and (2) an incorrect assumption.

chapter
9

Themes on
(I) Imagery,
and (II) Symbolism
and Allegory

Imagery, on the one hand, and symbolism and allegory, on the other, are closely related because both use elements of literary works to deepen meaning or to stand for something else. Because of their similarities, they are included here together, but because of their differences, two separate kinds of themes are described.

I. Imagery

Imagery is a broad term referring to the comparison of something known—a description of an object or action—with something to be communicated—a situation or emotional state. It is the means by which authors reach directly into the experience and imagination of their readers to create a desired response.

Imagery works by means of *analogy*, i.e., "This is like that." At the heart of an author's use of imagery is this assumption:

> Not only do I want you to understand my descriptions of this character's attitudes or of that scene or object, but I want you to come close to *feeling* them too. Therefore I will make an analogy—an image—which, by its similarity to your own experience or by its ability to touch your imagination, will intensify your perceptions and heighten your emotions.

For example, to communicate a character's joy and excitement, the sentence "She was happy" is not effective. A writer can get at these feelings better by using an image like this one: "She felt as if she had just inherited five million tax-free dollars." Because readers can easily *imagine* the combination of excitement, disbelief, and joy that such a happening would bring, they can deepen their awareness of these emotions. It is the *image* that evokes this perception—something that no simple description can quite accomplish.

As a literary parallel, let us use John Keats's poem "On First Looking Into Chapman's Homer." Keats wrote the poem after he first read Chapman's translation of Homer, the ancient Greek epic poet. His main idea is that Chapman not only translated Homer's words but also transmitted his greatness. A paraphrase of the poem is this:

> I have read much literature and have been told that Homer is the best writer of all, but not knowing Greek, I could not appreciate his works until I discovered them in Chapman's translation. To me, this experience was exciting and awe-inspiring.

This paraphrase also destroys Keats' poetry. Contrast the second sentence of the paraphrase with the last six lines of the sonnet as Keats wrote them:

> Then felt I like some watcher of the skies
> When a new planet swims into his ken;
> Or like stout Cortez when with eagle eyes
> He stared at the Pacific—and all his men
> Looked at each other with a wild surmise—
> Silent, upon a peak in Darien.

If Keats had written only the sentence in the paraphrase, we would probably not read him with interest because we would find no descriptions of objects from which we could derive his emotion. But we can readily respond to the imagery of the last six lines; namely, we can *imagine* how we would have felt if we had been the first astronomers to discover a new planet, or the first explorers to see the Pacific.

SOME DEFINITIONS

IMAGE, IMAGERY. The word *image* refers to single comparisons. Keats's reference to the "watcher of the skies" is an image. *Imagery* is a broader term referring to all the images within a passage ("the imagery of line 5, or of stanza 6"), an entire work ("the imagery of Eliot's 'Prufrock' "), a group of works ("the imagery of Shakespeare's Roman plays"), or an entire body of works ("the development of Shakespeare's imagery").

VEHICLE, TENOR. To describe the relationship between a writer's ideas and the images chosen to objectify them, two useful terms have been coined by I. A. Richards (in *The Philosophy of Rhetoric*). First is the *tenor,* which is the total of ideas and attitudes not only of the literary speaker but also of the author. Second is the *vehicle,* or the details that carry the tenor. The vehicle of the five million dollar image is the description of the inheritance. Similarly, the tenor of the last six lines of Keats' sonnet is awe and wonder; the vehicle is the reference to astronomical and geographical discovery.

Characteristics of Literary Imagery

It would be difficult to find any good piece of writing that does not employ imagery to at least some extent. Imagery is most vital, however, in imaginative writing, where it promotes understanding and shapes the reader's responses.

Usually, imagery is embodied in words or descriptions denoting sense experience that leads to many associations. A single word naming a flower, say *rose,* evokes a positive response. A person might think of the color of a rose, recall its smell, associate it with the summer sun and pleasant days, and recall the love and respect that a bouquet of roses means as a gift. But *rose* is not an image until its associations are used as an analogy, as in these lines by Robert Burns:

> O, my luve's like a red, red rose
> That's newly sprung in June.

Once Burns has made this comparison, he evokes pleasant thoughts and feelings about roses. These become the tenor of the image. That a rose may have unpleasant associations, perhaps because of its thorns, should not be considered. Such an extension of meaning, although truthful, would likely be a misreading of the image.

It would, that is, unless the writer deliberately calls some of these less happy ideas to mind. In one of the most famous poems about a rose, by Edmund Waller ("Go Lovely Rose," in which the speaker addresses a rose that he is about to send to his sweetheart), the speaker observes that roses, when cut, die:

> Then die—that she
> The common fate of all things rare
> May read in thee:
> How small a part of time they share
> That are so wondrous sweet and fair.

Here the poet is directing the reader's responses to the original comparison of the rose with the sweetheart. The structure of the poem is the full development of the image. In this poem, the tenor is an awareness that life is both lovely and fragile.

Imagery is most vivid when it appeals directly to sense experience. References to senses like sight and touch will produce an immediate imaginative response. More complex and intellectualized images require greater effort to reconstruct. Matthew Arnold stated in "Dover Beach" that the world seemed "to lie before us like a land of dreams," a figurative image that has caused much speculation. Shakespeare's line, "And summer's lease hath all too short a date," from Sonnet 18, makes the reader think about the renting and leasing of property. Despite such variety, the common element in imagery is the attempt by writers to convey ideas by referring to sense impressions, objects, and situations that readers can imaginatively reconstruct and to which they can emotionally and intellectually respond.

Imagery and Rhetorical Devices

The vehicles of imagery have been classified rhetorically. The two most important types are the *simile* and the *metaphor*.

SIMILE. In a simile the vehicle is introduced by *like* or *as*. The second of these two lines is a simile:

> It glows and glitters in my cloudy breast
> Like stars upon some gloomy grove.

In the six lines from the Keats sonnet on Chapman's Homer, quoted on p. 97, there are two similes, each conveying the tenor of the excitement of discovery.

METAPHOR. In a metaphor the comparison is made in the form of a direct equation, without the use of *like* or *as*. The tenor is implied in the vehicle. A metaphor may consist of a single word, as in the word *choirs* in Shakespeare's sonnet "That Time of Year":

> Bare ruined choirs where late the sweet birds sang

Here the word *choirs* refers to a section of a church which has been destroyed. This word in turn affects the meaning of "sweet birds," for on the one hand they are real birds, but on the other they are human singers who sang in the choirs before the destruction.

A metaphor may also be more extensive, as in Shakespeare's sonnet "Poor Soul, the Center of My Sinful Earth," when the speaker equates his body with a house ("mansion") and his soul with a tenant renting the house:

> Why so large cost, having so short a lease,
> Dost thou upon thy fading mansion spend?

Less common forms of imagery are *synecdoche, metonymy, personification,* and *controlling image*.

SYNECDOCHE. In a synecdoche, which is a special kind of metaphor, a small part stands for a large part, usually as a way of stressing a particular aspect of something. The following expression illustrates a synecdoche: "Each day they had the task of attending to four hungry mouths." This is a means of emphasizing that the parents in question were having difficulty in caring for all the needs of four very dependent children.

METONYMY. A metonym, also a metaphor, is a term that stands for something with which it is closely associated. The President, for example, is closely associated with the White House, so that "news from the White House" is news of actions and policies of the President. Similar to this are "the Pentagon," "Broadway," "Haight Ashbury," and so on.

PERSONIFICATION. In personification, something abstract is given human attributes, as in this example from Keats' ode "To Autumn," where the season is personified as a woman:

> Who hath not seen thee oft amid thy store?
>   Sometimes whoever seeks abroad may find
> Thee sitting careless on a granary floor
>   Thy hair soft-lifted by the winnowing wind;

CONTROLLING IMAGE. A controlling image is one that is so thoroughly developed in a work, or is so vital and pervasive, that one may interpret the work in the light of this image. At the beginning of John of Gaunt's speech in Shakespeare's *Richard II*, for example (II.i.33–70), there is a controlling image when Gaunt compares himself to a "prophet." The entire speech is colored by the idea that the speaker giving it, being close to death and therefore close to God and the riddles of the universe, is presenting an accurate forecast of the future, just as the Old Testament prophets did.

II. Symbolism and Allegory

Symbolism and allegory are closely related to metaphor. A metaphor indicates an analogy by momentarily equating the two things being compared. Symbols and allegories actually *stand* for something else.

Symbolism

A symbol may be a thing, place, action, person, or concept. In a literary work it has its own objective reality—if it did not have such validity, it would be artificial and therefore weak—but it is used to carry greater meaning than its simple presence might indicate. When a symbol is introduced, it is understood to signify the very specific things intended by the writer. Once it is established in a work, it is often reintroduced like a theme with variations.

To judge whether something is symbolic, you should try to determine if it serves as the vehicle for a significant idea or emotion. Thus, the character Sisyphus, in the ancient myth of Sisyphus, is a symbol. Sisyphus is doomed in the afterlife to roll a large rock up a high hill. Just as he gets it to the top it rolls down, and he then must roll it back up again, and again, and again, for the rock always rolls down as he gets it to the top. His plight has been taken as a symbol for the human condition: A person rarely if ever completes anything. Work must always be done over and over, and the same problems recur without any final solution. But at least people, like Sisyphus, are involved and active and hence can gain satisfaction from their activity.

Some symbols, like the myth of Sisyphus, are generally or universally recognized. Authors referring to them rely on this recognition and understanding. Thus water used in the sacrament of baptism is recognized as a symbol of life. When it spouts up as a fountain, water may symbolize optimism (as upwelling, bubbling life). In a brackish pool, it may symbolize life being polluted or diminished. With the trend toward psychological interpretations of symbols, water may be construed as a reference to sexuality. Thus, lovers may meet by a quiet lake, a cascading waterfall, a purling stream, a wide river, or a stormy sea. The condition of the water in each instance could be interpreted as a symbol of their romantic relationships. Another generally recognized symbol is the serpent, which represents Satan. In "Young Goodman Brown," Nathaniel Hawthorne refers to a walking-stick that resembles a serpent, in this way instantly evoking the image of Satanic evil. But because the stick only "seems" to "wriggle like a serpent," it may also symbolize human tendencies to see evil where it does not exist. (Please see the second sample theme, on Hawthorne's use of this symbol.)

Many more objects and descriptions do not have this generally established rank as symbols. They can be symbols only within their works. For example, the jug of beer (porter) carried by Jackie's grandmother in "First Confession" is one of the things that symbolize for Jackie the grandmother's peasant-like and boorish habits. The porter is symbolic only within the work; a reference to it elsewhere would not carry the symbolic meaning that O'Connor gives it in the story.

In determining whether references like these are symbols, you need to make decisions based on your judgment of the total importance of the references. If they seem of great significance, you can justify claiming them as symbols as long as you can demonstrate their scope. Thus, at the end of "A Worn Path" Phoenix buys a toy windmill for her sick grandson. It is slight, and she pays for it with all the money she has. It will break soon, like her life and that of her grandson, but it is an attempt to give him some small pleasure despite her poverty and the hopelessness of her life. For all these reasons it is correct to interpret the windmill as a symbol of her strong character, generous nature, and pathetic existence.

Allegory

An allegory is to a symbol as a motion picture is to a still picture. The allegory puts symbols into action. In form the allegory is a complete and self-sufficient narrative, but it also signifies another series of events or conditions of life as expressed in a religion or philosophy. While some works are allegories from beginning to end, many works that are not allegories contain sections or episodes that may be considered allegorically.

If you write about allegory or an allegorical reading, you are to show how the entire story, or an extensive and self-contained episode, may be applied. Thus, John Bunyan's *The Pilgrim's Progress* is a story about Christian's difficult journey from his home in the City of Destruction to his new home in the Heavenly City. The specific application of this allegory is to the rigors and trials of Christian life as Bunyan understood them. The story may also be applied in a secular context, and to make such an application you would need to show that it is relevant to the growth and problems of most people working toward a goal. Bunyan probably intended his episode of the "Slough of Despond," to name only one section in *The Pilgrim's Progress*, to allegorize the doubt and depression that even the firmest Christian believers sometimes have about their faith. In applying the episode generally it would be proper to take the Slough as meaning those moments of doubt, discouragement, and depression that sometimes plague people seeking an education, a work goal, the good life, or whatever. As long as your parallels are close, as this one is, your allegorical reading will have validity.

FABLE, PARABLE, AND MYTH

Three forms that you might encounter that are close to allegory are *fable*, *parable*, and *myth:*

FABLE. A fable is a short story, often featuring animals with human traits, to which writers and editors attach "morals" or explanations. The fable of "The Fox and the Grapes," for example, signifies the tendency to demean those things we cannot have.

PARABLE. Parables are most often associated with Jesus Christ, who used them in his teaching. They are extremely short narratives which exemplify religious truths and insights. Parables like those of the Good Samaritan and the Prodigal Son are interpreted to show God's active love, concern, understanding, and forgiveness for human beings.

MYTH. Myths are stories, either short or long, that are often associated with religion and philosophy, and also, in anthropological or psychological terms, with various races or cultures. Myths embody scientific truths for pre-scientific societies, and codify the social and cultural values of the civilization in which they were written. In the past the word *mythical* was a way of saying that something was untrue. Today, however, it is proper to be more sympathetic to myths, for the truths are to be found not literally in the stories themselves, but figuratively in the interpretations.

Allusiveness in Imagery, Symbolism, and Allegory

These modes are often complicated by the *allusion* to other things, such as the classics, the Bible, or contemporary politics. The original source then becomes a vital part of the writer's image. In John Donne's sonnet "I Am a Little World Made Cunningly," for example, the concluding lines are:

> . . . burn me, O Lord, with a fiery zeal
> Of Thee and Thy house, which doth in eating heal.

Reading the last line is made possible if you realize that the metaphor is an allusion to *Psalms* 69.9: "For the zeal of thine house hath eaten me up." Until the Biblical reference is known, however, the line is difficult if not impossible to understand.

This example brings up the problem of how much background you need for understanding imagery or symbols. For the most part your attempt to imagine the experience described or suggested will be enough. But an allusive image, like the Biblical one in Donne's poem, or an archaic symbol, may require a dictionary or other reference work. The scope of your Collegiate Dictionary will surprise you. If you cannot find an entry in your dictionary, however, try an encyclopedia, or ask your reference librarian about standard reference guides such as *The Oxford Companion to English Literature, The Oxford Companion to Classical Literature,* or William Rose Benet's *The Reader's Encyclopaedia.* If you continue to have trouble after using sources like these, see your instructor.

Preparing for Your Theme

You will need to be alert and to employ all facilities that can aid your understanding and appreciation. Study the poem or passage word by word. Try to discover individual images and patterns of imagery. Take careful notes, and write your reactions as they occur to you. A good thing to do is to make visual aids, trying to bring images to life by drawing diagrams or sketches. In Shakespeare's Sonnet 146, for example, line 13 offers a challenge to the imagination that might be aided by a sketch:

So shalt thou [the speaker's Soul] feed on Death that feeds on
men.

Just how far does this metaphor invite visualization? Do *feed* and *feeds*
suggest an eater who, while eating, is being eaten, or should the words
be read without the attempt to imagine specific feeders? In the age of *Jaws*
and *Jaws II*, one student made the following drawing for these lines:

This drawing vividly shows the relationships involved, though it tends to
demean Soul, Death, and Men (perhaps the student was thinking that
human beings, in this case, are "poor fish"). Whether or not you carry
your visualization this far, it is clear that Shakespeare's speaker is calling
Death voracious because it seizes human beings for prey. But he is also
claiming that the Soul can be equally voracious and stronger than Death,
even though it is also dependent on Death in this graphic food chain.

A particularly helpful aid for symbolism is a list. The idea is to show
how qualities of the symbol may be paralleled with qualities of a character
or action. Such a list can give you the substance for much in your theme,
and it can also help you in thinking more deeply about the effectiveness
of the symbol. Here is such a list, for the symbol of the toy windmill in
Welty's "A Worn Path":

Qualities in the Windmill	Comparable Qualities in Phoenix and her Life
1. Cheap	1. Poor, but she gives all she has for the windmill
2. Breakable	2. Old, and not far from death
3. A gift	3. Generous
4. Not practical	4. Needs some relief from reality and practicality
5. Colorful	5. Same as 4

An aid for figuring out an allegory or allegorical passage can work well
with a diagram of parallel lines. Along these lines you can place corresponding events, as follows:

PILGRIM'S PROGRESS	Christian's Burden	Slough of Despond	Valley of the Shadow of Death
CHRISTIAN APPLICATION	Original Sin	Doubt and Despair	Danger of the Loss of the Soul
GENERAL APPLICATION	Problems, Shortcomings, Poverty, etc.	Depression, Despondency	General risks and dangers of living

Some persons might object to making such sketches or diagrams because they might limit your responses too narrowly. But if these aids genuinely help you, go right ahead and use them. You might wish to modify your aids, as you make progress with them, by crossing some things out and by putting others in. As long as what you do can be supported in your work, you will stay on the right track and can even improve the accuracy and forcefulness of your theme.

Organizing Your Theme

INTRODUCTION

Whether you are discussing imagery or symbolism and allegory, you should try to relate your topic to the general nature of the work. Thus, images or symbols of suffering might be appropriate to a religious, redemptive work, while those of sunshine and cheer might be right for a romantic one. You should also try to justify any claims that you make about images or symbols. In Swift's *A Modest Proposal*, for example, the eating of infants is proposed: How can this action be viewed as a symbol? Your introduction is the place to establish ideas and justifications of this sort. Your central idea and thesis sentence should be here, too, to guide your reader for the remainder of your theme.

BODY

A. IMAGERY. There are a number of approaches for discussing imagery. They are not mutually exclusive, and you may combine them as you wish.

1. *The meaning and effect of the imagery.* Here you explain your interpretation of the various images. In Eve Merriam's poem "Robin Hood," for example, Robin Hood comes back to Sherwood Forest to establish the forest as a preserve next to the "Hood enterprises / for Sherwood Homesights."

as a preserve next to the "Hood enterprises / for Sherwood Homesights." In explaining this action as metaphor, you would say that modern commercialism has preempted the sense of adventure, romance, and justice that we associate with earlier times. In determining the effect of the metaphor, you would probably draw attention to its combination of cynicism, derision, and amusement.

2. *The frames of reference of the imagery, and the appropriateness of the imagery to the subject matter.* Here you might show the locations from which the images are derived. Does the writer favor images from Nature, science, warfare, politics, business, reading? Are these images appropriate to the subject matter? If the subject is the dreariness of a 9-to-5 office routine, for example, would an image of paper clips and commas be appropriate (see Theodore Roethke's poem "Dolor")? Similarly, in a tragedy, would it be appropriate to refer to images drawn from joyous springtime rituals?

3. *The frequency and the types of images.* Does the writer characteristically express himself or herself in imagery? How many images are there? How often do they occur? Does the writer use images appealing to one sense (sight, hearing, smell, taste, touch) rather than to another? Does he or she record colors, sounds, shapes? Do the images function integrally in the ideas of the work, or in the type of work? How fully does the author rely on the associations of sensuous imagery? (Do references to green plants and trees, for example, suggest that life may be rich and full, or do references to touch suggest amorous warmth?) What conclusions can you draw about the author's—or the speaker's—taste or sensibility as a result of your study?

4. *The effect of one image, or series of images, on the other images and ideas in the work.* Usually you will pick an image that occurs early in the work and determine whether this image acts as a controlling image over the ideas or mood of the work. Thus, the first paragraph of Jonathan Swift's *Battle of the Books* contains a demeaning image about the behavior of sexually aroused dogs. In this way, Swift conveys the impression that the claims to superiority of modern writers and thinkers has a physiological origin that is anything but flattering. In an analysis of this sort, you would try to show the importance of the controlling image throughout the work.

B. SYMBOLS, SYMBOLISM

1. *The meaning of a major symbol.* Here you interpret the symbol and try to show what it stands for both inside and outside the work. A few of the questions you might pursue are these: How do you determine that the symbol is really a symbol? How do you derive from the work the exact meaning of the symbol? What is the extent of the meaning? Does the symbol undergo any modification if it reappears in the work? How? Does the author create any ironies by using the symbol? Does the symbol give any special strength to the work?

2. *The meaning and relationship of a number of symbols.* What are the symbols? Do they have any specific connection or common bond? Do they suggest a unified reading or a contradictory one? Are the symbols of general significance, or do they operate only in the context of the work? Do the symbols control the form of the work? How? Do they fit naturally into the narrative, or do they seem to be drawn in artificially? Does their use make for any unique qualities or excellences in the work?

C. ALLEGORY (FABLE, PARABLE, MYTH)

1. *The application of the allegory.* Does the allegory (fable, parable, myth) refer to anything or anyone specific? Does it refer to an action or particular period of history? Or does the allegory refer to human tendencies or ideas? Does it illustrate, point by point, particular philosophies or religions? If so, what are these? If the original meaning of the allegory seems outdated, how much can be salvaged for people living today?

2. *The consistency of the allegory.* Is the allegory maintained consistently throughout the work, or is it intermittently used and dropped? Explain and detail this use. Would it be correct to call your work *allegorical* rather than *an allegory*? Are there any unnatural or arbitrary events that are introduced because of the allegory (such as the albatross' being hung around the neck of Coleridge's Ancient Mariner to show that he must carry the burden of his crime)?

CONCLUSION

In your conclusion you might summarize your main points, describe your general impressions, try to describe the impact of the images or symbolic methods, indicate your personal responses, or show what might further be done along the lines you have been developing in the body. You might also try to assess the quality of the images and to make a statement about their appropriateness.

First Sample Theme
(Imagery in a Poem)

A Study of Shakespeare's Imagery in Sonnet 30

When to the sessions of sweet silent thought,	1
I summon up remembrance of things past,	2
I sigh the lack of many a thing I sought,	3
And with old woes new wail my dear time's waste:	4
Then can I drown an eye (un-used to flow)	5

For precious friends hid in death's dateless night,   6
And weep afresh love's long since cancelled woe,   7
And moan th'expense of many a vanished sight.   8
Then can I grieve at grievances foregone,   9
And heavily from woe to woe tell o'er   10
The sad account of fore-bemoaned moan,   11
Which I new pay, as if not paid before.   12
    But if the while I think on thee (dear friend)   13
    All losses are restored, and sorrows end.   14

[1] In this sonnet Shakespeare, the speaker, stresses the sadness and regret of remembered experience, but he states that a person with these feelings may be cheered by the thought of a friend. His imagery, cleverly used, creates new and fresh ways of seeing personal life in this perspective.* He presents images drawn from the public and business world of the courtroom, money, and banking or money-handling.†

[2] The courtroom image of the first four lines shows that the past is alive in the present. Like a justice at a hearing, Shakespeare "summons" his memory of "things past" to appear on trial before him. This image suggests that people are their own judges and that their ideals and morals are like laws by which they measure themselves. Shakespeare finds himself guilty of wasting his time in the past. Removing himself, however, from the strict punishment that the image would require, he does not condemn himself for his "dear time's waste," but instead laments it (line 4).

[3] With the closely related image of money, Shakespeare shows that living is a lifelong investment and is valuable for this reason. It is not money that is spent, but emotions and commitment. Thus, his dead friends are "precious" because he invested time and love in them, and the "sights" that have "vanished" from his eyes make him "moan" because he went to great "expense" for them (8).

[4] Like the money image, the reference to banking or money-handling emphasizes the fact that life's experiences are on deposit in the mind. They are recorded there, and may be withdrawn in moments of "sweet silent thought" just as money may be withdrawn. Thus Shakespeare states that he counts out his woes just as a teller counts money. He pays with new woe the accounts that he had already paid with old woe in the past. The imagery suggests that the past is so much a part of the present that a person never finishes paying both the principal and interest of past emotional investments. Because of this combination of banking and legal imagery, Shakespeare indicates that his memory puts him in double jeopardy, for the thoughts of his losses overwhelm him in the present just as much as they did in the past.

[5] The legal, financial, and money-handling images combine in the last two lines to show how a healthy present life may overcome past regrets. The "dear friend" being addressed in these lines has the resources (financial) to settle all the emotional judgments that the speaker makes against himself (legal). It is as though the friend is a rich patron who rescues him from emotional bank-

*Central idea
†Thesis sentence

ruptcy (legal and financial) and the possible sentence of emotional misery (legal).

<u>Shakespeare's images are drawn from everyday public and business actions, but his use of them is creative, unusual, and excellent.</u> In particular, the tenor of line 8 ("And moan th'expense of many a vanished sight") stresses that people spend much emotional energy on others. Without emotional commitment, one cannot have precious friends and loved ones. In keeping with this image of money and investment, one could measure life not in months or years, but in the spending of emotion and involvement in personal relationships. Shakespeare, by inviting readers to explore the values brought out by his images, gives a new sense of the value of life itself.

[6]

Commentary on the Theme

This theme treats the three classes of images that Shakespeare introduces in Sonnet 30. It thus illustrates the second approach (p. 106). But the aim of the discussion is not to explore the extent and nature of the comparison between the images and the personal situations spoken about in the poem. Instead the goal is to explain how the images develop Shakespeare's meaning. This method therefore illustrates the first approach (pp. 105–106).

The introduction provides a brief description of the sonnet, the central idea, and the thesis sentence. Paragraph 2 deals with the meaning of Shakespeare's courtroom image. His money image is explained in paragraph 3. Paragraph 4 considers the banking, or money-handling image. The fifth paragraph shows how Shakespeare's last two lines bring together the three separate strands, or classes of images.

The conclusion comments generally on the creativity of Shakespeare's images. It also amplifies the way in which the money image creates an increased understanding and valuation of life.

Second Sample Theme (Allegory and Symbolism in a Story)

Allegory and Symbolism in Hawthorne's "Young Goodman Brown"

It is hard to read beyond the third paragraph of "Young Goodman Brown" without finding allegory and symbolism. The opening seems realistic—Goodman Brown, a young Puritan, leaves his home in colonial Salem to take an overnight trip—but his wife's name, "Faith," immediately suggests a symbolic reading. Before long, Brown's walk into the dreamlike forest seems like an allegorical trip into evil. The idea that Hawthorne shows by this trip is that rigid

[1]   belief destroys the best human qualities, such as understanding and love.* He develops this thought in the allegory and in many symbols, particularly the sunset, the walking-stick, and the path.†

The allegory is about how people develop destructive ideas. Most of the story seems dreamlike and unreal, and therefore the ideas that Brown gains seem unreal. After the weird night he thinks of his wife and neighbors not with love, but with hatred for their sins during the "witch meeting" deep in the dream forest. For this wrong cause, really no cause at all, he condemns everyone around him, and he lives out his life in unforgiving harshness. This story may

[2]   be applied allegorically to the pursuit of any ideal or system beyond human love and forgiveness. No matter what *ism* people follow, to the degree that for that *ism* they condemn human beings, take hostages, accept political repression of others, and destroy people and land, they are like Goodman Brown. With his bitterness and distrust, he has destroyed the best in himself—his ability to love and forgive.

The attack on such dehumanizing belief is found not just in the allegory, but also in Hawthorne's many symbols. The seventh word in the story, *sunset,* may be seen as a symbol. Sunset indicates the end of the day. Coming at the

[3]   beginning of the story, however, it suggests that Goodman Brown is beginning the long night of his hatred, his spiritual death. For him the night will never end because his final days are shrouded in "gloom" (p. 166). Hawthorne indicates that Brown, like anyone else who gives up on human beings, is cut off, locked in an inner prison of bitterness.

The next symbol, the walking-stick, suggests the ambiguous and arbitrary standard by which Brown judges his neighbors. The stick is carried by the guide who looks like Brown's father, but it is more. Hawthorne writes that it "might almost be seen to twist and wriggle itself like a living serpent" (p. 157). The serpent is a clear symbol for Satan, who tempted Adam and Eve. The stick is also still a walking-stick, however, and in this respect it is innocent.

[4]   Hawthorne seems to be using it to symbolize human tendencies to see evil where evil does not really exist. This double meaning squares with his statement about "the instinct that guides mortal man to evil" (p. 162). This instinct is not just the temptation to do bad things, but also the invention of wrongs for arbitrary reasons, and, more dangerously, the condemnation of those who have "done" these wrongs even though they have done nothing more than lead their own quiet lives.

In the same vein, the path through the forest is a major symbol of the evil of the mental confusion to which Brown is subject. As he walks, the path before him grows "wilder and drearier, and more faintly traced," and "at length" it

[5]   vanishes (p. 162). This is like the description of the "broad" Biblical way that leads "to Destruction" (Matthew, VII.13). As a symbol, the path shows that most human acts are bad, while a small number, like the "narrow" way to life

*Central idea
†Thesis sentence
For the text of this story, please see Appendix C, pp. 156–166.

(Matthew, VII.14), are good. Goodman Brown's path is at first clear, as though sin is at first unique and unusual, but soon it is so indistinct that he can see only sin wherever he turns. The symbol thus suggests that, as people follow evil, their moral vision becomes blurred and they cannot choose the right way even if it is in front of them. With such vision, they can hardly be anything other than destructive of their best instincts.

Through Hawthorne's allegory and symbols, then, the story presents a paradox: How can a seemingly good system lead to bad results? How can noble beliefs backfire so destructively? Goodman Brown dies in gloom because he believes strongly that his wrong vision is real. This form of evil is the hardest to stop, no matter what outward set of beliefs it takes, because wrongdoers [6] who are convinced of their own goodness are beyond reach. Such a blend of evil and self-righteousness causes Hawthorne to write that "the fiend in his own shape is less hideous than when he rages in the breast of man" (p. 162). Young Goodman Brown thus becomes Hawthorne's main symbol. He is one of those who walk in darkness but have forever barred themselves from the light.

Commentary on the Theme

The introduction justifies the treatment of allegory and symbolism because of the way in which Hawthorne early in the story invites a symbolic reading. The central idea relates Hawthorne's method to the idea that rigid belief destroys the best human qualities. The thesis sentence outlines two major areas of discussion: (1) allegory, and (2) symbolism.

Paragraph two considers the allegory not just as Hawthorne intended it—as a criticism of rigid Puritan morality—but as a general criticism of *isms* pursued to the point of dehumanization. Paragraphs three, four, and five deal with three major symbols: the sunset, the walking-stick, and the path. The aim of this discussion is to show the meaning and application of these symbols for Hawthorne's attack on rigidity of belief. Throughout these three paragraphs the central idea—the relationship of rigidity to destructiveness—is stressed. The concluding paragraph raises questions that lead to the idea that Brown himself is a symbol of Hawthorne's idea that the primary cause of evil is the inability to separate reality from unreality.

chapter
10

The Themes of Comparison-Contrast and Extended Comparison-Contrast

The comparison theme may be used to compare and contrast different authors, two or more works by the same author, different drafts of the same work, or characters, incidents, and ideas within the same work or in different works. Not only is comparison-contrast popular in literature courses, but it is one of the commonest approaches you will find in other disciplines. The ideas of two philosophers may be compared, or the approaches of two schools of psychology, or two conflicting economic theories. The possibilities for using comparison-contrast are extensive.

Comparison-Contrast as a Way to Knowledge

Comparison and contrast are important means to gaining understanding. For example, suppose that you are having trouble understanding separately the poems "War is Kind" by Stephen Crane and "The Fury of Aerial Bombardment" by Richard Eberhart. When you start comparing the two poems, however, you will immediately notice things that you may not have noticed at first. Both of them treat the horrors of war, but they do so differently. Crane is ironic, whereas Eberhart is quietly bitter. Though Eberhart's topic is the "fury" of bombardment, he does not describe explosions and anguished death, but rather draws attention to human stupidity and to the regrettable deaths of persons with great potential. Crane, on the other hand, achieves his ironic effect by speaking of "slaughter" and "corpses" while at the same time he also speaks of war being "kind." Both poems ultimately agree on the irrationality of war. Making a comparison and contrast in this way enables you to see each poem in perspective, and therefore more clearly. The comparison-contrast method is similarly rewarding whenever you apply it, for perhaps the quickest way to get at the essence of an artistic work is to compare it with another work. Similarities are brought out by comparison, and differences are shown by contrast.

The comparison-contrast method is closely related to the study of *defi-nition*, because definition aims at the description of a particular thing by identifying its properties while also isolating it from everything else. Comparison-contrast is also closely allied with Plato's idea that we learn a thing best by reference to its opposite; that is, one way of finding out what a thing *is* is to find out what it is *not*.

Clarify Your Intention

Your first problem in this theme is to decide on a goal, for you may use the comparison-contrast method in a number of ways. One objective can be the equal and mutual illumination of both (or more) works. Thus, a theme comparing O'Connor's "First Confession" and Hawthorne's "Young Goodman Brown" might be designed (1) to compare ideas, characters, or methods in these stories equally, without stressing or favoring either. But you might also wish (2) to emphasize "Young Goodman Brown," and therefore you would use "First Confession" as material for highlighting Hawthorne's work. You might also use the comparison-contrast method (3) to show your liking of one work (at the expense of another), or (4) to emphasize a method or idea that you think is especially noteworthy or appropriate.

Your first task is therefore to decide where to place your emphasis. The first sample theme reflects a decision to give "equal time" to both works being considered, without any claims for the superiority of either. Unless you wish to pursue a different rhetorical goal, you will find this theme a suitable model for most comparisons.

Find Common Grounds
for Comparison

Your second problem is to select the proper material—the grounds of your discussion. It is useless to try to compare dissimilar things, for then your conclusions will be of limited value. You need to put the works or writers you are comparing onto common ground. Compare like with like: idea with idea, characterization with characterization, imagery with imagery, point of view with point of view, problem with problem. Nothing can be learned from a comparison of "Welty's view of courage and Shakespeare's view of love," but a comparison of "The relationship of love to stability and courage in Shakespeare and Welty" suggests common ground, with points of both likeness and difference. (Please see the second sample theme for the use of this basis for comparison in an extended theme of comparison-contrast.)

In searching for common ground, you may have to use your ingenuity a bit. But just as adding 3/4 and 2/3 may be done by changing these fractions to 9/12 and 8/12 to get 1 5/12, you can usually find a basis for your comparison. Thus De Maupassant's "The Necklace" and Chekhov's *The Bear* at first may seem to be as different as they can be. Yet common grounds do exist for these works, such as "The Treatment of Self-Deceit," "The Effects of Chance on Human Affairs," or "The View of Women." As you can see, apparently unlike works can be put into a frame of reference that permits analytical comparison and contrast. Much of your success in this theme will depend on your ingenuity in finding a workable basis—a "common denominator"—for comparison.

Methods of Comparison

Let us assume that you have decided on your rhetorical purpose and on the basis or bases of your comparison: you have done your reading, taken your notes, and know what you want to say. The remaining problem is the treatment of your material. Here are two acceptable ways.

A common, but inferior, way is to make your points first about one work and then do the same for the other. This method makes your paper seem like two big lumps, and it also involves much repetition because you must repeat the same points as you treat your second subject. This first method is only satisfactory.

The superior method is to treat your main idea in its major aspects and to make references to the two (or more) writers as the reference illustrates and illuminates your main idea. Thus you would be constantly referring to both writers, sometimes within the same sentence, and would be reminding your reader of the point of your discussion. There are reasons for the superiority of the second method: (1) you do not repeat your points needlessly, for you document them as you raise them; (2) by constantly referring to the two works in relation to your common ground of comparison, you make your points without requiring a reader with a poor memory to reread previous sections. Frequently such readers do not bother to reread, and as a result they are never clear about what you have said.

As a good example, here is a paragraph from a student theme on "Nature as a basis of comparison in William Wordsworth's 'The World Is Too Much with Us' and Gerard Manley Hopkins' 'God's Grandeur.' " The virtue of the paragraph is that it uses material from both poets as a means of development; the material is synthesized by the student (sentence numbers in brackets) as follows:

> [1] Hopkin's ideas are Christian, though not genuinely other-worldly. [2] God is a God of the world for Hopkins, and "broods with warm breast and with ah! bright wings" (line 14); Hopkins is convinced that God is here and everywhere, for his first line triumphantly proclaims this. [3] Wordsworth, by contrast, is able to perceive the beauty of Nature, but feels that God in the Christian sense has deserted him. [4] Wordsworth is to be defended here, though, because his wish to see Proteus or to hear Triton is not pagan. [5] He wants, instead, to have faith, to have the conviction that Hopkins so confidently claims. [6] Even if the faith is pagan, Wordsworth would like it just so he could have firm, unshakable faith. [7] As a matter of fact, however, Wordsworth's perception of Nature contradicts the lack of faith he claims. [8] His God is really Nature itself. [9] Hopkins' more abstract views of Nature make me feel that the Catholic believes that Nature is only a means to the worship of God. [10] For Hopkins, God is supreme; for Wordsworth, Nature is.

Letting *H* stand for ideas about Hopkins, and *W* for ideas about Wordsworth, the paragraph may be schematized as follows (numbers refer to sentences):

$$1 = H. \quad 2 = H. \quad 3 = W. \quad 4 = W. \quad 5 = W.H. \quad 6 = W.$$
$$7 = W. \quad 8 = W. \quad 9 = H. \quad 10 = H.W.$$

The interweaving of subject material gives the impression that the student has learned both poems well enough to think of them at the same time. Mental "digestion" has taken place. Thus Wordsworth's ideas of Nature are linked with ideas on the same topic by Hopkins, sometimes within the same sentence. You can learn from this example: If you develop your theme by putting your two subjects constantly together, you will write more economically and clearly than you would by the first method (this statement is true of tests as well as themes). Beyond that, if you have actually digested the material as successfully as this method would show, you will be demonstrating that you have fulfilled one of the primary goals of education—the assimilation and *use* of material. Too often education as presented in a course-by-course and writer-by-writer approach seems to be compartmentalized. You should always be trying to synthesize the materials you acquire, to put them together through comparison and contrast so that you can accustom yourself to seeing things not as *fragments* but as parts of *wholes*.

Avoid the "Tennis-Ball" Method

As you make your comparison, do not confuse an interlocking method with a "tennis-ball" method, in which you bounce your subject back and forth constantly and repetitively. The tennis-ball method is shown in the following example from a comparison of A. E. Housman's "On Wenlock Edge" and Theodore Roethke's "Dolor":

> Housman talks about the eternal nature of human troubles whereas Roethke talks about the "dolor" of modern business life. Housman uses details of woods, gales, snow, leaves, and hills, whereas Roethke selects details of pencils, boxes, paper-weights, mucilage, and lavatories. Housman's focus is therefore on the torments of people close to Nature; Roethke's on civilized, ordered, duplicated, gray-flanneled humanity. Housman states that the significance of human problems fades in the perspective of eternity; Roethke does not mention eternity but makes human problems seem even smaller by showing that business life has virtually erased human emotion.

Imagine the effect of reading an entire theme presented in this fashion. Aside from its power to bore, the tennis-ball method does not give you the chance to develop your points. You should not feel so cramped that you cannot take several sentences to develop a point about one writer or subject before you bring in comparison with another. If you remember to interlock the two points of comparison, however, as in the example comparing Hopkins and Wordsworth, your method will be satisfactory.

The Extended Comparison-Contrast

For a longer theme, such as a limited research paper or the sort of extended theme required at the end of the semester, the technique of comparison-contrast may be used for many works. The extended theme may also be adapted for tests that deal with general, comprehensive questions. Such questions require that you treat ideas or methods in a number of works.

For themes of this larger scope, you will still need to develop common grounds for comparison, although with more works to discuss you will need to modify the method.

Let us assume that you have been assigned not just two works but five or six. You need first to find a common ground among them which you will use as your central, unifying idea. This is the same as for a comparison of just two works. When you take your notes, sketch out your ideas, make your early drafts, and rearrange and shape your developing materials, try to bring all the works together on your major points. Thus in the second sample theme, all the works are treated on the common basis that they speak about the nature of love and devoted service.

When you contrast the works, you should try to make groups based on variations or differences. Let us assume that three or four works treat a topic in one way while one or two do it in another. Here you treat the topic itself in a straightforward contrast method but may wish to use details from the groups on either side of the issue to support your points. Again, it is desirable to use the analysis of a particular point based on one work so that you can make your theme concrete and vivid. But once you have exemplified your point, there is no need to go into any more detail from the other works than seems necessary to get your point across. In this way, you can keep your theme within limits; if you group your works on points of similarity, you do not need to go into excessive and unproductive detail.

As an example of how works may be grouped in this way, please see the second sample theme. There, four works are grouped into a general category of how love and service may offer guidance and stability for living. This group is contrasted with another group of three works (including two characters from one of the works in the first group), in which love is shown as an escape or retreat.

Documentation and the Extended Comparison-Contrast Theme

For the longer comparison-contrast theme you may find a problem in documentation. Generally you will not need to locate page numbers for references to major traits, ideas, or actions. For example, if you refer to the end of "First Confession," where the priest gives Jackie some candy, you may assume that your reader also knows this action. You do not need to do any more than make the reference.

But if you are quoting lines or passages, or if you are making any special or unusual reference, you may need to use footnotes or parenthetical references. For page numbers, the second sample theme uses the parenthetical abbreviation system described in Appendix B. For lines of poetry, or parts of lines, the theme uses parenthetical line numbers. Be guided by this principle: If you make a specific reference that you think your reader might want to examine in more detail, provide the line or page number. If you are referring to minor details that might easily be forgotten or not noticed, supply the line or page number. Otherwise, if you are referring to major ideas, actions, or characterizations, be sure that your reference within your theme is sufficiently clear that your reader can easily recall it from his or her own memory of the work. Then you will not need to provide line or page numbers.

Organizing Your Theme

First you must narrow your subject into a topic you can handle conveniently within the limits of the assignment. For example, if you have been assigned a comparison of Wordsworth and Hopkins, pick out one or two poems of each poet and write your theme about them. You must be wary, however, of the limitations of this selection: generalizations made from one or two works may not apply to the broad subject originally proposed.

INTRODUCTION

State what works, authors, characters, and ideas are under consideration, then show how you have narrowed the basis of your comparison. Your central idea will be a brief statement of what can be learned from your paper: the general similarities and differences that you have observed from your comparison and/or the superiority of one work or author over another. Your thesis sentence should anticipate the body of your theme.

BODY

The body of your theme depends on the points you have chosen for comparison. You might be comparing two works on the basis of *point of view* or *imagery*, two authors on *ideas*, or two characters on *character traits*. In your discussion you would necessarily use the same methods that you would use in writing about a single work, except that here (1) you are exemplifying your points by reference to more subjects than one, and (2) your main purpose is to shed light on the subjects on which your comparison is based. In this sense, the methods you use in talking about point of view or imagery are not "pure" but are instead subordinate to your aims of comparison-contrast. Let us say that you are comparing the ideas in two different works. The first part of your theme might be devoted to analyzing and describing the similarities and dissimilarities of the ideas *as* ideas. Your interest here is not so much to explain the ideas of either work separately as to explain the ideas of both works in order to show points of agreement and disagreement. A second part might be given over to the influences of the ideas on the point of view of the particular works; that is, you might discuss how the ideas help make the works similar or dissimilar. If you are comparing characters, your points might be to show similarities and dissimilarities of mental and spiritual qualities and of activities in which the characters engage.

CONCLUSION

Here you are comparatively free to reflect on other ideas in the works you have compared, to make observations on comparative qualities, or to summarize briefly the basic grounds of your comparison. The conclusion of an extended comparison-contrast theme should represent a final bringing together of the materials. In the body of the theme you may not have referred to all the works in each paragraph; however, in the conclusion you should try to refer to them all, if possible.

If your writers belonged to any "period" or "school," you also might wish to show in your conclusion how they relate to these larger movements. References of this sort provide a natural common ground for comparison.

First Sample Theme
(Two Works)

The Treatment of the Need for Understanding in "Young Goodman Brown" by Nathaniel Hawthorne and "First Confession" by Frank O'Connor

---

[1] The major difference between "Young Goodman Brown" and "First Confession" is that O'Connor's story is comic, farcical, and pleasant, while Hawthorne's is serious, demonic, and grim. Yet there are many similarities. Both deal with religious materials. Both have episodes that are vivid and dramatic. Both have journeys, one to a forest and the other to a church. And both have major figures who are being initiated into life—one a child and the other a newly married man. A most important agreement is that both works stress that understanding, tolerating, and forgiving people is better than condemning them.* This point is made in the sinful actions, the attitudes, and the conclusions of both works.†

[2] Sinfulness, or what passes for sinfulness, emphasizes the need for understanding. Things are much worse in "Young Goodman Brown" than in "First Confession." Real sins and punishable crimes (such as infant murder, political corruption, and poisoning) are mentioned by the "sable form" in Hawthorne's demonic forest ritual (p. 164). Above these is Goodman Brown's condemnation of his wife and neighbors. By contrast, Jackie's "sins" of kicking his grandmother and waving the bread knife at Nora are no more than the actions of a confused child. Yet both sets of actions show that there is a need for trying to understand the motives of the sinner. Without understanding, there can be nothing but outright condemnation, which for Hawthorne and O'Connor seems to be a greater sin than any the devil can mention.

[3] Just like the treatment of sinful actions, the attitudes of the major characters in both works underscore the need for sympathy and understanding. By the end of the story, Goodman Brown shows a complete intolerance of others because he believes that everyone is lost in sin. Where things seem good, he sees only hypocrisy, and he views everyone with mistrust and hatred. Mrs.

*Central idea
†Thesis sentence
For the texts of these stories, please see Appendix C, pp. 156–166 and 174–180 respectively.

Ryan and Nora are very much like Goodman Brown. Nora is suspicious of everything Jackie does and tries to get him punished regularly. In a way, Mrs. Ryan is slightly worse than Goodman Brown, because she teaches children her philosophy of fear and punishment, while Goodman Brown hurts only himself. The negative views of all three, however, show the need for something human and compassionate, the attempt to understand and correct rather than to condemn.

[4]

The conclusions of the stories may be read as both positive and negative illustrations of the advantages of compassion and understanding. In "First Confession" the priest gives Jackie a complete audience, hears his worst secrets, makes sympathetic comments, and gives the boy candy with only three Hail Marys as penance. What could be a more positive model than this for showing the practical benefits of understanding? In contrast, Goodman Brown's vision of evil is obsessive and destructive. He listens to no one sympathetically, as the priest does, and he tries to speak to no one about his troubles, as Jackie finally does. While Jackie confesses his anger and fear, and thus will no longer need to brood about them, Goodman Brown is left alone, in the gloom of his own mind. He goes to his grave convinced that everyone around him is evil, and he never even gives his friends and neighbors a chance. He gets the worst that his religion has to offer, with none of the better parts that Jackie receives.

[5]

There are many other points of comparison that are related to the issue of tolerance and understanding. A major one is the point of view. O'Connor could not get as serious as Hawthorne without disturbing his comedy. Thus his first-person point of view, by which Jackie as an adult tells about his first confession as a seven-year-old, keeps things close to the surface, on a child's level. This outlook makes understanding and forgiveness seem not just possible, but absolutely necessary. Hawthorne, by contrast, writes in the third-person point of view but never enters his character. Brown therefore remains distant, never as close and friendly and as easy to forgive as Jackie is. Although both stories make similar points about the need for human understanding and toleration, they are different and unique.

Commentary on the Theme

Although this theme points out a number of possible subjects on which the two works could be compared (religion, dramatic scenes, journeys, and characters undergoing initiation), the point chosen for comparison (the central idea) is the need for understanding and forgiveness. The effect of pointing out these subjects in the introduction is to give the reader the impression that the two works have been studied thoroughly and that the subject chosen for comparison has been selected because of its major importance. In other words, there is rhetorical value in this approach to the introduction. The thesis sentence defines three areas in which the central idea is to be examined.

Paragraph two compares the sinful actions in the two stories, stressing the point of agreement and demonstrating that the actions in "Young Goodman Brown" are worse than those in "First Confession." The third paragraph carries the comparison to Goodman Brown, on the one hand, and Nora and Mrs. Ryan, on the other, showing how their negative attitudes fit into the claim about the need for understanding. The fourth paragraph compares the happy ending of "First Confession" with the bleak one in "Young Goodman Brown."

The conclusion does not summarize the major headings of the theme, but stresses instead how the points of view in the two stories can be related to the central idea.

In each of the paragraphs, this theme shows how the two works may be connected by the topic idea. Paragraph three, for example, contains seven sentences. Three show points of similarity and one shows a point of difference. While the remaining three are on single works (two on Hawthorne, one on O'Connor), they are designed to emphasize points of comparison. All the sentences, therefore, carry out the goal of comparison and contrast.

Second Sample Theme
(Extended Comparison-Contrast)

*The Complexity of Love and Devoted Service
as Shown in Six Works*

---

[1]

On the surface, at least, love and devotion are simple, and their results should be good. A person loves someone, or serves someone or something. This love may be romantic or familial, and the service may be religious or national. But love is not simple. It is complex, and its results are not uniformly good.* Love and devotion should be ways of saying "yes," but ironically they sometimes become ways of saying "no," too. This idea can be traced in a comparison of six works: Shakespeare's Sonnet 116, Arnold's "Dover Beach," Hardy's "Channel Firing," Chekhov's *The Bear*, O'Connor's "First Confession," and Welty's "A Worn Path." The complexity in these works is that love and devotion do not operate in a vacuum but rather in the context of personal, philosophical, economic, and national difficulties. The works show that love and devotion may be forces for stability and refuge, but also for harm.†

Ideal and stabilizing love, along with service performed out of love, is shown by Shakespeare in Sonnet 116 and by O'Connor in "First Confession." Shake-

---

*Central idea
†Thesis sentence
For the texts of these works, please see Appendix C.

speare states that love gives lovers strength and stability in a complex world
of opposition and difficulty. Such love is like a "star" that guides wandering
ships (line 7), and like a "fixed mark" that stands against the shaking of life's
tempests (lines 5 and 6). A character who is similarly aware of human tempests
[2]   and conflicts is the "young priest" who hears Jackie's confession in "First
Confession." He is clearly committed to service, and is "intelligent above the
ordinary" (p. 178). With service to God as his "star," to use Shakespeare's
image, he is able to talk sympathetically with Jackie and to send the boy home
with a clear and happy mind.

For both Shakespeare and O'Connor, love and service grow out of a great
human need for stability and guidance. To this degree love is a simplifying
[3]   force, but it simplifies primarily because the "tempests" complicating life are
so strong. Such love is one of the best things that happen to human beings,
because it fulfills them and prepares them to face life.

The desire for love of this kind is so strong that it can also be the cause for
people to do strange and funny things. The two major characters in Chekhov's
short comedy-farce The Bear are examples. At the play's start, Chekhov shows
that Mrs. Popov and Smirnov are following some of the crack-brained and
negative guides that people often confuse for truth. She is devoted to the
[4]   memory of her dead husband, while he is disillusioned and cynical about
women. But Chekhov makes them go through hoops for love. As the two argue,
insult each other, and reach the point of dueling with real pistols, their need
for love overcomes all their other impulses. It is as though love happens despite
everything going against it, because the need for the stabilizing base is so
strong. Certainly love here is not without at least some complexity.

Either seriously or comically, then, love is shown as a rudder, guiding people
[5]   in powerful and conflicting currents. The three works studied so far show that
love shapes lives and makes for sudden and unexpected changes.

This thought is somewhat like the view presented by Eudora Welty in "A
Worn Path." Unlike Chekhov and Shakespeare, and more like O'Connor, Welty
tells a story of service performed out of love. A poor grandmother, Phoenix
Jackson, has a hard life in caring for her incurably ill grandson. The walk she
[6]   takes along the "worn path" to Natchez symbolizes the hardships she endures
because of her single-minded love. Her service is the closest thing to pure
simplicity that may be found in all the works examined, with the possible
exception of the love in Chekhov's play.

But even her love is not without its complexity. Hardy in "Channel Firing"
and Arnold in "Dover Beach" describe a joyless, loveless, insecure world
overrun by war. Phoenix's life is just as grim. She is poor and ignorant, and
her grandson has nowhere to go but down. If she would only stop to think
[7[deeply about her condition, she might be as despairing as Arnold and Hardy.
But her strength may be her ability either to accept her difficult life or to ignore
the grimness of it. With her service as her "star" and "ever-fixed mark," she
is able to keep cheerful and to live in friendship with the animals and the
woods. Her life has meaning and dignity.

Arnold's view of love and devotion under such bad conditions is different
from the views of Shakespeare, Chekhov, O'Connor, and Welty. For Arnold,
[8]   the public world seems to be so far gone that there is nothing left but personal
relationships. Thus love is not so much a guide as a refuge, a place of sanity

and safety. After describing what he considers the worldwide shrinking of the "Sea of Faith," he states:

> Ah, love, let us be true
> To one another! for the world, which seems
> To lie before us like a land of dreams,
> So various, so beautiful, so new,
> Hath really neither joy, nor love, nor light,
> Nor certitude, nor peace, nor help for pain;
> And we are here as on a darkling plain
> Swept with confused alarms of struggle and flight
> Where ignorant armies clash by night.

—lines 29–37

Here the word *true* should be underlined, as Shakespeare emphasizes "true minds" and as O'Connor's priest is a *true* servant of God. "True" to Arnold seems to involve a pledge to create a small area of certainty in the mad world like that of "Channel Firing," where there is no certainty. Love is not so much a guide as a last place of hope, a retreat where truth can still have meaning.

[9]   In practice, perhaps, Arnold's idea of love as a refuge is not very different from the view that love is a guide. Once the truthful pledge is made, it is a force for goodness, at least for the lovers making the pledge, just as love works for goodness in Shakespeare, O'Connor, Chekhov, and Welty. Yet Arnold's view is weaker. It does not result from an inner need or conviction, but rather from a conscious decision to let everything else go and to look out only for the small relationship. In an extreme form, this could lead to total withdrawal. Such a passive relationship to other affairs could be harmful by omission.

[10]   The idea that love and devotion as a refuge could be actively harmful is explored by O'Connor in other characters in "First Confession." Nora and Mrs. Ryan seem to think only of sinfulness and punishment. They seek the love of God out of a desire for protection. Their devotion is therefore a means to an end, not the pure goal which operates in Shakespeare, Welty, and O'Connor's own priest. As Jackie says of Mrs. Ryan:

> She . . . wore a black cloak and bonnet, and came every day to school at three o'clock when we should have been going home, and talked to us of hell. She may have mentioned the other place as well, but that could only have been by accident, for hell had the first place in her heart (p. 175).

[11]   Love and devotion for her and for Nora take the form of observing ritual and following rules, such as being sure that all confessions are "good" (that is, complete, with no sins held back). If this obedience were only personal, it would be a force for security, as it is on the personal level for Arnold. But from the safety of their refuge, Mrs. Ryan confuses children like Jackie by describing devilish, sadistic tortures, while Nora tells her father about the bread knife and thus brings down punishment (the "flaking") and a "scalded" heart on Jackie. Even though Mrs. Ryan is not a bad soul, and Nora is no more than a young girl, their use of religion is negative. Fortunately, their influence is counterbalanced by the priest.

    Mrs. Ryan and Nora are minor compared with those unseen, unnamed, and distant persons firing the big guns during the "gunnery practice out at sea" in Hardy's "Channel Firing" (line 10). Hardy does not treat the gunners as individuals but as an evil collective force made up of persons who, under the sheltering claim of devotion to country and obedience of orders, are "striving strong to make / Red war yet redder" (lines 13, 14). For them, love of country [12]   is a refuge, just like the love of God for Mrs. Ryan and Nora and the true pledge to love for Arnold's speaker. As members of the military they obey orders and, as Hardy's God says, they are not much better than the dead because they do nothing "for Christés sake" (line 15). They operate the ships and fill the columns of Arnold's "ignorant armies," for Hardy makes clear that their target practice takes place at night (line 1).

In summary, love and devotion as seen in these various works may be compared with a continuous line formed out of the human need for love and for the stability and guidance that love offers. At one end love is totally good and ideal; at the other it is totally bad. Shakespeare, Welty, Chekhov, and [13]   O'Connor (in the priest) show the end that is good. Still at the good end, but moving toward the center, is Arnold's use of love as a refuge. On the other side of the line are Mrs. Ryan and Nora of "First Confession," while all the way at the bad end are the insensible and invisible gunners in "Channel Firing."

The difficulty noted in all the works, and a major problem in life, is to devote oneself to the right, stabilizing, constructive part of the line. Although in his farce Chekhov makes love win against almost impossible odds, he shows the problem most vividly of all the authors studied. Under normal conditions, peo- [14]   ple like Mrs. Popov and Smirnov would not find love. Instead, they would continue following their destructive and false guides. They would be unhappy and disillusioned, or else they might become more like Mrs. Ryan and spread talk about their own confused ideas (as Smirnov actually does almost right up to his conversion to love). Like the military and naval forces of Arnold and Hardy, they would then wind up at the destructive end of the line.

Change, opposition, confusion, anger, resignation, economic difficulty— these are only some of the forces that attack people as they try to find the benefits of love. If they are lucky they find meaning and stability in love and [15]   service, as in Sonnet 116, "First Confession," *The Bear*, "A Worn Path," and, to a small degree, "Dover Beach." If confusion wins, they are locked into harmful positions, like the gunners in "Channel Firing" and Mrs. Ryan and Nora in "First Confession." Thus love is complicated by circumstances, and it is not the simple force for good that it should ideally be. The six works compared and contrasted here have shown these difficulties and complexities.

Commentary on the Theme

This theme compares and contrasts six works—three poems, two stories, and a play—on the common ground or central idea of the complexity of love and service. The complexity is caused by life's difficulties ("tempests," as Shakespeare calls them) and by bad results. The theme develops the central idea in terms of love as an ideal and guide (paragraphs two–seven) and love as a refuge or escape (eight–twelve), with a sub-category of love as a cause of harm (ten–twelve).

The various works are introduced as they are grouped according to these sections. For example, Sonnet 116, "First Confession" (because of the priest), *The Bear*, and "A Worn Path" are together in the first group—love as an ideal and guide. Because "Dover Beach" and "Channel Firing" are in the second group, these works are brought in earlier, during the discussion of the first group. For this reason, both poems are used regularly for comparison and contrast throughout the theme.

The use of the various works within groups may be seen in paragraph eight. There, the principal topic is the use of love as a refuge or retreat, and the central work of the paragraph is "Dover Beach." However, the first sentence contrasts Arnold's view with the four works in the first group; the fifth sentence shows how Arnold is similar in one respect to Shakespeare and O'Connor; and the sixth sentence shows a similarity of Arnold and Hardy. The paragraph thus brings together all the works being studied in the theme.

The technique of comparison-contrast used in this way shows how the various works may be defined and distinguished in relation to the common idea. Paragraph thirteen, the first in the conclusion, attempts to summarize these distinctions by suggesting a continuous line along which each of the works may be placed. Paragraphs fourteen and fifteen continue the summary by showing the prominence of complicating difficulties, and, by implication, the importance of love. Thus, the effect of the comparison of all the works collectively is the enhanced understanding of each of the works separately.

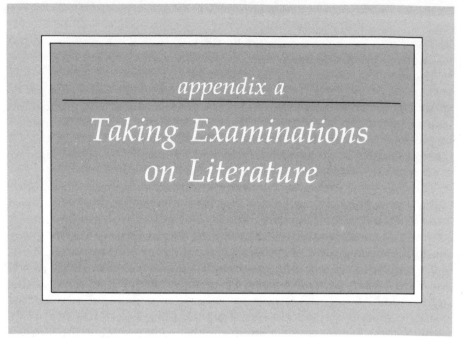

appendix a

Taking Examinations
on Literature

Taking an examination on literature is not difficult if you prepare in the right way. Preparing means (1) studying the material assigned, studying the comments made in class by your instructor and by fellow students in discussion, and studying your own thoughts; (2) anticipating the questions by writing some of your own on the material to be tested and by writing practice answers to these questions; and (3) understanding the precise function of the test in your education.

You should realize that the test is not designed to plague you or to hold down your grade. The grade you receive is in fact a reflection of your achievement at a given point in the course. If your grades are low, you can probably improve them by studying in a coherent and systematic way. Those students who can easily do satisfactory work might do superior work if they improve their method of preparation. From whatever level you begin, you can increase your achievement by improving your method of study.

Your instructor has three major concerns in evaluating your tests (assuming literate English): (1) to see the extent of your command over the subject material of the course ("How good is your retention?"), (2) to see how well you are able to think about the material ("How well are you educating yourself?"), and (3) to see how well you can actually respond to a question or address yourself to an issue.

There are many elements that go into writing good answers on tests, but this last point, about responsiveness, is perhaps the most important of all. A major cause of low exam grades is that students really do not *answer* the questions asked. Does that seem surprising? The problem is that some students do no more than retell the story, never confronting the issues in the question. This is the common problem that has been treated throughout this book. Therefore, if you are asked, "Why does . . . ," be sure to emphasize the *why*, and use the *does* only to exemplify the *why*. If the question is about organization, focus on that. If a problem has been raised, deal with the problem. In short, always *respond* directly to the question or instruction. Let us compare two answers to the same question:

Q. How does the setting of Stephen Crane's "Horses—One Dash" contribute to the action of the story?

A

The setting is essential to the action of "Horses—One Dash." The scene opens on the Mexican desert. It is lovely, with mesquite and distant hills that are beautiful in the setting sun. Richardson and Jose, his servant and guide, are riding through this desert. As night comes on, so do the shadows and the cold, so Richardson and Jose go to a nearby village for shelter. The village looks ghostly in the twilight gloom. The men find a house, an inn, in which to spend the night. There, Richardson's expensive looking gun and saddle excite the local gang of men, who apparently decide to rob him and likely kill him. There is a good deal of tension in the house as Richardson believes that the men are closing in, but the main action is that Jose is beaten. Soon the gang is distracted by guitar music and laughing women, and so Richardson gets some disturbed sleep. In the early morning it is back to the horses for Richardson and Jose, who flee into the surrounding desert and hills. They push their horses to topmost speed and they are pursued closely by the bandits from the village. It is in the hills that the two men are about to be caught and killed, but a patrol of *Rurales* (soldiers) stops the chase and makes the rescue. "Horses—One Dash" is an action story, and the setting is indispensable in this action.

B

The setting is both a cause and location for the action of "Horses—One Dash." The coldness and darkness of the Mexican desert at night force Richardson and Jose into the nearby village to find a house or inn (cause). This inn, with its force of young men, hoodlums really, is the location for the first part of the action. The men aim to rob and likely kill Richardson and Jose for Richardson's expensive equipment (cause). Because the inn also supplies music and women, however (cause), the locals settle at first for beating poor Jose (location). But the inn is not a refuge for long, and the threat makes Richardson wake Jose and ride away before sunup (cause). The desert and nearby hills are the natural place of their flight, and thus the scene of action (location). Fortunately, the isolation and lawlessness of this natural setting justify the patrolling *Rurales* (cause). Therefore, just as the chase is about to end in death for Richardson and Jose, the *Rurales* stop the pursuers (location). "Horses—One Dash" is an action story, and the setting is indispensable to the action both as a cause and a location.

While column *A* relates the action to the various scenes of the story, it does not focus on the relationship. It is also cluttered by details that have no bearing on the question. Column *B*, on the other hand, focuses directly on the connection and uses parenthetical words for emphasis. Because of this emphasis, *B* is shorter than *A*. That is, with the focus directly on the issue, there is no need for irrelevant narrative details. Thus, *A* is unresponsive and unnecessarily long, while *B* is responsive and includes only enough detail to exemplify the major points.

Preparation

Your problem is how best to prepare yourself to have a knowledgeable and ready mind at examination time. If you simply cram facts into your head for the examination in hopes that you will be able to adjust to whatever questions are asked, you will likely flounder.

READING AND REREADING

Above all, keep in mind that your preparation should begin not on the night before the exam but as soon as the course begins. When each assignment is given, you should complete it by the date due, for you will understand your instructor's lecture and the classroom discussion only if you know the material being discussed. Then, about a week before the exam, you should review each assignment, preferably rereading everything completely. With this preparation, your study on the night before the exam will be fruitful, for it might be viewed as a climax of preparation, not the entire preparation itself.

MAKE YOUR OWN QUESTIONS: GO ON THE ATTACK

Just to read or reread is too passive to give you the masterly preparation you want for an exam. You should instead go on the attack by trying to anticipate the specific conditions of the test. The best way to reach this goal is to compose and answer your own practice questions. Do not waste your time trying to guess the questions you think your instructor might ask. That might happen—and wouldn't you be happy if it did?—but do not turn your study into a game of chance. What is of greatest importance is to arrange the subject matter by asking yourself questions that help you get things straight.

How can you make your own questions? It is not as hard as you might think. Your instructor may have announced certain topics or ideas to be tested on the exam. You might develop questions from these. Or you might apply general questions to the specifics of your assignments, as in the following examples:

1. About a character: What sort of character is *A*? How does *A* grow, or change, in the work? What does *A* learn, or not learn, that brings about the conclusion? To what degree is *A* the representative of any particular type?
2. About the interactions of characters: How does *B* influence *A*? Does a change in *C* bring about any corresponding change in *A*?
3. About events or situations: What relationship does episode *A* have with situation *D*? Does *C's* thinking about situation *D* have any influence on the outcome of event *E*?
4. About a problem: Why is character *A* or situation *X* this way, and not that way? Is the conclusion justified by the ideas and events leading up to it?

ADAPT YOUR NOTES TO MAKE QUESTIONS

Perhaps the best way to construct questions is to use your classroom notes, for notes are the fullest record you have about your instructor's views of the subject material. As you work with your notes, you should refer to passages from the text that were studied by the class or mentioned by your instructor. If there is time, try to memorize as many important phrases or lines as you can; plan to incorporate these into your answers as evidence to support the points you make. Remember that it is good to work not only with main ideas from your notes, but also with matters such as style, imagery, and organization.

Obviously you cannot make questions from all your notes, and you will therefore need to select from those that seem most important. As an example, here is a short but significant note from a class about John Dryden's poem *Absalom and Achitophel* (1681): "A political poem—unintelligible unless one knows the politics of the time." It is not difficult to use this note to make two practice questions:

1. Why is *Absalom and Achitophel* unintelligible unless one knows the politics of the time?
2. What knowledge of the politics of the time is needed to make *Absalom and Achitophel* intelligible?

The first question consists of the simple adaptation of the word *why* to the phrasing of the note. For the second, the word *what* has been adapted. Either question would force pointed study. The first would require an explanation of how various parts of Dryden's poem become clear only when they are related to aspects of the politics of 1681. The second would emphasize the politics, with less reference to the poem. If you spent fifteen or twenty minutes writing practice answers to these questions, you could be confident in taking an examination on the material. It is likely that you could adapt your preparation to any question related to the politics of the poem.

WORK WITH QUESTIONS EVEN
WHEN TIME IS SHORT

Whatever your subject, it is important that you spend as much study time as possible making and answering your own questions. Of course, you will have limited time and will not be able to write extensive answers indefinitely. Even so, do not give up on the question method. If time is too short for full answers, write out the main heads, or topics, of an answer. When the press of time (or the need for sleep) no longer permits you to make even such a brief outline answer, keep thinking of questions, and think about the answers on the way to the exam. Try never to read passively or unresponsively, but always with a creative, question-and-answer goal. Think of studying as a potential writing experience.

Whatever time you spend in this way will be of great value, for as you practice, you will develop control and therefore confidence. If you have ever known anyone who has had difficulty with tests, or who has claimed a phobia about them, you may find that a major cause has been passive rather than active preparation. The process is about like this: A passively prepared student finds that test questions compel thought, arrangement, and responsiveness; but the student is not ready for this challenge and therefore writes answers that are both unresponsive and filled with summary. The grade, needless to say, is low, and the student's general fear of tests is reinforced. It seems clear that active, creative study is the best way to break any such long-standing patterns of fear or uncertainty, because it is the best form of preparation. There is no moral case to make against practice question-and-answer study, either, for everyone has the right and obligation to prepare—and all of this is preparation—in the best way possible.

STUDY WITH A FELLOW STUDENT

Often the thoughts of another person can help you understand the material to be tested. Try to find a fellow student with whom you can work, for both of you can help each other. In view of the need for steady preparation throughout a course, keep in mind that regular conversations (over coffee or some other beverage to your liking) are a good idea. Also, you might wish to make your joint study genuinely systematic, and thus might set aside a specific evening or afternoon for detailed work sessions.

Make the effort; working with someone else can be stimulating and rewarding.

Two Basic Types of Questions About Literature

There are two types of questions that you will find on any examination about literature. Keep them in mind as you prepare. The first type is *factual*, or *mainly objective*, and the second is *general, comprehensive, broad, or mainly subjective*. In a literature course, very few questions are purely objective, except multiple-choice questions.

FACTUAL QUESTIONS

MULTIPLE-CHOICE QUESTIONS. These are the most purely factual questions. In a literature course your instructor will most likely reserve them for short quizzes, usually on days when an assignment is due, to make sure that you are keeping up with the reading. Multiple choice can test your knowledge of facts, and it also can test your ingenuity in perceiving subtleties of phrasing in certain choices, but on a literature exam this type of question is rare.

IDENTIFICATION QUESTIONS. These questions are decidedly of more interest. They test not only your factual knowledge but also your ability to relate this knowledge to your understanding of the work assigned. This type of question will frequently be used as a check on the depth and scope of your reading. In fact, an entire exam could be composed of only identification questions, each demanding perhaps five minutes to write. Typical examples of what you might be asked to identify are:

1. *A Character*, for example, Nora in O'Connor's "First Confession." It is necessary to describe briefly the character's position and main activity (i.e., she is Jackie's older sister who gets him in trouble at home and who takes him to his confession). You should then go on to emphasize the character's importance (i.e., her values help keep Jackie confused throughout most of the story, but by the end it is clear that O'Connor shows that it is really her values that are confused).
2. *Incidents or Situations*, which may be illustrated as follows: "A woman mourns the death of her husband." After the location of the situation or incident (Mrs. Popov in Chekhov's play *The Bear*), try to demonstrate its significance in the work. (That is, Mrs. Popov is mourning the death of her husband when the play opens, and in the course of the play Chekhov uses her feelings to show amusingly

that life with real emotion is stronger than devotion or duty to the dead.)

3. *Things, places,* and *dates.* Your instructor may ask you to identify an "overcoat" (Gogol's "Overcoat"), or a train station (Cheever's "The Five Forty-Five"), or the date of *Paradise Lost* (1672). For dates, you might often be given a leeway of five or ten years if you must guess.

4. *Quotations.* Theoretically, you should remember enough of the text to identify a passage taken from it, or at least to make an informed guess. Generally, you should try to locate the quotation, if you remember it, or else to describe the probable location, and to show the ways in which the quotation is typical of the work you have read, with regard to both content and style. You can often salvage much from a momentary lapse of memory by writing a reasoned and careful explanation of your guess, even if the guess is incorrect.

TECHNICAL AND ANALYTICAL QUESTIONS AND PROBLEMS. In a scale of ascending importance, the third and most difficult type of factual question is on those matters with which this book has been concerned: technique, analysis, and problems. You might be asked to discuss the *setting, images, point of view,* or *principal idea* of a work; you might be asked about a *specific problem;* you might be asked to analyze a poem that may or may not be duplicated for your benefit (if it is not duplicated, woe to students who have not studied their assignments). Questions like these are difficult, because they usually assume that you have a fairly technical knowledge of some important terms, while they also ask you to examine the text quite rigidly within the limitations imposed by the terms.

Obviously, technical questions will occur more frequently in advanced courses than in elementary ones, and the questions will become more subtle as the courses become more advanced. Instructors of elementary courses may frequently use main-idea or special-problem questions but will probably not use many of the others unless they specifically state their intentions to do so in advance, or unless technical terms have been studied in class.

Questions of this type are fairly long, perhaps with from fifteen to twenty-five minutes allowed for each. If you have two or more of these questions to write, try to space your time sensibly; do not devote 80 percent of your time to one question and leave only 20 percent for the rest.

BASIS OF JUDGING
FACTUAL QUESTIONS

IDENTIFICATION QUESTIONS. In all factual questions, literate English being assumed, your instructor is testing (1) your factual command, and (2) your quickness in relating a part to the whole. Thus, suppose that you are identifying the incident "A woman refuses to go on tour with a traveling show" (assuming that you are being quizzed on Dreiser's novel *Sister Carrie*). You would identify Sister Carrie as the woman and say that she is advised by her friend Lola to stay in New York (where the big opportunity is) and not to go on tour, where nobody important will see her. You would also try to show that the incident occurs when Carrie is just a minor dancer, during her early years in show business. But more important, you should show that her decision leaves her in New York, where a new opportunity develops, quickly enabling Carrie to become a star. You should conclude by saying that the incident prepares the way for all Carrie's later successes and shows how far she has advanced above Hurstwood's deteriorating state, monetarily speaking. The incident can therefore be seen as one of the most significant in the entire novel.

Your answers should all take this general pattern. Always try to show the *significance* of the things you are identifying. Significance, of course, works in many directions, but for a short identification question you should try to refer to (1) major events in the book, (2) major ideas, (3) the structure of the work, and (4) for a quotation, the style. Time is short; therefore you must be selective, but if you can set your mind toward producing answers along these lines, you will probably approach what your instructor expects.

Here are three answers that were written to an identification question. The students were asked to identify "The thing which was not," from the fourth voyage of Swift's *Gulliver's Travels*.

Answer 1. This quotation serves as an example of a typical saying in the language of the Houyhnhnms. It means that the thing was false. It shows their roundabout method of saying things.

Answer 2. This quotation is found in Chapter IV of "A Voyage to the Country of the Houyhnhnms." Gulliver is told this by his Master, one of the Houyhnhnms (a horse). It is brought out when the two of them are discussing their own customs and culture, and Gulliver is telling his Master how he sailed over to this country. The Master finds it hard to believe. He tells Gulliver that lying is altogether foreign to the culture of the Houyhnhnms. He says speech is for the purpose of being understood and he cannot comprehend lying and is unfamiliar with doubt. He goes on to say that if someone says "the thing which was not," the whole end of speech is defeated. I think what the Master has said to Gulliver clearly illustrates Swift's thought that people should use language as a means to communicate truth or otherwise its purpose is defeated. We can also see Swift's thought that this very beautiful concept of language and its use is not taken up by people. This degrades humankind.

Answer 3. The thing which was not, a variation on "*is* not," is used throughout the fourth voyage of Gulliver by the Houyhnhnm Master as a term for lying—telling a thing contrary to fact. The term is interesting

because it shows a completely reasonable reaction (represented by that
of the Houyhnhnm Master) toward a lie, with all the subtle variations on
the word we have in English. By whatever term we use, a lie is <u>a thing
which is not</u> (except in the mind of the person who tells it) and destroys
the chief end of speech—truthful communication. The term is therefore
an integral part of Swift's attack in *Gulliver* on the misuse of reason. A
lie misleads the reason, and thereby destroys all the processes of reason
(e.g., logic, science, law) by supplying it with nonexistent things. Because our civilization depends on the reasonable pursuit of truth, a lie
about anything is thus actually an attack on civilization itself. Swift's
Houyhnhnms have this value, then, that they provide us with a reasonable
basis for judging elements in our own life, and for improving them where
reason can improve them.

The first answer is not satisfactory, since it is inaccurate in sentences one
and three and does not indicate much thought about the meaning of the
quotation. The second answer is satisfactory; despite faults of style, it
shows knowledge of the conditions under which the quotation is delivered,
and it also indicates some understanding of the general meaning of the
quotation. The third answer is superior, for it relates the quotation to
Swift's satiric purposes in *Gulliver's Travels* and also shows how lying becomes a perversion of language and reason. The distinguishing mark of
the third answer is that it shows *thorough* understanding.

One thing is clear from these sample answers: *really superior answers
cannot be written if your thinking originates entirely at the time you are faced with
the question;* the more thinking and practicing you do before the exam, the
better your answers will be. Obviously the writer of the third answer was
not caught unprepared. You should reduce surprise on an exam to an
absolute minimum.

LONGER FACTUAL QUESTIONS.   The more extended factual questions also
require more thoroughly developed organization. Remember that here your
knowledge of essay writing is important, for the quality of your composition
will determine a major share of your instructor's evaluation of your answers. It is therefore best to take several minutes to gather your thoughts
together before you begin to write, because a ten-minute planned answer
is preferable to a twenty-five-minute unplanned answer. You do not need
to write down every possible fact on each particular question. Of greater
significance is the use to which you put the facts you know and the organization of your answer. When the questions are before you, use a sheet
of scratch paper to jot down the facts you remember and your ideas about
them in relation to the question. Then put them together, phrase a thesis
sentence, and use your facts to illustrate or prove your thesis.

It is always necessary to begin your answer pointedly, using key words
or phrases from the question or direction if possible, so that your answer
will have thematic shape. You should never begin an answer with "Because" and then go on from there without referring again to the question.

To be most responsive during the short time available for writing an exam, you should use the question as your guide for your answer. Let us suppose that you have the following question on your test: "What are some reasons for which Dick Diver loses his professional abilities and therefore his strength and security?" (Fitzgerald's novel *Tender Is the Night*). You should use some of the phrases here to launch yourself. Here are some possible opening sentences, with phrases from the question underlined:

> Dick Diver <u>loses his professional abilities</u> for at least two <u>reasons.</u> Fitzgerald indicates that Nicole absorbs Dick's <u>strength</u> as he <u>loses</u> it by helping her back to mental health. A more plausible <u>reason</u> is the sapping of his <u>strength and security</u> by his living so superficially among the international set.

From this opening you could go on to develop Fitzgerald's reason (Dick's relationship with his wife) and then your own (Dick's lifestyle among the wealthy). What is important here is that these first three sentences have set the aims and limits of the answer, so that the entire response will be self-contained. The problem with many answers is that they are not self-contained; they seem to exist in a vacuum, totally apart from the question. Your reader or readers must always know what you are about, and there is no way they can know unless *you* tell them. Your best approach is to think of every one of your answers as an essay, no matter how short, demanding good thinking, clear organizing, and pointed writing.

For comparison, here are two paragraphs from a twenty-five-minute question on Fitzgerald's story "The Rich Boy." The question was: "What do Anson's two love affairs contribute to your understanding of his character?" Both paragraphs are about Anson's first love affair, with Paula Legendre:

1	2
The Paula affair helps understand Anson. Paula best understood him through their relationship. Anson was searching for stability and security in life; he felt he could achieve these with Paula. This was shown through the following idea: if only he could be with Paula he would be happy. Paula saw him as a mixture of solidity and self-indulgence and cynicism. She deeply loved him, but it was impossible for him to form a lasting relationship with her. The reason for this was his drinking and his code of superiority. This was shown in the fact that he felt hopeless despair before his pride and his self-knowl-	Fitzgerald brings out Anson's strength and weakness through the Paula affair. In one way, Anson sees in Paula everything he needs for a full, satisfying life: love, equal social and economic position, a purpose in life, and conservatism. His earnest, low talks with her show how positive his life could be if he were to marry her. But Paula also brings out Anson's weakness. Because his life as a rich boy has been without motivation or responsibility, he is a man of shallow and superficial emotions. Thus, he cannot face the responsibility of marriage with Paula. He gets drunk and embarrasses her. He delays pro-

knowledge. His superiority can be further observed through his physical and
emotional relationship with Paula. His
entire relationship with Paula was
based on his feelings that emotion was
sufficient, and why should he commit
himself? Her marriage greatly affected
Anson; it made a cynic out of him.

posing to her at the right moment, and
therefore the right moment is lost forever. When Paula marries another man,
Anson is deeply disturbed, but secretly
he is happy. He is really no better than
a child, for his emotions are undevel-
oped. Paula is his opportunity, and he
knows it, but he cannot summon the
necessary strength to come to grips
with maturity, and thus he becomes an
emotional failure.

Column 2 is superior to column 1. If column 1 were judged as part of
an outside-class theme, it would be a failure, but as part of a test it would
probably receive a passing grade. Column 2 is clearer; it develops its point
well and uses evidence more accurately to illustrate its point.

GENERAL OR COMPREHENSIVE QUESTIONS

General or comprehensive questions are particularly important on final
examinations, when your instructor is interested in testing your total comprehension of the course material. You have much freedom of choice in
deciding what to write, but you must constantly bear in mind that your
instructor is looking for intelligence and knowledge in what you choose
to say.

Considerable time is usually allowed for answering a comprehensive
question, perhaps forty-five minutes or more, depending on the scope and
depth that your instructor expects. Questions may be phrased in a number
of ways:

1. A direct question asking about philosophy, underlying attitudes,
   "schools" of literature or literary movements, main ideas, characteristics of style, backgrounds, and so on. Here are some typical
   questions in this category: "Define and characterize Metaphysical
   poetry," or "Discuss the influences of science on literature in the
   Restoration," or "Describe the dramatic prose of the Jacobean dramatists."
2. A "comment" question, usually based on an extensive quotation,
   borrowed from a critic or written by your instructor for the occasion,
   about a broad class of writers, or about a literary movement, or the
   like. Your instructor may ask you to treat this question broadly (taking
   in many writers) or else to apply the quotation to a specific writer.

3. A "suppose" question, such as "Suppose Rosalind were in Desdemona's place; what would she do when Othello accused her of infidelity?" or "What would Pope say about Joyce's *Ulysses*?"

BASIS OF JUDGING
GENERAL QUESTIONS

In dealing with a broad, general question you are in fact dealing with an unstructured situation, and you must not only supply an *answer* but—almost more important—must also create a *structure* within which your answer can have meaning. You might say that you make up your own question, which will be derived from the original, broadly expressed question. If you were asked to "Consider Shakespeare's thoughts about the ideal monarch," for example, you would do well to structure the question by narrowing its limits. A possible narrowing might be put as follows: "Shakespeare dramatizes thoughts about the ideal monarch by setting up a contrast between, on one side, monarchs who fail either by alienating their close supporters or by becoming tyrannical, and, on the other side, monarchs who succeed by securing faithful supporters and by creating confidence in themselves." With this sort of focus, you would be able to proceed point by point, introducing supporting data as you went. Without such a structure, you would experience difficulty.

As a general rule, the best method to adopt in answering a comprehensive question is that of comparison-contrast. The reason is that in dealing with, say, a general question on Yeats, Eliot, and Auden, it is too easy to write three separate essays rather than one. Thus, you should force yourself to consider a topic like "The Treatment of Alienation," or "The Attempt to Find Truth," and then to treat such a topic point by point rather than author by author. If you were answering the question posed on Shakespeare's thoughts about the ideal monarch, you might try to show the failures of Richard II and Richard III against the successes of Henry IV and Henry V. It would also be relevant to introduce, by way of comparison and contrast, references to Antony, and even to King Lear or to Prospero (from *The Tempest*). By moving from point to point, you would bring in these references as they are germane to your topic. But if you treated each figure separately, your comprehensive answer would become diffuse and ineffective. For further ideas on this method, see Chapter 10 (pp. 112–125).

In judging your response to a general question, your instructor is interested in seeing: (1) how intelligently you select material, (2) how well you organize your material, (3) how adequate and intelligent are the generalizations you make about the material, and (4) how relevant are the facts you select for illustration.

Bear in mind that in comprehensive questions, though you are ostensibly free, the freedom you have been extended has been that of creating your own structure. The underlying idea of the comprehensive, general question is that you personally possess special knowledge and insights that cannot be discovered by more factual questions. You must therefore try to formulate your own responses to the material and to introduce evidence that reflects your own particular insights and command of information.

appendix b

A Note on Documentation

This section will not present a complete discussion of documentation, but only as much as is necessary for typical themes about literature. You will find complete discussions in most writing handbooks and guidebooks to research, and in the latest edition of the *MLA Style Sheet*. Whenever you are in doubt about documentation, always ask your instructor.

In any writing not derived purely from your own mind, you must document your facts. In writing about literature, you must base your conclusions on material in particular literary works and must document this material. If you refer to secondary sources, you must be especially careful to document your facts. To document properly, you must use illustrative material in your discussion and mention your sources either in your discussion or in footnotes to it.

Integration and Mechanics of Quotations

DISTINGUISH YOUR THOUGHTS FROM THOSE OF YOUR AUTHOR. Ideally your themes should reflect your own thought as it is prompted and illustrated by an author's work. Sometimes a problem arises, however, because it is hard for your reader to know when *your* ideas have stopped and your *author's* have begun. You must therefore arrange things to make the dis-

tinction clear, but you must also create a constant blending of materials
that will make your themes easy to follow. You will be moving from paraphrase, to general interpretation, to observation, to independent application of everything you choose to discuss. It is not always easy to keep
these various elements integrated. Let us see an example in which the
writer moves from reference to an author's ideas—really paraphrase—to
an independent application of the idea:

> [1] In the "Preface to the Lyrical Ballads," Wordsworth stated that the
> language of poetry should be the same as that of prose. [2] That is,
> poetic diction should not be artificial or contrived in any sense, but should
> consist of the words normally used by people in their everyday lives (pp.
> 791–93). [3] If one follows this principle in poetry, then it would be
> improper to refer to the sun as anything but *the sun*. [4] To call it a
> *heavenly orb* or the *source of golden gleams* would be inadmissible
> because these phrases are not used in common speech.

Here the first two sentences present a paraphrase of Wordsworth's ideas
about poetic diction, the second going so far as to locate a particular spot
where the idea is developed. The third and fourth sentences apply Wordsworth's idea to examples chosen by the writer. Here the blending is provided by the transitional clause, "If one follows this principle," and the
reader is thus not confused about who is saying what.

INTEGRATE MATERIAL BY USING QUOTATION MARKS. Sometimes you will
use short quotations from your author to illustrate your ideas and interpretations. Here the problem of distinguishing your thoughts from the
author's is solved by quotation marks. In this sort of internal quotation you
may treat prose and poetry in the same way. If a poetic quotation extends
from the end of one line to the beginning of another, however, indicate
the line break with a virgule (/), and use a capital letter to begin the next
line, as in the following:

> Wordsworth states that in his boyhood all of nature seemed like his own
> personal property. Rocks, mountains, and woods were almost like food
> to him, and he claimed that "the sounding cataract/Haunted . . . [him]
> like a passion" (76–80).

BLEND QUOTATIONS INTO YOUR OWN SENTENCES. Making internal quotations still creates the problem of blending materials, however, for quotations should never be brought in unless you prepare your reader for
them in some way. Do not, for example, bring in quotations in the following
manner:

> The sky is darkened by thick clouds, bringing a feeling of gloom that is
> associated with the same feeling that can be sensed at a funeral. "See
> gloomy clouds obscure the cheerful day."

This abrupt quotation throws the reader off balance. It is better to prepare the reader to move from the discourse to the quotation, as in the following revision:

> The scene is marked by sorrow and depression, as though the spectator, who is asked to "See gloomy clouds obscure the cheerful day," is present at a funeral.

Here the quotation is made an actual part of the sentence. This sort of blending is satisfactory, provided the quotation is brief.

SET AND INDENT LONG QUOTATIONS. The standard for how to place quotations should be not to quote within your own sentence any passage longer than 20 or 25 words. Quotations of greater length demand so much separate attention that they interfere with your own sentence. When your quotation is long, you should set it off separately, remembering to introduce it in some way. It is possible but not desirable to have one of your sentences conclude with an extensive quotation, but you should never make an extensive quotation in the middle of your sentence. By the time you finish such an unwieldy sentence, your reader will have lost sight of how it began.

The physical layout of extensive quotations should be as follows: Leave three blank lines between your own discourse and the quotation. Single-space the quotation and make a special indention for it to set it off from the rest of your theme. After the quotation leave a three-line space again and resume your own discourse. Here is a specimen, from a theme about John Gay's *Trivia,* an early eighteenth-century poem:

> In keeping with this general examination of the anti-heroic side of life, Gay takes his description into the street, where constant disturbance and even terror were normal conditions after dark. A person trying to sleep was awakened by midnight drunkards, and the person walking late at night could be attacked by gangs of thieves and cutthroats who waited in dark corners. The reality must have been worse than Gay implies in his description of these sinister inhabitants of the darkened streets:
>
>> Now is the time that rakes their revels keep;
>> Kindlers of riot, enemies of sleep.
>> His scattered pence the flying Nicker flings,
>> And with the copper shower the casement rings.
>> Who has not heard the Scourer's midnight fame?
>> Who has not trembled at the Mohock's name?
>> —lines 321–326
>
> Gay mentions only those who have "trembled" at the Mohocks, not those who have experienced their brutality.

This same layout applies also when you are quoting prose passages. When quoting lines of poetry, always remember to quote them *as lines*. Do not run them together. When you set off the quotation by itself, as in the example above, you do *not* need quotation marks.

USE THREE SPACED PERIODS (AN ELLIPSIS) TO SHOW OMISSIONS. Whether your quotation is long or short, you will often need to change some of the material in it to conform to your own thematic requirements. You might wish to omit something from the quotation that is not essential to your point. Indicate such omissions with three spaced periods (. . .). If your quotation is very brief, however, do not use spaced periods, as they might be more of a hindrance than a help. See, for example, the absurdity of using an ellipsis in a sentence like this one:

> Keats asserts that "a thing of beauty . . ." always gives joy.

USE SQUARE BRACKETS FOR YOUR OWN WORDS WITHIN QUOTATIONS

If you add words of your own to integrate your quotation into your own train of discourse, or to explain words that may seem obscure, put square brackets around these words, as in the following passage:

> In the "Tintern Abbey Lines," Wordsworth refers to a trance-like state of illumination, in which the "affections gently lead . . . [him] on." He is un-questionably describing a state of extreme relaxation, for he mentions that the "motion of . . . human blood [was]/Almost suspended [his pulse slowed]" and that in these states he became virtually "a living soul" (lines 42–49).

DO NOT CHANGE YOUR SOURCE

Always reproduce your source exactly. Because most freshman anthol-ogies and texts modernize the spelling in works that are old, you may never see any old-spelling editions. But if you use an unmodernized text, as in many advanced courses, duplicate everything exactly as you find it, even if this means spelling words like *achieve* as *atchieve* or *joke* as *joak*. A student once spelled out fully the word *an* in the construction "an I were" in an Elizabethan text. The result was unnecessary confusion, because *an* really meant *if* (or *and if*) and not *and*. Difficulties like this one are rare, but you will avoid them if you reproduce the text as you find it. Should you think that something is either misspelled or confusing as it stands, you may do one of two things:

1. Within brackets, clarify or correct the confusing word or phrase, as in the following:
   In 1714, fencing was considered a "Gentlemany [i.e., gentlemanly] subject."
2. Use the word *sic* (Latin for *thus*, meaning "It is this way in the text") immediately after the problematic word or obvious mistake:
   He was just finning [sic] his way back to health when the next disaster struck.

DO NOT OVERQUOTE. A word of caution: Do not use too many quotations. You will be judged on your own thought and on the continuity and development of your own theme. It is tempting to use many quotations on the theory that you need to use examples from the text to illustrate your ideas. Naturally, it is important to illustrate your ideas, but please remember that too many quotations can disturb the flow of your own thought.

Formal Documentation

It is essential to acknowledge any source from which you have derived factual or interpretive information. If you fail to grant recognition, you run the risk of being challenged for representing as your own the results of other people's work. To indicate the source of all derived material, you must, formally, use footnotes at the bottom of your page or at the end of your theme, or, informally, embody some form of recognition in the body of your paper. Although the care necessary for noting book titles and page numbers can be annoying, you should realize that footnotes and informal references exist to help your readers. First, your readers may want to consult your source in order to assure themselves that you have not misstated any facts. Second, they may dispute your conclusions and wish to see your source in order to arrive at their own conclusions. Third, they may become so interested in one of your points that they might wish to read more about it for their own pleasure or edification. For these reasons, you must show the sources of all material that you use.

If you are using many sources in a research report, the standard method is to document your paper formally. The procedures discussed here will be sufficient for most papers requiring formal documentation. For especially difficult problems, consult the latest edition of the *MLA Style Sheet*, or the section on documentation in your writing handbook.

The first time you quote from a source or refer to the source, you should provide a footnote giving the following information in the order listed below.

FOR A BOOK

1. The author's name, first name or initials first.
2. The title: in quotation marks for a story or poem; underlined for a book.
3. The edition (if indicated) abbreviated thus: *2nd ed., 3rd ed.*, etc.
4. The name of the editor or translator. Abbreviate "editor" or "edited by" as *ed.*; "editors" as *eds.* Use *trans.* for "translator" or "translated by."
5. The publication facts should be given in parentheses in the following order:
   (a) City (not the state) of publication, followed by a colon (the state need not be included unless the city might be confused with another).
   (b) Publisher. This information is frequently not given, but it is wise to include it.[1]
   (c) Year of publication.
6. The page number(s), for example, *p. 65, pp. 65f., pp. 6–10.* For books commonly reprinted (like *Gulliver's Travels*) and for well-known long poems (like *Paradise Lost*) you should include the chapter or part number and the line numbers, so that readers using a different edition may be able to locate your quotation.

FOR A MAGAZINE ARTICLE

1. The author, first name or initials first.
2. The title of the article, in quotation marks.
3. The name of the magazine, underlined.
4. The volume number, in Arabic numerals (no longer Roman).
5. The year of publication, within parentheses.
6. The page number(s), for example, *65, 65f., 6–10.* (It is not necessary to include *p.* or *pp.* when you have included the volume number of the periodical.)

To prepare for subsequent footnotes, mention at the end of the first footnote that you will hereafter use a shortened reference to the source, such as the author's last name, or the title of the work, or some abbreviation, according to your preference. This practice is illustrated in the sample footnotes below.

---

[1] If faced with a choice, some editors prefer citing the publisher rather than the city of publication, on the assumption that several publishers in cities like London or New York will often have published editions of the same work. For identification purposes, citing the publisher is therefore more helpful than citing the city, but as yet this practice has not been widely adopted. In this as in all matters connected with your course, be guided by the advice of your instructor.

Footnotes may be positioned either at the bottom of each page (separated from the text by a line) or else at the end of the theme in a list. Some instructors request that each footnote go right into the text at the appropriate position, with lines setting the footnote apart from the text. Ask your instructor about the practice you should adopt.

The first line of a footnote should be paragraph indented, and continuing lines should be flush with the left margin of your theme. Footnote numbers are positioned slightly above the line. Generally, you may single-space footnotes, but be sure to ask your instructor about how to proceed.

SAMPLE FOOTNOTES

In the examples below, book titles and periodicals, which are usually italicized in print, are shown underlined, as they would be in your typewritten paper.

[1]Joseph Conrad, The Rescue: A Romance of the Shallows (New York: Doubleday & Co., Inc., 1960), p. 103. Hereafter cited as The Rescue.

[2]George Milburn, "The Apostate," An Approach to Literature, 3rd ed., Cleanth Brooks, John Thibaut Purser, and Robert Penn Warren, eds. (New York: Appleton-Century-Crofts, Inc., 1952), p. 74. Hereafter cited as "The Apostate."

[3]Carlisle Moore, "Conrad and the Novel as Ordeal," Philological Quarterly, 42 (1963), 59. Hereafter cited as Moore.

[4]Moore, p. 61.

[5]The Rescue, p. 171.

[6]"The Apostate," p. 76.

As a general principle, you do not need to repeat in a footnote any material that you have already incorporated into your theme. For example, if in your theme you mention the author and title of your source, then your footnote should merely give the data about publication. Here is an example:

In *Charles Macklin: An Actor's Life*, William W. Appleton points out that Macklin had been "reinstated at Drury Lane" by December 19, 1744, and that he was playing his stellar role of Shylock.[7]

[7](Cambridge, Mass.: Harvard University Press, 1961), p. 72.

Informal Documentation

Opinion today among many editors and persons who pay printing bills is that writers should put as many references as possible within the text of a paper. If you are using many sources, of course, formal footnotes avoid much ambiguity. Even so, you should include the names of authors, articles, and books in the body of your theme whenever possible, as in the example just given.

When you are writing about only one work of literature—as you will be in most of your themes—it is desirable to include virtually all documentation within the text of the theme. The principle is to give complete documentation but to avoid footnotes which distract your reader for no other reason than to list page numbers. This principle has been applied in most of the sample themes in this book.

The method is easy: In a single footnote (the only one you will need), state that all later page numbers, parenthetical and otherwise, will refer to the work you are citing in the footnote:

[1]Lucian, *True History and Lucius or the Ass,* trans. Paul Turner (Bloomington: Indiana University Press, 1958), p. 49. All page numbers in this theme refer to this edition.

The next time you refer to the source, do the following:

1. For an indented (set off) quotation, indicate the page number, line number, or chapter number, preceded by a dash, immediately below the quotation, as follows:

   Nobody grows old there, for they all stay the age they were when they first arrived, and it never gets dark. On the other hand, it never gets really light either, and they live in a sort of perpetual twilight, such as we have just before sunrise.
   —p. 39

2. For a quotation blended into your own discussion:
   a. If your sentence ends with the quotation, put the reference in parentheses immediately following the quotation marks and immediately before the period concluding your sentence:

   Sidney uses the example that "the Romaine lawes allowed no person to be carried to the warres but hee that was in the Souldiers role" (p. 189).

   b. If the quotation ends near the conclusion of your sentence, put the reference in parentheses at the end of your sentence before the period:

   William Webbe states that poetry originated in the needs for "eyther exhortations to vertue, dehortations from vices, or the prayses of some laudable thing"; that is, in public needs (p. 248).

c. If the quotation ends far from the end of your sentence, put the reference in parentheses immediately following the quotation mark but before your own punctuation mark:

If we accept as a truth Thomas Lodge's statement, "Chaucer in pleasant vein can rebuke sin vncontrold" (p. 69), then satire and comedy are the most effective modes of moral persuasion in literature.

Shorter Reference Systems

Some instructors recommend shorter reference systems like the above even when many works are being used, as in an extended research theme. The mechanics are simple. First, a first-page list of references should contain all the works—and *only* those works—used in the theme, arranged alphabetically according to abbreviations that stand for the works. All necessary bibliographical information should be included in this list, in the following order:

For a book:
Author, last name first, period.
Title, underlined, period.
City of publication, colon; publisher, comma; and date, period.
For an article:
Author, last name first, period.
Title of article, in quotation marks, period.
Name of journal, underlined, comma; volume number, together with series number if there is one, in Arabic numerals, no punctuation; year of publication, including month and day of weekly or daily publications, all within parentheses, comma; and inclusive page numbers, period.

Here is a model entry:

Sp   Spacks, Patricia Meyer. An Argument of Images: The Poetry of
        Alexander Pope. Cambridge: Harvard University Press, 1971.

Whenever a reference to this book is necessary, the abbreviation *Sp* followed by the page number should appear within parentheses, for example: (Sp, 24). The following is a short list of references arranged in this manner:

D   Dixon, Peter. The World of Pope's Satires. London: Methuen,
        1968.
G   Gneiting, Teona Tone. "Pictorial Imagery and Satiric Inversion
        in Pope's Dunciad." Eighteenth-Century Studies, 8 (1975),
        420–430.
K   Kallich, Martin I. Heav'ns First Law. DeKalb: Northern
        Illinois University Press, 1967.

R   Russo, John. Alexander Pope: Tradition and Identity. Cam-
         bridge: Harvard University Press, 1972.
Sit   Sitter, John E. The Poetry of Pope's Dunciad. Minneapolis: Uni-
         versity of Minnesota Press, 1971.
Sp   Spacks, Patricia Meyer. An Argument of Images: The Poetry of
         Alexander Pope. Cambridge: Harvard University Press, 1971.
W   Wellington, James E. "Pope and Charity." Philological Quarterly,
         46 (1967), 225–235.

NOTE: When references are made to page numbers in these works, the
abbreviations and the page numbers are given in parentheses; e.g., "(D,
24)" refers to page 24 in Peter Dixon's book.

Some instructors prefer that the reference list be numbered and that the
numbers be used with the appropriate pages. Let us assume that we number our list, with D as 1 and Sp as 6. Then the parenthetical references
"(3, 45)" and "(6, 64)" would refer to page 45 of the Nicolson-Rousseau
book, and to page 64 of the Spacks book.

Here is a sample paragraph showing the use of the abbreviation system,
based on our list of references:

> In the midst of fragmentation and disunity, Alexander Pope held to the
> ideal that the universe was a whole, an entirety, which provided a "viable
> benevolent system for the salvation of everyone who does good," as
> Martin Kallich has stated (K, 24). Pope's view was therefore positive, but
> it was not passive. It required that people in power use their Christian
> charity to help the poor, who did not have power (W, 235). In this way,
> the system worked through an intricate network of human dependency.
> Pope saw a "common humanity" in life (Sp, 149), and therefore he was
> tolerant of persons incapable of reason, like Sir Plume, but he was also
> filled with "a sense of outrage" against those who attempted to destroy
> art and beauty (G, 421).

The Reference Method
of the American Psychological
Association (APA)

A system of references is detailed in the Publication Manual of the American
Psychological Association, 2nd edn. (Washington: American Psychological
Association, 1974, with "Change Sheets" dated 1975 and 1977). The
method, used in all the APA journals and in many other publications in
the social and natural sciences, is the "author-date method of citation"
(p. 58). By this method, all footnotes are eliminated, and the last name of
the author or authors, date of publication, and page numbers are included
within the article itself. This information may all be included within pa-

rentheses, or some of it may appear as part of the discourse, as in the example to follow. The full bibliographical data for each reference are to be found in the bibliography at the end of the article (arranged by the last names of the authors). Nothing is to be included in this list that is not used in the article. Here is a sample paragraph employing the APA method, based on the previous list of seven references:

> Underlying Pope's satires was a complex set of intellectual, psychological, and moral ideals. In the intellectual sphere, Pope measured contemporary wits against the "Augustan conception of cultural progress" (Sitter, 1971, p. 100) and satirized them when they did not measure up. On the personal level, there was a need, in Russo's words, for the "active harmonization of conflicting emotions and ideas" (1972, p. 204). To go too far either toward emotion or reason was to cause psychological disharmony, and therefore to become the butt of Pope's satiric attack. Dixon, in 1968, drew attention to the standards of "genuine hospitality" and "human dignity" (p. 58) that determined whether Pope's subjects were failing in their moral obligations to love and respect one another, not only personally but socially.

Final Words

As long as all that you want from a reference is the page number of a quotation or of a paraphrase, any of the shorter methods is suitable and easy, but always remember to use them consistently. They save your reader the trouble of glancing to the bottom of your page or of thumbing through pages to find a long list of footnotes. Obviously, these systems are not adequate if you wish to add more details or if you wish to refer your reader to additional materials that you are not using directly in your theme. In such cases you must use full footnotes.

Whatever method you use, there is an unchanging need to grant recognition to sources. Remember that whenever you begin to write and to make references, you might forget a number of specific details about documentation, and you will certainly discover that you have many questions. Be sure then to ask your instructor, who is your final authority.

Works Used
for the
Sample Themes

William Shakespeare (1564–1616)

Sonnet 116

Let me not to the marriage of true minds	1
Admit impediments. Love is not love	2
Which alters when it alteration finds,	3
Or bends with the remover to remove:	4
O, no! it is an ever-fixed mark,	5
That looks on tempests and is never shaken;	6
It is the star to every wand'ring bark,	7
Whose worth's unknown, although his height be taken.	8
Love's not Time's fool, though rosy lips and cheeks	9
Within his bending sickle's compass come;	10
Love alters not with his brief hours and weeks,	11
But bears it out even to the edge of doom:—	12
If this be error and upon me proved,	13
I never writ, nor no man ever loved.	14

Matthew Arnold (1822–1888)

Dover Beach

The sea is calm to-night.	1
The tide is full, the moon lies fair	2
Upon the straits:—on the French coast the light	3
Gleams and is gone; the cliffs of England stand,	4
Glimmering and vast, out in the tranquil bay.	5
Come to the window, sweet is the night air!	6
Only, from the long line of spray	7
Where the sea meets the moon-blanched land,	8
Listen! you hear the grating roar	9
Of pebbles which the waves draw back, and fling,	10
At their return, up the high strand,	11
Begin, and cease, and then again begin,	12
With tremulous cadence slow, and bring	13
The eternal note of sadness in.	14
Sophocles long ago	15
Heard it on the Ægean, and it brought	16
Into his mind the turbid ebb and flow	17
Of human misery; we	18
Find also in the sound a thought,	19
Hearing it by this distant northern sea.	20
The Sea of Faith	21
Was once, too, at the full, and round earth's shore	22
Lay like the folds of a bright girdle furled.	23
But now I only hear	24
Its melancholy, long, withdrawing roar,	25
Retreating, to the breath	26
Of the night wind, down the vast edges drear	27
And naked shingles of the world.	28
Ah, love, let us be true	29
To one another! for the world, which seems	30
To lie before us like a land of dreams,	31

So various, so beautiful, so new,   32
Hath really neither joy, nor love, nor light,   33
Nor certitude, nor peace, nor help for pain;   34
And we are here as on a darkling plain   35
Swept with confused alarms of struggle and flight   36
Where ignorant armies clash by night.   37

Thomas Hardy (1840–1928)

Channel Firing

That night your great guns unawares,	1
Shook all our coffins as we lay,	2
And broke the chancel window squares.	3
We thought it was the Judgment-day	4
And sat upright. While drearisome	5
Arose the howl of wakened hounds:	6
The mouse let fall the altar-crumb,	7
The worms drew back into the mounds,	8
The glebe cow drooled. Till God called, "No;	9
It's gunnery practice out at sea	10
Just as before you went below;	11
The world is as it used to be:	12
"All nations striving strong to make	13
Red war yet redder. Mad as hatters	14
They do no more for Christés sake	15
Than you who are helpless in such matters.	16
"That this is not the judgment-hour	17
For some of them's a blessed thing,	18
For if it were they'd have to scour	19
Hell's floor for so much threatening . . .	20
"Ha, ha. It will be warmer when	21
I blow the trumpet (if indeed	22
I ever do; for you are men,	23
And rest eternal sorely need)."	24
So down we lay again. "I wonder,	25
Will the world ever saner be,"	26
Said one, "than when He sent us under	27
In our indifferent century!"	28

And many a skeleton shook his head.   *29*
"Instead of preaching forty year,"   *30*
My neighbor Parson Thirdly said,   *31*
"I wish I had stuck to pipes and beer."   *32*

Again the guns disturbed the hour,   *33*
Roaring their readiness to avenge,   *34*
As far inland as Stourton Tower,   *35*
And Camelot, and starlit Stonehenge.   *36*

April 1914

Robert Frost (1875–1963)

Desert Places

Snow falling and night falling fast, oh, fast	1
In a field I looked into going past,	2
And the ground almost covered smooth in snow,	3
But a few weeds and stubble showing last.	4
The woods around it have it—it is theirs.	5
All animals are smothered in their lairs.	6
I am too absent-spirited to count;	7
The loneliness includes me unawares.	8
And lonely as it is that loneliness	9
Will be more lonely ere it will be less—	10
A blanker whiteness of benighted snow	11
With no expression, nothing to express.	12
They cannot scare me with their empty spaces	13
Between stars—on stars where no human race is.	14
I have it in me so much nearer home	15
To scare myself with my own desert places.	16

Nathaniel Hawthorne (1804–1864)

Young Goodman Brown

Young Goodman Brown came forth at sunset, into the street of Salem village, but put his head back, after crossing the threshold, to exchange a parting kiss with his young wife. And Faith, as the wife was aptly named, thrust her own pretty head into the street, letting the wind play with the pink ribbons of her cap, while she called to Goodman Brown.

"Dearest heart," whispered she, softly and rather sadly, when her lips were close to his ear, "prithee, put off your journey until sunrise, and sleep in your own bed to-night. A lone woman is troubled with such dreams and such thoughts, that she's afeard of herself, sometimes. Pray, tarry with me this night, dear husband, of all nights in the year!"

"My love and my Faith," replied young Goodman Brown, "of all nights in the year, this one night must I tarry away from thee. My journey, as thou callest it, forth and back again, must needs be done 'twixt now and sunrise. What, my sweet, pretty wife, dost thou doubt me already, and we but three months married!"

"Then God bless you!" said Faith with the pink ribbons, "and may you find all well, when you come back."

"Amen!" cried Goodman Brown. "Say thy prayers, dear Faith, and go to bed at dusk, and no harm will come to thee."

So they parted; and the young man pursued his way, until, being about to turn the corner by the meeting-house, he looked back and saw the head of Faith still peeping after him, with a melancholy air, in spite of her pink ribbons.

"Poor little Faith!" thought he, for his heart smote him. "What a wretch am I, to leave her on such an errand! She talks of dreams, too. Methought, as she spoke, there was trouble in her face, as if a dream had warned her what work is to be done to-night. But no, no! 't would kill her to think it. Well; she's a blessed angel on earth; and after this one night, I'll cling to her skirts and follow her to Heaven."

With this excellent resolve for the future, Goodman Brown felt himself justified in making more haste on his present evil purpose. He had taken a dreary road, darkened by all the gloomiest trees of the forest, which barely stood aside to let the narrow path creep through, and closed immediately behind. It was all as lonely as could be; and there is this peculiarity in such a solitude, that the traveller knows not who may be concealed by the innumerable trunks and the thick boughs overhead; so that, with lonely footsteps, he may yet be passing through an unseen multitude.

"There may be a devilish Indian behind every tree," said Goodman Brown to himself; and he glanced fearfully behind him, as he added, "What if the devil himself should be at my very elbow!"

His head being turned back, he passed a crook of the road, and looking forward again, beheld the figure of a man, in grave and decent attire, seated at the foot of an old tree. He arose at Goodman Brown's approach, and walked onward, side by side with him.

"You are late, Goodman Brown," said he. "The clock of the Old South was striking, as I came through Boston; and that is full fifteen minutes agone."

"Faith kept me back awhile," replied the young man, with a tremor in his voice, caused by the sudden appearance of his companion, though not wholly unexpected.

It was now deep dusk in the forest, and deepest in that part of it where these two were journeying. As nearly as could be discerned, the second traveller was about fifty years old, apparently in the same rank of life as Goodman Brown, and bearing a considerable resemblance to him, though perhaps more in expression than features. Still, they might have been taken for father and son. And yet, though the elder person was as simply clad as the younger, and as simple in manner too, he had an indescribable air of one who knew the world, and would not have felt abashed at the governor's dinner-table, or in King William's court, were it possible that his affairs should call him thither. But the only thing about him that could be fixed upon as remarkable, was his staff, which bore the likeness of a great black snake, so curiously wrought, that it might almost be seen to twist and wriggle itself like a living serpent. This, of course, must have been an ocular deception, assisted by the uncertain light.

"Come, Goodman Brown!" cried his fellow-traveller, "this is a dull pace for the beginning of a journey. Take my staff, if you are so soon weary."

"Friend," said the other, exchanging his slow pace for a full stop, "having kept covenant by meeting thee here, it is my purpose now to return whence I came. I have scruples, touching the matter thou wot'st of."

"Sayest thou so?" replied he of the serpent, smiling apart. "Let us walk on, nevertheless, reasoning as we go, and if I convince thee not, thou shalt turn back. We are but a little way in the forest, yet."

"Too far, too far!" exclaimed the goodman, unconsciously resuming his walk. "My father never went into the woods on such an errand, nor his father before him. We have been a race of honest men and good Christians, since the days of the martyrs. And shall I be the first of the name of Brown that ever took this path and kept—"

"Such company, thou wouldst say," observed the elder person, interrupting his pause. "Well said, Goodman Brown! I have been as well acquainted with your family as with ever a one among the Puritans; and that's no trifle to say. I helped your grandfather, the constable, when he lashed the Quaker woman so smartly through the streets of Salem. And it was I that brought your father a pitch-pine knot, kindled at my own hearth, to set fire to an Indian village, in King Philip's war. They were my good friends, both; and many a pleasant walk have we had along this path, and returned merrily after midnight. I would fain be friends with you, for their sake."

"If it be as thou sayest," replied Goodman Brown, "I marvel they never spoke of these matters. Or, verily, I marvel not, seeing that the least rumor of the sort would have driven them from New England. We are a people of prayer, and good works to boot, and abide no such wickedness."

"Wickedness or not," said the traveller with twisted staff, "I have a very general acquaintance here in New England. The deacons of many a church have drunk the communion wine with me; the selectmen, of divers towns, make me their chairman; and a majority of the Great and General Court are firm supporters of my interest. The governor and I, too—but these are state secrets."

"Can this be so!" cried Goodman Brown, with a stare of amazement at his undisturbed companion. "Howbeit, I have nothing to do with the governor and council; they have their own ways, and are no rule for a simple husbandman like me. But, were I to go on with thee, how should I meet the eye of that good old man, our minister, at Salem village? Oh, his voice would make me tremble, both Sabbath-day and lecture-day!"

Thus far, the elder traveller had listened with due gravity, but now burst into a fit of irrepressible mirth, shaking himself so violently, that his snake-like staff actually seemed to wriggle in sympathy.

"Ha! ha! ha!" shouted he, again and again; then composing himself, "Well, go on, Goodman Brown, go on; but, prithee, don't kill me with laughing!"

"Well, then, to end the matter at once," said Goodman Brown, considerably nettled, "there is my wife, Faith. It would break her dear little heart; and I'd rather break my own!"

"Nay, if that be the case," answered the other, "e'en go thy ways, Goodman Brown. I would not, for twenty old women like the one hobbling before us, that Faith should come to any harm."

As he spoke, he pointed his staff at a female figure on the path, in whom Goodman Brown recognized a very pious and exemplary dame, who had taught him his catechism in youth, and was still his moral and spiritual adviser, jointly with the minister and Deacon Gookin.

"A marvel, truly, that Goody Cloyse should be so far in the wilderness, at nightfall!" said he. "But, with your leave, friend, I shall take a cut through the woods, until we have left this Christian woman behind. Being a stranger to you, she might ask whom I was consorting with, and whither I was going."

"Be it so," said his fellow-traveller. "Betake you to the woods, and let me keep the path."

Accordingly, the young man turned aside, but took care to watch his companion, who advanced softly along the road, until he had come within a staff's length of the old dame. She, meanwhile, was making the best of her way, with singular speed for so aged a woman, and mumbling some indistinct words, a prayer, doubtless, as she went. The traveller put forth his staff, and touched her withered neck with what seemed the serpent's tail.

"The devil!" screamed the pious old lady.

"Then Goody Cloyse knows her old friend?" observed the traveller, confronting her, and leaning on his writhing stick.

"Ah, forsooth, and is it your worship, indeed?" cried the good dame. "Yea, truly is it, and in the very image of my old gossip, Goodman Brown, the grandfather of the silly fellow that now is. But, would your worship believe it? My broomstick hath strangely disappeared, stolen, as I suspect, by that unhanged witch, Goody Cory, and that, too, when I was all anointed with the juice of smallage and cinque-foil and wolf's-bane—"

"Mingled with fine wheat and the fat of a new-born babe," said the shape of old Goodman Brown.

"Ah, your worship knows the recipe," cried the old lady, cackling aloud. "So, as I was saying, being all ready for the meeting, and no horse to ride on, I made up my mind to foot it; for they tell me there is a nice young man to be taken into communion to-night. But now your good worship will lend me your arm, and we shall be there in a twinkling."

"That can hardly be," answered her friend. "I will not spare you my arm, Goody Cloyse, but here is my staff, if you will."

So saying, he threw it down at her feet, where, perhaps, it assumed life, being one of the rods which its owner had formerly lent to the Egyptian Magi. Of this fact, however, Goodman Brown could not take cognizance. He had cast up his eyes in astonishment, and looking down again, beheld neither Goody Cloyse nor the serpentine staff, but his fellow-traveller alone, who waited for him as calmly as if nothing had happened.

"That old woman taught me my catechism!" said the young man; and there was a world of meaning in this simple comment.

They continued to walk onward, while the elder traveller exhorted his companion to make good speed and persevere in the path, discoursing so aptly, that his arguments seemed rather to spring up in the bosom of his auditor, than to be suggested by himself. As they went he plucked a branch of maple, to serve for a walking-stick, and began to strip it of the twigs and little boughs, which were wet with evening dew. The moment his fingers touched them, they became strangely withered and dried up, as with a week's sunshine. Thus the pair proceeded, at a good free pace, until suddenly, in a gloomy hollow of the road, Goodman Brown sat himself down on the stump of a tree, and refused to go any farther.

"Friend," said he, stubbornly, "my mind is made up. Not another step will I budge on this errand. What if a wretched old woman do choose to go to the devil, when I thought she was going to Heaven! Is that any reason why I should quit my dear Faith, and go after her?"

"You will think better of this by and by," said his acquaintance, composedly. "Sit here and rest yourself a while; and when you feel like moving again, there is my staff to help you along."

Without more words, he threw his companion the maple stick, and was as speedily out of sight as if he had vanished into the deepening gloom. The young man sat a few moments by the roadside, applauding himself greatly, and thinking with how clear a conscience he should meet the minister, in his morning walk, nor shrink from the eye of good old Deacon Gookin. And what calm sleep would be his, that very night, which was to have been spent so wickedly, but purely and sweetly now, in the arms of Faith! Amidst these pleasant and praiseworthy meditations, Goodman Brown heard the tramp of horses along the road, and deemed it advisable to conceal himself within the verge of the forest, conscious of the guilty purpose that had brought him thither, though now so happily turned from it.

On came the hoof-tramps and the voices of the riders, two grave old voices, conversing soberly as they drew near. These mingled sounds appeared to pass along the road, within a few yards of the young man's hiding-place; but owing, doubtless, to the depth of the gloom, at that particular spot, neither the travellers nor their steeds were visible. Though their figures brushed the small boughs by the wayside, it could not be seen that they intercepted, even for a moment, the faint gleam from the strip of bright sky, athwart which they must have passed. Goodman Brown alternately crouched and stood on tiptoe, pulling aside the branches, and thrusting forth his head as far as he durst, without discerning so much as a shadow. It vexed him the more, because he could have sworn, were such a thing possible, that he recognized the voices of the minister and Deacon Gookin, jogging along quietly, as they were wont to do, when bound to some ordination or ecclesiastical council. While yet within hearing, one of the riders stopped to pluck a switch.

"Of the two, reverend Sir," said the voice like the deacon's, "I had rather miss an ordination dinner than to-night's meeting. They tell me that some of our community are to be here from Falmouth and beyond, and others from Connecticut and Rhode Island; besides several of the Indian powwows, who, after their fashion, know almost as much deviltry as the best of us. Moreover, there is a goodly young woman to be taken into communion."

"Mighty well, Deacon Gookin!" replied the solemn old tones of the minister. "Spur up, or we shall be late. Nothing can be done, you know, until I get on the ground."

The hoofs clattered again, and the voices, talking so strangely in the empty air, passed on through the forest, where no church had ever been gathered, nor solitary Christian prayed. Wither, then, could these holy men be journeying, so deep into the heathen wilderness? Young Goodman Brown caught hold of a tree, for support, being ready to sink down on the ground, faint and over-burthened with the heavy sickness of his heart. He looked up to the sky, doubting whether there really was a Heaven above him. Yet, there was the blue arch, and the stars brightening in it.

"With Heaven above, and Faith below, I will yet stand firm against the devil!" cried Goodman Brown.

While he still gazed upward, into the deep arch of the firmament, and had lifted his hands to pray, a cloud, though no wind was stirring, hurried across the zenith, and hid the brightening stars. The blue sky was still visible, except directly overhead, where this black mass of cloud was sweeping swiftly northward. Aloft in the air, as if from the depths of the cloud, came a confused and doubtful sound of voices. Once, the listener fancied that he could distinguish the accents of town's-people of his own, men and women, both pious and ungodly, many of whom he had met at the communion-table, and had seen others rioting at the tavern. The next moment, so indistinct were the sounds, he doubted whether he had heard aught but the murmur of the old forest, whispering without a wind. Then came a stronger swell of those familiar tones, heard daily in the sunshine, at Salem village, but never, until now, from a cloud at night. There was one voice, of a young woman, uttering lamentations, yet with an uncertain sorrow, and entreating for some favor, which, perhaps, it would grieve her to obtain. And all the unseen multitude, both saints and sinners, seemed to encourage her onward.

"Faith!" shouted Goodman Brown, in a voice of agony and desperation; and the echoes of the forest mocked him, crying—"Faith! Faith!" as if bewildered wretches were seeking her, all through the wilderness.

The cry of grief, rage, and terror was yet piercing the night, when the unhappy husband held his breath for a response. There was a scream, drowned immediately in a louder murmur of voices fading into far-off laughter, as the dark cloud swept away, leaving the clear and silent sky above Goodman Brown. But something fluttered lightly down through the air, and caught on the branch of a tree. The young man seized it and beheld a pink ribbon.

"My Faith is gone!" cried he, after one stupefied moment. "There is no good on earth, and sin is but a name. Come, devil! for to thee is this world given."

And maddened with despair, so that he laughed loud and long, did

Goodman Brown grasp his staff and set forth again, at such a rate, that he seemed to fly along the forest path, rather than to walk or run. The road grew wilder and drearier, and more faintly traced, and vanished at length, leaving him in the heart of the dark wilderness, still rushing onward, with the instinct that guides mortal man to evil. The whole forest was peopled with frightful sounds; the creaking of the trees, the howling of wild beasts, and the yell of Indians; while, sometimes, the wind tolled like a distant church bell, and sometimes gave a broad roar around the traveller, as if all Nature were laughing him to scorn. But he was himself the chief horror of the scene, and shrank not from its other horrors.

"Ha! ha! ha!" roared Goodman Brown, when the wind laughed at him. "Let us hear which will laugh loudest! Think not to frighten me with your deviltry! Come witch, come wizard, come Indian powwow, come devil himself! and here comes Goodman Brown. You may as well fear him as he fear you!"

In truth, all through the haunted forest, there could be nothing more frightful than the figure of Goodman Brown. On he flew, among the black pines, brandishing his staff with frenzied gestures, now giving vent to an inspiration of horrid blasphemy, and now shouting forth such laughter, as set all the echoes of the forest laughing like demons around him. The fiend in his own shape is less hideous, than when he rages in the breast of man. Thus sped the demoniac on his course, until, quivering among the trees, he saw a red light before him, as when the felled trunks and branches of a clearing have been set on fire, and throw up their lurid blaze against the sky, at the hour of midnight. He paused, in a lull of the tempest that had driven him onward, and heard the swell of what seemed a hymn, rolling solemnly from a distance, with the weight of many voices. He knew the tune. It was a familiar one in the choir of the village meeting-house. The verse died heavily away, and was lengthened by a chorus, not of human voices, but of all the sounds of the benighted wilderness, pealing in awful harmony together. Goodman Brown cried out; and his cry was lost to his own ear, by its unison with the cry of the desert.

In the interval of silence, he stole forward, until the light glared full upon his eyes. At one extremity of an open space, hemmed in by the dark wall of the forest, arose a rock, bearing some rude, natural resemblance either to an altar or a pulpit, and surrounded by four blazing pines, their tops aflame, their stems untouched, like candles at an evening meeting. The mass of foliage, that had overgrown the summit of the rock, was all on fire, blazing high into the night, and fitfully illuminating the whole field. Each pendent twig and leafy festoon was in a blaze. As the red light arose and fell, a numerous congregation alternately shone forth, then disappeared in shadow, and again grew, as it were, out of the darkness, peopling the heart of the solitary woods at once.

"A grave and dark-clad company!" quoth Goodman Brown.

In truth, they were such. Among them, quivering to-and-fro, between gloom and splendor, appeared faces that would be seen, next day, at the council-board of the province, and others which, Sabbath after Sabbath, looked devoutly heavenward, and benignantly over the crowded pews, from the holiest pulpits in the land. Some affirm that the lady of the governor was there. At least, there were high dames well known to her, and wives of honored husbands, and widows a great multitude, and ancient maidens, all of excellent repute, and fair young girls, who trembled lest their mothers should espy them. Either the sudden gleams of light, flashing over the obscure field, bedazzled Goodman Brown, or he recognized a score of the church members of Salem village, famous for their especial sanctity. Good old Deacon Gookin had arrived, and waited at the skirts of that venerable saint, his reverend pastor. But, irreverently consorting with these grave, reputable, and pious people, these elders of the church, these chaste dames and dewy virgins, there were men of dissolute lives and women of spotted fame, wretches given over to all mean and filthy vice, and suspected even of horrid crimes. It was strange to see, that the good shrank not from the wicked, nor were the sinners abashed by the saints. Scattered, also, among their pale-faced enemies, were the Indian priests, or powwows, who had often scared their native forest with more hideous incantations than any known to English witchcraft.

"But, where is Faith?" thought Goodman Brown; and, as hope came into his heart, he trembled.

Another verse of the hymn arose, a slow and mournful strain, such as the pious love, but joined to words which expressed all that our nature can conceive of sin, and darkly hinted at far more. Unfathomable to mere mortals is the lore of fiends. Verse after verse was sung, and still the chorus of the desert swelled between, like the deepest tone of a mighty organ. And, with the final peal of that dreadful anthem, there came a sound, as if the roaring wind, the rushing streams, the howling beasts, and every other voice of the unconverted wilderness were mingling and according with the voice of guilty man, in homage to the prince of all. The four blazing pines threw up a loftier flame, and obscurely discovered shapes and visages of horror on the smoke-wreaths, above the impious assembly. At the same moment, the fire on the rock shot redly forth, and formed a glowing arch above its base, where now appeared a figure. With reverence be it spoken, the apparition bore no slight similitude, both in garb and manner, to some grave divine of the New England churches.

"Bring forth the converts!" cried a voice, that echoed through the field and rolled into the forest.

At the word, Goodman Brown stepped forth from the shadow of the trees, and approached the congregation, with whom he felt a loathful brotherhood, by the sympathy of all that was wicked in his heart. He could have well-nigh sworn, that the shape of his own dead father beckoned him to advance, looking downward from a smoke-wreath, while a woman, with dim features of despair, threw out her hand to warn him back. Was it his mother? But he had no power to retreat one step, nor to resist, even in thought, when the minister and good old Deacon Gookin seized his arms, and led him to the blazing rock. Thither came also the slender form of a veiled female, led between Goody Cloyse, that pious teacher of the catechism, and Martha Carrier, who had received the devil's promise to be queen of hell. A rampant hag was she! And there stood the proselytes, beneath the canopy of fire.

"Welcome, my children," said the dark figure, "to the communion of your race! Ye have found, thus young, your nature and your destiny. My children, look behind you!"

They turned; and flashing forth, as it were, in a sheet of flame, the fiend-worshippers were seen; the smile of welcome gleamed darkly on every visage.

"There," resumed the sable form, "are all whom ye have reverenced from youth. Ye deemed them holier than yourselves, and shrank from your own sin, contrasting it with their lives of righteousness and prayerful aspirations heavenward. Yet, here are they all, in my worshipping assembly! This night it shall be granted you to know their secret deeds; how hoary-bearded elders of the church have whispered wanton words to the young maids of their households; how many a woman, eager for widow's weeds, has given her husband a drink at bedtime, and let him sleep his last sleep in her bosom; how beardless youths have made haste to inherit their father's wealth; and how fair damsels—blush not, sweet ones!—have dug little graves in the garden, and bidden me, the sole guest, to an infant's funeral. By the sympathy of your human hearts for sin, ye shall scent out all the places—whether in church, bed-chamber, street, field, or forest—where crime has been committed, and shall exult to behold the whole earth one stain of guilt, one mighty blood-spot. Far more than this! It shall be yours to penetrate, in every bosom, the deep mystery of sin, the fountain of all wicked arts, and which inexhaustibly supplies more evil impulses than human power—than my power, at its utmost!—can make manifest in deeds. And now, my children, look upon each other."

They did so; and, by the blaze of the hell-kindled torches, the wretched man beheld his Faith, and the wife her husband, trembling before that unhallowed altar.

"Lo! there ye stand, my children," said the figure, in a deep and solemn tone, almost sad, with its despairing awfulness, as if his once angelic nature could yet mourn for our miserable race. "Depending upon one another's hearts, ye had still hoped that virtue were not all a dream! Now are ye undeceived!—Evil is the nature of mankind. Evil must be your only happiness. Welcome, again, my children, to the communion of your race!"

"Welcome!" repeated the fiend-worshippers, in one cry of despair and triumph.

And there they stood, the only pair, as it seemed, who were yet hesitating on the verge of wickedness, in this dark world. A basin was hollowed, naturally, in the rock. Did it contain water, reddened by the lurid light? or was it blood? or, perchance, a liquid flame? Herein did the Shape of Evil dip his hand, and prepare to lay the mark of baptism upon their foreheads, that they might be partakers of the mystery of sin, more conscious of the secret guilt of others, both in deed and thought, than they could now be of their own. The husband cast one look at his pale wife, and Faith at him. What polluted wretches would the next glance show them to each other, shuddering alike at what they disclosed and what they saw!

"Faith! Faith!" cried the husband. "Look up to Heaven, and resist the Wicked One!"

Whether Faith obeyed, he knew not. Hardly had he spoken, when he found himself amid calm night and solitude, listening to a roar of the wind, which died heavily away through the forest. He staggered against the rock, and felt it chill and damp, while a hanging twig, that had been all on fire, besprinkled his cheek with the coldest dew.

The next morning, young Goodman Brown came slowly into the street of Salem village staring around him like a bewildered man. The good old minister was taking a walk along the grave-yard, to get an appetite for breakfast and meditate his sermon, and bestowed a blessing, as he passed, on Goodman Brown. He shrank from the venerable saint, as if to avoid an anathema. Old Deacon Gookin was at domestic worship, and the holy words of his prayer were heard through the open window. "What God doth the wizard pray to?" quoth Goodman Brown. Goody Cloyse, that excellent old Christian, stood in the early sunshine, at her own lattice, catechising a little girl, who had brought her a pint of morning's milk. Goodman Brown snatched away the child, as from the grasp of the fiend himself. Turning the corner by the meetinghouse, he spied the head of Faith, with the pink ribbons, gazing anxiously forth, and bursting into such joy at sight of him that she skipt along the street, and almost kissed her husband before the whole village. But Goodman Brown looked sternly and sadly into her face, and passed on without a greeting.

Had Goodman Brown fallen asleep in the forest, and only dreamed a wild dream of a witch-meeting?

Be it so, if you will. But, alas! it was a dream of evil omen for young Goodman Brown. A stern, a sad, a darkly meditative, a distrustful, if not a desperate man did he become, from the night of that fearful dream. On the Sabbath day, when the congregation were singing a holy psalm, he could not listen, because an anthem of sin rushed loudly upon his ear, and drowned all the blessed strain. When the minister spoke from the pulpit, with power and fervid eloquence, and with his hand on the open Bible, of the sacred truths of our religion, and of saint-like lives and triumphant deaths, and of future bliss or misery unutterable, then did Goodman Brown turn pale, dreading lest the roof should thunder down upon the gray blasphemer and his hearers. Often, awaking suddenly at midnight, he shrank from the bosom of Faith, and at morning or eventide, when the family knelt down at prayer, he scowled, and muttered to himself, and gazed sternly at his wife, and turned away. And when he had lived long, and was borne to his grave, a hoary corpse, followed by Faith, an aged woman, and children and grandchildren, a goodly procession, besides neighbors not a few, they carved no hopeful verse upon his tombstone; for his dying hour was gloom.

Guy de Maupassant (1850–1893)*

The Necklace

She was one of those pretty and charming women, born, as if by an error of destiny, into a family of clerks and copyists. She had no dowry, no prospects, no way of getting known, courted, loved, married by a rich and distinguished man. She finally settled for a marriage with a minor clerk in the Ministry of Education.

She was a simple person, without the money to dress well, but she was as unhappy as if she had gone through bankruptcy, for women have neither rank nor race. In place of high birth or important family connections, they can rely only on their beauty, their grace, and their charm. Their inborn finesse, their elegant taste, their engaging personalities, which are their only power, make working-class women the equals of the grandest duchesses.

She suffered constantly, feeling herself destined for all delicacies and luxuries. She suffered because of her grim apartment with its drab walls, threadbare furniture, ugly curtains. All such things, which most other women in her situation would not even have noticed, tortured her and filled her with despair. The sight of the young country girl who did her simple housework awakened in her only a sense of desolation and lost hopes. She daydreamed of large, silent anterooms, decorated with oriental tapestries and lighted by high bronze floor lamps, with two elegant valets in short culottes dozing in large armchairs under the effects of forced-air heaters. She visualized large drawing rooms draped in the most expensive silks, with fine end tables on which were placed knickknacks of inestimable value. She dreamed of the perfume of dainty private rooms, which were designed only for intimate tête-à-têtes with the closest friends, who because of their achievements and fame would make her the envy of all other women.

When she sat down to dinner at her round little table covered with a cloth that had not been washed for three days, in front of her husband who opened the kettle while declaring ecstatically, "Oh boy, beef stew, my favorite," she dreamed of expensive banquets with shining placesettings, and wall hangings depicting ancient heroes and exotic birds in an en-

*translated by Edgar V. Roberts

167

chanted forest. She imagined a gourmet-prepared main course carried on the most exquisite trays and served on the most beautiful dishes, with whispered gallantries which she would hear with a sphinxlike smile as she dined on the pink meat of a trout or the delicate wing of a quail.

She had no decent dresses, no jewels, nothing. And she loved nothing but these; she believed herself born only for these. She burned with the desire to please, to be envied, to be attractive and sought after.

She had a rich friend, a comrade from convent days, whom she did not want to see anymore because she suffered so much when she returned home. She would weep for the entire day afterward with sorrow, regret, despair, and misery.

Well, one evening, her husband came home glowing and carrying a large envelope.

"Here," he said, "this is something for you."

She quickly tore open the envelope and took out a card engraved with these words:

> The Chancellor of Education and Mrs. George Ramponneau request that Mr. and Mrs. Loisel do them the honor of coming to dinner at the Ministry of Education on the evening of January 8.

Instead of being delighted, as her husband had hoped, she threw the invitation spitefully on the table while muttering:

"What do you expect me to do with this?"

"But Honey, I thought you'd be glad. You never get to go out, and this is a special occasion! I had a lot of trouble getting the invitation. Everyone wants one; the demand is high and not many clerks get invited. Everyone important will be there."

She looked at him angrily and stated impatiently:

"What do you want me to wear to go there?"

He had not thought of that. He stammered:

"But your theatre dress. That seems nice to me . . . "

He stopped, amazed and bewildered, as his wife began to cry. Large tears fell slowly from the corners of her eyes to her mouth. He said falteringly:

"What's wrong? What's wrong?"

But with a strong effort she had recovered, and she answered calmly as she wiped her damp cheeks:

"Nothing, except that I have nothing to wear and therefore can't go to the party. Give your invitation to someone else at the office whose wife will have nicer clothes than mine."

Distressed, he responded:

"Well, okay, Mathilde. How much would a nice new dress cost, something you could use at other times, but not anything fancy?"

She thought for a few moments, adding things up and thinking also of an amount that she could ask without getting an immediate refusal and a frightened outcry from the frugal clerk.

Finally she responded tentatively:

"I don't know exactly, but it seems to me that I could get by on four hundred francs."

He blanched slightly at this, because he had set aside just that amount to buy a shotgun and go with a few friends to Nanterre on Sundays the next summer to shoot larks.

However, he said:

"Okay, you've got four hundred francs, but make it a pretty dress."

As the day of the party drew near, Mrs. Loisel seemed sad, uneasy, anxious, even though her dress was all ready. One evening her husband said to her:

"What's up? You've been acting strangely for several days."

She answered:

"It's awful, but I don't have any jewels, not a single stone, nothing for matching jewelry. I'm going to look impoverished. I'd almost rather not go to the party."

He responded:

"You can wear a corsage of cut flowers. This year that's really the in thing. For no more than ten francs you can get two or three gorgeous roses."

She was not convinced.

"No . . . there's nothing more humiliating than to look ragged in the middle of rich women."

But her husband exclaimed:

"God, but you're silly! Go to your friend Mrs. Forrestier, and ask her to lend you some jewelry. You know her well enough to do that."

She uttered a cry of joy:

"That's right. I hadn't thought of that."

The next day she went to her friend's house and described her problem.

Mrs. Forrestier went to her glass-plated wardrobe, took out a large jewel box, opened it, and said to Mrs. Loisel:

"Choose, my dear."

She saw bracelets, then a pearl necklace, then a Venetian cross of finely worked gold and gems. She tried on the jewelry in front of a mirror, and hesitated, unable to make up her mind about which ones to give back. She kept asking:

"Do you have anything else?"

"Certainly. Look to your heart's content. I don't know what will please you most."

Suddenly she found, in a black satin box, a superb diamond necklace, and her heart throbbed with desire for it. Her hands shook as she took it up. She fastened it around her neck, watched it gleam at her throat, and looked at herself ecstatically.

Then she asked, haltingly and anxiously:

"Could you lend me this, nothing but this?"

"Why yes, certainly."

She jumped up, hugged her friend joyfully, then hurried away with her treasure.

The day of the party came. Mrs. Loisel was a success. She was prettier than anyone else, stylish, graceful, smiling, and wild with joy. All the men saw her, asked her name, and sought to be introduced. All the important administrators stood in line to waltz with her. The Chancellor watched her.

She danced joyfully, passionately, intoxicated with pleasure, thinking of nothing but the moment, in the triumph of her beauty, in the glory of her success, in a cloud-nine of happiness made up of all the admiration, of all the aroused desire, of this victory so complete and so sweet to the heart of any woman.

She did not leave until four o'clock in the morning. Her husband, since midnight, had been sleeping in a little empty room with three other men whose wives had also been enjoying themselves.

He threw over her shoulders the shawl that he had brought for the trip home, modest clothing from everyday life, the poverty of which contrasted sharply with the elegance of the party dress. She felt it and hurried away to avoid being noticed by the other women who luxuriated in rich furs.

Loisel tried to hold her back:

"Wait a while. You'll catch cold outdoors. I'll call a cab."

But she paid no attention and hurried down the stairs. When they reached the street they found no carriages. They began to look for one, shouting at cabmen passing by at a distance.

They walked toward the Seine, desperate, shivering. Finally, on a quay, they found one of those old night-going buggies that are seen in Paris only after dark, as if they were ashamed of their wretched appearance in day-light.

It took them to their door, on the Street of Martyrs, and they sadly climbed the stairs to their flat. For her, it was finished. As for him, he could think only that he had to begin work at the Ministry of Education at ten o'clock.

She took the shawl off her shoulders, in front of the mirror, to see herself once more in her glory. But suddenly she cried out. The necklace was no longer around her neck!

Her husband, already half undressed, asked:

"What's wrong with you?"

She turned toward him frantically:

"I . . . I . . . I no longer have Mrs. Forrestier's necklace."

He stood up, bewildered:

"What! . . . How! . . . It's not possible!"

And they looked in the folds of the dress, in the creases of the shawl, in the pockets, everywhere. They found nothing.

He asked:

"You're sure you still had it when you left the party?"

"Yes. I checked it in the vestibule of the Ministry."

"But if you had lost it in the street, we would have heard it fall. It must be in the cab."

"Yes, probably. Did you notice the number?"

"No. Did you see it?"

"No."

Overwhelmed, they looked at each other. Finally, Loisel got dressed again:

"I'm going out to retrace all our steps," he said, "to see if I can find the necklace that way."

And he went out. She stayed in her evening dress, without the energy to get ready for bed, prostrated in a chair, drained of strength and thought.

Her husband came back at about seven o'clock. He had found nothing.

He went to Police Headquarters and to the newspapers to announce a reward. He went to the small cab companies, and finally he followed up even the slightest hopeful lead.

She waited the entire day, in the same enervated state, in the face of this frightful disaster.

Loisel came back in the evening, his face pale and haggard. He had found nothing.

"You'll have to write to your friend," he said, "that you broke a fastening on her necklace and that you will have it fixed. That will give us time to look around."

She wrote as he dictated.

At the end of a week they had lost all hope.

And Loisel, seemingly five years older, declared:

"We'll have to see about replacing the jewels."

The next day, they took the case which had contained the necklace, and went to the jeweler whose name was inside. He looked at his books:

"I wasn't the one, Madam, who sold the necklace. I only made the case."

Then they went from jeweler to jeweler, searching for a necklace like the other one, racking their memories, both of them sick with worry and anguish.

In a shop in the Palais-Royal, they found a string of diamonds that seemed to them exactly like the one they were seeking. It was priced at forty thousand francs. They could buy it for thirty-six thousand.

They got the jeweler to promise not to sell it for three days. And they made an agreement that he would buy it back for thirty-four thousand francs if the original was recovered before the end of February.

Loisel had saved eighteen thousand francs that his father had left him. He would have to borrow the rest.

He borrowed asking a thousand francs from one, five hundred from another, five louis[1] here, three louis there. He made promissory notes, undertook ruinous obligations, did business with loan sharks and the whole tribe of finance companies. He compromised himself for the remainder of his days, risked his signature without knowing whether he would be able to honor it, and, terrified by anguish over the future, by the black misery that was about to descend on him, by the prospect of all kinds of physical deprivations and moral tortures, he went to get the new necklace, and put down thirty-six thousand francs on the jeweler's counter.

Mrs. Loisel took the necklace back to Mrs. Forrestier, who said with an offended tone:

"You should have brought it back sooner, because I might have needed it."

She did not open the case, as her friend feared she might. If she had noticed the substitution, what would she have thought? What would she have said? Would she not have taken her for a thief?

Mrs. Loisel soon discovered the horrible life of the needy. She did her share, however, completely, heroically. That horrifying debt had to be paid. She would pay. They dismissed the maid; they changed their address; they rented an attic flat.

She learned to do heavy housework, dirty kitchen jobs. She washed the dishes, wearing away her manicured fingernails on greasy pots and encrusted baking dishes. She handwashed dirty linen, shirts, and dish towels that she hung out on the line to dry. Each morning, she took the garbage down to the street, and she carried up water, stopping at each floor to catch her breath. And, dressed in cheap house dresses, she went to the fruit dealer, the grocer, the butcher, with her basket under her arms, haggling, insulting, defending her measly cash penny by penny.

They had to make installment payments every month, and, to buy more time, to refinance loans.

The husband worked evenings to make fair copies of tradesmen's accounts, and late into the night he made copies at five cents a page.

And this life lasted ten years.

At the end of ten years, they had paid back everything—everything—including the extra charges imposed by loan sharks and the accumulation of compound interest.

---

[1]A louis was a twenty-franc coin.

Mrs. Loisel seemed old now. She had become the strong, hard, and rude woman of poor households. Her hair unkempt, with uneven skirts and rough, red hands, she spoke loudly, washed floors with large buckets of water. But sometimes, when her husband was at work, she sat down near the window, and she dreamed of that evening so long ago, of that party, where she had been so beautiful and so admired.

What would life have been like if she had not lost that necklace? Who knows? Who knows? Life is so peculiar, so uncertain. How little a thing it takes to destroy you or to save you!

Well, one Sunday, as she had gone on a stroll along the Champs-Elysées to relax from the cares of the week, she suddenly noticed a woman walking with a child. It was Mrs. Forrestier, always youthful, always beautiful, always attractive.

Mrs. Loisel felt moved. Would she speak to her? Yes, certainly. And now that she had paid, she could tell all. Why not?

She walked closer.

"Hello, Jeanne."

The other did not recognize her at all, being astonished to be addressed so intimately by this working woman. She stammered:

"But . . . Madam! . . . I don't know. . . . You must have made a mistake."

"No. I'm Mathilde Loisel."

Her friend cried out:

"Oh! . . . My poor Mathilde, you've changed so much."

"Yes. I've had some hard times since I saw you last; in fact, miseries . . . and all this because of you! . . . "

"Of me . . . how so?"

"You remember the diamond necklace that you lent me to go to the party at the Ministry of Education?"

"Yes. What then?"

"Well, I lost it."

"How, since you gave it back to me?"

"I brought back another exactly like it. And for ten years we've been paying for it. You understand that this wasn't easy for us, who have nothing. . . . Finally it's over, and I'm mighty damned glad."

Mrs. Forrestier stopped her.

"You say that you bought a diamond necklace to replace mine?"

"Yes. You didn't notice it, eh? They were exactly like yours."

And she smiled with proud and childish joy.

Mrs. Forrestier, deeply moved, took both her hands.

"Oh, my poor Mathilde! But mine was false. At the most, it was worth five hundred francs! . . . "

Frank O'Connor (1903–1966)

First Confession

ALL the trouble began when my grandfather died and my grandmother—
my father's mother—came to live with us. Relations in the one house are
a strain at the best of times, but, to make matters worse, my grandmother
was a real old countrywoman and quite unsuited to the life in town. She
had a fat, wrinkled old face, and, to Mother's great indignation, went
round the house in bare feet—the boots had her crippled, she said. For
dinner she had a jug of porter and a pot of potatoes with—sometimes—a
bit of salt fish, and she poured out the potatoes on the table and ate them
slowly, with great relish, using her fingers by way of a fork.

Now, girls are supposed to be fastidious, but I was the one who suffered
most from this. Nora, my sister, just sucked up to the old woman for the
penny she got every Friday out of the old-age pension, a thing I could not
do. I was too honest, that was my trouble; and when I was playing with
Bill Connell, the sergeant-major's son, and saw my grandmother steering
up the path with the jug of porter sticking out from beneath her shawl I
was mortified. I made excuses not to let him come into the house, because
I could never be sure what she would be up to when we went in.

When Mother was at work and my grandmother made the dinner I
wouldn't touch it. Nora once tried to make me, but I hid under the table
from her and took the bread-knife with me for protection. Nora let on to
be very indignant (she wasn't, of course, but she knew Mother saw through
her, so she sided with Gran) and came after me. I lashed out at her with
the bread-knife, and after that she left me alone. I stayed there till Mother
came in from work and made my dinner, but when Father came in later
Nora said in a shocked voice: "Oh, Dadda, do you know what Jackie did
at dinnertime?" Then, of course, it all came out; Father gave me a flaking;
Mother interfered, and for days after that he didn't speak to me and Mother
barely spoke to Nora. And all because of that old woman! God knows, I
was heart-scalded.

Then, to crown my misfortunes, I had to make my first confession and
communion. It was an old woman called Ryan who prepared us for these.

She was about the one age with Gran; she was well-to-do, lived in a big house on Montenotte, wore a black cloak and bonnet, and came every day to school at three o'clock when we should have been going home, and talked to us of hell. She may have mentioned the other place as well, but that could only have been by accident, for hell had the first place in her heart.

She lit a candle, took out a new half-crown, and offered it to the first boy who would hold one finger—only one finger!—in the flame for five minutes by the school clock. Being always very ambitious I was tempted to volunteer, but I thought it might look greedy. Then she asked were we afraid of holding one finger—only one finger!—in a little candle flame for five minutes and not afraid of burning all over in roasting hot furnaces for all eternity. "All eternity! Just think of that! A whole lifetime goes by and it's nothing, not even a drop in the ocean of your sufferings." The woman was really interesting about hell, but my attention was all fixed on the half-crown. At the end of the lesson she put it back in her purse. It was a great disappointment; a religious woman like that, you wouldn't think she'd bother about a thing like a half-crown.

Another day she said she knew a priest who woke one night to find a fellow he didn't recognize leaning over the end of his bed. The priest was a bit frightened—naturally enough—but he asked the fellow what he wanted, and the fellow said in a deep, husky voice that he wanted to go to confession. The priest said it was an awkward time and wouldn't it do in the morning, but the fellow said that last time he went to confession, there was one sin he kept back, being ashamed to mention it, and now it was always on his mind. Then the priest knew it was a bad case, because the fellow was after making a bad confession and committing a mortal sin. He got up to dress, and just then the cock crew in the yard outside, and— lo and behold!—when the priest looked round there was no sign of the fellow, only a smell of burning timber, and when the priest looked at his bed didn't he see the print of two hands burned in it? That was because the fellow had made a bad confession. This story made a shocking impression on me.

But the worst of all was when she showed us how to examine our conscience. Did we take the name of the Lord, our God, in vain? Did we honour our father and our mother? (I asked her did this include grandmothers and she said it did.) Did we love our neighbours as ourselves? Did we covet our neighbour's goods? (I thought of the way I felt about the penny that Nora got every Friday.) I decided that, between one thing and another, I must have broken the whole ten commandments, all on account of that old woman, and so far as I could see, so long as she remained in the house I had no hope of ever doing anything else.

I was scared to death of confession. The day the whole class went I let on to have a toothache, hoping my absence wouldn't be noticed; but at three o'clock, just as I was feeling safe, along comes a chap with a message from Mrs. Ryan that I was to go to confession myself on Saturday and be at the chapel for communion with the rest. To make it worse, Mother couldn't come with me and sent Nora instead.

Now, that girl had ways of tormenting me that Mother never knew of. She held my hand as we went down the hill, smiling sadly and saying how sorry she was for me, as if she were bringing me to the hospital for an operation.

"Oh, God help us!" she moaned. "Isn't it a terrible pity you weren't a good boy? Oh, Jackie, my heart bleeds for you! How will you ever think of all your sins? Don't forget you have to tell him about the time you kicked Gran on the shin."

"Lemme go!" I said, trying to drag myself free of her. "I don't want to go to confession at all."

"But sure, you'll have to go to confession, Jackie," she replied in the same regretful tone. "Sure, if you didn't, the parish priest would be up to the house, looking for you. 'Tisn't, God knows, that I'm not sorry for you. Do you remember the time you tried to kill me with the bread-knife under the table? And the language you used to me? I don't know what he'll do with you at all, Jackie. He might have to send you up to the bishop."

I remember thinking bitterly that she didn't know the half of what I had to tell—if I told it. I knew I couldn't tell it, and understood perfectly why the fellow in Mrs. Ryan's story made a bad confession; it seemed to me a great shame that people wouldn't stop criticizing him. I remember that steep hill down to the church, and the sunlit hillsides beyond the valley of the river, which I saw in the gaps between the houses like Adam's last glimpse of Paradise.

Then, when she had manoeuvred me down the long flight of steps to the chapel yard, Nora suddenly changed her tone. She became the raging malicious devil she really was.

"There you are!" she said with a yelp of triumph, hurling me through the church door. "And I hope he'll give you the penitential psalms, you dirty little caffler."

I knew then I was lost, given up to eternal justice. The door with the coloured-glass panels swung shut behind me, the sunlight went out and gave place to deep shadow, and the wind whistled outside so that the silence within seemed to crackle like ice under my feet. Nora sat in front of me by the confession box. There were a couple of old woman ahead of her, and then a miserable-looking poor devil came and wedged me in at the other side, so that I couldn't escape even if I had the courage. He joined his hands and rolled his eyes in the direction of the roof, muttering aspirations in an anguished tone, and I wondered had he a grandmother too. Only a grandmother could account for a fellow behaving in that heartbroken way, but he was better off than I, for he at least could go and confess his sins; while I would make a bad confession and then die in the night and be continually coming back and burning people's furniture.

Nora's turn came, and I heard the sound of something slamming, and then her voice as if butter wouldn't melt in her mouth, and then another slam, and out she came. God, the hypocrisy of women! Her eyes were lowered, her head was bowed, and her hands were joined very low down on her stomach, and she walked up the aisle to the side altar looking like a saint. You never saw such an exhibition of devotion; and I remembered the devilish malice with which she had tormented me all the way from our door, and wondered were all religious people like that, really. It was my turn now. With the fear of damnation in my soul I went in, and the confessional door closed of itself behind me.

It was pitch-dark and I couldn't see priest or anything else. Then I really began to be frightened. In the darkness it was a matter between God and me, and He had all the odds. He knew what my intentions were before I even started; I had no chance. All I had ever been told about confession got mixed up in my mind, and I knelt to one wall and said: "Bless me, father, for I have sinned; this is my first confession." I waited for a few minutes, but nothing happened, so I tried it on the other wall. Nothing happened there either. He had me spotted all right.

It must have been then that I noticed the shelf at about one height with my head. It was really a place for grown-up people to rest their elbows, but in my distracted state I thought it was probably the place you were supposed to kneel. Of course, it was on the high side and not very deep, but I was always good at climbing and managed to get up all right. Staying up was the trouble. There was room only for my knees, and nothing you could get a grip on but a sort of wooden moulding a bit above it. I held on to the moulding and repeated the words a little louder, and this time something happened all right. A slide was slammed back; a little light entered the box, and a man's voice said: "Who's there?"

" 'Tis me, father," I said for fear he mightn't see me and go away again. I couldn't see him at all. The place the voice came from was under the moulding, about level with my knees, so I took a good grip of the moulding and swung myself down till I saw the astonished face of a young priest looking up at me. He had to put his head on one side to see me, and I had to put mine on one side to see him, so we were more or less talking to one another upside-down. It struck me as a queer way of hearing confessions, but I didn't feel it my place to criticize.

"Bless me, father, for I have sinned; this is my first confession," I rattled off all in one breath, and swung myself down the least shade more to make it easier for him.

"What are you doing up there?" he shouted in an angry voice, and the strain the politeness was putting on my hold of the moulding, and the shock of being addressed in such an uncivil tone, were too much for me.

I lost my grip, tumbled, and hit the door an unmerciful wallop before I found myself flat on my back in the middle of the aisle. The people who had been waiting stood up with their mouths open. The priest opened the door of the middle box and came out, pushing his biretta back from his forehead; he looked something terrible. Then Nora came scampering down the aisle.

"Oh, you dirty little caffler!" she said. "I might have known you'd do it. I might have known you'd disgrace me. I can't leave you out of my sight for one minute."

Before I could even get to my feet to defend myself she bent down and gave me a clip across the ear. This reminded me that I was so stunned I had even forgotten to cry, so that people might think I wasn't hurt at all, when in fact I was probably maimed for life. I gave a roar out of me.

"What's all this about?" the priest hissed, getting angrier than ever and pushing Nora off me. "How dare you hit the child like that, you little vixen?"

"But I can't do my penance with him, father," Nora cried, cocking an outraged eye up at him.

"Well, go and do it, or I'll give you some more to do," he said, giving me a hand up. "Was it coming to confession you were, my poor man?" he asked me.

" 'Twas, father," said I with a sob.

"Oh," he said respectfully, "a big hefty fellow like you must have terrible sins. Is this your first?"

" 'Tis, father," said I.

"Worse and worse," he said gloomily. "The crimes of a lifetime. I don't know will I get rid of you at all today. You'd better wait now till I'm finished with these old ones. You can see by the looks of them they haven't much to tell."

"I will, father," I said with something approaching joy.

The relief of it was really enormous. Nora stuck out her tongue at me from behind his back, but I couldn't even be bothered retorting. I knew from the very moment that man opened his mouth that he was intelligent above the ordinary. When I had time to think, I saw how right I was. It only stood to reason that a fellow confessing after seven years would have more to tell than people that went every week. The crimes of a lifetime, exactly as he said. It was only what he expected, and the rest was the cackle of old women and girls with their talk of hell, the bishop, and the penitential psalms. That was all they knew. I started to make my examination of conscience, and barring the one bad business of my grandmother it didn't seem so bad.

The next time, the priest steered me into the confession box himself and left the shutter back the way I could see him get in and sit down at the further side of the grille from me.

"Well, now," he said, "what do they call you?"

"Jackie, father," said I.

"And what's a-trouble to you, Jackie?"

"Father," I said, feeling I might as well get it over while I had him in good humour, "I had it all arranged to kill my grandmother."

He seemed a bit shaken by that, all right, because he said nothing for quite a while.

"My goodness," he said at last, "that'd be a shocking thing to do. What put that into your head?"

"Father," I said, feeling very sorry for myself, "she's an awful woman."

"Is she?" he asked. "What way is she awful?"

"She takes porter, father," I said, knowing well from the way Mother talked of it that this was a mortal sin, and hoping it would make the priest take a more favourable view of my case.

"Oh, my!" he said, and I could see he was impressed.

"And snuff, father," said I.

"That's a bad case, sure enough, Jackie," he said.

"And she goes round in her bare feet, father," I went on in a rush of self-pity, "and she know I don't like her, and she gives pennies to Nora and none to me, and my da sides with her and flakes me, and one night I was so heart-scalded I made up my mind I'd have to kill her."

"And what would you do with the body?" he asked with great interest.

"I was thinking I could chop that up and carry it away in a barrow I have," I said.

"Begor, Jackie," he said, "do you know you're a terrible child?"

"I know, father," I said, for I was just thinking the same thing myself. "I tried to kill Nora too with a bread-knife under the table, only I missed her."

"Is that the little girl that was beating you just now?" he asked.

" 'Tis, father."

"Someone will go for her with a bread-knife one day, and he won't miss her," he said rather cryptically. "You must have great courage. Between ourselves, there's a lot of people I'd like to do the same to but I'd never have the nerve. Hanging is an awful death."

"Is it, father?" I asked with the deepest interest—I was always very keen on hanging. "Did you ever see a fellow hanged?"

"Dozens of them," he said solemnly. "And they all died roaring."

"Jay!" I said.

"Oh, a horrible death!" he said with great satisfaction. "Lots of the fellows I saw killed their grandmothers too, but they all said 'twas never worth it."

He had me there for a full ten minutes talking, and then walked out the chapel yard with me. I was genuinely sorry to part with him, because he was the most entertaining character I'd ever met in the religious line.

Outside, after the shadow of the church, the sunlight was like the roaring of waves on a beach; it dazzled me; and when the frozen silence melted and I heard the screech of trams on the road my heart soared. I knew now I wouldn't die in the night and come back, leaving marks on my mother's furniture. It would be a great worry to her, and the poor soul had enough.

Nora was sitting on the railing, waiting for me, and she put on a very sour puss when she saw the priest with me. She was mad jealous because a priest had never come out of the church with her.

"Well," she asked coldly, after he left me, "what did he give you?"

"Three Hail Marys," I said.

"Three Hail Marys," she repeated incredulously. "You mustn't have told him anything."

"I told him everything," I said confidently.

"About Gran and all?"

"About Gran and all."

(All she wanted was to be able to go home and say I'd made a bad confession.)

"Did you tell him you went for me with the bread-knife?" she asked with a frown.

"I did to be sure."

"And he only gave you three Hail Marys?"

"That's all."

She slowly got down from the railing with a baffled air. Clearly, this was beyond her. As we mounted the steps back to the main road she looked at me suspiciously.

"What are you sucking?" she asked.

"Bullseyes."

"Was it the priest gave them to you?"

" 'Twas."

"Lord God," she wailed bitterly, "some people have all the luck! 'Tis no advantage to anybody trying to be good. I might just as well be a sinner like you."

Eudora Welty (1909–   )

A Worn Path

It was December—a bright frozen day in the early morning. Far out in the country there was an old Negro woman with her head tied in a red rag, coming along a path through the pinewoods. Her name was Phoenix Jackson. She was very old and small and she walked slowly in the dark pine shadows, moving a little from side to side in her steps, with the balanced heaviness and lightness of a pendulum in a grandfather clock. She carried a thin, small cane made from an umbrella, and with this she kept tapping the frozen earth in front of her. This made a grave and persistent noise in the still air, that seemed meditative like the chirping of a solitary little bird.

She wore a dark striped dress reaching down to her shoe tops, and an equally long apron of bleached sugar sacks, with a full pocket: all neat and tidy, but every time she took a step she might have fallen over her shoe-laces, which dragged from her unlaced shoes. She looked straight ahead. Her eyes were blue with age. Her skin had a pattern all its own of numberless branching wrinkles and as though a whole little tree stood in the middle of her forehead, but a golden color ran underneath, and the two knobs of her cheeks were illumined by a yellow burning under the dark. Under the red rag her hair came down on her neck in the frailest of ringlets, still black, and with an odor like copper.

Now and then there was a quivering in the thicket. Old Phoenix said, "Out of my way, all you foxes, owls, beetles, jack rabbits, coons and wild animals! . . . Keep out from under these feet, little bob-whites. . . . Keep the big wild hogs out of my path. Don't let none of those come running my direction. I got a long way." Under her small black-freckled hand her cane, limber as a buggy whip, would switch at the brush as if to rouse up any hiding things.

On she went. The woods were deep and still. The sun made the pine needles almost too bright to look at, up where the wind rocked. The cones dropped as light as feathers. Down in the hollow was the mourning dove—it was not too late for him.

The path ran up a hill. "Seem like there is chains about my feet, time I get this far," she said, in the voice of argument old people keep to use with themselves. "Something always take a hold of me on this hill—pleads I should stay."

After she got to the top she turned and gave a full, severe look behind her where she had come. "Up through pines," she said at length. "Now down through oaks."

Her eyes opened their widest, and she started down gently. But before she got to the bottom of the hill a bush caught her dress.

Her fingers were busy and intent, but her skirts were full and long, so that before she could pull them free in one place they were caught in another. It was not possible to allow the dress to tear. "I in the thorny bush," she said. "Thorns, you doing your appointed work. Never want to let folks pass, no sir. Old eyes thought you was a pretty little *green* bush."

Finally, trembling all over, she stood free, and after a moment dared to stoop for her cane.

"Sun so high!" she cried, leaning back and looking, while the thick tears went over her eyes. "The time getting all gone here."

At the foot of this hill was a place where a log was laid across the creek.

"Now comes the trial," said Phoenix.

Putting her right foot out, she mounted the log and shut her eyes. Lifting her skirt, leveling her cane fiercely before her, like a festival figure in some parade, she began to march across. Then she opened her eyes and she was safe on the other side.

"I wasn't as old as I thought," she said.

But she sat down to rest. She spread her skirts on the bank around her and folded her hands over her knees. Up above her was a tree in a pearly cloud of mistletoe. She did not dare to close her eyes, and when a little boy brought her a plate with a slice of marble-cake on it she spoke to him. "That would be acceptable," she said. But when she went to take it there was just her own hand in the air.

So she left that tree, and had to go through a barbed-wire fence. There she had to creep and crawl, spreading her knees and stretching her fingers like a baby trying to climb the steps. But she talked loudly to herself: she could not let her dress be torn now, so late in the day, and she could not pay for having her arm or her leg sawed off if she got caught fast where she was.

At last she was safe through the fence and risen up out in the clearing. Big dead trees, like black men with one arm, were standing in the purple stalks of the withered cotton field. There sat a buzzard.

"Who you watching?"

In the furrow she made her way along.

"Glad this not the season for bulls," she said, looking sideways, "and the good Lord made his snakes to curl up and sleep in the winter. A pleasure I don't see no two-headed snake coming around that tree, where it come once. It took a while to get by him, back in the summer."

She passed through the old cotton and went into a field of dead corn. It whispered and shook and was taller than her head. "Through the maze now," she said, for there was no path.

Then there was something tall, black, and skinny there, moving before her.

At first she took it for a man. It could have been a man dancing in the field. But she stood still and listened, and it did not make a sound. It was as silent as a ghost.

"Ghost," she said sharply, "who be you the ghost of? For I have heard of nary death close by."

But there was no answer—only the ragged dancing in the wind.

She shut her eyes, reached out her hand, and touched a sleeve. She found a coat and inside that an emptiness, cold as ice.

"You scarecrow," she said. Her face lighted. "I ought to be shut up for good," she said with laughter. "My senses is gone. I too old. I the oldest people I ever know. Dance, old scarecrow," she said, "while I dancing with you."

She kicked her foot over the furrow, and with mouth drawn down, shook her head once or twice in a little strutting way. Some husks blew down and whirled in streamers about her skirts.

Then she went on, parting her way from side to side with the cane, through the whispering field. At last she came to the end, to a wagon track where the silver grass blew between the red ruts. The quail were walking around like pullets, seeming all dainty and unseen.

"Walk pretty," she said. "This the easy place. This the easy going."

She followed the track, swaying through the quiet bare fields, through the little strings of trees silver in their dead leaves, past cabins silver from weather, with the doors and windows boarded shut, all like old women under a spell sitting there. "I walking in their sleep," she said, nodding her head vigorously.

In a ravine she went where a spring was silently flowing through a hollow log. Old Phoenix bent and drank. "Sweet-gum makes the water sweet," she said, and drank more. "Nobody know who made this well, for it was here when I was born."

The track crossed a swampy part where the moss hung as white as lace from every limb. "Sleep on, alligators, and blow your bubbles." Then the track went into the road.

Deep, deep the road went down between the high green-colored banks. Overhead the live-oaks met, and it was as dark as a cave.

A black dog with a lolling tongue came up out of the weeds by the ditch. She was meditating, and not ready, and when he came at her she only hit him a little with her cane. Over she went in the ditch, like a little puff of milkweed.

Down there, her senses drifted away. A dream visited her, and she reached her hand up, but nothing reached down and gave her a pull. So she lay there and presently went to talking. "Old woman," she said to herself, "that black dog come up out of the weeds to stall you off, and now there he sitting on his fine tail, smiling at you."

A white man finally came along and found her—a hunter, a young man, with his dog on a chain.

"Well, Granny!" he laughed. "What are you doing there?"

"Lying on my back like a June-bug waiting to be turned over, mister," she said, reaching up her hand.

He lifted her up, gave her a swing in the air, and set her down. "Anything broken, Granny?"

"No sir, them old dead weeds is springy enough," said Phoenix, when she had got her breath. "I thank you for your trouble."

"Where do you live, Granny?" he asked, while the two dogs were growling at each other.

"Away back yonder, sir, behind the ridge. You can't even see it from here."

"On your way home?"

"No sir, I going to town."

"Why, that's too far! That's as far as I walk when I come out myself, and I get something for my trouble." He patted the stuffed bag he carried, and there hung down a little closed claw. It was one of the bob-whites, with its beak hooked bitterly to show it was dead. "Now you go on home, Granny!"

"I bound to go to town, mister," said Phoenix. "The time come around."

He gave another laugh, filling the whole landscape. "I know you old colored people! Wouldn't miss going to town to see Santa Claus!"

But something held old Phoenix very still. The deep lines in her face went into a fierce and different radiation. Without warning, she had seen with her own eyes a flashing nickel fall out of the man's pocket onto the ground.

"How old are you, Granny?" he was saying.

"There is no telling, mister," she said, "no telling."

Then she gave a little cry and clapped her hands and said, "Git on away from here, dog! Look! Look at that dog!" She laughed as if in admiration. "He ain't scared of nobody. He a big black dog." She whispered, "Sic him!"

"Watch me get rid of that cur," said the man. "Sic him, Pete! Sic him!"

Phoenix heard the dogs fighting, and heard the man running and throwing sticks. She even heard a gunshot. But she was slowly bending forward by that time, further and further forward, the lids stretched down over her eyes, as if she were doing this in her sleep. Her chin was lowered almost to her knees. The yellow palm of her hand came out from the fold of her apron. Her fingers slid down and along the ground under the piece of money with the grace and care they would have in lifting an egg from under a setting hen. Then she slowly straightened up, she stood erect, and the nickel was in her apron pocket. A bird flew by. Her lips moved. "God watching me the whole time. I come to stealing."

The man came back, and his own dog panted about them. "Well, I scared him off that time," he said, and then he laughed and lifted his gun and pointed it at Phoenix.

She stood straight and faced him.

"Doesn't the gun scare you?" he said, still pointing it.

"No, sir, I seen plenty go off closer by, in my day, and for less than what I done," she said, holding utterly still.

He smiled, and shouldered the gun. "Well, Granny," he said, "you must be a hundred years old, and scared of nothing. I'd give you a dime if I had any money with me. But you take my advice and stay home, and nothing will happen to you."

"I bound to go on my way, mister," said Phoenix. She inclined her head in the red rag. Then they went in different directions, but she could hear the gun shooting again and again over the hill.

She walked on. The shadows hung from the oak trees to the road like curtains. Then she smelled wood-smoke, and smelled the river, and she saw a steeple and the cabins on their steep steps. Dozens of little black children whirled around her. There ahead was Natchez shining. Bells were ringing. She walked on.

In the paved city it was Christmas time. There were red and green electric lights strung and crisscrossed everywhere, and all turned on in the daytime. Old Phoenix would have been lost if she had not distrusted her eyesight and depended on her feet to know where to take her.

She paused quietly on the sidewalk where people were passing by. A lady came along in the crowd, carrying an armful of red-, green- and silver-wrapped presents; she gave off perfume like the red roses in hot summer, and Phoenix stopped her.

"Please, missy, will you lace up my shoe?" She held up her foot.

"What do you want, Grandma?"

"See my shoe," said Phoenix. "Do all right for out in the country, but wouldn't look right to go in a big building."

"Stand still then, Grandma," said the lady. She put her packages down on the sidewalk beside her and laced and tied both shoes tightly.

"Can't lace 'em with a cane," said Phoenix. "Thank you, missy. I doesn't mind asking a nice lady to tie up my shoe, when I gets out on the street."

Moving slowly and from side to side, she went into the big building, and into a tower of steps, where she walked up and around and around until her feet knew to stop.

She entered a door, and there she saw nailed up on the wall the document that had been stamped with the gold seal and framed in the gold
frame, which matched the dream that was hung up in her head.

"Here I be," she said. There was a fixed and ceremonial stiffness over
her body.

"A charity case, I suppose," said an attendant who sat at the desk before
her.

But Phoenix only looked above her head. There was sweat on her face,
the wrinkles in her skin shone like a bright net.

"Speak up, Grandma," the woman said. "What's you name? We must
have your history, you know. Have you been here before? What seems to
be the trouble with you?"

Old Phoenix only gave a twitch to her face as if a fly were bothering
her.

"Are you deaf?" cried the attendant.

But then the nurse came in.

"Oh, that's just old Aunt Phoenix," she said. "She doesn't come for
herself—she has a little grandson. She makes these trips just as regular as
clockwork. She lives away back off the Old Natchez Trace." She bent down.
"Well, Aunt Phoenix, why don't you just take a seat? We won't keep you
standing after your long trip." She pointed.

The old woman sat down, bolt upright in the chair.

"Now, how is the boy?" asked the nurse.

Old Phoenix did not speak.

"I said, how is the boy?"

But Phoenix only waited and stared straight ahead, her face very solemn
and withdrawn into rigidity.

"Is his throat any better?" asked the nurse. "Aunt Phoenix, don't you
hear me? Is your grandson's throat any better since the last time you came
for the medicine?"

With her hands on her knees, the old woman waited, silent, erect and
motionless, just as if she were in armor.

"You mustn't take up our time this way, Aunt Phoenix," the nurse said.
"Tell us quickly about your grandson, and get it over. He isn't dead, is
he?"

At last there came a flicker and then a flame of comprehension across
her face, and she spoke.

"My grandson. It was my memory had left me. There I sat and forgot
why I made my long trip."

"Forgot?" The nurse frowned. "After you came so far?"

Then Phoenix was like an old woman begging a dignified forgiveness
for waking up frightened in the night. "I never did go to school, I was too
old at the Surrender," she said in a soft voice. "I'm an old woman without

an education. It was my memory fail me. My little grandson, he is just the same, and I forgot it in the coming."

"Throat never heals, does it?" said the nurse, speaking in a loud, sure voice to old Phoenix. By now she had a card with something written on it, a little list. "Yes. Swallowed lye. When was it?—January—two, three years ago—"

Phoenix spoke unasked now. "No, missy, he not dead, he just the same. Every little while his throat begin to close up again, and he not able to swallow. He not get his breath. He not able to help himself. So the time come around, and I go on another trip for the soothing medicine."

"All right. The doctor said as long as you came to get it, you could have it," said the nurse. "But it's an obstinate case."

"My little grandson, he sit up there in the house all wrapped up, waiting by himself," Phoenix went on. "We is the only two left in the world. He suffer and it don't seem to put him back at all. He got a sweet look. He going to last. He wear a little patch quilt and peep out holding his mouth open like a little bird. I remembers so plain now. I not going to forget him again, no, the whole enduring time. I could tell him from all the others in creation."

"All right." The nurse was trying to hush her now. She brought her a bottle of medicine. "Charity," she said, making a check mark in a book.

Old Phoenix held the bottle close to her eyes, and then carefully put it into her pocket.

"I thank you," she said.

"It's Christmas time, Grandma," said the attendant. "Could I give you a few pennies out of my purse?"

"Five pennies is a nickel," said Phoenix stiffly.

"Here's a nickel," said the attendant.

Phoenix rose carefully and held out her hand. She received the nickel and then fished the other nickel out of her pocket and laid it beside the new one. She stared at her palm closely, with her head on one side.

Then she gave a tap with her cane on the floor.

"This is what come to me to do," she said. "I going to the store and buy my child a little windmill they sells, made out of paper. He going to find it hard to believe there such a thing in the world. I'll march myself back where he waiting, holding it straight up in this hand."

She lifted her free hand, gave a little nod, turned around, and walked out of the doctor's office. Then her slow step began on the stairs, going down.

Anton Chekhov (1860–1904)

The Bear:
A Joke in One Act

Cast of Characters

Mrs. Popov. *A widow of seven months,* Mrs. Popov *is small and pretty, with dimples. She is a landowner. At the start of the play, she is pining away in memory of her dead husband.*

Grigory Stepanovich Smirnov. *Easily angered and loud,* Smirnov *is older. He is a landowner, too, and a gentleman farmer of some substance.*

Luka. Luka *is* Mrs. Popov's *footman (a servant whose main tasks were to wait table and attend the carriages, in addition to general duties). He is old enough to feel secure in telling* Mrs. Popov *what he thinks.*

Gardener, Coachman, Workmen, *who enter at the end.*

The drawing room of MRS. POPOV'S *country home.*

(MRS. POPOV, *in deep mourning, does not remove her eyes from a photograph.*)

LUKA. It isn't right, madam . . . you're only destroying your-self. . . . The chambermaid and the cook have gone off berry picking; every living being is rejoicing; even the cat knows how to be content, walking around the yard catching birds, and you sit in your room all day as if it were a convent, and you don't take pleasure in anything. Yes, really! Almost a year has passed since you've gone out of the house!

MRS. POPOV. And I shall never go out. . . . What for? My life is already ended. *He* lies in his grave; I have buried myself in these four walls . . . we are both dead.

LUKA. There you go again! Your husband is dead, that's as it was meant to be, it's the will of God, may he rest in peace. . . . You've done your mourning and that will do. You can't go on weeping and mourning forever. My wife died when her time came, too. . . . Well? I grieved, I wept for a month, and that was enough for her; the old lady wasn't worth a second more. *(Sighs.)* You've forgotten all your neighbors. You don't go anywhere or accept any calls. We live, so to speak, like spiders. We never see the light. The mice have eaten my livery. It isn't as if there weren't any nice neighbors—the district is full of them . . . there's a regiment stationed at

*Slightly altered from the Bantam Press edition of *Ten Great One-Act Plays,* Morris Sweet-kind, ed. (1968). With minor slight verbal alterations.

Riblov, such officers—they're like candy—you'll never get your fill of them! And in the barracks, never a Friday goes by without a dance; and, if you please, the military band plays music every day. . . . Yes, madam, my dear lady: you're young, beautiful, in the full bloom of youth—if only you took a little pleasure in life . . . beauty doesn't last forever, you know! In ten years' time, you'll be wanting to wave your fanny in front of the officers— and it will be too late.

MRS. POPOV *(determined)*. I must ask you never to talk to me like that! You know that when Mr. Popov died, life lost all its salt for me. It may seem to you that I am alive, but that's only conjecture! I vowed to wear mourning to my grave and not to see the light of day. . . . Do you hear me? May his departed spirit see how much I love him. . . . Yes, I know, it's no mystery to you that he was often mean to me, cruel . . . and even unfaithful, but I shall remain true to the grave and show him I know how to love. There, beyond the grave, he will see me as I was before his death. . . .

LUKA. Instead of talking like that, you should be taking a walk in the garden or have Toby or Giant harnessed and go visit some of the neighbors . . .

MRS. POPOV. Ai! *(She weeps.)*

LUKA. Madam! Dear lady! What's the matter with you! Christ be with you!

MRS. POPOV. Oh, how he loved Toby! He always used to ride on him to visit the Korchagins or the Vlasovs. How wonderfully he rode! How graceful he was when he pulled at the reins with all his strength! Do you remember? Toby, Toby! Tell them to give him an extra bag of oats today.

LUKA. Yes, madam.

(Sound of loud ringing.)

MRS. POPOV *(shudders)*. Who's that? Tell them I'm not at home!

LUKA. Of course, madam. *(He exits.)*

MRS. POPOV *(alone. Looks at the photograph)*. You will see, Nicholas, how much I can love and forgive . . . my love will die only when I do, when my poor heart stops beating. *(Laughing through her tears.)* Have you no shame? I'm a good girl, a virtuous little wife. I've locked myself in and I'll be true to you to the grave, and you . . . aren't you ashamed, you chubby cheeks? You deceived me, you made scenes, for weeks on end you left me alone . . .

LUKA *(enters, alarmed)*. Madam, somebody is asking for you. He wants to see you. . . .

MRS. POPOV. But didn't you tell them that since the death of my husband, I don't see anybody?

LUKA. I did, but he didn't want to listen; he spoke about some very important business.

MRS. POPOV. I am *not at home!*

LUKA. That's what I told him . . . but . . . the devil . . . he cursed and pushed past me right into the room . . . he's in the dining room right now.

MRS. POPOV *(losing her temper)*. Very well, let him come in . . . such manners! (LUKA *goes out.*) How difficult these people are! What does he want from me? Why should he disturb my peace? *(Sighs.)* But it's obvious I'll have to go live in a convent. . . . *(Thoughtfully.)* Yes, a convent. . . .

SMIRNOV *(to* LUKA). You idiot, you talk too much. . . . Ass! *(Sees* MRS. POPOV *and changes to dignified speech.)* Madam, may I introduce myself: retired lieutenant of the artillery and landowner, Grigory Stepanovich Smirnov! I feel the necessity of troubling you about a highly important matter. . . .

MRS. POPOV *(refusing her hand)*. What do you want?

SMIRNOV. Your late husband, whom I had the pleasure of knowing, has remained in my debt for two twelve-hundred-ruble notes. Since I must pay the interest at the agricultural bank tomorrow, I have come to ask you, madam, to pay me the money today.

MRS. POPOV. One thousand two hundred. . . . And why was my husband in debt to you?

SMIRNOV. He used to buy oats from me.

MRS. POPOV *(sighing, to* LUKA). So, Luka, don't you forget to tell them to give Toby an extra bag of oats.

    (LUKA *goes out.*)

(To SMIRNOV.) If Nikolai, my husband, was in debt to you, then it goes without saying that I'll pay; but please excuse me today. I haven't any spare cash. The day after tomorrow, my steward will be back from town and I will give him instructions to pay you what is owed; until then I cannot comply with your wishes. . . . Besides, today is the anniversary— exactly seven months ago my husband died, and I'm in such a mood that I'm not quite disposed to occupy myself with money matters.

SMIRNOV. And I'm in such a mood that if I don't pay the interest tomorrow, I'll be owing so much that my troubles will drown me. They'll take away my estate!

MRS. POPOV. You'll receive your money the day after tomorrow.

SMIRNOV. I don't want the money the day after tomorrow. I want it today.

MRS. POPOV. You must excuse me. I can't pay you today.

SMIRNOV. And I can't wait until after tomorrow.

MRS. POPOV. What can I do, if I don't have it now?

SMIRNOV. You mean to say you can't pay?

MRS. POPOV. I can't pay. . . .

SMIRNOV. Hm! Is that your last word?

MRS. POPOV. That is my last word.

SMIRNOV. Positively the last?

MRS. POPOV. Positively.

SMIRNOV. Thank you very much. We'll make a note of that. *(Shrugs his shoulders.)* And people want me to be calm and collected! Just now, on the way here, I met a tax officer and he asked me: why are you always so angry, Grigory Stepanovich? Goodness' sake, how can I be anything but angry? I need money desperately . . . I rode out yesterday early in the morning, at daybreak, and went to see all my debtors; and if only one of them had paid his debt . . . I was dog-tired, spent the night God knows where—a Jewish tavern beside a barrel of vodka. . . . Finally I got here, fifty miles from home, hoping to be paid, and you treat me to a "mood." How can I help being angry?

MRS. POPOV. It seems to me that I clearly said: My steward will return from the country and then you will be paid.

SMIRNOV. I didn't come to your steward, but to you! What the hell, if you'll pardon the expression, would I do with your steward?

MRS. POPOV. Excuse me, my dear sir, I am not accustomed to such unusual expressions nor to such a tone. I'm not listening to you any more. *(Goes out quickly.)*

SMIRNOV *(alone).* Well, how do you like that? "A mood." . . . "Husband died seven months ago"! Must I pay the interest or mustn't I? I ask you: Must I pay, or must I not? So, your husband's dead, and you're in a mood and all that finicky stuff . . . and your steward's away somewhere; may he drop dead. What do you want me to do? Do you think I can fly away from my creditors in a balloon or something? Or should I run and bash my head against the wall? I go to Gruzdev—and he's not at home; Yaroshevich is hiding, with Kuritsin it's a quarrel to the death and I almost throw him out the window; Mazutov has diarrhea, and this one is in a "mood." Not one of these swine wants to pay me! And all because I'm too nice to them. I'm a sniveling idiot, I'm spineless, I'm an old lady! I'm too delicate with them! So, just you wait! You'll find out what I'm like! I won't let you play around with me, you devils! I'll stay and stick it out until she pays. Brr! . . . How furious I am today, how furious! I'm shaking inside from rage and I can hardly catch my breath. . . . Damn it! My God, I even feel sick! *(He shouts.)* Hey, you!

LUKA *(enters).* What do you want?

SMIRNOV. Give me some beer or some water! (LUKA *exits.*) What logic is there in this! A man needs money desperately, it's like a noose around his neck—and she won't pay because, you see, she's not disposed to occupy herself with money matters! . . . That's the logic of a woman! That's why I never did like and do not like to talk to women. I'd rather sit on a keg of gunpowder than talk to a woman. Brr! . . . I even have goose pimples, this broad has put me in such a rage! All I have to do is see one of those spoiled bitches from a distance, and I get so angry it gives me a cramp in the leg. I just want to shout for help.

LUKA *(entering with water)*. Madam is sick and won't see anyone.

SMIRNOV. Get out! (LUKA *goes*.) Sick and won't see anyone! No need to see me . . . I'll stay and sit here until you give me the money. You can stay sick for a week, and I'll stay for a week . . . if you're sick for a year, I'll stay a year. . . . I'll get my own back, dear lady! You can't impress me with your widow's weeds and your dimpled cheeks . . . we know all about those dimples! *(Shouts through the window.)* Semyon, unharness the horses! We're not going away quite yet! I'm staying here! Tell them in the stable to give the horses some oats! You brute, you let the horse on the left side get all tangled up in the reins again! *(Teasing.)* "Never mind" . . . I'll give you a never mind! *(Goes away from the window.)* Shit! The heat is unbearable and nobody pays up. I slept badly last night and on top of everything else this broad in mourning is "in a mood" . . . my head aches . . . *(Drinks, and grimaces.)* Shit! This is water! What I need is a drink! *(Shouts.)* Hey, you!

LUKA *(enters)*. What is it?

SMIRNOV. Give me a glass of vodka. (LUKA *goes out*.) Oof! *(Sits down and examines himself.)* Nobody would say I was looking well! Dusty all over, boots dirty, unwashed, unkempt, straw on my waistcoat. . . . The dear lady probably took me for a robber. *(Yawns.)* It's not very polite to present myself in a drawing room looking like this; oh well, who cares? . . . I'm not here as a visitor but as a creditor, and there's no official costume for creditors. . . .

LUKA *(enters with vodka)*. You're taking liberties, my good man. . . .

SMIRNOV *(angrily)*. What?

LUKA. I . . . nothing . . . I only . . .

SMIRNOV. Who are you talking to? Shut up!

LUKA *(aside)*. The devil sent this leech. An ill wind brought him. . . . (LUKA *goes out*.)

SMIRNOV. Oh how furious I am! I'm so mad I could crush the whole world into a powder! I even feel faint! *(Shouts.)* Hey, you!

MRS. POPOV *(enters, eyes downcast)*. My dear sir, in my solitude, I have long ago grown unaccustomed to the masculine voice and I cannot bear shouting. I must request you not to disturb my peace and quiet!

SMIRNOV. Pay me my money and I'll go.

MRS. POPOV. I told you in plain language: I haven't any spare cash now; wait until the day after tomorrow.

SMIRNOV. And I also told you respectfully, in plain language: I don't need the money the day after tomorrow, but today. If you don't pay me today, then tomorrow I'll have to hang myself.

MRS. POPOV. But what can I do if I don't have the money? You're so strange!

SMIRNOV. Then you won't pay me now? No?

MRS. POPOV. I can't. . . .

SMIRNOV. In that case, I can stay here and wait until you pay. . . . *(Sits down.)* You'll pay the day after tomorrow? Excellent! In that case I'll stay here until the day after tomorrow. I'll sit here all that time . . . *(Jumps up.)* I ask you: Have I got to pay the interest tomorrow, or not? Or do you think I'm joking?

MRS. POPOV. My dear sir, I ask you not to shout! This isn't a stable!

SMIRNOV. I wasn't asking you about a stable but about this: Do I have to pay the interest tomorrow or not?

MRS. POPOV. You don't know how to behave in the company of a lady!

SMIRNOV. No, I don't know how to behave in the company of a lady!

MRS. POPOV. No, you don't! You are an ill-bred, rude man! Respectable people don't talk to a woman like that!

SMIRNOV. Ach, it's astonishing! How would you like me to talk to you? In French, perhaps? *(Lisps in anger.)* Madame, je vous prie* . . . how happy I am that you're not paying me the money. . . . Ah, pardon, I've made you uneasy! Such lovely weather we're having today! And you look so becoming in your mourning dress. *(Bows and scrapes.)*

MRS. POPOV. That's rude and not very clever!

SMIRNOV *(teasing).* Rude and not very clever! I don't know how to behave in the company of ladies. Madam, in my time I've seen far more women than you've seen sparrows. Three times I've fought duels over women; I've jilted twelve women, nine have jilted me! Yes! There was a time when I played the fool; I became sentimental over women, used honeyed words, fawned on them, bowed and scraped. . . . I loved, suffered, sighed at the moon; I became limp, melted, shivered . . . I loved passionately, madly, every which way, devil take me, I chattered away like a magpie about the emancipation of women, ran through half my fortune as a result of my tender feelings; but now, if you will excuse me, I'm on to your ways! I've had enough! Dark eyes, passionate eyes, ruby lips, dimpled cheeks; the moon, whispers, bated breath—for all that I wouldn't give a good goddamn. Present company excepted, of course, but all women, young and old alike, are affected clowns, gossips, hateful, consummate liars to the marrow of their bones, vain, trivial, ruthless, outrageously illogical, and as far as this is concerned *(taps on his forehead),* well, excuse my frankness, any sparrow could give pointers to a philosopher in petticoats! Look at one of those romantic creatures: muslin, ethereal demigoddess, a thousand raptures, and you look into her soul—a common crocodile! *(Grips the back of a chair; the chair cracks and breaks.)* But the most revolting part of it all is that this crocodile imagines that she has, above everything, her own privilege, a monopoly on tender feelings. The hell with it—you can hang me upside down by that nail if a woman is capable of loving anything besides a lapdog. All she can do when she's in love is slobber! While the man suffers and sacrifices, all her love is expressed in playing with her skirt and trying to lead him around firmly by the nose. You have the misfortune of being a woman, you know yourself what the nature of a woman is like.

*Madam, I beg you.

Tell me honestly: Have you ever in your life seen a woman who is sincere, faithful, and constant? You never have! Only old and ugly ladies are faithful and constant! You're more liable to meet a horned cat or a white woodcock than a faithful woman!

MRS. POPOV. Pardon me, but in your opinion, who is faithful and constant in love? The man?

SMIRNOV. Yes, the man!

MRS. POPOV. The man! (Malicious laugh.) Men are faithful and constant in love! That's news! (Heatedly.) What right have you to say that? Men are faithful and constant! For that matter, as far as I know, of all the men I have known and now know, my late husband was the best. . . . I loved him passionately, with all my being, as only a young intellectual woman can love; I gave him my youth, my happiness, my life, my fortune; he was my life's breath; I worshiped him as if I were a heathen, and . . . and, what good did it do—this best of men himself deceived me shamelessly at every step of the way. After his death, I found his desk full of love letters; and when he was alive—it's terrible to remember—he used to leave me alone for weeks at a time, and before my very eyes he paid court to other women and deceived me. He squandered my money, made a mockery of my feelings . . . and, in spite of all that, I loved him and was true to him . . . and besides, now that he is dead, I am still faithful and constant. I have shut myself up in these four walls forever and I won't remove these widow's weeds until my dying day. . . .

SMIRNOV (laughs contemptuously). Widow's weeds! . . . I don't know what you take me for! As if I didn't know why you wear that black outfit and bury yourself in these four walls! Well, well! It's so secret, so romantic! When some fool of a poet passes by this country house, he'll look up at your window and think: "Here lives the mysterious Tamara, who, for the love of her husband, buried herself in these four walls." We know these tricks!

MRS. POPOV (flaring). What? How dare you say that to me?

SMIRNOV. You may have buried yourself alive, but you haven't forgotten to powder yourself!

MRS. POPOV. How dare you use such expressions with me?

SMIRNOV. Please don't shout. I'm not your steward! You must allow me to call a spade a spade. I'm not a woman and I'm used to saying what's on my mind! Don't you shout at me!

MRS. POPOV. I'm not shouting, you are! Please leave me in peace!

SMIRNOV. Pay me my money and I'll go.

MRS. POPOV. I won't give you any money!

SMIRNOV. Yes, you will.

MRS. POPOV. To spite you, I won't pay you anything. You can leave me in peace!

SMIRNOV. I don't have the pleasure of being either your husband or your fiancé, so please don't make scenes! (Sits down.) I don't like it.

MRS. POPOV *(choking with rage).* You're sitting down?

SMIRNOV. Yes, I am.

MRS. POPOV. I ask you to get out!

SMIRNOV. Give me my money . . . *(Aside.)* Oh, I'm so furious! Furious!

MRS. POPOV. I don't want to talk to impudent people! Get out of here! *(Pause.)* You're not going? No?

SMIRNOV. No.

MRS. POPOV. No?

SMIRNOV. No!

MRS. POPOV. We'll see about that. *(Rings.)*

(LUKA *enters.*)

Luka, show the gentleman out!

LUKA *(goes up to* SMIRNOV). Sir, will you please leave, as you have been asked. You mustn't . . .

SMIRNOV *(jumping up).* Shut up! Who do you think you're talking to? I'll make mincemeat out of you!

LUKA *(his hand to his heart).* Oh my God! Saints above! *(Falls into chair.)* Oh, I feel ill! I feel ill! I can't catch my breath!

MRS. POPOV. Where's Dasha? Dasha! *(She shouts.)* Dasha! Pelagea! Dasha! *(She rings.)*

LUKA. Oh! They've all gone berry picking . . . there's nobody at home . . . I'm ill! Water!

MRS. POPOV. Will you please get out!

SMIRNOV. Will you please be more polite?

MRS. POPOV *(clenches her fist and stamps her feet).* You're nothing but a crude bear! A brute! A monster!

SMIRNOV. What? What did you say?

MRS. POPOV. I said that you were a bear, a monster!

SMIRNOV *(advancing toward her).* Excuse me, but what right do you have to insult me?

MRS. POPOV. Yes, I am insulting you . . . so what? Do you think I'm afraid of you?

SMIRNOV. And do you think just because you're one of those romantic creations, that you have the right to insult me with impunity? Yes? I challenge you!

LUKA. Lord in Heaven! Saints above! . . . Water!

SMIRNOV. Pistols!

MRS. POPOV. Do you think just because you have big fists and you can bellow like a bull, that I'm afraid of you? You're such a bully!

SMIRNOV. I challenge you! I'm not going to let anybody insult me, and I don't care if you are a woman, a delicate creature!

MRS. POPOV *(trying to get a word in edgewise).* Bear! Bear! Bear!

SMIRNOV. It's about time we got rid of the prejudice that only men must pay for their insults! Devil take it, if women want to be equal, they should behave as equals! Let's fight!

MRS. POPOV. You want to fight! By all means!

SMIRNOV. This minute!

MRS. POPOV. This minute! My husband had some pistols . . . I'll go and get them right away. *(Goes out hurriedly and then returns.)* What pleasure I'll have putting a bullet through that thick head of yours! The hell with you! *(She goes out.)*

SMIRNOV. I'll shoot her down like a chicken! I'm not a little boy or a sentimental puppy. I don't care if she is delicate and fragile.

LUKA. Kind sir! Holy father! *(Kneels.)* Have pity on a poor old man and go away from here! You've frightened her to death and now you're going to shoot her?

SMIRNOV *(not listening to him)*. If she fights, then it means she believes in equality of rights and the emancipation of women. Here the sexes are equal! I'll shoot her like a chicken! But what a woman! *(Imitates her.)* "The hell with you! . . . I'll put a bullet through that thick head of yours! . . ." What a woman! How she blushed, her eyes shone . . . she accepted my challenge! To tell the truth, it was the first time in my life I've seen a woman like that. . . .

LUKA. Dear sir, please go away! I'll pray to God on your behalf as long as I live!

SMIRNOV. That's a woman for you! A woman like that I can understand! A real woman! Not a sour-faced nincompoop but fiery, gunpowder! Fireworks! I'm even sorry to have to kill her!

LUKA *(weeps)*. Dear sir . . . go away!

SMIRNOV. I positively like her! Positively! Even though she has dimpled cheeks, I like her! I'm almost ready to forget about the debt. . . . My fury has diminished. Wonderful woman!

MRS. POPOV *(enters with pistols)*. Here they are, the pistols. Before we fight, you must show me how to fire. . . . I've never had a pistol in my hands before . . .

LUKA. Oh dear Lord, for pity's sake. . . . I'll go and find the gardener and the coachman. . . . What did we do to deserve such trouble? *(Exit.)*

SMIRNOV *(examining the pistols)*. You see, there are several sorts of pistols . . . there are special dueling pistols, the Mortimer with primers. Then there are Smith and Wesson revolvers, triple action with extractors . . . excellent pistols! . . . they cost a minimum of ninety rubles a pair. . . . You must hold the revolver like this . . . *(Aside.)* What eyes, what eyes! A woman to set you on fire!

MRS. POPOV. Like this?

SMIRNOV. Yes, like this . . . then you cock the pistol . . . take aim . . . put your head back a little . . . stretch your arm out all the way . . . that's right . . . then with this finger press on this little piece of goods . . . and that's all there is to do . . . but the most important thing is not to get excited and aim without hurrying . . . try to keep your arm from shaking.

MRS. POPOV. Good . . . it's not comfortable to shoot indoors. Let's go into the garden.

SMIRNOV. Let's go. But I'm giving you advance notice that I'm going to fire into the air.

MRS. POPOV. That's the last straw! Why?

SMIRNOV. Why? . . . Why . . . because it's my business, that's why.

MRS. POPOV. Are you afraid? Yes? Aahhh! No, sir. You're not going to get out of it that easily! Be so good as to follow me! I will not rest until I've put a hole through your forehead . . . that forehead I hate so much! Are you afraid?

SMIRNOV. Yes, I'm afraid.

MRS. POPOV. You're lying! Why don't you want to fight?

SMIRNOV. Because . . . because you . . . because I like you.

MRS. POPOV *(laughs angrily)*. He likes me! He dares say that he likes me! *(Points to the door.)* Out!

SMIRNOV *(loads the revolver in silence, takes cap and goes; at the door, stops for half a minute while they look at each other in silence; then he approaches* MRS. POPOV *hesitantly)*. Listen. . . . Are you still angry? I'm extremely irritated, but, do you understand me, how can I express it . . . the fact is, that, you see, strictly speaking . . . *(He shouts.)* Is it my fault, really, for liking you? *(Grabs the back of a chair, which cracks and breaks.)* Why the hell do you have such fragile furniture! I like you! Do you understand? I . . . I'm almost in love with you!

MRS. POPOV. Get away from me—I hate you!

SMIRNOV. God, what a woman! I've never in my life seen anything like her! I'm lost! I'm done for! I'm caught like a mouse in a trap!

MRS. POPOV. Stand back or I'll shoot!

SMIRNOV. Shoot! You could never understand what happiness it would be to die under the gaze of those wonderful eyes, to be shot by a revolver which was held by those little velvet hands. . . . I've gone out of my mind! Think about it and decide right away, because if I leave here, then we'll never see each other again! Decide . . . I'm a nobleman, a respectable gentleman, of good family. I have an income of ten thousand a year. . . . I can put a bullet through a coin tossed in the air . . . I have some fine horses. . . . Will you be my wife?

MRS. POPOV *(indignantly brandishes her revolver)*. Let's fight! I challenge you!

SMIRNOV. I'm out of my mind . . . I don't understand anything . . . *(Shouts.)* Hey, you, water!

MRS. POPOV *(shouts)*. Let's fight!

SMIRNOV. I've gone out of my mind. I'm in love like a boy, like an idiot! *(He grabs her hand, she screams with pain.)* I love you! *(Kneels.)* I love you as I've never loved before! I've jilted twelve women, nine women have jilted me, but I've never loved one of them as I love you. . . . I'm weak, I'm a limp rag. . . . I'm on my knees like a fool, offering you my hand. . . . Shame, shame! I haven't been in love for five years, I vowed I wouldn't; and suddenly I'm in love, like a fish out of water. I'm offering my hand in marriage. Yes or no? You don't want to? You don't need to! *(Gets up and quickly goes to the door.)*

MRS. POPOV. Wait!

SMIRNOV *(stops).* Well?

MRS. POPOV. Nothing . . . you can go . . . go away . . . wait. . . . No, get out, get out! I hate you! But—don't go! Oh, if you only knew how furious I am, how angry! *(Throws revolver on table.)* My fingers are swollen from that nasty thing. . . . *(Tears her handkerchief furiously.)* What are you waiting for? Get out!

SMIRNOV. Farewell!

MRS. POPOV. Yes, yes, go away! *(Shouts.)* Where are you going? Stop. . . . Oh, go away! Oh, how furious I am! Don't come near me! Don't come near me!

SMIRNOV *(approaching her).* How angry I am with myself! I'm in love like a student. I've been on my knees. . . . It gives me the shivers. *(Rudely.)* I love you! A lot of good it will do me to fall in love with you! Tomorrow I've got to pay the interest, begin the mowing of the hay. *(Puts his arm around her waist.)* I'll never forgive myself for this. . . .

MRS. POPOV. Get away from me! Get your hands away! I . . . hate you! I . . . challenge you!

>   *(Prolonged kiss.* LUKA *enters with an ax, the* GARDENER *with a rake, the*
>   COACHMAN *with a pitchfork, and* WORKMEN *with cudgels.)*

LUKA *(catches sight of the pair kissing).* Lord in heaven! *(Pause.)*

MRS. POPOV *(lowering her eyes).* Luka, tell them in the stable not to give Toby any oats today.

CURTAIN

Index

CHAUCER, GEOFFREY, 147; *Troilus and Criseyde*, 82
CHEEVER, JOHN, "The Five Forty-Eight," 132
CHEKHOV, ANTON, *The Bear*, 55, 57, 58, 79, 114, 131; complete play, 188–98; Sample theme (major idea) on the idea of the strength of love in *The Bear*, with commentary, 85–86; Sample theme (extended comparison-contrast) comparing *The Bear* and five other works, with commentary, 121–25
Climax, 42
COLERIDGE, SAMUEL TAYLOR, "The Rime of the Ancient Mariner," 107
Comedy, 5
Commentaries; commentaries on the sample themes explained, 21; Commentaries appear after each sample theme.
Comparison-contrast, 8, 9; Chapter 10, The Themes of Comparison-Contrast and Extended Comparison-Contrast, 112–25; Sample comparison-contrast theme on Williams' *The Glass Menagerie* and Miller's *All My Sons*, 28–30
Condensation; Chapter 1, The Précis Theme, or Abstract, 35–40
Conflict, 42, 49
CONRAD, JOSEPH, *The Rescue*, 145
Controlling image, 99f.
CRANE, STEPHEN, "The Bride Comes to Yellow Sky," 74; "Do Not Weep, Maiden," 80; "Horses—One Dash," 84, 127f.; "War is Kind," 112f.

D

DE MAUPASSANT, GUY, 67; "The Necklace," 9, 48ff., 55, 66, 81, 82, 119; complete story, 167–73; sample theme (likes and dislikes) with commentary, 52–53; sample theme (character) with commentary, 60–62; sample theme (setting) with commentary, 76–78
Development; developing ideas in a theme, 30ff.
DIXON, PETER, 147, 149
Documentation; Appendix B: A Note on Documentation, 139–49
DONNE, JOHN, "I Am a Little World Made Cunningly," 103
Drama, 5
Dramatic monologue, 5
Dramatic point of view, 66–67
DREISER, THEODORE, *Sister Carrie*, 133
DRYDEN, JOHN, *Absalom and Achitophel*, 129f.

E

EBERHART, RICHARD, "The Fury of Aerial Bombardment," 112f.
ELIOT, T.S., 137; "The Love Song of J. Alfred Prufrock," 84, 97
Ellipsis (omissions within quotations), 142
Epic, 4, 5; mock epic, 5
Epitome; Chapter 1, The Précis Theme, or Abstract, 35–40
Essay, 6
Evidence; use of literary works as evidence in developing a theme, 23ff.; evidence and point of view, 67
Examinations; Appendix A: Taking Examinations on Literature, 126–38; multiple-choice questions, 131; identification questions, 131f.; technical and analytical questions and problems, 132; longer factual questions, 134ff.; general or comprehensive questions, 136f.

F

Fable, 102
Farce, 5
Fiction, narrative, 4–5
FIELDING, HENRY, *Tom Jones*, 30ff.
Film script, 5
First-person point of view, 65–66
FITZGERALD, F. SCOTT, *The Great Gatsby*, 65–66, 69; "The Rich Boy," 135f., *Tender is the Night*, 135
Footnotes; need for footnotes, 143; form of footnotes, 144; sample footnotes, 145
Formal documentation, 143–45
FORSTER, E.M., "The Machine Stops," 32f.; *A Passage to India*, 74, 82
FROST, ROBERT, "Desert Places," 89; complete poem, 155; sample theme (problem) with commentary, 93–94

G

GAY, JOHN, *Trivia*, 141
GNEITING, TEONA TONE, 147, 148
Goals of writing themes, 1
GOGOL, NICOLAI, "The Overcoat," 132
Growth; developing the ideas in a theme, 30ff.

H

Habits; reading habits, 2, 10
HAIGHT ASHBURY, as a metonym, 100
Hansel and Gretel (children's story), and the Précis Theme, 36, 37